WORLD HANDBOOK OF

POLITICAL AND SOCIAL INDICATORS

WORLD HANDBOOK OF POLITICAL AND SOCIAL INDICATORS

by

BRUCE M. RUSSETT

and

Hayward R. Alker, Jr., Karl W. Deutsch, Harold D. Lasswell

with the assistance of
Robert Bunselmeyer, James Eisenstein, Robert Grey
Russell Murphy, John Shingler, Seth Singleton, Stephen Stephens

New Haven and London, Yale University Press

Preface

The Universal Declaration of Human Rights proclaims a wide variety of fundamental prerogatives for the peoples of the world. They include

Political rights: "to take part in the government . . . directly or through freely chosen representatives," and to "a social and international order."

Rights to *information:* "to seek, receive, and impart information and ideas through any media and regardless of frontiers."

Economic rights: "to own property," "to protection against unemployment," and "to just and favorable remuneration insuring for himself and his family an existence worthy of human dignity."

Rights to *health:* "to a standard of living adequate for the health and well-being of himself and of his family, including . . . medical care."

Rights to *learning:* "to education." "Education shall be free, at least in the elementary and fundamental stages. Elementary education shall be compulsory."

Rights to *family and personal relations:* "to marry and to found a family," and "to leave any country, including his own, and to return to his country."

Rights to *respect and dignity:* "the economic, social, and cultural rights indispensable for his dignity and the free development of his personality."

Religious rights: "to freedom of thought, conscience, and religion . . . to manifest his religion or belief in teaching, practice, worship, and observance."

These rights are not, of course, universally in effect. They were proclaimed as norms to guide aspirations. In the words of the preamble, they are part of "a common standard of achievement for all peoples and all nations, to the end that every individual and every organ of society, keeping this Declaration constantly in mind, shall strive by teaching and education to promote respect for these rights and freedoms and by progressive measures, national and international, to secure their universal and effective recognition and observance . . ." Not all peoples subscribe fully to all these prescriptions, and the values placed on different rights vary immensely. But since an international and very diverse body of representatives did adopt the Declaration, it seems appropriate to compare nations as to their relative implementation of the asserted rights.

The foregoing list represents a selection from the Declaration of some of the rights the achievement of which can perhaps fairly adequately be measured. This book is an attempt to compare nations on a great variety of politically relevant indices. The kinds of questions that can be investigated—the interrelationships of different levels of political, economic, social, and cultural development are myriad. In this volume we try to present some of the data necessary for the further development of a science of comparative and international politics, and to illustrate some of the means for analyzing the data. It is meant to be a scientific work, but one for practitioners of science who would compare nations in terms of widely held values. While perhaps of special use to political scientists, this *Handbook* is also directed toward other social scientists, such as

v

economists and sociologists, who may find it useful for germinating or testing hypotheses about cross-cultural comparisons.

As is clear from the title page, the book is the result of a cooperative effort. It is one product of the Yale Political Data Program, established in 1962 by a grant from the National Science Foundation. Additional support in preparing this volume has come from the United Nations Educational, Scientific, and Cultural Organization and the International Social Science Council. This book is the first in a series, entitled *Tools and Methods of Comparative Research*, to be sponsored by the International Social Science Council and the International Committee for Social Science Documentation. The individuals listed on the title page contributed in a number of ways. The *Handbook* stems from the long-term interests of Deutsch and Lasswell, who did much to formulate its basic purpose, content, and organization. Bunselmeyer, Grey, Murphy, and Singleton undertook much of the labor of data collection. Alker, Eisenstein, Stephens, and Shingler assumed the responsibility for computation. Other essential help came from Judith Ann Alker, who carefully edited the manuscript, Lotte Doverman, Truus Koopmans, and Robert Norris, who collected several of the series, and Kay Latona, who was primarily responsible for preparing the copy. With one exception, however, the manuscript was written by Russett, and only he should be held responsible for the form of the final product. The exception is Hayward Alker, to whom belongs all or part of the blame for those sections of Part B of which he appears as sole author or co-author.

The volume also owes a great debt to the American, Asian, and European participants in the International Conference on the Use of Quantitative Political, Social, and Cultural Data in Cross-National Comparisons held at Yale University in September 1963 under the auspices of the International Social Science Council and the Yale Data Program. The constructive criticism offered by this group was extremely useful, and we only regret the impossibility of using it all. Mattei Dogan must be singled out for special thanks in this respect, as must Stein Rokkan for his continuing help after the conference. Many ideas of conference participants for the use and improvement of the data will be incorporated in a companion volume, *Comparing Nations: The Use of Quantitative Data in Cross-National Research*, edited by Richard L. Merritt and Stein Rokkan, which is based on the papers presented to the conference.

The data in this book have been reproduced on punch cards. Decks and code books may be obtained either from the Inter-University Consortium for Political Research (P.O. Box 1248, Ann Arbor, Michigan 48106) on its usual terms, or from the Yale Political Data Program (89 Trumbull Street, New Haven, Connecticut 06520) for a nominal fee. Copies of most of the computer programs used are also available from the Data Program. In furnishing this material we realize that we are making it easy for the reader to second-guess us. Though such an arrangement may be unusual to many readers, we trust that it will bring benefits both to us and to future users. This *Handbook* represents a first effort which we hope will be expanded, improved, and, where necessary, corrected in later editions.

New Haven, Connecticut
February 1964

Contents

Government and Politics (cont.)

Contents   ix

Tables

Figures

Introduction

Empirical social analysis can be divided broadly into two types: examination in depth of a single case or at most a very few cases, and the more general comparison of many similar though not identical cases. Too often these two approaches are treated as exclusive and incompatible. Actually each type has serious limitations, but the limitations of one are often precisely the strengths of the other. Used in tandem they can complement each other in important ways.

Attention to a single case may take several forms. One may look at a particular social or political unit (like a nation) or a particular event (like a war) and examine the many variables that seem to be associated with certain outcomes. But scrutiny of the single case can never be pursued exclusively. One can know where to look and what kinds of relationships to seek out only by making at least implicit comparison with other cases. It may be tempting to say that what one finds after analysis is unique, relevant only to the peculiar circumstances of the particular instance, but one can *know* this, if at all, only after comparing the results with what has been found for other partly similar, partly dissimilar cases. Concentration on the single case always involves the loss of important information.

An escape from this quandary may involve the examination of a single variable (such as class structure) and the search for its apparent effects in many societies. This type of analysis approaches the general comparative method, but the primary focus on a single independent variable imposes severe limits on the wide applicability and productivity of the analysis. Social scientists have now well learned that truly valid, generalizable results can best be obtained through the study of many variables—and many units and many events. This clearly can lead to inundation by too much data, a situation where neither mind nor even computer can absorb and sort out the information. Furthermore, broad comparative analysis can lead to serious difficulties in identifying causal relationships, as contrasted with mere correlations. While some mathematical and statistical means have been developed for dealing in part with this problem,[1] the fact remains that the single case study, which loses other types of information, is often uniquely valuable in the identification of cause, at least in the particular case.

In other words, each approach leads eventually to the other; the social scientist who discards one does no service either to himself or to his readers. The priorities may of course work either way. Perhaps one observes the individual case, develops a theory, and then tests it against information from many other cases. Or one may start with the large body of data and then move to the case study to better identify details and causal relationships.

---

1. Cf. H. A. Simon, "Spurious Correlation: A Causal Interpretation," *Journal of the American Statistical Association, 49* (September 1954), 467–79; H. M. Blalock, "Four Variable Causal Models and Partial Correlations," *American Journal of Sociology, 58* (September 1962), 182–94; and Blalock, "Making Causal Inferences for Unmeasured Variables from Correlations Among Indicators," *American Journal of Sociology, 59* (July 1963), 53–62.

In political science, nevertheless, and especially in comparative and international politics, broad comparison has frequently been neglected. Even comparative politics, despite its name, has usually been limited to the comparison of only a few political systems at a time. The reason for this neglect stems only partly from gaps in our conceptual apparatus; a more serious handicap has been the absence of reliable, valid, and comparable data to make the comparison of many polities possible. It is that gap which, in some measure, this book attempts to fill.

This discussion suggests another possible distinction in social science—between the use of data for testing existing theory and the use of data as an active element in the process of theory building. The latter is sometimes inelegantly referred to as "fishing," that is, going to the data without a clearly formulated hypothesis and letting the data themselves suggest relationships. This course is often scorned; at best it is a preliminary, not a final step in theory construction because of the possibility that an apparent relationship exists only by chance, not because of any true association. Yet the activity should not be disdained, particularly if it takes the form of a constant dialogue between theory and data. The theorist may begin with a set of hypotheses. Examination of data bears out some to a limited extent, while others are not supported. Close scrutiny of the failures as well as of the successes suggests modifications of the hypotheses, which must be tested further with new data.

The information presented in this volume was selected with reference to existing theories of international and comparative politics. Each of the series represents an attempt to operationalize a variable central to several important theories of political or social change. In some cases it seems fairly clear that a given index accurately represents a basic underlying variable of concern; in other cases the adequacy of the index is more doubtful. Where there is most doubt we have tried to include two or more alternative measures or we have broken down a complex concept into several simpler ones.

In addition to the demands of theoretical importance, our data series were selected according to the criteria of accuracy and availability. Problems of accuracy involve two separate questions: Are the numbers *reliable,* neither exaggerations nor underestimates, and are they *comparable*? That is, are the definitions of the relevant event the same in different countries? We have tried to estimate the probable error in the data and to compare it with the permissible error that can still be tolerated in relation to the inferences to be drawn from the data. This permissible error is in part related to the range of the series. When the value of a variable in two countries differs by 20 percentage points, an error margin of 15 points will have crippling effects; if they should differ by 40 or 50 percentage points an error margin of 15 points, while damaging, may nonetheless be tolerable.

In deciding whether to collect a given series at all we had to make a preliminary judgment about the data's accuracy. We have attempted further, and this was a difficult and uncertain task given the paucity of existing information, to assess for most of the series fairly precise error margins. Few previous data collections have made more than the grossest assessments, perhaps warning the reader to use the data only with caution and due regard for incomparabilities. Obviously it is not easy to give any precise error margin either for a single datum or for a whole series. There is always the danger that such an attempt, meant to give only a very general order of magnitude, may be taken too seriously by the reader.

Nevertheless it seemed to us that refusal to make any quantitative estimate of error when presenting series of this sort would be an abdication of responsibility. Publication of figures merely with the admonition to be cautious does not tell the reader how cautious he must be or how much confidence he can attach to the resulting calculations. He is free to draw his own conclusions, but this may be a poor kind of freedom if the information available to him is—as is usually the case—less than that available to the original compilers of the data.

Some of the specific problems affecting data accuracy are discussed with each series. In general it may be stated that there is a clear tendency for the quality and availability of data to rise with the level of economic development in a country. This is simply a matter of resources. The collection and evaluation of adequate data is an expensive process requiring skilled personnel; in many countries neither the human nor the financial raw material is available. This is particularly true in small countries and with respect to data normally collected by sample survey methods. With a population of a million or more inhabitants the size of the sample needed for reliable data collection is not responsive to the size of the total population. The results of a sample survey of, say, five thousand individuals are virtually as reliable for a country of two hundred million as for a country of one million. The costs of the survey are not very different in the large country, but the burden on the small country may be relatively great, especially if it is not wealthy. Thus sample surveys, which can form an important supplement to decennial censuses, are often not undertaken in smaller states.

Another problem stems from the lack of international agreement on the definition of certain items. The United Nations has performed a major service in attempting to establish standard definitions for census-taking, accounting, and other data-gathering and data analysis procedures. Yet the task is far from complete, and often one cannot be sure that standard definitions were used in published data.

A final major difficulty is the deliberate or semi-deliberate distortion of data by national governments. Sometimes a government does not want to admit that certain data are unavailable; such an admission may seem to reflect on its own competence or the state of the nation's development. In these cases "data" may be created without much empirical referent. This may even occur within one branch of a government with respect to another. A regional office faced with a demand for data beyond its resources to collect may find quite ingenious ways of reporting something. And, on a national scale, the appearance of economic strength or rapid development or a literate and healthy population may be an important asset in international politics. Where the true data indicate otherwise, they may be modified, and it may be extraordinarily difficult for an independent researcher to determine the presence or degree of modification. Some governments, like some businessmen, keep two sets of books.

Despite these difficulties, wherever we have had any reasonable basis at all for estimating an error margin we have done so. Where we have used data gathered by some other individual or agency our suggested error margins have been very approximate. Our assessments are admittedly rough and subject to improvement.

Finally, our data-gathering efforts have been unavoidably influenced by availability. For many series the basic data, or occasionally even the finished series, were already available in studies published by governments, international organizations, or private agencies. In a few such cases we simply made whatever adjustments were possible to improve comparability, rank-ordered the countries, computed summary measures such as the mean and median, and exhibited the distribution. More often we had to calculate the ratios or percentages or rates of change essential to make comparison meaningful. Frequently it was necessary to modify certain items of data substantially to make them more nearly comparable to the other items in the series. For a great number of series that seemed highly interesting theoretically, however, preexisting compilations were absent, and we had to build up the series largely or exclusively from private studies and national statistical yearbooks. We tried, however, to go considerably beyond the original sources in processing the data in order to bring out important characteristics of the distributions.

Our emphasis has been on the collection and analysis of quantitative data and of data that would be replicable by other scholars. Thus we have tried to state our definitions clearly and to include all the information necessary to permit any researcher to see just what was collected and, where we modified existing data, how we modified it. Ambiguity or the absence of full discussion in our sources sometimes made this impossible; nevertheless it was our aim. This meant that many series that would have been most interesting theoretically had to be excluded because we felt that different analysts would have made quite different judgments about the same country.

This is *not* to imply that we think all important variables for political and social analysis can be expressed as precise and replicable quantities. Our position is quite the contrary. What we do think is that quantification can proceed further than it has, and in a very modest way we have attempted to push the frontier of quantification forward a little. Any analyst will be aware of many less readily quantifiable variables that should be used in any extensive use of these data. Because we have not put such data in this book does not mean either that we are not aware of them or that we would ignore them in our own analysis. Our goal has been the limited one of trying to quantify where quantification looked promising.

Many important types of data could not be included because they did not exist on a comparable basis for a sufficient number of countries. Our rule of thumb (violated in a few cases) was to include only series for which adequate information seemed to exist for at least thirty separate political units, and in most instances we demanded more units. This ruled out most data derived from such sources as survey research and content analysis; as these methods are used more widely, later editions of this work will perhaps be able to include them.

The rule also necessitated the omission (except for income and land distribution) of data on differences *within* countries. It should be clear to the reader, as it is to us, that this is a major omission. The importance of the distribution of values within a country can hardly be overstated. One country may have only a moderate number of radio receivers, but they may be reasonably well distributed around the countryside. Another state, with about the same overall proportion of radios to population, may have them concentrated in urban areas while the countryside remains almost inaccessible to modern ideas. The situations are very different. Or a country may have a relatively high *average* income while the majority of the population lives in poverty. Again, the implications are quite different from those of a more egalitarian distribution of income. In principle one would desire not just the *mean* of a certain value for a country, but also the *median,* the *mode,* and the *range* of the distribution, as well as the frequency and the physical and social location of various levels of the distribution. Obviously this is an impossible demand at the moment; even for countries where these data might possibly be available governments may have a clear interest in suppressing them. For the present we can do little more than state their desirability for social research and try to encourage this kind of data collection and analysis.

Thus in a sense we describe the book as "beginnings." By no means all the series that would be relevant to important theories are included here. Many are not at this stage quantifiable at all; some could have been gathered only with very substantial effort; others, though available, were discarded because of lack of space. This last is particularly true of the indicators of economic development and of mass communications media; we tried to select from the number available several that might not be too closely correlated and thus might enlighten us about different aspects of reality. We have reservations also about the quality of some of the data we have presented. While we have tried to reduce errors to a minimum, some undoubtedly remain, and we shall welcome corrections. We hope that one of the major results of this study will be to emphasize the gaps in existing data and the problems of comparability of those data that do exist.

To discuss our effort in terms of "beginnings" is not to imply that it has no intellectual ancestry. Previous compilations of data were indispensable, the most important obviously being the works of the United Nations and its specialized agencies.[2] Others are acknowledged in the tables. But we wish to mention here not existing *collections,* but past and current attempts to *analyze* this kind of data. In discussing these contributions we shall group them into four general categories, defined by the interests of the authors and the variables concerned.

1. *Primarily economic.* Several economists have made systematic cross-national comparisons. The leader in this field is undoubtedly Simon Kuznets, who has published a number of studies comparing the character-

---

2. Cf. also the two-volume work of W. S. Woytinsky and E. S. Woytinsky (*World Commerce and Governments*, New York, 1955, and *World Population and Production*, New York, 1955). Norton Ginsburg (*Atlas of Economic Development*, Chicago, 1961) has produced an important compilation in some ways similar to Part A of this book. The major difference is our attempt to go beyond economic development variables to the broader analysis of social and especially political factors.

istics of 60 or more nations.[3] Charles Wolf has developed a sophisticated model and computed indices of "self-help" on the part of foreign aid recipients.[4] The variables included in these analyses are such explicitly economic ones as the relative shares in Gross National Product of foreign trade, private consumption, and gross capital formation, foreign aid received, the relative contribution of various sectors of the economy to total production, and the distribution of income within countries. An acquaintance with this work is essential to further exploration, and most of these variables are included in this volume. Nevertheless a wider scope is necessary for political and social research.

2. *Economic growth,* including such indicators of social change as urbanization and the spread of the mass media. A number of analyses have explored the question of stages of political and social development, and factor analysis has been used to establish basic patterns. Brian J. L. Berry performed a factor analysis on 43 variables for 90 countries.[5] The variables were principally economic ones, but included also indices of urbanization, literacy, education, and development of the mass media. He found that four factors accounted for most of the variation and that the factor accounting for by far the greatest variation was one related to economic development. And Leo Schnore examined cross-national data on 11 variables.[6] He too derived a major factor related to economic development and urbanization.

Daniel Lerner has presented models of modern, transitional, and traditional societies, supported by social, economic, and demographic data for 54 countries.[7] He examined several of the latter—urbanization, literacy, media participation, plus political participation—in terms of their mutual interaction, especially their multiple correlations with each other. His conclusion was that the correlations were so high as to demonstrate that the relationship among the sectors *is* systemic. Further analysis, such as examining the relation between literacy and urbanization controlling for a third variable such as population density, added appreciable refinements to the basic model. A UNESCO report also found high simple correlations between indices of communication and literacy, urbanization, income, and industrialization.[8] A number of broadly comparative studies on urban areas have come from the International Urban Research of the University of California at Berkeley.[9]

---

3. Cf. his "A Comparative Appraisal," in Abram Bergson and Simon Kuznets, eds., *Economic Trends in the Soviet Union* (Cambridge, Mass., 1963), pp. 333-72, and further references there to his articles in *Economic Development and Cultural Change.*

4. Charles Wolf, Jr., *Savings and the Measurement of "Self-Help" in Developing Countries,* RAND Monograph RM-3586-ISA (Santa Monica, Cal., 1963).

5. Brian J. L. Berry, "An Inductive Approach to the Regionalization of Economic Development," in Norton Ginsburg, ed., *Essays on Geography and Economic Development* (Chicago, 1960), pp. 78-107; and Berry, "Basic Patterns of Economic Development," in Ginsburg, *Atlas*, pp. 110-19.

6. Leo F. Schnore, "The Statistical Measurement of Urbanization and Economic Development," *Land Economics, 37* (August 1961), 230-45.

7. Daniel Lerner, *The Passing of Traditional Society* (Glencoe, Ill., 1958), ch. 2.

8. *Freedom of Information: Development of Information Media in Under-developed Countries,* Report by the Director General of UNESCO (Paris, 1961), pp. 38ff.

9. For the basic data cf. International Urban Research, *The World's Metropolitan Areas* (Berkeley, Cal., 1959).

Several interesting analyses have explored the question of stages of economic and social development. A recent United Nations study examined the relative standing of 74 countries and territories on indices of income, health, literacy, and food consumption.[10] The report found that certain levels of social and economic development were usually associated; where the discrepancy was wide, especially where economic growth seemed to outpace social development, political strain and instability were likely to be quite marked. Similarly Karl W. Deutsch produced a provocative analysis which, though based on a smaller number of countries, included data on rates of change over a longer time span.[11] And Irma Adelman has presented a most interesting analysis of the relation between several economic and social variables and age-specific fertility and mortality rates.[12]

3. *Social and cultural,* usually including economic data. The most massive effort yet undertaken is in anthropology: the Human Relations Area Files collection of data on a sample of the world's societies.[13] Many important analytical projects have depended on the collection in this repository. The files incorporate information on societies at all levels of development, but the effort to apply anthropological techniques of data gathering and codification to nation-states has not been fully successful. Most comparisons have been limited to nonliterate tribes.

Students of sociology and social psychology have produced several valuable cross-national comparisons for a substantial number of countries. The pioneering effort, though it was for years virtually ignored, was that of Pitirim Sorokin on social mobility data.[14] A more recent effort at rigorous comparison is S. M. Miller's analysis of occupational mobility and stratification for 18 countries.[15] Also to be noted is the attempt by David C. McClelland to relate content analysis data on basic attitudes in 41 countries to demographic and social variables.[16] The most thoroughly validated of McClelland's measures, the Achievement Motive, is included in the series given in this book.

In this context the work of R. B. Cattell must also be mentioned. Cattell factor-analyzed a very wide variety of data—72 variables—first for 69 countries and then later for only 40 countries. In each study he derived 12 separate factors. Factor analysis requires a substantial amount of interpretation in identifying the meaning of the resulting factors; Cattell's interpretation is subject to a variety of evaluations. The quality of his data seems also not to have been high; at the time it was done much of it was necessarily derived from old League of Nations material.[17]

10. U. N., *Report on the World Social Situation* (New York, 1961), ch. 3.

11. Karl W. Deutsch, "Social Mobilization and Political Development," *American Political Science Review,* 55 (September 1961), 493–514.

12. Irma Adelman, "An Econometric Analysis of Population Growth," *American Economic Review,* 53 (June 1963), 314–39.

13. For the code used in classifying information cf. G. P. Murdoch et al., *An Outline of Cultural Materials* (4th ed. New Haven, 1961), and for the list of societies cf. Murdoch, *An Outline of World Cultures* (3d ed. New Haven, 1963).

14. Pitirim Sorokin, *Social Mobility* (London, 1927; reprinted Glencoe, Ill., 1959).

15. S. M. Miller, "Comparative Social Mobility," *Current Sociology,* 9 (1960), 1–89.

16. David C. McClelland, *The Achieving Society* (Princeton, 1961).

17. Raymond B. Cattell, "The Dimensions of Culture Patterns of Factorization of National Characters," *Journal of Abnormal and Social Psychology,* 44 (1949), 215–53; and Raymond B. Cattell, H. Breul, and H. Parker Hartman, "An Attempt at More Refined Definition of the Cultural Dimensions of Syntality of Modern Nations," *American Sociological Review,* 17 (1951), 408–21.

4. *Political,* including some economic and social variables. One of the most ambitious is Arthur Banks' and Robert Textor's recently published study, *A Cross-Polity Survey.*[18] This effort represents a rating of 115 separate political entities on 57 different political and social characteristics and offers tables showing the degree of association between variables. Some of the basic characteristics measured were "hard," quantifiable items like literacy or national income; others were "soft," judgmental variables like interest articulation or the political role of the police. This is the first difference between their study and this volume. We have limited ourselves, in the tables, to quantifiable variables. The Banks–Textor approach has obvious advantages in terms of inclusiveness; it has equally obvious disadvantages in terms of reproducibility. In addition Banks and Textor chose to dichotomize their variables. Sometimes this was the only reasonable option—it was not possible to draw fine distinctions in the political importance of the police from country to country. At other times this meant the loss of important information, as in the case of literacy or national income where more precise measurement is possible. The loss of information placed severe limits on the kind and sophistication of analytical techniques open to them; in addition it limited the ability of the reader to use the data himself and try different combinations and different cutting points for dichotomization. To us the importance of the Banks–Textor effort, and less ambitious works of a similar type, is complementary rather than competitive to the one undertaken here.

A similar approach is characteristic of work by Lyle W. Shannon. Shannon also dichotomized his series into high and low groups of countries, but his analysis included the creation of Guttman scales as well as simple indices of the degree of association between paired variables.[19] One major limitation, however, is the restriction of the political part of the analysis to "self-governing" or "non-self-governing."

In a seminal study Seymour Martin Lipset examined the social prerequisites of democracy, comparing the characteristics of democratic and nondemocratic states in Western Europe and Latin America. "Stable democracies," "unstable democracies," and "dictatorships" were distinguished, and a relatively high level of economic development was usually found associated with the former, especially when region (Europe or Latin America) was controlled. Except for the control for region Lipset's technique was basically a simple correlation of various indices of economic development with a dichotomized variable of political system, though he did not compute any statistical measures of association.[20] A similar effort for more countries was done by Gabriel Almond and James Coleman.[21]

---

18. Arthur S. Banks and Robert Textor, *A Cross-Polity Survey* (Cambridge, Mass., 1963).

19. Lyle W. Shannon, "Socio-economic Development and Political Status," *Social Problems,* Fall 1959, pp. 157–69; "Is Level of Development Related to Capacity for Self-Government?" *The American Journal of Economics and Sociology,* 17, no. 3 (1958), pp. 367–81; "The Demographic Characteristics of Non-Self-Governing Areas," *Planning Outlook,* 5,/no. 3 (1960); and further references there.

20. Seymour Martin Lipset, "Some Social Requisites of Democracy: Economic Development and Political Legitimacy," *American Political Science Review,* 53 (March 1959), 69–105.

21. Gabriel A. Almond and James S. Coleman, *The Politics of the Developing Areas* (Princeton, 1960), pp. 579–81.

A more recent study by Feierabend, Feierabend, and Nesvold examined 84 countries for the relationship between various indices of social and economic development and what is basically a seven-step index of political stability.[22] Although they also presented an analysis in terms of a ratio of want formation to want satisfaction, the major part of the paper related to the degree of association between the political index and each of the economic and social ones. A tabular presentation also brought out the fact that the highest levels of instability are associated with *middle* levels of economic development. Another examination of the explicitly political aspects of national growth is that of Phillips Cutright.[23] Dissatisfied with the efforts of Lipset and Shannon, he created his own index of political development. His index is not, and seems not intended to be, a satisfactory measure of democracy; it is a measure of the complexity of political institutions and is a much more refined and replicable index than most earlier attempts. Furthermore, he applies such methods as multiple regression analysis to bring out some of the implications of his data.

It is clear that many aspects of economic development—the growth of income, literacy, education, health facilities, urbanization, industrialization—bear some fairly close relationship to political development. But to sort out the nature of the relationship one must add other variables to the analysis. In a study published elsewhere Bruce Russett has applied multiple regression with partial success in discriminating the effects of different variables, including the degree of equality in the distribution of agricultural land.[24] This study of 47 countries concluded that inequality clearly is associated with political instability, especially when other influences such as per capita G. N. P. and the percentage of the labor force engaged in agriculture are taken into account. Nevertheless theories that place a great deal of emphasis on the inequality problem leave much to be explained. A major attempt to include a wide variety of indices in a factor analysis, not limited to measures of economic development, is Rudolph Rummel's Dimensionality of Nations Project. One study from this project has so far appeared; it attempts to identify patterns of domestic and international conflict.[25]

One other effort to broaden the theoretical scope of political cross-national analyses can be found in an article in which Karl Deutsch proposes certain indices for background data on the stability and capabilities of governments.[26] He suggests that the background conditions for stability may be expressed as a ratio of governmental burdens to capabilities: the former might be measured by the percentage of the population literate, the percentage of political participation, and the extent of inequality of income

22. Ivo K. Feierabend, Rosalind L. Feierabend, and Betty A. Nesvold, "Correlates of Political Stability," Paper Presented at the 1963 Annual Meeting of the American Political Science Association, Sept. 4-7, 1963.

23. Phillips Cutright, "National Political Development: Measurement and Analysis," *American Sociological Review*, 28 (April 1963), 253-64.

24. Bruce M. Russett, "Inequality and Instability: The Relation of Land Tenure to Politics," *World Politics*, 16 (April 1964), 442-53.

25. Rudolph J. Rummel, "Dimensions of Conflict Behavior Within and Between Nations," *General Systems*, Yearbook of the Society for the Advancement of General Systems Theory, Ann Arbor, Mich., 1963.

26. Karl W. Deutsch, "Toward an Inventory of Basic Trends and Patterns in Comparative International Politics," *American Political Science Review*, 54 (March 1960), 34-57.

distribution. Governmental capabilities might, he suggests, be measured by per capita national income and by the share of the government sector in total national income. He presents only a little data, and emphasizes the need for empirical investigation and refinement of the concepts. Much of the data needed for such an investigation can be found in this volume.

Several other studies might be mentioned, but this listing probably includes most of the important ones using a number of countries and several different variables. In any case it should now be clear that we have built upon the work of others in this field. Our first emphasis has been methodological—the use of techniques to supplement the computation of simple indices of correlation—in order better to find leads and lags and to identify deviant cases. We have not analyzed all our data fully in this respect, but we have tried at least to illustrate the possible uses of a number of techniques.

Our second objective has been to include a great number of different social, cultural, and economic variables in the book—variables that seem for one reason or another to be politically relevant. The most difficult variables to obtain data on, or frequently even to conceptualize in operational terms, have been the explicitly political ones like political stability. We hope that any shortcomings in this respect will be recognized as stemming in some part from the still exploratory nature of this kind of research. Most of our intellectual predecessors too have had least success with the political variables. On the other hand, the easiest variables to measure are usually those most closely related to economic development. Nevertheless we made a deliberate effort to include indices which did not seem necessarily to be part of an overall pattern of economic development. Still, one cannot be sure whether a given variable is associated with economic development until the data have been gathered and analyzed. In any case the degree of association, the deviant cases, and the relationship with third variables are always instructive.

Section A contains 75 series of data for all those countries for which we have been able to discover reasonably reliable information. The series are "profiled," that is, the countries are ranked from highest to lowest on the index, and simple statistical summary measures are presented. This method of presentation will enable the reader to ascertain very quickly the relative positions of various states, and to compare rankings on one series with those on another.

The summary measures given are range, mean, median, standard deviation, case deciles and data deciles, and modal decile. The range is simply the difference between the highest and the lowest value given, and measures the amount of dispersion. The mean is the average; the median represents the middle state in the range, i.e. the country with an equal number of states above and below it.

One important characteristic to be ascertained about any series is its distribution—not just the mean or median and the range, but the number of states to be found at various points within the range. A distribution may be normal, that is, most of the states may be found in the middle of the range, with the remainder distributed about equally on either side of the mean. In that case the average, the median, the mode, and the midpoint of

the range all coincide. Or it may be bimodal, with a large proportion of
the states at one point on the range and another large segment grouped at
another point, with few between. Or it may be skewed, with most of the
states concentrated at one end of the range. Other distributions, with important statistical properties, include the Yule and Poisson distributions.
In this book the population and per capita G. N. P. series neatly illustrate
highly skewed distributions, the Roman Catholic series is bimodal, while
the Achievement Motive series approximates a normal distribution.

The properties of these distributions may be identified in several ways.
One measure of skewness takes advantage of the fact that the greater the
skewness the larger is the difference between the mean and the median.
Using the summary measures given at the top of each table one can calcu-
late skewness as equal to $3(\overline{X}-Md)/s$ where $\overline{X}$ is the mean, Md the median,
and s the standard deviation. To identify the direction in which the distribution is skewed, or to see whether perhaps it is bimodal or even trimodal,
one can look at the range deciles along the right-hand side of the listing.
The range deciles simply divide the range into tenths, and one can easily
see how many cases fall into each tenth of the range. The decile with the
most cases, or modal decile, is identified at the top of the page. Finally,
a small graph at the top of each table shows the distribution function. The
range of the series is given in descending order from left to right, and the
number of cases in each decile is given along the vertical axis.[27]

As the comparison of countries' rankings in different series would be
complicated by the wide variation in the number of countries represented
in each table (varying between 11 and 134), we have given several additional
aids. One is the listing of case deciles at the far left of the table. The
number of cases in the series is divided by ten, and the beginning of each
tenth marked with a Roman numeral. The twentieth rank is relatively very
much lower in a short table than in a long one, but the second tenth, or
second decile, will be much more comparable in each. As a further aid
we note at the left of each table the points near which 25 per cent, 50 per
cent, and 75 per cent of the total population of the countries represented in
the table are reached. Also, at the upper right of the table we give the
percentage of the world's population which is represented by the countries
in the table, allowing the reader to see how complete it is.

We have presented data for a basic list of 133 countries. They include
all members of the United Nations (except Byelorussian S. S. R. and Ukrai-
nian S. S. R.), colonies for which data are generally available, and independent states not members of the United Nations (East and West Germany,
North and South Korea, North and South Vietnam, and Mainland China, but
not very small states like Monaco and Andorra). Each table is preceded
by a discussion of the comparability and reliability of the data. Wherever
possible we have made an estimate, at least in terms of a general order
of magnitude, of the error in the series.

———

27. The scale of the vertical axis is adjusted so as to avoid distortion of the curve by small Ns.
The height of the vertical axis is calculated according to the formula N/2 rounded to the nearest
ten = length of vertical axis.

N. B.   With the exception of a single table (8:   Annual Percentage Rate of Increase in Population) to be discussed in the introduction to that table, a percentage error margin applies to a *percentage of the datum,* whether that figure is itself a percentage or an absolute number.   Thus an error margin of ±10 per cent means, when applied to a figure listed as 60 per cent, that the error range is from 54 per cent to 66 per cent, not from 50 per cent to 70 per cent.[28]

Part B of this volume represents a preliminary analysis of the data.   It begins with a table of simple correlations (the correlation of each series with every other series), and then illustrates a variety of more complex analytical techniques as applied to some of the material.

------

28.   For reasons that will be apparent the data in Table 1 for Total Population, 1961, are given with an error *range* (total error) rather than an error *margin* (error on either side).

Part A
Distribution Profiles

Human Resources

1. TOTAL POPULATION, 1961

The following population estimates are based on what the United Nations calls the "modified de facto," or "international conventional total." This is defined as "the total number of persons present in the country at the time of the census, excluding foreign military, naval, and diplomatic personnel and their families located in the country but including military, naval, and diplomatic personnel of the country and their families located abroad and merchant seamen resident in the country but at sea at the time of the census."[1] In principle the totals also include data for such groups as jungle tribes, aborigines, nomadic peoples, displaced persons and refugees, and exclude enemy prisoners of war stationed inside the country. Most of the cases where the U. N. data deviate from this basic definition are trivial, although occasionally, as in some Latin American countries, exclusion of the Indian jungle population underestimates the total by 5% or more. Where the United Nations has not adjusted the reported totals to conform with this definition, and where we have had the information necessary to make at least an approximate adjustment, we have done so.

A much more serious source of inaccuracy and incomparability stems not from different definitions but from different methods and periods of data collection. Three sources of error in total population estimates can be identified: the base, such as the census total, from which later annual estimates must be calculated; the method of adjusting for population increase; and the period of time from the base date for which an approximate adjustment must be made.

It is hardly possible to know precisely how much error is introduced by a given data collection or adjustment method, but the United Nations has provided the following four-part code, with approximate error *ranges* as typical:[2]

I. Nature of base data (error ranges in per cent of estimated population—these error ranges are especially approximate, since the quality of different national census methods varies widely)
   A. Complete census of individuals
      1.0% in censuses taken at least decennially;
      2.0% in censuses taken sporadically;
      3.5% in censuses taken for the first time (no distinction is made among these three different types in this part of the code, but the nature of the census can nevertheless usually be deduced from its date and the rest of the code).

---

1. U. N., *Demographic Yearbook, 1960* (New York, 1961), p. 17.
2. Ibid., pp. 1–8.

    B. Sample census or survey—5.0%
    C. Partial census or registration; annual count (apparently this is the same as an "unconventional count"; e.g., a count of dwellings, or a count from voting or tax registers)—10.0%
    D. Conjecture—20.0%
    .. nature of base data undetermined

II. Recency of base data

A numeral suffix to the first part of the code, indicating the number of years since the base data were established.

III. Method of time adjustment

    a Adjustment by a continuous population register of births and deaths;
    b Adjustment based on a calculated balance of births, deaths, and migration;
    c Adjustment by assumed rate of increase;
    d No adjustment; base data held constant;
    x Adjustment derived from regional population estimates; e.g., an estimate for Saudi Arabia based on the rate of increase in other Middle Eastern countries;
    .. Method of adjustment not determined.

IV. Quality of time adjustment

Adjustments of types a and b:
    1 Population balance adequately accounted for;[3]
    2 Adequacy of population balance not determined;
    3 Population balance not adequately accounted for.

Adjustments of type c:
    1 Two or more decennial censuses;
    2 Two or more censuses taken at intervals exceeding ten years;
    3 One census or none.

Approximate error ranges for Parts III and IV are:

a1 — 0.1%	c1 — 0.6%
a2 — 0.2%	c2 — 0.8%
a3 — 0.4%	c3 — 1.2%
b1 — 0.2%	d — 1.6%
b2 — 0.4%	x — 1.0%
b3 — 0.8%	.. — 1.2%

From this code and the corresponding error ranges one can calculate for the complete estimate an error range (E) with the following formula: $E = B + t(T)$, where B is the range of per cent error imputed to the base data, t the number of years since the base data were established, and T the range of annual per cent error imputed to the time adjustment. Most error arises from underestimation, so three-quarters of the error range applies above the estimate, one quarter below it.

The United Nations suggests these error calculations and includes the necessary codes in the *Demographic* and *Statistical Yearbooks*, but nowhere are the error ranges actually calculated. In the following table we have

---

3. For a definition of "adequate" see ibid., p. 21.

indicated our calculation of the error range in parentheses after the name of the country. In only one type of situation will the error range not correspond to the code given by the United Nations. In a number of instances the source does not give an estimate for 1961, but only for an earlier year, or it gives an estimate but indicates that the estimate is really for a previous base year which was not adjusted. When this occurred we made our own adjusted estimate for 1961; the rate used was either that estimated for the country by the *Statistical Yearbook* or one we calculated from data applying to apparently similar countries in the region. We have assumed that this adjustment was subject to an error range of 1% a year. In no instance have we calculated indicated total error ranges greater than 20% (the range for conjecture).

Let us take Libya as an example. The base data are derived from a 1954 census which was the first of its kind to be taken; it was at least recent enough to be of use in calculating rates of change (base data error of 3.5%). The adjustment was made by means of an assumed rate of increase obviously not derived from the data of two or more censuses (adjustment error of 1.2% a year, for seven years). Combining the two results gives an error range of 11.9%.

It should be observed that the error ranges so derived seem quite generous. While it is not possible to estimate the probability that the actual population total does fall within this error range, it would appear that the probability is high. The major exception occurs in some underdeveloped countries which have taken a decennial census. According to the United Nations code an error range of 1% should be assigned in such instances. This would often seem to be too narrow, but we lack the detailed information to judge particular cases. Also, in a very few cases of the grossest conjecture, even a range of 20% may be too small.

TABLE 1

Total Population, 1961
(mid-year)

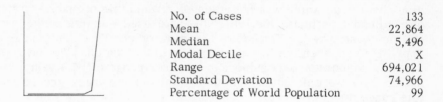

No. of Cases	133
Mean	22,864
Median	5,496
Modal Decile	X
Range	694,021
Standard Deviation	74,966
Percentage of World Population	99

% of Table Population	Case Deciles	Rank	Country	Population (thousands)	Range Deciles
22.9	I	1	China (Mainland) (20.0)	694,200	I–III
		2	India (1.0)[1]	442,195	IV–VI
		3	U.S.S.R. (5.9)	218,000	VII
50.8		4	United States (1.2)	183,742	VIII
		5	Indonesia (3.5)	95,655	IX
		6	Pakistan (1.0)	94,547	
		7	Japan (1.2)	94,050	
		8	Brazil (1.6)[2]	73,238	
		9	West Germany (1.0)	54,027	X
		10	United Kingdom (1.0)	52,925	
		11	Italy (1.0)	49,455	
		12	France (2.4)	45,960	
		13	Mexico (1.6)	36,091	
		14	Nigeria (14.3)	35,752	
	II	15	Spain (1.6)	30,559	
		16	Poland (1.2)	29,965	
74.6		17	Philippines (2.6)	28,727	
		18	Turkey (1.6)	28,602	
		19	Thailand (2.6)	27,181	
		20	Egypt (4.3)	26,593	
		21	South Korea (1.8)	25,375	
		22	Ethiopia (20.0)[3]	22,122	
		23	Burma (19.5)	21,527	
		24	Iran (7.4)	20,678	
		25	Argentina (2.2)	20,346	
		26	Yugoslavia (1.0)	18,607	
	III	27	Romania (5.0)	18,567	
		28	Canada (1.0)	18,269	
		29	North Vietnam (4.5)	16,690	
		30	South Africa (1.6)	16,249	
		31	East Germany (7.9)	16,061	
		32	South Vietnam (12.0)	14,520	
		33	Congo (Leopoldville) (12.2)	14,464	
		34	Colombia (11.5)	14,443	

TABLE 1 (continued)

% of Table Population	Case Deciles	Rank	Country	Population (thousands)	Range Deciles
		35	Afghanistan (20.0)	14,204	
		36	Czechoslovakia (1.0)	13,776	
		37	Sudan (11.0)	12,109	
		38	Morocco (2.2)	11,925	
		39	Netherlands (3.4)	11,637	
	IV	40	Algeria (1.8)	10,989	
		41	Taiwan (1.5)	10,971	
		42	Peru (2.0)[2]	10,820	
		43	Australia (1.0)[4]	10,547	
		44	Ceylon (2.6)	10,167	
		45	Hungary (1.2)	10,028	
		46	Tanganyika (5.9)	9,399	
		47	Nepal (1.0)	9,388	
		48	Belgium (1.0)	9,184	
		49	Portugal (1.6)	8,992	
		50	North Korea (20.0)	8,649	
		51	Rhodesia & Nyasaland (20.0)	8,520	
		52	Kenya (4.7)	8,485	
		53	Greece (1.0)	8,402	
	V	54	Bulgaria (3.0)	7,943	
		55	Chile (1.4)	7,827	
		56	Venezuela (1.0)[2]	7,621	
		57	Sweden (1.0)	7,520	
		58	Iraq (8.3)	7,263	
		59	Malaya (2.6)	7,137	
		60	Austria (1.0)	7,081	
		61	Ghana (2.2)	6,943	
		62	Cuba (8.3)	6,933	
		63	Uganda (4.4)	6,845	
		64	Mozambique (2.0)	6,650	
		65	Saudi Arabia (20.0)	6,313	
		66	Madagascar (16.0)	5,577	
	VI	67	Switzerland (1.2)	5,496	
		68	Cambodia (20.0)	5,335	
		69	Yemen (20.0)	5,000	
		70	Syria (3.9)[5]	4,903	
		71	Angola (2.0)	4,870	
		72	Denmark (1.6)	4,617	
		73	Finland (1.2)	4,467	
		74	Ecuador (12.3)[6]	4,455	
		75	Upper Volta (5.0)	4,405	
		76	Tunisia (4.0)	4,254	
		77	Haiti (7.9)	4,249	
		78	Cameroun (20.0)	4,135	
		79	Mali (20.0)	4,100	
	VII	80	Guatemala (6.4)	3,886	
		81	Norway (3.1)	3,611	
		82	Bolivia (16.7)	3,500	
		83	Ivory Coast (9.8)	3,300	
		84	Hong Kong (3.5)	3,178	

TABLE 1 (continued)

% of Table Population	Case Deciles	Rank	Country	Population (thousands)	Range Deciles
		85	Dominican Republic (1.8)	3,116	
		86	Senegal (6.2)	2,980	
		87	Uruguay (20.0)	2,867	
		88	Ireland (1.0)	2,815	
		89	Guinea (20.0)	2,800	
		90	Rwanda (20.0)	2,743	
		91	Chad (16.0)	2,680	
		92	El Salvador (1.0)	2,501	
		93	Niger (20.0)	2,492	
	VIII	94	Sierra Leone (20.0)	2,450	
		95	New Zealand (1.0)	2,420	
		96	Puerto Rico (1.2)	2,409	
		97	Burundi (20.0)	2,262	
		98	Israel (1.0)	2,185	
		99	Dahomey (5.0)	2,050	
		100	Somalia (20.0)	2,030	
		101	Honduras (3.5)	1,893	
		102	Laos (13.6)	1,850	
		103	Lebanon (20.0)	1,817	
		104	Paraguay (16.7)	1,812	
		105	Jordan (20.0)	1,690	
		106	Singapore (2.6)	1,687	
	IX	107	Albania (2.2)	1,660	
		108	Jamaica (2.2)	1,631	
		109	Nicaragua (10.8)	1,526	
		110	Togo (7.1)	1,480	
		111	Liberia (20.0)	1,290	
		112	Central African Republic (7.4)	1,227	
		113	Costa Rica (6.4)	1,225	
		114	Libya (11.9)	1,216	
		115	Aden (20.0)	1,210	
		116	Panama (1.6)	1,109	
		117	Mongolian People's Republic (9.5)	968	
		118	Congo (Brazzaville) (20.0)	917	
		119	Trinidad & Tobago (2.2)	859	
	X	120	Sarawak (2.8)	760	
		121	Mauritania (20.0)	659	
		122	Mauritius (5.3)	656	
		123	British Guiana (2.2)	582	
		124	Cyprus (2.4)	577	
		125	South West Africa (1.6)	534	
		126	Gabon (20.0)	448	
		127	Malta & Gozo (2.6)	329	
		128	Kuwait (20.0)	322	
		129	Surinam (12.3)	321	
		130	Luxembourg (2.4)	317	
		131	Barbados (2.2)	236	
		132	Netherlands Antilles (2.4)	194	
		133	Iceland (3.1)	179	

TABLE 1 (continued)

[1] Includes Kashmir-Jammu and former Portuguese India; excludes Northeast Frontier Agency.

[2] Adjusted to include Indian jungle population.

[3] This figure is perhaps at least 25% too high, regardless of the U. N. error estimate. Paul Rosenstein-Rodan (*International Aid for Underdeveloped Countries*, Cambridge, Mass., 1961, p. 20) uses an estimate of 15 million, which he regards as, if anything, on the high side.

[4] Adjusted to include aborigines.

[5] Adjusted to include Palestinian refugees.

[6] Excludes Indian jungle population (number unknown).

[7] Adjusted to include Indians and Negroes living in tribes.

Source: U. N., *Statistical Yearbook, 1962* (New York, 1963).

2. PERCENTAGE OF POPULATION OF WORKING AGE (15–64)

The following data will be used as bases from which various ratios will later be calculated. These ratios include both information involving the working-age population (such as wage and salary earners as a percentage of population aged 15–64), and information involving other age groups (such as voting age) where the base data are calculated in essentially the same manner as is working-age population. The totals presented in this table are useful in themselves in that they give an approximate indication of the proportionate size of the potentially productive, as compared with the dependent, segment of the population. Of course defining "working age" as 15–64 is artificial and subject in practice to considerable variation among countries. Not all the working-age population is in the labor force.

Four major sources of error affect the following figures:

1. The accuracy of the original base estimate, discussed in the introduction to Table 1.

2. Underenumeration of particular age groups. Children seem to be underenumerated everywhere, to varying degrees. It may be assumed that this kind of error is associated with error in estimates of total population, but it is impossible to know the degree of error and the strength of the relationship.

3. The completeness of the age breakdown published. In the majority of instances data were given for the age groups necessary to compute directly the 15–64 age group. These countries are coded I in the table.

In a number of cases the published data included figures for ages 0–14, but data for older people were given only for some other age group, such as 60–70. Where this occurred the population aged 60–64 had to be estimated from whatever age breakdown was available; these countries are coded II.

Sometimes an age breakdown of some sort was available, but the data did not coincide with either end of the 15–64 group. For these countries data for both the 0–14 and 65-and-over groups had to be estimated from some other age breakdown, and the countries are coded III.

There were several instances in which no detailed age breakdowns were available, yet we wanted to have some estimate for the country to serve as a base for further calculations. When possible we applied to that country the age breakdown available for another country which seemed culturally related and at a similar stage of economic development (e.g. the age breakdown for Turkey was applied to Lebanon). But in most cases (all low-income countries), no satisfactory data for a sufficiently similar country were available. Here we simply calculated the mean (56.0%) working-age population for those low-income countries for which data were available, and applied it. All such indirect estimates are coded IV.

4. Misstatement of age to the census or sample-survey taker in the country. For various reasons, including economic and political ones, a person may deliberately misstate his age. In addition, there is the problem of semi-deliberate misstatement of age by a year or two; i.e., the tendency of some individuals to give their age in a digit ending in five or

zero. There is no satisfactory way of estimating the frequency of the first kind of deliberate misstatement, but a measure known as Whipple's Index can be used to determine the latter. It is calculated by summing the age returns for the years 23 through 62 years and multiplying by five the percentage which is made up by the total of returns for years ending with five and zero. Thus no preference at all for digits ending in five and zero would produce an index of 100; perfect concentration on them would give an index of 500. The United Nations *Demographic Yearbook* presents 91 age distributions for which Whipple's Index has been calculated, grouped as follows:[1]

A. Less than 105
B. 105–109.9
C. 110–124.9
D. 125–174.9
E. 175 and over

These may be recalculated as percentage error margins by subtracting 100 and dividing the remainder by four. Thus an Index of 105 indicates that 1.25% more age returns than one would expect are concentrated on ages ending in the digits five and zero.

Whipple's Index is a measure of digit preference, and not other kinds of error on age returns. Only to the extent that such digit preference is usually connected with other sources of inaccuracy does Whipple's Index give a general indication of the comparative quality of national estimates. In any case, the error margin calculated from the Index would appear to overstate other kinds of error. It is useful for providing a general ranking of national estimates but cannot give a reliable absolute error margin.

In the table, each country is followed by at least a one- and often a two-part code. The first part indicates the completeness of the basic age breakdown as defined above (codes I–IV); the second gives Whipple's Index group for those countries for which the United Nations has provided it as just described (A–E).[2] Thus the data for the United States are coded I,B—complete age breakdowns, with some but not marked digit preference. The estimate for Lebanon, however, was imputed from the age structure of another country and is merely coded IV.

We may in a general way suggest the maximum error introduced into a series of data by mistakes in age-structure information. As will be clear from the table, the range of age distributions for the 15–64 bracket is relatively narrow—only about 20%, from 70.0% to 49.3%. Furthermore, a fairly clear pattern appears. Most developed countries, with low birth and death rates, have 60% or more of the population in the 15–64 bracket. Most poor but developing countries, where modern public health procedures have cut the death rate without significantly affecting the birth rate, are found to have between 50% and 55%. Underdeveloped countries that have only recently or perhaps not even yet had the benefit of drastically lowered death rates tend to fall somewhere in between 55% and 60%.

---

1. U. N., *Demographic Yearbook, 1960* (New York, 1961), pp. 18–19.
2. In some cases the *Demographic Yearbook* gives Whipple's Index as calculated for an earlier estimate or census of a country than we have used here. When that happened we nevertheless assumed it would apply to the later census as well.

These general patterns, coupled with the fairly narrow overall range, suggest that errors exceeding ±10% are quite rare (e.g., a 15–64 age group estimated at 50% of the total population is very unlikely in fact to be more than 55% or less than 45%, however crude the estimating procedure). Similarly, a ratio derived from that base (such as military personnel as a percentage of working-age population) should not have an error margin exceeding ±10%, providing the numerator is accurate. Thus error in such a table is at least as much, if not more, a function of errors in the total population estimate as in the age-structure estimate.

The percentage of the population of working age clearly is of great consequence for a nation's productivity and not insignificant for its military strength. Or, if one takes the proportion *not* of working age, one has the dependent population, i.e., those who, in general, must be supported by the productive age groups. Cursory inspection of the table will show that the top of the list is composed almost entirely of the economically advanced countries. Even so, there is substantial variation even within this group. West Germany, for instance, is given as 67.7% and New Zealand as only 58.5%; the proportion of Germany's population in the productive age span is thus about 15% greater than New Zealand's.

A further refinement of the data, of obvious interest in predicting future age distributions, would be the percentage composed of children and the percentage in the older age group. For one thing, age distributions may be supposed to be politically relevant. There is evidence that in many respects older people tend to be more conservative; one might expect the political culture of countries with a large elderly population to be more conservative than in countries with young populations. Or conceivably, at least with regard to welfare policies, the countries with older populations might be further "left." A later edition of the *Handbook* may contain this information, but given the current quality and availability of age-distribution statistics it seems desirable here to give only the information of greatest theoretical relevance: working-age population.

TABLE 2

Percentage of Population of Working Age (15–64)

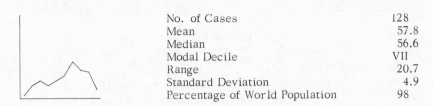

No. of Cases	128
Mean	57.8
Median	56.6
Modal Decile	VII
Range	20.7
Standard Deviation	4.9
Percentage of World Population	98

% of Table Population	Case Deciles	Rank	Country	% Working Age	Range Deciles
I	I	1	Luxembourg (I,A)	70.0	I
		2	Gabon (III)	68.2	
		3	West Germany (I,B)	67.7	II
		4	Uruguay (I)	67.2[a]	
		5	Austria (I,A)	66.5	
		6	Bulgaria (I)	66.4	
		7.5	Italy (I)	66.2	
		7.5	Switzerland (I,A)	66.2	
		9	Romania (I)	66.1[b]	
		10	Sweden (I,A)	66.0	
		11	Greece (I,D)	65.8	III
		12	Hungary (I,A)	65.7	
	II	13	United Kingdom (I,A)	65.3	
		14	East Germany (I,A)	65.1	
		15	Argentina (I,A)	64.9[b]	
		16	Belgium (I,A)	64.5	
		17.5	Mauritania (III)	64.4	
		17.5	Spain (I,C)	64.4[b]	
		19	Japan (I,A)	64.2	
		20.5	Aden (III)	64.1	
		20.5	Mongolian People's Republic (II)	64.1[b]	
		22	French Cameroons (III)	64.0	
		23.5	Czechoslovakia (I)	63.9	
		23.5	Denmark (I,A)	63.9	
		25	Burma (II)	63.6[b]	IV
III	III	26	Portugal (I,C)	63.4	
		27	Norway (I,A)	63.2	
		28.5	Finland (I,A)	62.6	
		28.5	Mali (III)	62.6	
		31	France (I,A)	62.4	
		31	Poland (I)	62.4	
		31	Yugoslavia (I,A)	62.4	
		33	Kuwait (I)	61.8	
		34	Australia (I,A)	61.4	V

TABLE 2 (continued)

% of Table Population	Case Deciles	Rank	Country	% Working Age	Range Deciles
		35	Dahomey (II)	61.3	
		36	Netherlands (I,A)	61.0	
		37.5	Barbados (I,B)	60.2	
		37.5	Indonesia (I)	60.2[c]	
22.3	IV	39	Central African Republic (II)	59.9	
		40.5	China (Mainland) (I)	59.7[d]	
51.8		40.5	United States (I,B)	59.7	
		42	Cuba (I)	59.4	VI
		43.5	Canada (I)	59.1	
		43.5	Israel (I,B)	59.1	
		46	Congo (Brazzaville) (II)	59.0	
		46	India (I)	59.0	
		46	Ireland (I,A)	59.0	
		48.5	Cyprus (I,E)	58.6	
		48.5	Egypt (I,E)	58.6	
		50	New Zealand (I,A)	58.5	
		51	Chile (I)	58.4	
	V	52	Syria (IV)	58.0	
		53.5	Angola (I)	57.9	
		53.5	Nepal (I)	57.9	
		55	Haiti (I,E)	57.8	
		56	South Africa (I,D)	57.7	
		57	Madagascar (I)	57.5	VII
		58	Ceylon (I,D)	57.4	
		60	Iceland (I,A)	57.1	
		60	Lebanon (IV)	57.1	
71.8		60	Turkey (I,E)	57.1	
		62	U.S.S.R. (II)	57.0[b]	
		63	Mozambique (I)	56.8	
		64	Laos (I)	56.7[c]	
	VI	65	Uganda (I)	56.5	
		66.5	Bolivia (I,E)	56.1	
		66.5	Malta & Gozo (I,B)	56.1	
		74	Afghanistan (IV)	56.0	
		74	Chad (II)	56.0	
		74	Ethiopia (IV)	56.0	
		74	Liberia (IV)	56.0	
		74	Niger (III)	56.0	
		74	Ruanda-Urundi (III)	56.0	
		74	Sierra Leone (IV)	56.0	
		74	Somalia (IV)	56.0	
		74	Saudi Arabia (IV)	56.0	
	VII	74	Tanganyika (III)	56.0	
		74	Togo (II)	56.0	
		74	Yemen (IV)	56.0	
		80.5	El Salvador (I,E)	55.8	
		80.5	Libya (I)	55.8	
		82	Upper Volta (I)	55.7	
		83	Brazil (I,D)	55.6	
		84.5	Algeria (I)	55.4	VIII
		84.5	Morocco (I)	55.4	
		87	Guatemala (I,E)	55.3	
		87	Thailand (I,C)	55.3	

TABLE 2 (continued)

% of Table Population	Case Deciles	Rank	Country	% Working Age	Range Deciles
		87	Venezuela (I,D)	55.3	
		89	Singapore (I)	55.0	
	VIII	90	Hong Kong (I)	54.9	
		91	Ivory Coast (II)	54.8	
		93	Albania (I)	54.6	
		93	South Korea (I)	54.6[b]	
		93	Tunisia (II)	54.6	
		96	Guinea (I)	54.5	
		96	Jamaica (I)	54.5[b]	
		96	Congo (Leopoldville) (II)	54.4	
		98.5	British Cameroons (II)	54.3	
		98.5	Colombia (I)	54.3	
		100	Trinidad & Tobago (I,D)	54.1	
		101	Ecuador (I,E)	54.0	
		102	Iran (I)	53.8	
	IX	103	Malaya (I)	53.4	
		104	Cambodia (I)	53.1	IX
		105.5	Panama (I,D)	52.9	
		105.5	Peru (I)	52.9	
		107	Mauritius (I,D)	52.8	
		108	Dominican Republic (I,E)	52.6	
		109	Sarawak (I)	52.5	
		110.5	Rhodesia & Nyasaland (III)	52.4	
		110.5	Taiwan (I)	52.4	
		113	Ghana (I)	52.3[b]	
		113	Nicaragua (I,E)	52.3	
		113	Nigeria (II)	52.3	
		115	Mexico (I,E)	52.2[b]	
	X	116.5	British Guiana (I,C)	52.1	
		116.5	Puerto Rico (I,D)	52.1	
		118.5	Pakistan (II)	51.9[b]	
		118.5	Senegal (III)	51.9[b]	
		120.5	Philippines (I,D)	51.3	X
		120.5	Sudan (I)	51.3	
		122	Surinam (I)	51.1	
		123	Costa Rica (I,D)	50.9[b]	
		124	Paraguay (I)	50.8	
		125	Kenya (III)	50.0	
		126	Iraq (I)	49.9[b]	
		127.5	Honduras (I)	49.3[b]	
		127.5	Jordan (II)	49.3	

Sources: Unless otherwise noted, U. N., *Demographic Yearbook, 1961* (New York, 1962); and *1960* (New York, 1961).

[a] U. N. E. C. L. A., *Economic Bulletin for Latin America, VI, Suplemento Estadistico*, November 1961, p. 9.

[b] U. N., *Compendium of Social Statistics, 1963* (New York, 1963).

[c] U. N., Department of Economic and Social Affairs, *The Population of South-East Asia (Including Ceylon and China: Taiwan)* (New York, 1958), pp. 114, 116.

[d] U. N., Department of Economic and Social Affairs, *The Future Growth of World Population* (New York, 1958), p. 56.

3. WAGE AND SALARY EARNERS AS A PERCENTAGE OF WORKING-AGE POPULATION

These data can be used to measure the relative size of the employee, as compared with the self-employed, sector of the economy. The absolute figures from which these percentages were derived will be used below as a base for one indicator of the impact of unemployment. For the preceding tables it was possible to calculate rather precise error margins; here the necessary information simply does not exist. Since with only a very few exceptions these data are derived from censuses or sample surveys they should be of a fairly high quality—an extremely approximate error margin might be on the order of $\pm 15\%$. The denominator (working-age population) is of course subject independently to error of the magnitudes discussed in connection with Table 2. It must be noted that workers on collective farms are *not* counted as wage and salary earners for the purposes of this series. For certain theoretical purposes this decision might be reversed; for most of the countries where collectives are common the data are available to do so.

The proportion of wage and salary earners is of obvious relevance to theories of society, especially theories about the effect of employee (as compared with self-employed) status on job satisfaction, incentives, and alienation. Note, of course, that all nonemployees are not self-employed, for many are housewives.

Unemployed are in most countries included in the total of wage and salary earners. As mentioned with respect to the previous table, of course not all individuals of working-age population are in the labor force. National definitions of "labor force" vary so widely, however, that for most purposes working-age population seemed a more useful denominator.

28

TABLE 3

Wage and Salary Earners as a Percentage of
Working-Age Population

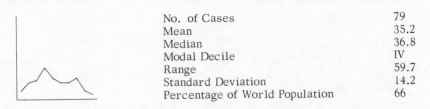

No. of Cases	79
Mean	35.2
Median	36.8
Modal Decile	IV
Range	59.7
Standard Deviation	14.2
Percentage of World Population	66

% of Table Population	Case Deciles	Rank	Country	W. & S. E. as % Pop.	Range Deciles	Year
	I	1	Barbados	62.3	I	1946
		2	United Kingdom	61.0		1951
		3	Sweden	57.1		1960
		4	Hong Kong	55.6	II	1961
		5	Denmark	55.4		1955
		6	Iceland	55.3		1950
		7	West Germany	54.2		1959
	II	8	East Germany	53.1		1946
		9	U.S.S.R.	52.4		1959
27.5		10	United States	51.9		1960
		11	Australia	51.7		1954
		12	Switzerland	51.1		1950
		13	Mauritius	50.7		1952
		14	New Zealand	50.1	III	1956
		15	Canada	48.5		1961
	III	16	British Guiana	48.2		1946
		17	Hungary	47.2		1960
		18	Austria	46.8		1959
		19	France	46.1		1957
		20	Finland	44.9		1950
		21	Norway	44.8		1960
		22	Czechoslovakia	44.5		1950
		23	Netherlands	44.1	IV	1947
	IV	24	Singapore	44.0		1957
		25	Belgium	43.8		1947
		26	Argentina	43.4		1947
		27	Portugal	43.1		1950
		28	Chile	42.5		1952
		29	Trinidad & Tobago	42.3		1956
		30	Costa Rica	42.2		1950
		31	Luxembourg	41.5		1947
	V	32.5	Ireland	40.8		1951
		32.5	Italy	40.8		1960
		34.5	Cuba	40.7		1953

TABLE 3 (continued)

% of Table Population	Case Deciles	Rank	Country	W. & S. E. as % Pop.	Range Deciles	Year
		34.5	Jamaica	40.7		1953
		36	Puerto Rico	39.5		1961
		37	Ceylon	38.5		1953
		38	Spain	38.2	V	1950
		39	Israel	37.8		1960
	VI	40	Ecuador	36.8		1950
		41	Poland	36.5		1950
		42	Malaya	36.2		1957
		43	Cyprus	36.1		1946
		44	El Salvador	34.8		1950
		45	Japan	34.7		1959
		46	Venezuela	33.5		1950
		47	Malta & Gozo	32.4		1948
	VII	48	Nicaragua	32.0	VI	1950
		49	Colombia	31.3		1951
50.1		50	Bulgaria	30.3		1956
		51	Brazil	30.0		1950
		52	Romania	28.1		1956
		53	Mexico	28.0		1958
		54	Peru	27.2		1940
		55	Iran	26.9		1956
	VIII	56	Algeria	24.8	VII	1954
		57	Panama	24.7		1950
		58	Egypt	24.6		1947
		59.5	Tunisia	23.3		1956
		59.5	Yugoslavia	23.3		1956
		61	Honduras	22.9		1961
		62	Pakistan	22.4		1956
		63	Greece	21.1		1951
	IX	64	Northern Rhodesia	20 3	VIII	1956
69.1		65	Taiwan	19.9		1956
		66	India	19.3		1961
		67	Philippines	19.2		1959
		68	Bolivia	19.0		1950
		69	Paraguay	18.4		1950
		70	Morocco	17.9		1952
		71	Congo (Leopoldville)	17.5		1955
	X	72	Kenya	17.3		1960
		73	Nepal	15.5		1954
		74	Haiti	12.0	IX	1950
		75	Turkey	11.8		1955
		76	Thailand	11.2		1960
		77	Ghana	9.5		1960
		78	South Korea	8.1	X	1955
		79	Nigeria	2.6		1959

Sources: I. L. O., *Yearbook of Labour Statistics, 1962* (Geneva, 1963); and *1961* (Geneva, 1962); Y. S. Yegnaraman, "Estimates of Employment and Underemployment at the Beginning of the Third Plan," *AIIC Economic Review, 14* (June 22, 1962), p. 32.

4. FEMALE WAGE AND SALARY EARNERS AS A PERCENTAGE OF TOTAL WAGE AND SALARY EARNERS

Figures for the percentage of women who are economically active, or the percentage of the labor force which is composed of women, are notoriously incomparable.[1] Very great differences in the statistical treatment of unpaid family workers force the analyst concerned with cross-national comparison to concentrate on actual wage and salary earners. Though restricting, this limitation produces much more comparable data. One can then use the percentages to draw inferences about social structure, the impact of female employment outside the home on child rearing, and the social mobilization of women. In advanced countries, at least, one can infer the existence of certain "reserves" of women who, though not normally employed, can be brought into the ranks of wage earners in an emergency.

The error margin should be approximately that for the preceding table, except that in a few countries, such as those with Islamic cultures, the employment of women may not be fully reported.

---

1. On some of the problems cf. U. N., *Demographic Aspects of Manpower: Sex and Age Patterns of Participation in Economic Activities* (New York, 1962), pp. 1-10.

31

TABLE 4

Female Wage and Salary Earners as Percentage of
Total Wage and Salary Earners

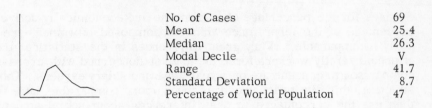

No. of Cases	69
Mean	25.4
Median	26.3
Modal Decile	V
Range	41.7
Standard Deviation	8.7
Percentage of World Population	47

% of Table Population	Case Deciles	Rank	Country	Female W. & S. E. as % Total	Range Deciles	Year
	I	1	U. S. S. R.	46.7	I	1959
		2	Barbados	42.3	II	1946
		3	Jamaica	40.5		1953
		4	Ecuador	40.4		1950
		5	Haiti	39.7		1950
		6	Finland	36.7	III	1950
	II	7	Philippines	35.6		1948
		8	Denmark	34.5		1955
		9	Austria	33.8	IV	1951
		10	West Germany	33.6		1960
		11.5	Poland	33.3		1950
25.5		11.5	Switzerland	33.3		1950
		13	Sweden	33.2		1960
	III	14	Nepal	32.9		1953
		15	United Kingdom	32.6		1951
		16	Hungary	32.0		1960
		17	Ireland	31.2		1951
		18	Panama	31.0		1950
		19	United States	30.5		1950
		20.5	France	30.3		1957
	IV	20.5	Japan	30.3		1960
53.8		22	Peru	30.1		1940
		23	Hong Kong	28.7	V	1961
		24	British Guiana	28.5		1946
		26	Norway	28.2		1950
		26	Czechoslovakia	28.2		1947
		26	Puerto Rico	28.2		1962
	V	28	Romania	27.9		1956
		29	Iceland	27.6		1950
		30	Bolivia	27.4		1950
		31	Bulgaria	27.3		1956
		32	New Zealand	27.0		1956
		33	Thailand	26.6		1960
		34	Ceylon	26.5		1953

TABLE 4 (continued)

% of Table Population	Case Deciles	Rank	Country	Female W. & S. E. as % Total	Range Deciles	Year
	VI	35	Canada	26.3		1962
		36	Italy	26.1		1961
		37	Portugal	26.0		1950
		38	Greece	25.2	VI	1961
		39	Australia	25.0		1954
		40	Venezuela	24.5		1950
		41	Malaya	24.4		1957
	VII	42	Israel	24.0		1961
		43	Chile	23.8		1952
		44	Netherlands	23.5		1947
		45.5	Belgium	23.4		1947
		45.5	Colombia	23.4		1951
		47	Honduras	23.3		1961
		48	Yugoslavia	22.4		1953
	VIII	49	Trinidad & Tobago	22.0		1956
74.2 -------------		50	Argentina	21.2	VII	1947
		51	Mauritius	21.0		1952
		52	Luxembourg	20.2		1947
		53	Costa Rica	19.9		1950
		54	El Salvador	19.5		1950
		55	Brazil	18.5		1950
	IX	56	Singapore	17.8		1957
		57.5	Nicaragua	17.1	VIII	1950
		57.5	Spain	17.1		1950
		59	Cuba	15.9		1953
		60	Taiwan	15.0		1956
		61	South Korea	14.3		1955
		62.5	Iran	12.4	IX	1956
	X	62.5	Turkey	12.4		1955
		64	Morocco	12.1		1952
		65	Malta & Gozo	11.9		1948
		66	Algeria	9.1		1954
		67	Egypt	8.0	X	1947
		68	Pakistan	6.4		1955
		69	Tunisia	5.0		1956

Source: I.L.O., *Yearbook of Labour Statistics, 1962* (Geneva, 1963).

5. LIVE BIRTHS PER 1,000 POPULATION

The accuracy of data on births is obviously heavily dependent on the requirements and means provided for birth registration and the degree to which national laws requiring registration are enforced. The United Nations groups its published data into three categories: "complete" (at least 90% coverage), "unreliable" (less than 90% coverage), and "reliability unknown." We have reproduced from the *Demographic Yearbook* only those items coded as "complete"; any existing error is of course in the direction of understatement, i.e., nonregistration. Thus the figures given here from the *Demographic Yearbook* would be accurate if inflated by a value of from 0 to 11%.

Elimination of all data not coded "reliable" has meant that the *Demographic Yearbook* data series is short; it is very incomplete for the underdeveloped countries and totally excludes the indigenous populations of sub-Saharan Africa. We have therefore added a number of estimates compiled by various independent efforts. Although it is virtually impossible in most cases to calculate adequate error margins, we have tried to include only those data which seemed accurate within 10%. These countries are labeled (E). But as these estimates were intended to replace unacceptable registration figures, the error margin represents a possible overstatement as well as an understatement.

In addition, a small amount of error is added by differences in national definitions of the relevant event. Some countries require "breathing" to establish a live birth; others simply recognize any "signs of life." A few countries do not register as a live birth any infant who dies within 24 hours of birth or, occasionally, before registration. Studies have shown, however, that these variations do not make a difference of more than about 1% in the number of live births recorded, and may safely be ignored.[1]

A final problem arises from the fact that a few countries give births by year of registration rather than year of occurrence. While most births are recorded within a year or two after the event, this is not always the case. Studies in the United States, Chile, Costa Rica, and the Dominican Republic have indicated that the majority of births are recorded no more than two to four years after taking place.[2] In a rapidly expanding population this can have a noticeable effect in reducing the reported birth rate. If, for example, all births are reported exactly two years late in a country where the population is expanding by 2% annually, the birth rate will be understated by 4%. It seems highly unlikely, however, that enough births are reported late enough to lower the apparent, as compared with the real, birth rate by more than 5% in any particular case.

Crude birth rates of course vary widely, in part according to the age structure of the population. Thus relatively young populations, with recently lowered death rates, will almost without exception have high crude

---

1. Cf. the discussion in U.N., *Handbook of Vital Statistics Methods*, ST/STAT/SER.F/7 (New York, 1954), pp. 46–53

2. U.N., *Demographic Yearbook, 1960* (New York, 1961), p. 24.

birth rates. It cannot be assumed, because one country's crude birth rate is higher than another's, that the rate for births per (married) woman of child-bearing age is higher, though this is often the case. Unfortunately adequate data for computing age-specific birth rates are not yet available for many countries, though they are becoming more common and probably can be included in future editions of the *Handbook*.

TABLE 5

Live Births per 1,000 Population

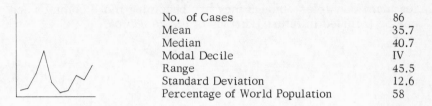

No. of Cases	86
Mean	35.7
Median	40.7
Modal Decile	IV
Range	45.5
Standard Deviation	12.6
Percentage of World Population	58

% of Table Population	Case Deciles	Rank	Country	Births per 1,000	Range Deciles	Year
	I	1	Guinea (E)	60.0[a]	I	1955
		2	Ivory Coast (E)	58.0[a]		1955
		3	Northern Rhodesia (E)	56.8[b]		1950
		4	Ghana (E)	54.0[a]	II	1952–53
		5	Senegal (E)	52.0[a]		1955
		6.5	Dominican Republic (E)	51.0[c]		1955–60
		6.5	Sudan (E)	51.0[a]		1956
		8	Egypt (E)	50.8	III	1956
	II	9	Guatemala (E)	50.0[c]		1955–59
		10	Nicaragua (E)	48.5[c]		1955–60
		11	Costa Rica	47.7		1955–59
		13.5	Ecuador (E)	47.5[c]		1955–60
		13.5	Honduras (E)	47.5[c]		1955–60
		13.5	Paraguay (E)	47.5[c]		1955–60
		13.5	Venezuela (E)	47.5[c]		1955–60
		16.5	Jordan (E)	47.4		1951–57
		16.5	El Salvador	47.4		1955–59
	III	18	Haiti (E)	46.5[c]		1956
		19	Mexico (E)	45.5[c]	IV	1955–59
		23.5	Algeria (E)[1]	45.0[a]		1954
		23.5	Angola (E)	45.0[a]		1950
		23.5	Brazil (E)	45.0[c]		1955–60
		23.5	Chad (E)	45.0[a]		1957
		23.5	Iran (E)	45.0[b]		1956–59
		23.5	Madagascar (E)	45.0[a]		1956
	IV	23.5	Nepal (E)	45.0[b]		1952–54
		23.5	Peru (E)	45.0[c]		1955–60
		28.5	Southern Rhodesia (E)	44.8[b]		1953–55
		28.5	Surinam[2]	44.8		1955–59
		30	Colombia (E)	44.5[c]		1955–60
		31	Malaya	44.4		1955–59
		33	British Guiana[3]	44.0		1955–58
		33	Ceylon (E)	44.0		1953
17.4		33	Congo (Leopoldville) (E)	44.0[a]		1954
	V	35.5	India (E)	43.2[d]		1951

TABLE 5 (continued)

% of Table Population	Case Deciles	Rank	Country	Births per 1,000	Range Deciles	Year
		35.5	Tunisia (E)	43.2[b]		1961
		37	Bolivia (E)	43.0[c]		1955–60
		38.5	Singapore	42.8		1955–59
		38.5	Taiwan	42.8		1955–59
		40.5	Ruanda-Urundi (E)	42.0[a]		1957
		40.5	Thailand (E)	42.0[b]		1956
		42	Mauritius	41.5	V	1955–59
	VI	43	Cambodia (E)	41.4[b]		1959
		44	Congo (Brazzaville) (E)	40.0[a]		1957
		45	Panama	39.9		1955–59
		46.5	Hong Kong	38.3		1955–59
		46.5	Trinidad & Tobago	38.3		1955–59
		48	Jamaica	37.7		1955–59
		49	Chile	35.5	VI	1955–59
		50	Puerto Rico	33.7		1955–59
		51	Cuba (E)	32.0[c]	VII	1955–60
	VII	52	Barbados	31.2		1955–59
		53	Iceland	28.3[e]		1955–59
		55	Canada	27.9	VIII	1955–59
		55	Cyprus	27.9		1950–54
49.2 ------------		55	Israel	27.9		1955–59
		57	Poland	27.4		1955–59
		58	Malta & Gozo	26.8		1955–59
		59	New Zealand	26.3		1955–59
		60	U. S. S. R.	25.3		1955–59
	VIII	61	Yugoslavia	24.8[e]		1955–59
		62	United States	24.6[e]		1955–59
75.3 ------------		63	Portugal	23.6		1955–59
		64	Argentina (E)	23.5[c]	IX	1955–60
		65	Romania	22.9		1955–59
		66	Australia	22.6		1955–59
		67	Spain	21.4		1955–59
		68	Netherlands	21.2		1955–59
	IX	69	Ireland	21.1		1955–59
		70	Uruguay (E)	20.5[c]		1955–60
		71	Finland	19.9		1955–59
		72	Bulgaria	18.7	X	1955–59
		73	Czechoslovakia	18.5		1955–59
		74	France	18.4		1955–59
		75	Japan	18.2		1955–59
		76.5	Italy	18.1		1955–59
		76.5	Norway	18.1		1955–59
	X	78	Hungary	17.8		1955–59
		79	Switzerland	17.5		1955–59
		80	Belgium	17.0		1955–59
		82	Austria	16.8		1955–59
		82	Denmark	16.8		1955–59
		82	West Germany	16.8		1955–59
		84	United Kingdom	16.4		1955–59
		85	Luxembourg	15.9		1955–59
		86	Sweden	14.5		1955–60

TABLE 5 (continued)

[1] Weighted average for Moslem and European population. European data from U. N., *Demographic Yearbook*.

[2] Excluding Amerindians.

[3] Excluding Indians and Negroes living in tribes.

Sources: Unless otherwise noted, U. N., *Demographic Yearbook, 1961* (New York, 1962).

[a] U. N. E. C. A., *Economic Bulletin for Africa*, June 1962, p. 74.

[b] U. N., *Population and Vital Statistics Report*, Statistical Papers, Series A, Vol. XV, Nos. 1–2 (New York, 1963).

[c] U. N. E. C. L. A., *Economic Bulletin for Latin America, Suplemento Estadistico*, October 1962, p. 8.

[d] A. Coale and E. Hoover, *Population Growth and Economic Development in Low Income Countries* (Princeton, 1958), ch. 5.

[e] U. N., *Compendium of Social Statistics, 1963* (New York, 1963), pp. 100, 103.

6. DEATHS PER 1,000 POPULATION

Errors in death registration statistics are, for all practical purposes, errors of underregistration. We have used only those official figures on registration which are identified by the United Nations as at least 90% complete. Where more precise estimates of the completeness of death statistics were available we have so revised the data given; where independent estimates of mortality were available and seemingly reliable within ±10% we have used them. Thus two different error margins are appropriate to the following data. Registration errors have a maximum error of 11% on the side of *underestimation* only. Estimates, labeled (E), should have a maximum error of ±10%. As with birth statistics, our insistence on this fairly high degree of reliability has meant that data for some countries, where the degree of completeness is unknown, had to be excluded.

A few countries have not included deaths of new-born infants dying before registration of birth, but according to studies this makes a difference of only about 1% and, compared with other possible errors, is unimportant.[1] Like crude birth rates, crude death rates are heavily affected by the age structure of the population, and the cautions about the previous table apply here.

---

1. U.N., *Handbook of Vital Statistics Methods*, ST/STAT/SER.F/7 (New York, 1954), pp. 46–53.

TABLE 6

Deaths per 1,000 Population

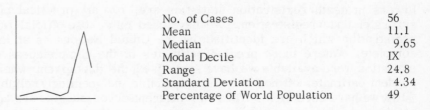

	No. of Cases	56
	Mean	11.1
	Median	9.65
	Modal Decile	IX
	Range	24.8
	Standard Deviation	4.34
	Percentage of World Population	49

% of Table Population	Case Deciles	Rank	Country	Deaths per 1,000	Range Deciles	Year
29.0	I	1	India (E)	31.0[a]	I–III	1951
		2	Bolivia (E)	22.5[b]	IV–V	1955–60
		3	Guatemala (E)	22.0[b]		1955–60
		4	Egypt (E)	21.2		1956
		5	Dominican Republic (E)	18.0[b]	VI	1955–60
	II	6	Colombia (E)	15.5[b]	VII	1955–60
		7	Mexico (E)	14.5[b]		1955–60
		8	El Salvador	13.2	VIII	1955–59
		9	Honduras (E)	13.1		1955–59
		10	Chile (E)	12.5[b]		1955–59
		11	Austria	12.4		1955–59
	III	13	Ceylon (E)	12.0		1953
		13	Ireland	12.0		1955–59
		13	Mauritius	12.0		1955–59
		15.5	Belgium	11.9[c]		1955–59
		15.5	Luxembourg	11.9		1955–59
	IV	17	France	11.8		1955–59
		18	United Kingdom	11.6		1955–59
		19	West Germany	11.4		1955–59
		20	Malaya	11.3		1955–59
		21.5	British Guiana[1]	11.2		1955–59
		21.5	Portugal	11.2		1955–59
	V	23	Yugoslavia	10.6	IX	1955–59
		24	Barbados	10.5		1955–59
50.1		25	Hungary	10.3		1955–59
		26	Switzerland	9.9[c]		1955–59
		27.5	Czechoslovakia	9.7[c]		1955–59
	VI	27.5	Romania	9.7		1955–59
		30.5	Costa Rica	9.6		1955–59
		30.5	Italy	9.6		1955–59
		30.5	Sweden	9.6		1955–59
		30.5	Trinidad & Tobago	9.6		1955–59
		33.5	Spain	9.4		1955–59
	VII	33.5	United States	9.4[c]		1955–59
		35.5	Jamaica	9.3		1955–58

TABLE 6 (continued)

% of Table Population	Case Deciles	Rank	Country	Deaths per 1,000	Range Deciles	Year
		35.5	Jordan (E)	9.3		1959
		38	Denmark	9.1		1955–59
		38	Finland	9.1		1955–59
		38	New Zealand	9.1		1955–59
	VIII	40	Poland	9.0		1955–59
		41.5	Bulgaria	8.9		1955–59
		41.5	Surinam[2]	8.9		1955–59
		44	Australia	8.8		1955–59
		44	Malta & Gozo	8.8		1955–59
	IX	44	Norway	8.8[c]		1955–59
75.1		46	Argentina (E)	8.5[b]	X	1955–60
		47	Canada	8.1		1955–59
		48	Taiwan	8.0		1955–59
		49	Japan	7.8[c]		1955–59
		50.5	Hong Kong	7.6		1955–59
	X	50.5	Netherlands	7.6		1955–59
		52	U.S.S.R.	7.5		1956–60
		53	Singapore	7.3		1955–60
		54.5	Iceland	7.1		1955–59
		54.5	Puerto Rico	7.1		1955–59
		56	Cyprus	6.2		1955–59

[1] Excludes Amerindians.

[2] Excludes Indians and Negroes living in trubes.

Sources: Unless otherwise noted, U. N., *Demographic Yearbook, 1961* (New York, 1962).

[a] A. Coale and E. Hoover, *Population Growth and Economic Development in Low Income Countries* (Princeton, 1958), ch. 5. This estimate appears high but accurate. The data are for a relatively early year (1951); since then the death rate may have declined. Also, India's per capita G. N. P. is lower than that of almost any other state in this table.

[b] U. N. E. C. L. A., *Economic Bulletin for Latin America; Suplemento Estadistico,* October, 1962, p. 8.

[c] U. N., *Compendium of Social Statistics, 1963* (New York, 1963), pp. 100–03.

7. NATURAL INCREASE OF POPULATION—ANNUAL RATE

The natural rate of population growth is obtained simply by subtracting the birth rate from the death rate. Accuracy, then, depends on the quality of the underlying rates, which have been discussed previously. The figures should be accurate within ±10%. This series is slightly longer than the preceding one for death rates; occasionally it is possible to estimate the overall rate of natural increase even when the components (births and deaths) are not known precisely.

TABLE 7

Natural Increase of Population—Annual Rate

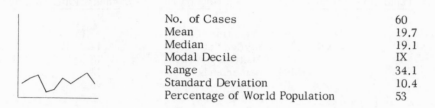

	No. of Cases	60
	Mean	19.7
	Median	19.1
	Modal Decile	IX
	Range	34.1
	Standard Deviation	10.4
	Percentage of World Population	53

% of Table Population	Case Deciles	Rank	Country	Natural Incr., Annual Rate	Range Deciles	Year
	I	1	Costa Rica	38.1	I	1955–59
		2	Jordan (E)	37.3		1957
		3	Surinam[1]	35.9		1955–59
		4	Singapore	35.5		1955–59
		5	Taiwan	34.8		1955–59
		6	El Salvador	34.2	II	1955–59
	II	7	Malaya	33.3		1955–59
		8	Dominican Republic (E)	33.0[a]		1955–60
		9	British Guiana[2]	32.8		1955–59
		10	Venezuela (E)	32.5[a]		1955–60
		11.5	Ceylon (E)	32.0		1953
		11.5	Mexico (E)	32.0[a]		1955–60
	III	13	Hong Kong	30.7	III	1955–59
		14	Egypt (E)	29.6		1956–60
		15	Mauritius	29.5		1955–59
		16	Colombia (E)	29.0[a]		1955–60
		17	Trinidad & Tobago	28.7		1955–59
		18	Honduras (E)	28.5[a]		1955–60
	IV	19	Jamaica	28.1		1955–58
		20	Guatemala (E)	28.0[a]		1955–60
		21	Puerto Rico	27.6	IV	1950–54
		22	Brazil (E)	25.5[a]		1955–60
		23	Chile (E)	23.0[a]	V	1955–60
		24	Israel	21.7		1955–59
	V	25	Iceland	21.2[b]		1955–59
		26	Cuba (E)	21.0[a]	VI	1955–60
		27	Barbados	20.7		1955–59
		28	Bolivia	20.5[a]		1955–60
		29	Cyprus	20.0		1957
		30	Canada	19.8		1955–59
	VI	31	Poland	18.3		1955–59
		32	Malta & Gozo	18.0		1955–59
31.0 - - - - - - - - - - - -		33	U.S.S.R.	17.4	VII	1959
		34	New Zealand	17.2		1955–59
		35	United States	15.2[b]		1955–59

TABLE 7 (continued)

% of Table Population	Case Deciles	Rank	Country	Natural Incr., Annual Rate	Range Deciles	Year
		36	Argentina (E)	15.0[a]		1955–60
	VII	37	Yugoslavia	14.2		1955–59
		38	Australia	13.8	VIII	1955–59
		39	Netherlands	13.6		1955–59
		40	Romania	13.2		1955–59
48.1 ------------		41	Portugal	12.4		1955–59
75.5 ------------		42	India	12.2[c]		1951
	VIII	43	Spain	12.0		1955–59
		44	Finland	10.8		1955–59
		45	Japan	10.4[b]	IX	1955–59
		46	Bulgaria	9.8		1955–59
		47	Norway	9.3[b]		1955–59
		48	Ireland	9.1		1955–59
	IX	49	Czechoslovakia	8.8[b]		1955–59
		50	Italy	8.5		1955–59
		51	Denmark	7.7		1955–59
		52	Switzerland	7.6[b]		1955–59
		53	Hungary	7.5		1955–59
		54	France	6.6	X	1955–59
	X	55	West Germany	5.8		1955–59
		56	Belgium	5.1[b]		1955–59
		57	Sweden	4.9		1955–57
		58	United Kingdom	4.8		1955–59
		59	Austria	4.4		1955–59
		60	Luxembourg	4.0		1955–59

[1] Excludes Indians and Negroes living in tribes.
[2] Excludes Amerindians.

Sources: Unless otherwise noted, U. N., *Demographic Yearbook, 1961* (New York, 1962).

[a] U. N. E. C. L. A., *Economic Bulletin for Latin America, Suplemento Estadistico,* October 1962, p. 8.

[b] U. N., *Compendium of Social Statistics, 1963* (New York, 1963), pp. 100–03.

[c] A. Coale and E. Hoover, *Population Growth and Economic Development in Low Income Countries* (Princeton, 1958), ch. 5.

8. ANNUAL PERCENTAGE RATE OF INCREASE IN POPULATION, 1958–1961

In the table for natural rate of population increase we limited our data to those that seemed reliable within an error margin of $\pm 10\%$. Here, in the interest of obtaining a longer series, we have abandoned that requirement. We have, however, calculated error margins by use of the same methods and data for which we derived error margins for our total population estimates. The formula[1] for the error range (e) in this case is: $e = T (1+E)$, where T is the error range imputed to the time adjustment and E the error range calculated for the population estimate (for T and E see the introduction to Table 1). Population change in this table is of course attributable to migration as well as to births and deaths.

Unlike the error calculations discussed elsewhere, the formula above gives an *absolute range* of per cent error—the error range *is without reference to the size of the datum presented*. Thus an error range of 0.6% means that a population increase rate given as 2.0% actually falls somewhere between 1.7% and 2.3%. Half the error *range* is the *absolute* error *margin* on either side. In a few cases data sufficient to calculate an error margin were not available.

---

1. U. N., *Demographic Yearbook, 1960* (New York, 1961), p. 8.

TABLE 8

Annual Percentage Rate of Increase in Population, 1958–1961

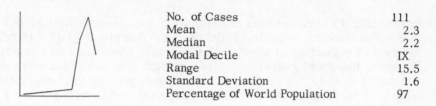

No. of Cases	111
Mean	2.3
Median	2.2
Modal Decile	IX
Range	15.5
Standard Deviation	1.6
Percentage of World Population	97

% of Table Population	Case Deciles	Rank	Country	% Annual Incr. in Pop.	Range Deciles
I	1	Kuwait	15.1	I–VI
		2	Sarawak (.83)	5.1	VII
		3	Syria (.4)	4.8	
		4	Surinam (.88)	4.5	
		5	Costa Rica (.43)	4.4	
		6	South Vietnam (.45)	3.9	VIII
		7	Cambodia (1.4)	3.8	
		8.5	Singapore (.4)	3.7	
		8.5	Taiwan (.1)	3.7	
		11	Brazil (.6)	3.6	
		11	El Salvador (.88)	3.6	
	II	11	Hong Kong (.4)	3.6	
		13	Nicaragua (.89)	3.5	
		14	Dominican Republic (.88)	3.4	
		16.5	Albania (1.2)	3.3	
		16.5	Iraq (1.29)	3.3	
		16.5	Philippines (.6)	3.3	
		16.5	Venezuela (.6)	3.3	
		19.5	Ecuador (.89)	3.2	
		19.5	Malaya (.41)	3.2	
		21.5	Guatemala (.43)	3.1	
		21.5	Mexico (.6)	3.1	
	III	25.5	Afghanistan (1.44)	3.0	
		25.5	British Guiana (.2)	3.0	
		25.5	Honduras (.8)	3.0	
		25.5	Israel	3.0	
		25.5	Mongolian People's Republic (1.31)	3.0	
		25.5	Thailand (.6)	3.0	
		30	South Korea (.83)	2.9	
		30	Trinidad & Tobago (.2)	2.9	
		30	Turkey (.6)	2.9	
		33.5	Madagascar (1.39)	2.8	
		33.5	Mauritius (.20)	2.8	
	IV	33.5	Morocco (1.22)	2.8	
		33.5	Sudan (1.33)	2.8	

TABLE 8 (continued)

% of Table Population	Case Deciles	Rank	Country	% Annual Incr. in Pop.	Range Deciles
		37.5	Ceylon (.2)	2.7	
		37.5	Laos (1.36)	2.7	
		37.5	Panama (.6)	2.7	
		37.5	Sierra Leone (1.4)	2.7	
		40.5	North Korea (1.20)	2.6	IX
		40.5	South Africa (.61)	2.6	
		42.5	Uganda (1.15)	2.5	
		42.5	Egypt (.8)	2.5	
		46	Angola (1.02)	2.4	
	V	46	Chile (.4)	2.4	
		46	Congo (Leopoldville) (1.3)	2.4	
		46	Paraguay (1.40)	2.4	
		46	Rhodesia & Nyasaland (1.44)	2.4	
18.8		49	Indonesia (1.24)	2.3	
		54	Australia	2.2	
		54	Canada (.2)	2.2	
		54	Colombia (.89)	2.2	
		54	Haiti (.43)	2.2	
		54	India (.6)	2.2	
		54	Ivory Coast (1.31)	2.2	
	VI	54	Kenya (1.26)	2.2	
		54	Mozambique (1.02)	2.2	
		54	South West Africa (.60)	2.2	
		60.5	Burma (.9)	2.1	
		60.5	Cuba (.64)	2.1	
		60.5	North Vietnam (1.04)	2.1	
40.3		60.5	Pakistan (.6)	2.1	
		65	China (Mainland)[1]	2.0	
		65	Iceland (.1)	2.0	
		65	Jordan	2.0	
		65	New Zealand (.2)	2.0	
	VII	65	Peru	2.0	
		69.5	Algeria (.8)	1.9	
		69.5	Central African Republic (1.28)	1.9	
		69.5	Nigeria (1.37)	1.9	
		69.5	Switzerland (.2)	1.9	
		73.5	Libya (1.34)	1.8	
		73.5	Nepal	1.8	
		73.5	Tanganyika (.8)	1.8	
76.2		73.5	U.S.S.R. (1.27)	1.8	
		77.5	Argentina (.2)	1.7	
		77.5	Iran (1.29)	1.7	
	VIII	77.5	Tunisia (.62)	1.7	
		77.5	United States (.2)	1.7	
		80.5	Jamaica (.2)	1.6	
		80.5	Puerto Rico (.2)	1.6	
		82.5	Bolivia (1.38)	1.4	
		82.5	Poland (.2)	1.4	
		84.5	Netherlands (.1)	1.3	
		84.5	Netherlands Antilles (.4)	1.3	

TABLE 8 (continued)

% of Table Population	Case Deciles	Rank	Country	% Annual Incr. in Pop.	Range Deciles
		86	West Germany (.2)	1.2	
		87.5	Cyprus (.4)	1.1	X
		87.5	Yugoslavia (.2)	1.1	
	IX	90	Chad (1.39)	1.0	
		90	France (.2)	1.0	
		90	Spain (.6)	1.0	
		93.5	Bulgaria (.2)	.9	
		93.5	Greece (.8)	.9	
		93.5	Japan (.2)	.9	
		93.5	Romania (.86)	.9	
		97.5	Finland (.2)	.8	
		97.5	Norway (.1)	.8	
		97.5	Portugal (.61)	.8	
		97.5	Somalia (1.44)	.8	
		102	Czechoslovakia (.2)	.7	
	X	102	Denmark (.1)	.7	
		102	Luxembourg (.4)	.7	
		102	Malta & Gozo (.4)	.7	
		102	United Kingdom (.2)	.7	
		106.5	Belgium (.2)	.5	
		106.5	Hungary (.2)	.5	
		106.5	Italy (.2)	.5	
		106.5	Sweden (.1)	.5	
		109	Austria (.2)	.3	
		110.5	Ireland	− .4	
		110.5	East Germany (.43)	− .4	

[1] For 1957–59.

Sources: Leo A. Orleans, *Professional Manpower and Education in Communist China* (Washington, 1961), p. 153; U.N., *Statistical Yearbook, 1962* (New York, 1963).

9-10. PERCENTAGE OF POPULATION IN CITIES OF OVER 20,000
POPULATION

The reliability and comparability of these statistics depend upon the same factors as the estimates of total population. In addition there is the problem of comparability in the definition of cities. Three general kinds of classification of localities have been used:[1]

A. Agglomerations or clusters of population without regard to official boundaries or administrative functions.

B. Localities having fixed boundaries and an administratively recognized town status usually characterized by some form of local government. Sometimes these are districts which include both the central agglomeration and whatever surrounding territory is administered from the central area.

C. Minor civil divisions, often the smallest administrative divisions, which have fixed boundaries and which together comprise the entire territory of the country. These units do not necessarily have local government or town status.

Where possible we have used data compiled by International Urban Research of the University of California at Berkeley.[2] These data in some cases differ from information published elsewhere, especially data belonging to class C. In some cases International Urban Research adjusted them to increase international comparability. Countries using either type A or type B definitions can, with a few exceptions, generally be compared with each other.[3] Comparisons of either with type C data are more hazardous. In those cases where we know the data corresponds to type C we have so identified them in the table. Fortunately the countries using this method appear to be few.

It is not possible to say precisely how much error is introduced by differences in definitions, though the work of International Urban Research in reducing and estimating error is extremely valuable. As stated, they do not in most cases regard the differences between types A and B as substantial. Perhaps a reasonable error margin for most of the following figures would be $\pm 10\%$. It is inevitably wider, however, for countries using the type C definition and for some of the least urbanized states.

We have used a population of 20,000 as our cut-off point. Other cut-off points, such as 10,000 or 100,000, would have been feasible, and would have produced somewhat different rankings. Gibbs and Davis, however, have found that the correlation among series using different cut-offs is quite high and the deviations not usually substantial.[4] It should also be noted that the "cities of over 20,000" classification gives far more comparable

---

1. Adapted from U. N., *Demographic Yearbook, 1960* (New York, 1961), p. 33.
2. Published in Norton Ginsburg, *Atlas of Economic Development* (Chicago, 1961), pp. 34-35.
3. J. P. Gibbs and Kingsley Davis, "Conventional vs. Metropolitan Data in the International Study of Urbanization," *American Sociological Review, 23* (October 1958), 504-14. International Urban Research (*The World's Metropolitan Areas*, Berkeley and Los Angeles, 1959) has discussed problems of delimitation and comparison at length. They have used a definition of "urban" which refers in part to the proportion of the population in nonagricultural occupations.
4. Ibid., p. 509.

results than an alternative often employed—simply the proportion of the population in areas classified by the countries in question as "urban."

The data for annual average changes are more reliable, as in most cases the definitions remain fairly constant over time within the same country. To achieve comparability within countries, the data and years in Table 10 are in a few instances not identical with those in Table 9. Time periods vary substantially. While we wanted change data since 1920, if possible, in a number of cases we had to be content with information on post-World War II years only. The average annual increase in Table 10 is simply the percentage in cities in the later year, minus the percentage in the earlier year, with the remainder divided by the number of years elapsed.

Urbanization data, along with information on literacy and mass media participation, provide a good measure of the relative proportion of the population exposed to modernity. (Obviously it is not an absolute measure, since some rural people will be more heavily exposed to modern life than some city dwellers). Cities are important in introducing a money economy, new social patterns, and the possibility of developing intellectual centers. But cities also may bring severe frustrations to their newer inhabitants. Unemployment is frequently a serious urban problem; the city dweller must learn to adjust to many new patterns of behavior; he often does not have the security of an extended family (or even a core family); the contrasts between rich and poor are likely to be especially striking.[5] The character of cities in newly developing areas varies greatly with the reasons behind their growth. A high rural population density may mean that people are *pushed* into cities; a lower density may mean that the new city dwellers are more likely to have been positively attracted, or *pulled*, to the cities. The latter type of individual is more often literate, or more knowledgeable about the step he is taking. In short, he is already more "modern," can make the move with fewer frustrations, and can make more of a contribution to modern life when he arrives.

---

5. Cf. Philip M. Hauser, ed., *Urbanization in Asia and the Far East* (Calcutta, 1957).

TABLE 9

Percentage of Population in Cities Over 20,000

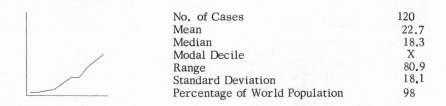

No. of Cases	120
Mean	22.7
Median	18.3
Modal Decile	X
Range	80.9
Standard Deviation	18.1
Percentage of World Population	98

% of Table Population	Case Deciles	Rank	Country	% Pop. in Cities Over 20,000	Deciles	Year
	I	1	Hong Kong	80.9[a]	I	1961
		2	Trinidad & Tobago	75.1[b]		1946
		3	Surinam[1]	72.4[b]	II	1950
		4	United Kingdom	66.9[c]		1961
		5	Israel	60.9[a]	III	1961
		6	New Zealand	59.7[a]		1961
		7	Australia	57.3		1955
		8	Barbados (C)	54.7[c]	IV	1960
		9	United States	52.0		1955
		10	Kuwait	50.6[b]		1957
		11	Netherlands	49.8		1955
	II	12	Denmark	48.5	V	1960
		13	Argentina	48.3		1955
		14	West Germany	47.6[a]		1961
		15	Venezuela	47.2[a]		1961
		16	Chile	46.3[b]		1959
		17	Japan	43.1		1955
		18	Sweden	40.8[a]		1960
		19	Iceland	40.5[b]		1957
		20.5	Austria	39.8	VI	1955
		20.5	Spain	39.8[b]		1950
		22	Canada	39.4[a]		1961
		23	Syria	38.8		1950
		24	Greece	37.4[a]		1961
	III	25	Hungary	37.0[b]		1960
		26	Cuba	36.5		1955
		27	East Germany (C)	36.2[b]		1959
		28	Ireland	35.6[a]		1961
26.5		29	U.S.S.R.	35.5[b]		1959
		30	Panama	33.1[c]		1960
		31	South Africa	32.9[b]		1960
		32	Norway	32.8[b]		1950
		33	Belgium	32.0[b]	VII	1947
		34	Poland	31.9[a]		1960
		35	Finland	31.2[b]		1958

TABLE 9 (continued)

% of Table Population	Case Deciles	Rank	Country	% Pop. in Cities Over 20,000	Deciles	Year
		36	Luxembourg (C)	30.6		1947
	IV	37	Italy	30.3		1955
		38	Switzerland	29.9[b]		1960
		39	France	29.8[d]		1954
		40	Egypt	29.1		1955
		41	Brazil	28.1[a]		1960
		42	Puerto Rico	28.0[a]		1960
		43	Mauritius	27.4[b]		1958
		44	Jordan	25.5		1952
		45	Czechoslovakia	25.3[c]		1952
		46	Morocco	24.2[c]	VIII	1960
		47.5	Mexico	24.0[a]		1950
	V	47.5	Taiwan	24.0		1958
		49	Iraq	23.6		1955
		50	Lebanon	23.0		1952
		51	Malaya	22.7[a]		1957
		52	Colombia	22.4		1955
		53	Iran	21.0[e]		1950
		54	North Korea	20.2		1950
		55	Nicaragua	20.1[b]		1957
		56	Tunisia	19.9		1955
		57	Bolivia	19.4		1955
		58	Yugoslavia	18.6[a]		1961
		59	South Korea	18.5		1950
		60	Libya	18.4		1955
	VI	61	Turkey	18.2[b]		1955
		62	Romania	18.0		1950
		63	British Guiana[1]	17.9[b]		1958
		64	Ecuador	17.8		1955
		65	Portugal	16.5[b]		1950
		66	Cambodia	16.0	IX	1955
		67.5	Congo (Brazzaville) (C)	15.4[b]		1950
		67.5	Costa Rica	15.4		1950
		69	Bulgaria	15.3		1955
		70	Paraguay	15.2		1955
		71	Algeria	14.1		1955
	VII	72.5	Mozambique	13.9[f]		1954
		72.5	Peru	13.9		1955
		74	Cyprus	13.6		1952
		75	Mongolian People's Republic	13.0		1955
		76	El Salvador	12.9		1955
		77	Philippines	12.7		1950
45.1 -------------		78	India	12.0[b]		1951
		79	Honduras (C)	11.5[c]		1961
		80	Ceylon	11.4		1955
		81.5	Guatemala	11.2		1955
		81.5	Rhodesia & Nyasaland[2]	11.2[b]		1951
		83	Dominican Republic	11.1[a]		1950
63.5 -------------		84	Nigeria	10.5		1955

TABLE 9 (continued)

% of Table Population	Case Deciles	Rank	Country	% Pop. in Cities Over 20,000	Deciles	Year
		85	Burma	10.0		1950
	VIII	85	China (Mainland)	10.0		1953
		85	Senegal	10.0[f]		1956
		88	Saudi Arabia	9.5		1955
		89.5	Congo (Leopoldville)	9.1[b]		1959
		89.5	Indonesia	9.1		1955
		91.5	Madagascar	8.0[b]	X	1959
		91.5	Pakistan	8.0		1955
		93	Thailand	7.7		1947
		94	Afghanistan	7.5		1950
		95	Malta & Gozo	7.3[a]		1957
		96	Sarawak	7.0		1947
	IX	97	Ivory Coast	6.8[f]		1956
		98	Ghana	6.4		1955
		99	Dahomey (A)	5.5[b]		1955
		100	South West Africa	5.4[b]		1958
		101.5	Guinea	5.1[f]		1955
		101.5	Haiti	5.1		1955
		103	Sudan	5.0		1955
		104	Angola	4.7		1955
		105	Togo	4.5[f]		1958
		106	Nepal	4.4		1950
		107	Cameroun	4.1[b]		1950
		108	Laos	4.0		1955
	X	109.5	Central African Republic (C)	3.9[b]		1950
		109.5	Somalia	3.9		1955
		111	Kenya	3.8		1955
		112	Tanganyika	3.3[b]		1957
		113	Sierra Leone	3.1		1955
		114	Upper Volta	2.3[f]		1956
		115	Mali	1.8[f]		1956
		116	Ethiopia	1.7		1955
		117	Chad (C)	1.0[b]		1950
		118	Uganda	.9		1955
		119	Yemen	.6		1955
		120	Liberia	.0		1955

[1] Population total adjusted to include Indian jungle population.

[2] Weighted average of Northern Rhodesia (1950), Southern Rhodesia (1951), and Nyasaland (1955; source: Ginsburg, *Atlas*).

Sources: Unless otherwise noted, Norton Ginsburg, *Atlas of Economic Development* (Chicago, 1961), p. 34.

[a] U. N., *Compendium of Social Statistics, 1963* (New York, 1963), pp. 72–80.

[b] U. N., *Demographic Yearbook, 1960* (New York, 1961), pp. 349–68.

[c] U. N., *Demographic Yearbook, 1962* (New York, 1963), pp. 380–96.

[d] J. P. Gibbs and Kingsley Davis, "Conventional vs. Metropolitan Data in the International Study of Urbanization," *American Sociological Review, 23* (October 1958), p. 509.

[e] U. N., *Report on the World Social Situation, 1957* (New York, 1957), p. 119.

[f] U. N. E. C. A., *Economic Bulletin for Africa,* June 1962, p. 63.

TABLE 10

Percentage of Population in Cities Over 20,000—Average Annual Increase

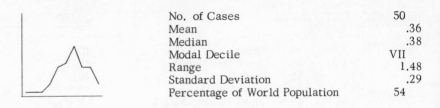

No. of Cases	50
Mean	.36
Median	.38
Modal Decile	VII
Range	1.48
Standard Deviation	.29
Percentage of World Population	54

% of Table Population	Case Deciles	Rank	Country	Avg. Ann. % Increase	Range Deciles	Years
	I	1	Venezuela	1.29	I	1936–61
		2	Panama	1.07	II	1950–60
		3	Poland	.90	III	1946–60
		4	Ireland	.75	IV	1946–61
		5	U. S. S. R.	.71		1926–59
	II	6	Nicaragua	.70		1950–57
		7	West Germany	.67	V	1946–61
		8	New Zealand	.65		1945–61
24.8		9	Japan	.64		1920–50
		10	Greece	.61		1940–61
	III	11	Mexico	.60		1940–50
		12	Cuba[1]	.58		1943–53
		13	Finland	.57		1940–58
		14	Iceland	.54	VI	1940–57
		15	Congo (Leopoldville)	.53		1946–59
	IV	16.5	Barbados	.52		1921–60
		16.5	Puerto Rico	.52		1940–60
		18	Yugoslavia	.49		1948–61
		19.5	Brazil	.47		1920–60
		19.5	Chile	.47		1920–59
	V	21	Spain	.44		1920–50
		23	Honduras	.39	VII	1950–61
		23	Israel	.39		1948–61
		23	South Africa	.39		1946–60
		25	Mauritius	.38		1931–58
	VI	26	Sweden	.37		1945–60
		27	East Germany	.36		1946–59
		28	Malaya	.34		1920–57
		29	Denmark	.32		1945–60
		30	Czechoslovakia	.31		1947–61
	VII	31	Pakistan[2]	.28		1951–61
		32	Dominican Republic	.27		1935–50
		33	Turkey	.26		1935–55
51.4		34	France	.24	VIII	1946–54
		35	Italy	.23		1936–51

TABLE 10 (continued)

% of Table Population	Case Deciles	Rank	Country	Avg. Ann. % Increase	Range Deciles	Years
	VIII	36	Canada	.22		1921–61
92.5 ---------------		37.5	India	.18		1921–51
		37.5	United States[1]	.18		1920–50
		39	Hungary	.15		1920–60
		40	Switzerland	.11		1941–60
	IX	41.5	South West Africa	.10	IX	1951–58
		41.5	United Kingdom	.10		1931–61
		43	Luxembourg	.08		1947–60
		44	Portugal	.05		1940–50
		45	Mozambique	.02		1940–56
	X	46	British Guiana	.003		1921–58
		47	Belgium	– .03		1930–47
		48	Malta & Gozo	– .07	X	1948–57
		49	Austria	– .08		1948–61
		50	Morocco	– .19		1951–60

[1] Cities of over 25,000 population.
[2] Cities of over 10,000 population.

Sources: Philip M. Hauser, ed., *Urbanization in Asia and the Far East* (Calcutta, 1957), p. 103; U. N., *Demographic Yearbook, 1962* (New York, 1963), pp. 380–96; *1960* (New York, 1961), pp. 349–67; U. N., *Compendium of Social Statistics, 1963* (New York, 1963), pp. 72–80.

Government and Politics

11-18. EXPENDITURE AND REVENUE OF CENTRAL AND GENERAL GOVERNMENT, SOCIAL SECURITY, AND PUBLIC ENTERPRISES AS A PERCENTAGE OF GROSS NATIONAL PRODUCT

Totals of central government revenue and expenditure are regularly given in the United Nations *Statistical Yearbook,* and totals for general government (including local and state or provincial governments) are usually to be found in the United Nations *Yearbook of National Accounts Statistics.* These figures are given, as a percentage of Gross National Product (G. N. P.), in Tables 11-14.

In most cases, however, these totals do not include complete data for social security funds, government enterprises, and public corporations.[1] If one is interested in establishing some kind of approximate measure of the actual or potential influence of the government in a national economy, these additional accounts must be included. Thus in Tables 15-18 we have tried to add them, and the percentages and rankings may be compared with the first set of tables.

To find a measure of the influence of the central government we have taken as a base the expenditures given in the budget accounts published in the United Nations *Statistical Yearbook.* We have added the following information where available in government yearbooks or in other reports:

1. That part of social security funds not covered by the government's contribution to the scheme, if the social security accounts were not already included in the government budget.

2. The total expenditure of the post office, telephone, telegraph, and railroad agencies where owned by the government, taking into consideration any subsidy previously reported in the accounts.

3. Nationalized industry accounts.

4. Special accounts of autonomous public agencies.

We have deducted taxes collected for local authorities wherever that was not done. Other transfer payments such as loans and grants, to state and local authorities were not deducted. Transfer payments to households have been kept as recorded in the United Nations *Statistical Yearbook.*

In compiling figures for G. N. P., double counting is eliminated; i.e., raw materials are not counted except in the value of the finished product. But in our totals of *government* expenditure and revenue all transactions of public enterprises, including purchases of raw materials, are included. Thus if very many industries were government-owned—e.g. coal mining, steelmaking, and automobile manufacture—the inputs at each stage would

---

1. The same is true of a special study presented in U. N., *Report on the World Social Situation* (New York, 1961), p. 70. Despite some ambiguities in the text, it is clear from conversation with members of the United Nations Secretariat that the figures apply only to budget reports.

be incorporated into the total of government expenditures, and so would total more than the *value added*. The percentage so arrived at—government expenditure as a percentage of G. N. P.—therefore must *not* be construed as the government's contribution to G. N. P. It is useful only as a measure of relative government influence in the economy. Accounts sufficiently detailed to permit estimates on the bases of value added are not publicly available.

Precise totals of government expenditure and revenue, including the public corporations, are difficult to arrive at due to great differences in accounting systems and the willingness or ability of governments to publish the relevant figures. Nevertheless, our totals represent a material improvement over those previously available and are probably accurate within an error margin of $\pm 10\%$. In one or two cases we have noted that they may be underestimates by somewhat more than 10% because of the difficulties in identifying all government corporations or all industries in which the government owns a substantial enough share to exert decisive influence— usually identified arbitrarily as at least half of all shares.

The *general* government figures for expenditure and revenue are gathered in part from the United Nations *Yearbook of National Account Statistics*. The totals there are for current transactions, including social security. We added to expenditures figures for interest on the public debt, and wherever possible we also added capital transfers to households and to corporations and the financing of gross capital formation in the noncorporate public sector. As in the case of the central government, the accounts of government enterprises and public corporations were added, as were corporations that were agencies of state (or provincial) and local governments.

To repeat, we compiled these figures as a measure of the actual or at least potential influence of government in the economy. They are relevant to many theories about the role of large government expenditures on incentives, saving, investment, and economic growth, and on the consequences for individual freedom in both the economic and political spheres. They also provide one measure of the capabilities available to a government to meet demands upon it.

The percentages clearly cannot be used mechanically for these purposes; control, especially of industrial corporations, may not be closely related to ownership. It has been said in some instances that a government controlled a given industry as effectively under regulation as under later public ownership. In many cases public ownership is in the hands of special autonomous corporations relatively immune from political influence; in other cases public ownership of even a minority of corporate shares may produce a very important element of control. Nevertheless it would seem that these series give at least a rough indication of potential government influence.

Note again that it is the series in Tables 15–18 that are significant in this respect. Tables 11–14 do not, on any consistent basis, include public enterprises and social security funds. Thus West Germany heads Table 11, but when public corporations are added it drops to ninth, more nearly where the informed observer might expect.

It has not been possible to list here all the references to the sources of the supplementary material, but this information, as well as certain notes on the calculations in individual cases, will be made available on request.

TABLE 11

Expenditure of General Government[1] as a Percentage of G. N. P.

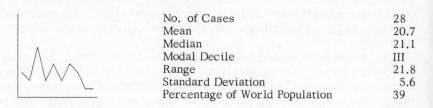

No. of Cases	28
Mean	20.7
Median	21.1
Modal Decile	III
Range	21.8
Standard Deviation	5.6
Percentage of World Population	39

% of Table Population	Case Deciles	Rank	Country	Expenditure/G. N. P.	Range Deciles
	I	1	West Germany	30.1	I
		2	Austria	28.8	
	II	3	France	28.7	
		4	Sweden	27.9	II
		5	Italy	26.9	
	III	6	United Kingdom	25.6	III
		7	Norway	25.2	
		8	Netherlands	24.4	
	IV	9	Finland	24.3	
19.4		10	Belgium	24.2	
		11	United States	23.8	
	V	12	Canada	22.8	IV
		13	New Zealand	21.9	
	VI	14	Denmark	21.3	V
		15	Ireland	20.9	
		16	Greece	20.3	
	VII	17	Congo (Leopoldville)	20.2	
		18	Brazil	18.9	VI
51.1		19	Pakistan	18.0	
	VIII	20	Burma	17.0	VII
		21	Portugal	16.4	
		22	Barbados	15.8	
	IX	23	Spain	15.3	
		24	Australia	14.7	VIII
		25	South Africa	14.6	
	X	26	Japan	13.9	
65.5		27	Jamaica	10.8	IX
		28	India	8.3	X

[1] General government includes central, state (or provincial), and local governments. Years are 1959 except Denmark, India, Ireland, and New Zealand (1958), and Spain (1957).

Sources: U. N., *Yearbook of National Account Statistics, 1959* (New York, 1960), *1960* (New York, 1961), *1961* (New York, 1962); U. N., *Statistical Yearbook, 1959* (New York, 1960), and *1961* (New York, 1962).

TABLE 12

Revenue of General Government as a Percentage of G. N. P.

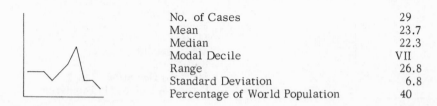

	No. of Cases	29
	Mean	23.7
	Median	22.3
	Modal Decile	VII
	Range	26.8
	Standard Deviation	6.8
	Percentage of World Population	40

% of Table Population	Case Deciles	Rank	Country	Revenue/G. N. P.	Range Deciles
	I	1	West Germany	36.4	I
		2	Finland	34.4	
	II	3	Austria	33.7	
		4	France	32.8	II
		5	Sweden	32.5	
	III	6	Norway	32.3	
		7	Italy	29.7	III
		8	Netherlands	29.6	
	IV	9	New Zealand	29.4	
		10	United Kingdom	26.7	IV
		11	Denmark	26.1	
19.0	V	12	United States	25.3	V
		13.5	Canada	25.0	
		13.5	Switzerland	25.0	
	VI	15	Belgium	22.3	VI
		16	Ireland	22.1	
		17	Greece	21.9	
	VII	18	Japan	20.4	
		19	Portugal	19.8	VII
		20	Australia	19.5	
	VIII	21	Spain	19.3	
		22	Barbados	18.4	
		23	Congo (Leopoldville)	18.0	
50.6	IX	24	South Africa	17.9	
		25	Brazil	17.2	VIII
		26	Burma	16.7	
	X	27	Jamaica	13.9	IX
		28	Pakistan	12.7	
65.5		29	India	9.6	X

Sources and dates: See Table 11.

TABLE 13

Expenditure of Central Government as a Percentage of G. N. P.[1]

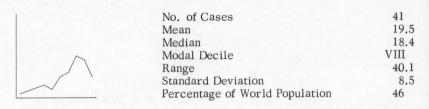

	No. of Cases	41
	Mean	19.5
	Median	18.4
	Modal Decile	VIII
	Range	40.1
	Standard Deviation	8.5
	Percentage of World Population	46

% of Table Population	Case Deciles	Rank	Country	Expenditure/G. N. P.	Range Deciles
	I	1	Jordan[2]	47.5	I–III
		2	Israel	33.5	IV
		3	Iraq	32.5	
		4	New Zealand	32.2	
	II	5	United Kingdom	29.9	V
		6	Austria	29.2	
		7	Venezuela	27.2	VI
		8	Egypt	26.7	
	III	9	Finland	26.3	
		10	Ireland	25.9	
		11	Sweden	25.7	
		12	Burma	23.4	VII
	IV	13	Belgium	23.0	
		14	Netherlands	21.1	
		15	France	20.5	
26.8		16	United States	20.4	
	V	17	Kenya	20.3	
		18.5	Greece	18.6	VIII
		18.5	Norway	18.6	
		20.5	Italy	18.4	
	VI	20.5	South Africa	18.4	
		22	Denmark	17.8	
		23	Argentina	17.0	
		24	Australia	16.4	
	VII	25	Uganda	16.3	
		26	Bolivia	16.1	
		27	Canada	15.8	
		28	West Germany	15.0	IX
	VIII	29	Portugal	14.9	
		30	Thailand	13.9	
49.7		31	Japan	13.6	
		32	Tanganyika	13.2	
	IX	33	Peru	13.1	
		34	Turkey	13.0	
		35	Spain	12.0	

TABLE 13 (continued)

% of Table Population	Case Deciles	Rank	Country	Expenditure/G. N. P.	Range Deciles
88.1 ---------------	X	36	India	11.8	X
		37	Pakistan	11.0	
		38	Brazil	10.4	
		39	Philippines	9.2	
		40	Afghanistan	8.0	
		41	Switzerland	7.4	

[1] Years are 1959 with the exception of Ireland, New Zealand, Denmark, West Germany, Canada, Japan, South Africa, and India (1958), and Iraq (1956).

[2] The high government expenditure ratio for Jordan is attributable to heavy foreign assistance.   Approximately one-fourth of Jordan's G. N. P. is devoted to defense.

Sources: U. N., *Statistical Yearbook, 1961* (New York, 1962), and *1958* (New York, 1959); U. N., *Yearbook of National Account Statistics, 1961* (New York, 1962), *1959* (New York, 1960), and *1958* (New York, 1959); U. N. E. C. A. F. E., *Economic Survey of Asia, 1959* (Bangkok, 1960).

TABLE 14

Revenue of Central Government as a Percentage of G. N. P.

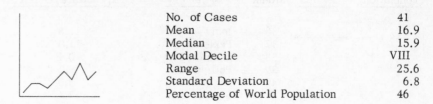

No. of Cases	41
Mean	16.9
Median	15.9
Modal Decile	VIII
Range	25.6
Standard Deviation	6.8
Percentage of World Population	46

% of Table Population	Case Deciles	Rank	Country	Revenue/G. N. P.	Range Deciles
	I	1	Iraq	32.3	I
		2	United Kingdom	29.4	II
		3	New Zealand	29.3	
		4	Egypt	27.8	
	II	5	Austria	26.9	III
		6	Israel	26.2	
		7	Finland	26.1	
		8	Ireland	23.3	IV
	III	9	Sweden	22.7	
		10	Venezuela	21.9	V
		11	France	21.0	
		12	Netherlands	20.4	
	IV	13	Norway	20.3	
		14	Denmark	18.7	VI
		15	Belgium	18.1	
25.8		16	United States	17.6	
	V	17	Australia	17.4	
		18	Italy	17.3	
		19	Burma	17.2	
		20	Kenya	16.2	VII
	VI	21	Greece	15.9	
		22	Uganda	15.1	
		23	West Germany	15.0	
		24.5	Canada	13.9	VIII
		24.5	South Africa	13.9	
	VII	26	Portugal	13.6	
		27	Turkey	13.4	
		28.5	Japan	12.8	
50.0		28.5	Thailand	12.8	
	VIII	30	Spain	12.7	
		31	Peru	12.4	
		32	Jordan	11.2	IX
	IX	33	Bolivia	11.1	
		34	Tanganyika	10.5	
		35	Argentina	9.8	
		36	Philippines	9.2	X
	X	37	Brazil	9.0	
		38	Switzerland	8.1	
		39	Pakistan	7.5	
69.9		40	Afghanistan	7.0	
		41	India	6.7	

Sources and dates: See Table 13.

TABLE 15

Expenditure of General Government, Social Security, and
Public Enterprises as a Percentage of G. N. P.[1]

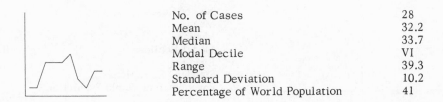

No. of Cases	28
Mean	32.2
Median	33.7
Modal Decile	VI
Range	39.3
Standard Deviation	10.2
Percentage of World Population	41

% of Table Population	Case Deciles	Rank	Country	Expenditure/G. N. P.	Range Deciles
	I	1	Sweden	52.9	I
		2	United Kingdom	45.3	II
	II	3	Austria[2]	43.8	III
		4	New Zealand	43.2	
		5	Japan	42.3	
	III	6	Netherlands	41.2	
		7	France	40.1	IV
		8	Italy	39.9	
25.6	IV	9	West Germany[2]	38.8	
		10	Canada	37.4	
		11	Finland	36.9	V
	V	12	Norway	36.5	
		13	South Africa	35.6	
	VI	14	Burma	34.3	
		15	Belgium	33.0	VI
		16	Congo (Leopoldville)	32.9	
	VII	17	Ireland	32.5	
		18	Australia	30.5	
		19	Denmark	29.9	
	VIII	20	United States	27.9	VII
		21	Greece	26.2	
49.5		22	Portugal	22.8	VIII
	IX	23	Brazil	18.9	IX
64.8		24	Pakistan	18.0	
		25	India	17.7	
	X	26	Barbados	15.8	X
		27	Spain	15.2	
		28	Jamaica	13.6	

[1] Years are 1959 except Denmark, India, Ireland, and New Zealand (1958), and
Spain (1957).
[2] Not all public enterprises included.

Sources: As in Table 11, plus national statistical yearbooks. Detailed list available on request.

TABLE 16

Revenue of General Government, Social Security, and
Public Enterprises as a Percentage of G. N. P.

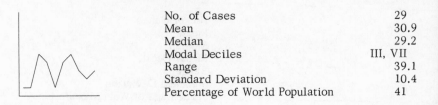

No. of Cases	29
Mean	30.9
Median	29.2
Modal Deciles	III, VII
Range	39.1
Standard Deviation	10.4
Percentage of World Population	41

% of Table Population	Case Deciles	Rank	Country	Revenue/G. N. P.	Range Deciles
	I	1	Sweden	51.8	I
		2	Japan	44.9	II
	II	3	New Zealand	43.4	III
		4	Austria[1]	43.1	
		5	Netherlands	42.7	
	III	6	West Germany[1]	41.3	
		7	United Kingdom	41.1	
		8	France	40.0	IV
	IV	9	Norway	39.6	
		10	Finland	38.9	
25.1	V	11	Italy	37.3	
		12	Canada	32.9	V
		13	Ireland	30.9	VI
		14	South Africa	30.4	
	VI	15	Denmark	29.2	
		16	Australia	28.5	
		17	Burma	28.1	VII
	VII	18	Belgium	28.0	
		19	United States	27.4	
		20	Congo (Leopoldville)	25.5	
	VIII	21	Switzerland	25.0	
		22	Portugal	24.3	VIII
49.7	IX	23	Greece	23.3	
		24	Spain	20.7	
		25.5	Barbados	17.2	IX
		25.5	Brazil	17.2	
58.1	X	27	Jamaica	14.3	X
		28	India	13.7	
		29	Pakistan	12.7	

[1] Not all public enterprises included.

Sources: As in Table 12, plus national statistical yearbooks. Detailed list available on request.

TABLE 17

Expenditure of Central Government, Social Security, and
Public Enterprises as a Percentage of G. N. P.[1]

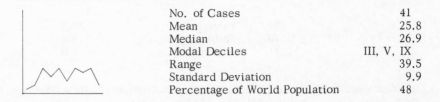

No. of Cases	41
Mean	25.8
Median	26.9
Modal Deciles	III, V, IX
Range	39.5
Standard Deviation	9.9
Percentage of World Population	48

% of Table Population	Case Deciles	Rank	Country	Expenditure/G. N. P.	Range Deciles
	I	1	Jordan	47.5	I
		2	France	40.0	II
		3	New Zealand	39.8	
		4	Sweden	39.1	III
	II	5	United Kingdom	38.8	
		6	Israel	38.2	
		7	Netherlands	37.0	
		8	Austria[2]	36.4	
	III	9	Egypt	36.1	
		10	Belgium	34.6	IV
		11	Japan	34.5	
		12	Italy	34.2	
	IV	13	Iraq	32.5	
		14.5	South Africa	31.1	V
		14.5	Ireland	31.1	
25.1		16	West Germany[2]	30.6	
	V	17	Finland	30.1	
		18	Burma	29.1	
		19	Norway	28.6	
		20	Venezuela	27.2	VI
	VI	21	Kenya	26.9	
		22	Turkey	23.8	
		23	Greece	23.6	
		24	Denmark	21.4	VII
	VII	25	Canada	21.3	
		26	Portugal	21.2	
		27	United States	21.0	
		28	Uganda	20.9	
	VIII	29	Australia	18.0	VIII
		30	Tanganyika	17.6	
49.7		31	Argentina[3]	17.0	
		32	Spain	16.5	
	IX	33	Bolivia[3]	16.1	
		34.5	Thailand	15.2	IX
		34.5	Switzerland	15.2	
84.5		36	India	13.9	
	X	37	Brazil	13.7	
		38	Peru	13.1	

TABLE 17 (continued)

% of Table Population	Case Deciles	Rank	Country	Expenditure/G. N. P.	Range Deciles
		39	Pakistan[4]	12.3	
		40	Philippines	9.2	X
		41	Afghanistan	8.0	

[1] Years are 1959 except Ireland, New Zealand, Denmark, West Germany, Canada, Japan, South Africa, and India (1958), and Iraq (1956).

[2] Not all public enterprises included.

[3] Social security not included.

[4] No data for state trading schemes and development corporations.

Sources: As in Table 13, plus national statistical yearbooks. Detailed list available on request.

TABLE 18

Revenue of Central Government, Social Security, and
Public Enterprises as a Percentage of G. N. P.

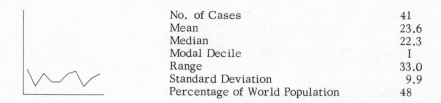

	No. of Cases	41
	Mean	23.6
	Median	22.3
	Modal Decile	I
	Range	33.0
	Standard Deviation	9.9
	Percentage of World Population	48

% of Table Population	Case Deciles	Rank	Country	Revenue/G. N. P.	Range Deciles
	I	1	Japan	40.0	I
		2	France	39.6	
		3	United Kingdom	38.3	
		4	Sweden	37.8	
	II	5	Egypt	37.1	
		6	New Zealand	37.0	
		7	Netherlands	36.0	II
		8	Austria[1]	34.9	
	III	9	Italy	32.8	III
		10	Iraq	32.3	
		11	West Germany[1]	31.9	
		12	Israel	30.9	
	IV	13	Belgium	30.6	
24.1		14	Ireland	28.8	IV
		15	Turkey	28.4	
		16	South Africa	28.1	
	V	17	Burma	26.4	V
		18.5	Finland	26.1	
		18.5	Norway	26.1	
		20	Kenya	22.9	VI
	VI	21	Denmark	22.3	
		22	Venezuela	21.9	
		23	Portugal	21.8	
		24	Greece	21.1	
	VII	25	Uganda	19.6	VII
		26	Australia	19.2	
		27	Canada	18.8	
		28	United States	18.2	
	VIII	29	Spain	17.3	
50.0		30	Switzerland	17.0	
		31	Tanganyika	14.9	VIII
		32	Thailand	14.2	
	IX	33	Brazil	12.7	IX
		34	Peru	12.4	
		35	Jordan	11.2	
		36	Bolivia[2]	11.1	
60.0	X	37	Argentina[2]	9.8	X

TABLE 18 (continued)

% of Table Population	Case Deciles	Rank	Country	Revenue/G. N. P.	Range Deciles
		38	India	9.5	
		39	Philippines	9.2	
		40	Pakistan[3]	8.8	
		41	Afghanistan	7.0	

[1] Not all public enterprises included.
[2] Social security not included.
[3] No data for state trading schemes and development corporations.

Sources: As in Table 14, plus national statistical yearbooks.   Detailed list available on request.

19-20. GOVERNMENT EMPLOYMENT AS A PERCENTAGE OF WORKING-AGE POPULATION

Tables 19-20 represent another attempt to measure the relative influence of government in the economy. Previous comments about the measurement of government expenditures and revenues apply here. Again it is believed that the error margin is approximately $\pm 10\%$, though again it is impossible to be sure that we have identified all the public enterprises.

TABLE 19

Employed by General Government and Public Enterprises as a
Percentage of Working-Age Population

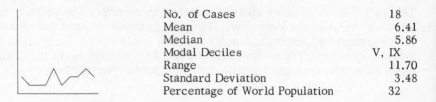

No. of Cases	18
Mean	6.41
Median	5.86
Modal Deciles	V, IX
Range	11.70
Standard Deviation	3.48
Percentage of World Population	32

% of Table Population	Case Deciles	Rank	Country	Govt. Emp. as % W.-A. Pop.	Range Deciles	Year
	I	1	New Zealand	12.86	I	1961
	II	2	Australia	12.52		1961
		3	United Kingdom	10.61	II	1960
	III	4	Denmark	9.76	III	1955
		5	Trinidad & Tobago	9.05	IV	1959
23.1	IV	6	United States	8.14	V	1960
		7	France	7.82		1956
	V	8	West Germany	7.15		1961
		9	Norway	5.88	VI	1960
	VI	10	Ghana	5.83	VII	1961
	VII	11	Malaya	5.47		1959
		12	Kenya	4.50	VIII	1960
	VIII	13	Japan	4.49		1958
		14	Taiwan	3.23	IX	1960
49.0	IX	15	Uganda	2.66		1959
93.4		16	India	2.49		1959
	X	17	South Korea	1.70	X	1961
		18	Nigeria	1.16		1959

Sources: National statistical yearbooks and individual studies. Detailed list available on request.

TABLE 20

Employed by Central Government and Public Enterprises as a
Percentage of Working-Age Population

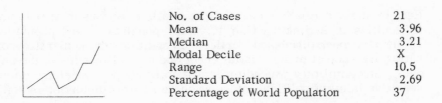

No. of Cases	21
Mean	3.96
Median	3.21
Modal Decile	X
Range	10.5
Standard Deviation	2.69
Percentage of World Population	37

% of Table Population	Case Deciles	Rank	Country	Govt. Emp. as % W.-A. Pop.	Range Deciles	Year
	I	1	Sweden	11.53	I–III	1957
		2	Trinidad & Tobago	7.90	IV	1959
	II	3	New Zealand	7.58		1961
		4	United Kingdom	7.37		1960
	III	5	France	6.28	V, VI	1956
		6	Ghana	4.94	VII	1961
	IV	7	South Africa	4.84		1960
		8	Belgium	3.69	VIII	1960
	V	9	Australia	3.50		1961
		10	Canada	3.26		1961
	VI	11	Mexico	3.21		1958
22.7		12	Italy	3.12	IX	1954
	VII	13	West Germany	2.94		1961
		14	Japan	2.48		1961
53.3	VIII	15	United States	2.16		1961
		16	Tanganyika[1]	1.73	X	1958
	IX	17	South Korea	1.56		1961
		18	Ivory Coast	1.53		1958
	X	19	Taiwan[2]	1.39		1960
60.3		20	Thailand	1.24		1958
		21	India	1.03		1959

[1] Africans only.
[2] The "central" government on Taiwan is the provisional government for all China; the "provincial" government is the actual government of the island. "Central government" as used here combines "central" and "provincial."

Sources: National statistical yearbooks and individual studies. Detailed list available on request.

21-23. EXPENDITURE ON DEFENSE AS A PERCENTAGE OF G. N. P.— MILITARY PARTICIPATION RATIOS

Each of these ratios is subject, first of all, to errors in the denominator. Difficulties in estimating G. N. P., total population, and population aged 15-64 have been discussed earlier. In addition, the numerators of these ratios are subject to substantial error due to inadequacies in the published data. Since military expenditures and military personnel are often highly sensitive items of political information, deliberate distortion is sometimes a factor.

No error margins can be furnished for the following data. Given the nature of their political systems, data for the Western democracies are most likely to be reliable. For the Soviet Union we have in Table 23 substituted the results of private study for the official figures.

The best means of ascertaining the reliability of the series is to compare the military expenditure ratios with those for military personnel as a percentage of working-age population. (Despite the additional error introduced by estimates of age breakdown, this series is preferable as a measure of economic benefits foregone.) Logarithms of these ratios are plotted against each other for 75 countries on the graph, and a regression line is plotted by the method of least squares. The dashed lines indicate values that differ by a factor of two (100% above or 50% below) the "predicted" level. Countries whose positions deviate substantially from the regression line should bear examination on the assumption, usually correct, that the two ratios generally vary together (they correlated with a fairly high r = .68 around the regression line, indicating that measurement error is probably not too serious. Note, however, that mere deviation from the regression line is not ipso facto proof of error in one of the estimates. Some underdeveloped countries, like Mexico, Liberia, or Nepal, may have large but poorly equipped military establishments. Jordan receives heavy external aid. Others, such as Indonesia, may have exceptionally high military expenditure ratios in one or two years of heavy spending for new equipment. In a later edition of the *Handbook* it would be preferable to give the average expenditure or participation ratios over several years.

The military participation or expenditure ratio for a given country may be high for many reasons. It may indicate tension with neighboring states; the data in these tables are essential in testing theories about arms races. Inspection of the tables will show a clear tendency for high ratios to be associated with alliance with one or the other of the major world power blocs. High levels of military expenditure are often made possible by substantial foreign assistance; this is clearly true for most of the smaller countries in the first case decile of the expenditure table. But a high rate of military expenditure or participation need not be directed externally. In many states it indicates substantial internal tension or repression.

The consequences may be as diverse as the causes. Large armies serve as a major source of social mobility in some countries where advancement through the ranks has long been one of the easiest means of moving up in the larger society. The army may also be a source of social mobilization;

it may bring into the modern and politically relevant sectors many people who would otherwise have remained in the traditionally oriented sectors. The levée en masse in Revolutionary France had enormous consequences for the French political system, and had major effects on the international system. Up to that time, most wars had been limited ones fought for limited aims. Armies were composed of professional soldiers. In the eighteenth-century economy, they were expensive to train and maintain; a king could ill afford to lose them by overreaching himself. Furthermore, as nonideological professionals they had a disconcerting tendency to desert under the stress of forced marches or heavy fighting. Mass armies of politically conscious and nationalistically motivated men vastly widened the horizons of ambitious rulers.[1]

Military conscription may provide an opportunity for many young men to become literate and skilled in modern technology. In some underdeveloped countries the primary source of such people is the army. Similarly, military careers, providing the experience of certain aspects of modern life, may produce in some men great dissatisfaction with civilian political control. The bargaining process, coupled with the apparent and often real inefficiency of democratic government, may be incomprehensible to one who has experienced the seemingly rational order of a military hierarchy. Young officers exposed to modern technology in the army may become impatient with civilian inefficiencies and step directly into politics. A large army created to suppress domestic opposition may turn against its creators. Large armies thus may indicate both actual domestic instability (opposition to be suppressed) and a potential instability on the part of the suppressors.

---

1. Cf. Richard N. Rosecrance, *Action and Reaction in International Politics* (Boston, 1963), ch. 2.

TABLE 21

Military Personnel as a Percentage of Total Population

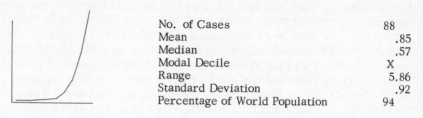

	No. of Cases	88
	Mean	.85
	Median	.57
	Modal Decile	X
	Range	5.86
	Standard Deviation	.92
	Percentage of World Population	94

% of Table Population	Case Deciles	Rank	Country	Military as % Total Pop.	Range Deciles	Year
	I	1	Taiwan	5.86[a]	I,II	1959
		2	North Korea	4.17[b]	III–V	1961
		3	Israel	2.86[e]	VI	1955
		4	South Korea	2.50[b]		1959
		5	France	2.28	VII	1959
		6	Albania	2.25		1959
		7	Yugoslavia	2.17[a]		1959
		8	Jordan	2.14[d]		1959
	II	9	Bulgaria	2.04		1959
		10.5	North Vietnam	1.75[b]	VIII	1961
		10.5	Turkey	1.75[b]		1961
		12	U.S.S.R.	1.72		1959
		13	Greece	1.66[a]		1959
		14	Czechoslovakia	1.62		1959
		15	Spain	1.59		1955
		16	Laos	1.42[a]		1959
		17	United States	1.41		1959
	III	18	Netherlands	1.22[b]		1961
		19	United Kingdom	1.21		1959
		20	Romania	1.18[b]		1961
25.2		21	South Vietnam	1.12	IX	1959
		23	Iran	1.04[e]		1959
		23	Mexico	1.04		1955
		23	Poland	1.04		1959
		25	Norway	1.02[b]		1961
		26.5	Sweden	1.01[e]		1955
	IV	26.5	Iraq	1.01		1959
		28	Syria	.99		1959
		29.5	Belgium	.95[e]		1959
		29.5	Finland	.95		1959
		31	Italy	.94[b]		1961
		32.5	Denmark	.93[b]		1961
		32.5	Luxembourg	.93		1959
		34	Portugal	.86[b]		1961
		35	Lebanon	.83		1959
	V	36	Cambodia	.79		1959
		37	Hungary	.75		1959
		38	Malaya	.73[f]		1957
		39	Canada	.69		1959
		41	East Germany	.62[b]		1961
		41	Chile	.62		1959

TABLE 21 (continued)

% of Table Population	Case Deciles	Rank	Country	Military as % Total Pop.	Range Deciles	Year
		41	New Zealand	.62		1959
		43	West Germany	.61[b]		1961
		44	Dominican Republic	.59		1959
	VI	45	Argentina	.54	X	1959
		46	Paraguay	.53		1959
		47	Cuba	.51		1959
		49	Nepal	.50		1959
		49	Thailand	.50[b]		1961
		49	Saudi Arabia	.50[d]		1959
		51	Australia	.49		1959
		52	Liberia	.48		1959
	VII	53.5	Afghanistan	.46		1959
		53.5	Ireland	.46		1959
		55	Yemen	.41[a]		1959
		57	Brazil	.39		1959
42.7		57	Egypt	.39		1959
		57	China (Mainland)	.39[b]		1961
		59	Libya	.38[d]		1959
		60	Ecuador	.37		1955
		61	Burma	.31[a]		1959
	VIII	62	Uruguay	.30[a]		1959
		63	Tunisia	.29[d]		1959
		64.5	Morocco	.27[d]		1959
		64.5	Venezuela	.27[e]		1959
		66	Japan	.25		1959
		67	Nicaragua	.23		1959
		68.5	Austria	.21[a]		1958
		68.5	Guatemala	.21		1959
		70	Pakistan	.19[b]		1961
76.3	IX	71	Haiti	.17		1959
		72.5	Colombia	.15		1959
		72.5	Indonesia	.15[c]		1955
		74.5	Ethiopia	.14[a]		1959
		74.5	Philippines	.14[a]		1959
		76.5	Honduras	.13		1959
		76.5	Peru	.13[a]		1956
		78	El Salvador	.12[a]		1959
		80	Sudan	.10[d]		1959
	X	80	Switzerland	.10[e]		1955
		80	Ghana	.10[h]		1960
		82	India	.09[e]		1955
		83	Senegal	.08[i]		1961
		84	South Africa	.06[a]		1955
		85.5	Bolivia	.03		1959
		85.5	Ceylon	.03[e]		1955
		87.5	Costa Rica	.00		1959
		87.5	Panama	.00[a]		1959

TABLE 21 (continued)

Sources: Unless otherwise noted, *Statesman's Yearbook of 1960-61* (New York, 1960).

[a] *Worldmark Encyclopedia of the Nations* (New York, 1960).

[b] Institute for Strategic Studies, *The Communist Bloc and the Western Alliances* (London, 1962), pp. 15, 24.

[c] U. S. Congress, *Congressional Record* (Washington, 1956), p. 14700.

[d] John J. Johnson, *The Role of the Military in Underdeveloped Countries* (Princeton, 1962), p. 292.

[e] *Annuaire Statistique de la Belgique et du Congo Belge, 81* (1960), p. 526.

[f] *1957 Population Census of the Federation of Malaya, Report No. 14* (Kuala Lumpur, 1960), p. 31.

[g] Edwin Lieuwin, *Venezuela* (New York, 1961), p. 161.

[h] W. F. Gutteridge, "The Armed Forces in Ghana Today,"*Canadian Army Journal*, September 1961, pp. 43-52.

[i] *Tropiques,* February 1962.

TABLE 22

Military Personnel as a Percentage of Population Aged 15–64

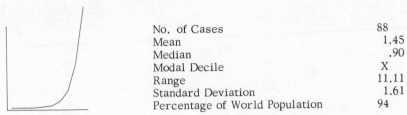

	No. of Cases	88
	Mean	1.45
	Median	.90
	Modal Decile	X
	Range	11.11
	Standard Deviation	1.61
	Percentage of World Population	94

% of Table Population	Case Deciles	Rank	Country	Milit. as % Pop. 15–64	Range Deciles	Year
	I	1	Taiwan	11.11	I–III	1959
		2	North Korea	7.16	IV,V	1961
		3	Israel	4.84	VI	1955
		4	South Korea	4.58		1959
		5	Jordan	4.34	VII	1959
		6	Albania	4.12		1959
		7	France	3.62		1959
		8	Yugoslavia	3.48		1959
	II	9	Bulgaria	3.07	VIII	1959
		10	Turkey	3.06		1961
		11	U.S.S.R.	3.02		1959
		12	North Vietnam	2.90		1961
		13	Czechoslovakia	2.54		1959
		14.5	Greece	2.52		1959
		14.5	Laos	2.52		1959
		16	Spain	2.39		1955
		17	United States	2.36		1959
	III	18	Iraq	2.02	IX	1959
		19.5	South Vietnam	2.00		1959
		19.5	Netherlands	2.00		1961
		21	Iran	1.94		1959
24.8		22	Mexico	1.92		1955
		23	United Kingdom	1.86		1959
		24	Romania	1.79		1961
		25	Syria	1.71		1959
		26	Poland	1.67		1959
	IV	27	Norway	1.62		1961
		28	Sweden	1.52		1955
		29	Finland	1.51		1959
		30	Cambodia	1.49		1959
		31.5	Belgium	1.46		1959
		31.5	Denmark	1.46		1961
		33	Italy	1.42		1961
		34	Malaya	1.37		1957
		35	Portugal	1.35		1961
	V	36	Luxembourg	1.32		1959
		37	Canada	1.16		1959
		38	Hungary	1.14		1959
		39	Dominican Republic	1.12		1959
		40	Chile	1.06	X	1959
		41	New Zealand	1.05		1959

TABLE 22 (continued)

% of Table Population	Case Deciles	Rank	Country	Milit. as % Pop. 15–64	Range Deciles	Year
		42	Paraguay	.96		1959
		43	East Germany	.95		1961
	VI	44.5	Thailand	.90		1961
		44.5	West Germany	.90		1961
		46	Liberia	.88		1959
		47	Nepal	.86		1959
		48	Cuba	.84		1959
		50	Argentina	.81		1959
		50	Saudi Arabia	.81		1959
		50	Afghanistan	.81		1959
		52	Australia	.79		1959
	VII	53	Ireland	.77		1959
		54	Yemen	.73		1959
		55	Brazil	.71		1959
		56.5	Libya	.69		1959
		56.5	Ecuador	.69		1955
42.9		58	Egypt	.67		1959
		59	China (Mainland)	.57		1961
		60	Tunisia	.54		1959
		61.5	Burma	.49		1959
	VIII	61.5	Venezuela	.49		1959
		63	Morocco	.48		1959
		64	Bolivia	.47		1959
		65	Uruguay	.45		1959
		66	Nicaragua	.43		1959
72.0		67	Japan	.39		1959
		68.5	Guatemala	.37		1959
		68.5	Pakistan	.37		1961
		70	Austria	.32		1958
	IX	71	Haiti	.29		1959
		72.5	Ethiopia	.28		1959
		72.5	Philippines	.28		1959
		74.5	Colombia	.27		1959
		74.5	Honduras	.27		1959
		76.5	Indonesia	.24		1955
		76.5	Peru	.24		1956
		78	El Salvador	.21		1959
		79.5	Ghana	.20		1960
	X	79.5	Sudan	.20		1959
		81	Senegal	.16		1961
		83	India	.15		1955
		83	Lebanon	.15		1959
		83	Switzerland	.15		1955
		85	South Africa	.11		1955
		86	Ceylon	.05		1955
		87.5	Costa Rica	.00		1959
		87.5	Panama	.00		1959

Sources: Military personnel as in preceding table; population aged 15–64 as in Table 3.

TABLE 23

Expenditure on Defense as a Percentage of G. N. P.

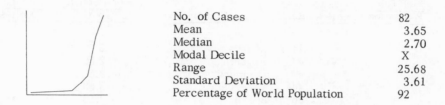

No. of Cases	82
Mean	3.65
Median	2.70
Modal Decile	X
Range	25.68
Standard Deviation	3.61
Percentage of World Population	92

% of Table Population	Case Deciles	Rank	Country	Expenditure on Defense as % of G. N. P.	Range Deciles	Year
	I	1	Jordan	25.70	I–V	1959
		2	Taiwan	12.30	VI	1959
		3	U. S. S. R.	10.40[a]		1955
		4	Laos	9.90	VII	1959
		5	United States	9.60		1959
		6	South Vietnam	8.30		1959
		7	Iraq	8.20		1956
		8	Cambodia	8.10		1959
	II	9	South Korea	7.50	VIII	1959
		10.5	Burma	7.30		1959
		10.5	Yugoslavia[1]	7.30		1959
		13	Indonesia	6.70		1959
		13	Egypt	6.70		1957
		13	United Kingdom	6.70		1959
24.4		15	Israel	6.30		1959
		16	France	5.90		1959
	III	17	Iran	5.60		1959
		18.5	Greece	5.10	IX	1959
		18.5	Libya	5.10		1959
		20	Syria	4.90		1959
		21	Sweden	4.70		1959
		22	Paraguay	4.50		1959
		23.5	Canada	4.40		1959
		23.5	Morocco	4.40		1959
	IV	25	Netherlands	4.00		1959
		26	Pakistan	3.90		1959
		27	West Germany	3.80		1959
55.7		28	China (Mainland)[1]	3.60[b]		1958
		29	Norway	3.50		1959
		30.5	Dominican Republic	3.20		1961
		30.5	Portugal	3.20		1959
		33.5	Belgium	3.00		1959
		33.5	Italy	3.00		1959
	V	33.5	Peru	3.00		1959
		33.5	Thailand	3.00		1959
		37	Cameroun	2.90		1960
		37	Haiti	2.90		1960
		37	Switzerland	2.90		1959
		39.5	Chile	2.80		1960
		39.5	Nicaragua	2.80		1960
		41.5	Australia	2.70		1959

TABLE 23 (continued)

% of Table Population	Case Deciles	Rank	Country	Expenditure on Defense as % of G. N. P.	Range Deciles	Year
		41.5	Malaya	2.70		1959
	VI	44	Argentina	2.60		1959
		44	Denmark	2.60		1959
		44	Venezuela	2.60		1959
		46	Brazil	2.50	X	1959
		47.5	Lebanon	2.40		1959
		47.5	Turkey	2.40		1959
		50	Ethiopia	2.20		1959
		50	New Zealand	2.20		1959
	VII	50	Spain	2.20		1959
		52	Bolivia	2.10		1959
		53.5	Finland	1.96		1959
74.0		53.5	Ecuador	1.96		1959
		55	India	1.89		1959
		56	Afghanistan	1.86		1960
		57	Somalia	1.84		1959
		58.5	Cuba	1.76		1957
	VIII	58.5	Tunisia	1.76		1959
		60	Philippines	1.61		1959
		61	Japan	1.60		1959
		62	El Salvador	1.58		1960
		63	Guatemala	1.52		1959
		64	Austria	1.48		1959
		65	Ireland	1.42		1958
		66	Sudan	1.31		1959
	IX	67	Honduras	1.30		1957
		68	Ceylon	1.21		1959
		69	Colombia	1.18		1959
		70	Uruguay	1.02		1960
		71	Rhodesia & Nyasaland	.88		1959
		72	South Africa	.79		1959
		73	Kenya	.74		1959
		74	Mexico	.72		1959
	X	75	Liberia	.65		1959
		76	Ghana	.63		1959
		77	Nepal	.59		1960
		78	Costa Rica	.53		1959
		79	Nigeria	.46		1959
		80	Panama	.27		1959
		81	Trinidad & Tobago	.23		1959
		82	Tanganyika	.04		1960
		83	Jamaica	.02		1960

[1] G. N. P. assumed equal to 110% of net material product.

Sources: Unless otherwise noted, A. I. D., *Economic Data Book* (Washington, 1962; looseleaf), and U. N., *Statistical Yearbook, 1961* (New York, 1962).

[a] Abram Bergson, *The Real National Income of Soviet Russia Since 1928* (Cambridge, Mass., 1961). This figure may well be low, as estimates vary widely.

[b] U. N. E. C. A. F. E., *Economic Survey of Asia and the Far East, 1960* (Bangkok, 1961), p. 83.

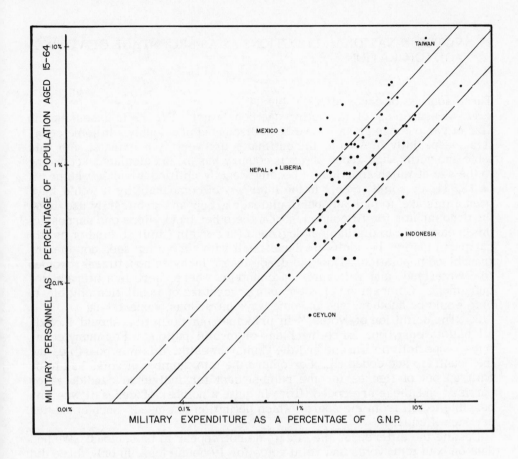

Figure A.1 Reliability Check for Military Participation Ratios and Defense Expenditure Ratios

24. VOTES IN NATIONAL ELECTIONS AS A PERCENTAGE OF VOTING-AGE POPULATION

Three sources of error affect Table 24:

1. Measurement of the voting-age population. Errors in assessing the size of various age groups have been discussed previously. In some countries, especially in Africa, the estimates are very approximate. For this table the voting-age group of each country has been calculated according to the age at which individuals become legally entitled to vote, whether it be 18, 21, or some other. In the interests of comparability it would have been a mistake to pick any particular age group and arbitrarily use it as the denominator for all countries. On the other hand, since one purpose of this measure is to distinguish degrees of a certain (limited) kind of political participation by adults we have dealt with the voting age, not the enfranchised population. Thus the denominator includes noncitizens, women in Switzerland, and illiterates in countries where there is a literacy requirement. Comparison of votes as a percentage of population eligible to vote would be another, and in some ways hazardous, undertaking.

2. The definition of "votes." In principal our definition should include all ballots cast, not excepting blank or invalid ballots. For many countries, especially in Europe and the Commonwealth, this was possible, and the countries are coded (I). For others the total number of votes had to be built up out of figures for the number cast for individual candidates or parties, and these are coded (III). In quite a number of cases it was impossible to tell from the source which definition was used; such countries are identified (II).

Despite the difference, the effects do not appear to be serious. We had data on both total votes and valid votes for 19 countries. In only three did the former datum exceed the latter by as much as 3%; except in Argentina the maximum difference was under 8%. Where there is evidence that large numbers of blank ballots were deliberately cast as evidence of support for a party not on the ballot (Argentina) the blanks have been included in the total vote.

3. Inaccurate reporting of the vote. In countries where party competition has been established over a period of two or more elections this is not a serious problem. Some reporting error and fraudulent electoral practices may exist, but they do not seem to be of a sort or magnitude that greatly affects reporting of the total vote, and certainly not in comparison with other sources of error in our data. But in countries holding elections for the first time, or especially where competition is not established, the published returns may not accurately reflect the number of votes cast. Even so this source of error would appear to be less important than the first, and probably less important than the second.

Countries where more than six years have elapsed since the most recent election are assigned a zero.

One major problem of comparability arises not from the data themselves, but from the relevant social and institutional context. In a number of countries it is a criminal offense, subject to fine, to fail to vote without good cause. Quite a few other states do not make nonvoting a crime, but nevertheless subject nonvoters to significant deprivations of one kind or another; in some nations failure to vote is virtually considered a sign of disloyalty to the regime. In all of these cases the voting participation rates are much higher than in countries where voting is encouraged but not made a virtual necessity. On the other hand in a few nations, principally the United States, voting rights are subject to certain requirements for a minimum period of residence in a city or state. People who are otherwise politically active are often temporarily denied the vote on this basis, thus artificially depressing the participation ratio. There is little that can be done other than simply to be aware of these problems; we have indicated with a footnote those states where nonvoting actually makes one subject to legal action.

Interpretation of the data requires some fairly complex hypotheses. In the United States and Western Europe it has generally been found that voting participation is highest among citizens of high education, income, and social status, and higher in the cities than in rural areas. The most cursory examination of the following table will show that this finding *within* countries does not apply in any consistent way *between* countries. There is a clear correlation between per capita G. N. P. and electoral turnout $(r = .47)$ but there are many obvious exceptions.[1]

It has been hypothesized that a fairly high level of political participation is essential for the development of an effective opposition, and furthermore that a society with many people outside politics is *potentially* more explosive than one where participation is high.[2] Alternatively, it has been suggested that extreme political interest "goes with extreme partisanship and might culminate in rigid fanaticism that could destroy democratic processes."[3] Thus a high level of voluntary participation might indicate tension. High voting rates are frequently observed during crises.[4] Great economic need, it has been said, may be mirrored in either high *or* low rates. Low economic status tends to diminish political participation unless access to information about the status of others, and the possibilities of improving one's status, are present.[5]

Some of these hypotheses have been very imperfectly tested even within states, and serve as examples of the kind of analysis that can be performed with the following data.

---

1. Daniel Lerner, *The Passing of Traditional Society* (Glencoe, Ill., 1958), pp. 61–62, finds a high multiple correlation $(r=.82)$ between voting and urbanization, literacy, and media participation. Part of the reason may lie in the limited nature of his sample, particularly the apparent exclusion of Communist states.

2. Seymour Martin Lipset, *Political Man* (Garden City, N.Y., 1960), p. 180.

3. Bernard Berelson, Paul Lazarsfeld, and William McPhee, *Voting* (Chicago, 1954), pp. 314–15.

4. Lipset, p. 187.

5. Ibid.

TABLE 24

Votes in National Elections as a Percentage of Voting-Age Population

No. of Cases	100
Mean	57.1
Median	60.3
Modal Decile	I
Range	99.6
Standard Deviation	30
Percentage of World Population	69

% of Table Population	Case Deciles	Rank	Country	Votes as % Vtg.-Age Pop.	Range Deciles	Year
	I	1	U.S.S.R. (II)	99.6	I	1958
		2	Bulgaria (I)	99.2		1957
		3	Czechoslovakia (I)	98.1		1960
		4	Romania (II)	97.9		1957
		5.5	East Germany (II)	97.3		1958
		5.5	Ivory Coast (II)	97.3[a]		1960
		7	Albania (I)	94.6		1958
		8	Rwanda (III)	93.7[b]		1961
		9	Hungary (II)	93.5		1958
		10	Italy (III)[1]	92.9[c]		1963
	II	11	Poland (I)	92.8		1957
		12	Nicaragua (III)	92.7[d]		1963
		13	Gabon (II)	92.6[e]		1958
		14	Netherlands (II)[1]	92.1[f]		1959
		15	Indonesia (II)	92.0[g]		1955
		16	Yugoslavia (II)	91.4		1958
		17	Austria (III)	90.4		1959
		18	France (II)	89.4[h]	II	1962
		19	Israel (I)	88.0[i]		1961
		20.5	Belgium (I)[1]	87.6[j]		1961
	III	20.5	Guinea (I)	87.6[a]		1958
25.3		22	West Germany (II)	86.9[k]		1961
		23	Iceland (III)	86.6		1959
		24	New Zealand (II)	86.4[l]		1960
		25	Australia (II)[1]	85.3[m]		1958
		26	Denmark (II)	84.0[n]		1960
		27	Venezuela (II)[1]	83.8[o]		1958
		28	Sweden (I)	83.1[p]		1960
		29	Liberia (III)	82.9[a]		1959
		30	Singapore (III)	82.3[q]		1959
	IV	31	Norway (I)	78.8[r]	III	1961
		32	United Kingdom (II)	78.0[s]		1959
		33.5	Canada (II)	74.2[t]		1958
		33.5	Haiti (II)	74.2[d]		1957
		35.5	Greece (III)[1]	73.3		1958
		35.5	Puerto Rico (III)	73.3[d]		1960
		37	Netherlands Antilles (II)	73.0[o]		1958
		38	Finland (III)	72.8		1958
		39	Turkey (III)	72.5[u]		1961

TABLE 24 (continued)

% of Table Population	Case Deciles	Rank	Country	Votes as % Vtg.-Age Pop.	Range Deciles	Year
		40	Cameroun (III)	72.2		1960
	V	41	Ireland (I)	71.6[v]		1957
		42	Japan (I)	71.2[w]		1960
		43	Luxembourg (III)	71.1		1954
		44	Jamaica (II)	70.6[o]		1962
		45	Cuba (II)	69.1[x]	IV	1954
		46	Burundi (II)	68.4[e]		1961
		47	Madagascar (III)	64.8[y]		1959
50.0		48	United States (II)	64.4[z]		1960
		49	Dominican Republic (III)	63.6[d]		1962
		50	Argentina (I)[1]	61.8		1960
	VI	51	Ceylon (III)	58.8	V	1960
		52	Senegal (I)	58.5[aa]		1959
		53	Uruguay (III)	58.3[d]		1962
		54	Costa Rica (II)	57.6[u]		1962
		55	Panama (III)	56.2[d]		1960
		56	Philippines (III)	55.1[bb]		1961
		57	Malaya (III)	54.8[q]		1959
		58	Burma (III)	54.5[cc]		1960
74.5		59	India (III)	52.6[dd]		1962
		60	British Guiana (II)	52.1[o]		1957
	VII	61	Bolivia (I)	51.4[d]		1962
		62	Tunisia (I)	49.9		1959
		63	Lebanon (II)	48.0[ee]	VI	1960
		64	Ghana (II)	43.9[c]		1957
		65	Mauritania (III)	42.8[ff]		1956
		66	Upper Volta (III)	41.9[ff]		1956
		67	Dahomey (III)	41.1		1959
		68	Nigeria (III)	40.4[gg]		1957
		69	Colombia (I)	40.2[d]		1962
		70	Peru (III)	39.2[u]	VII	1963
	VIII	71	Chile (III)	37.4[u]		1961
		72	Honduras (II)	36.5[o]		1957
		73	Mexico (II)	34.6[d]		1961
		74	Brazil (II)	34.4[d]		1960
		75	Tanganyika (III)	33.8[c]		1962
		76	South Korea (III)	31.3		1960
		77	Uganda (III)	31.0[c]		1961
		78	Central African Republic (III)	30.6[e]		1956
		79	El Salvador (I)	29.3[d]	VIII	1962
		80	Paraguay (I)	29.1[d]		1963
	IX	81	Kenya (I)	28.9[hh]		1961
		82	Ecuador (III)	28.4[d]		1960
		83	Switzerland (I)	28.0[ii]		1959
		84	Syria (III)	27.6[jj]		1961
		85	Guatemala (II)	27.5[o]		1958
		86	Mali (III)	25.1[ff]		1956
		87	Niger (III)	24.1[ff]		1956
		88	Portugal (II)	18.5[d]	IX	1958
		89	Sierra Leone (II)	16.7[aa]		1957

TABLE 24 (continued)

% of Table Population	Case Deciles	Rank	Country	Votes as % Vtg.-Age Pop.	Range Deciles	Year
		90	South West Africa (II)	11.0^c		1961
	X	91	South Africa (II)	10.4^{kk}		1961
		92	Rhodesia & Nyasaland (III)	1.9^{11}	X	1958
		96.5	Egypt	$.0^{mm}$		
		96.5	Iraq	$.0^{mm}$		
		96.5	Kuwait	$.0^{mm}$		
		96.5	Pakistan	$.0^{mm}$		
		96.5	Saudi Arabia	$.0^{mm}$		
		96.5	Spain	$.0^{mm}$		
		96.5	Sudan	$.0^{mm}$		
		96.5	Yemen	$.0^{mm}$		

[1] Voting legally required.

Sources: Unless otherwise noted, Institute of Electoral Research, *Review of Elections, 1954-58* (London, 1960), *1959* (London, 1961), *1960* (London, 1962).

[a] Gwendolyn Carter, ed., *African One-Party States* (Ithaca, N.Y., 1962), pp. 47, 169, 288, 361.

[b] *Africa Digest*, June 1960–February 1963.

[c] Italian Information Center, *Italy's General Elections* (New York, 1963).

[d] *Hispanic American Report*, October 1957–October 1963.

[e] Virginia Thompson and Richard Adloff, *The Emerging States of French Equatorial Africa* (Stanford, Cal., 1960), pp. 357, 392.

[f] Centraal Bureau voor de Statistick, *Jaarcijfers voor Nederland 1959-60* (Ziest, 1962), p. 57.

[g] Herbert Feith, *The Indonesian Elections of 1955* (Ithaca, N.Y., 1957), p. 58.

[h] *Encyclopedia Britannica Book of the Year 1963* (Chicago, 1963), p. 389.

[i] Central Bureau of Statistics, *Statistical Abstract of Israel 1962* (Jerusalem, 1962), p. 522.

[j] Institut National de Statistique, *Annuaire Statistique de la Belgique 1960* (Brussels, 1961), p. 509.

[k] Viggo Graf Blucher, *Der Prozess der Meinungsbildung* (Bielefeld, 1962), pp. 23, 24, 25A.

[l] Department of Statistics, *New Zealand Official Yearbook 1961* (Wellington, 1961), p. 1110.

[m] Commonwealth Bureau of Census and Statistics, *Official Yearbook of the Commonwealth of Australia 1960* (Canberra, 1960), p. 67.

[n] Det Statistiske Departement, *Statistisk Arbog 1961* (Copenhagen, 1962), p. 309.

[o] Center for Latin American Studies, U.C.L.A., *Statistical Abstract of Latin America, 1961* (Los Angeles, 1962), p. 17; *1962* (Los Angeles, 1963), p. 36.

[p] Central Bureau of Statistics, *Statistical Abstract of Sweden 1962* (Stockholm, 1962).

[q] K. C. Tregonning, "Malaya 1959," *Australian Quarterly*, June 1960.

[r] Central Bureau of Statistics of Norway, *Statistical Yearbook of Norway* (Oslo, 1962), p. 288.

[s] D. E. Butler and Richard Rose, *The British General Elections of 1959* (London, 1960), p. 204.

[t] Howard A. Scarrow, *Canada Votes* (New Orleans, La., 1962), p. 176.

[u] *The Europa Yearbook, 1963* (London, 1963).

[v] Central Statistics Office, *Statistical Abstract of Ireland, 1960* (Dubin, 1960), p. 60.

TABLE 24 (continued)

[w] Bureau of Statistics, Office of the Prime Minister, *Japan Statistical Yearbook, 1961* (Tokyo, 1962), p. 452.

[x] S. H. Steinberg, ed., *Statesman's Yearbook 1962-63* (London, 1962), p. 899.

[y] Raymond K. Kent, *From Madagascar to the Malagasy Republic* (New York, 1962), p. 149.

[z] U. S. Bureau of the Census, *Statistical Abstract of the U.S. 1962* (Washington, 1962), p. 359.

[aa] Agence France-Presse, *Bulletin Quotidien d'Information,* March 25, 1959.

[bb] *Asian Survey,* May 1962.

[cc] *Far Eastern Survey,* May 1960, p. 70.

[dd] Sundar Lai Poplai, *The 1962 General Elections in India* (Bombay, 1962), p. 42.

[ee] Jacob Landau, "Lebanese Elections," *Western Political Quarterly, 14* (March 1961).

[ff] *Paris-Dakar,* January 5, 1956, p. 3.

[gg] W. J. M. MacKenzie and Kenneth Robinson, *Five Elections in Africa* (Oxford, 1960).

[hh] George Bennett and Carl G. Rosenberg, *The Kenyatta Election, Kenya, 1960-61* (London, 1961), p. 217.

[ii] Bureau Federale de Statistique, *Annuaire Statistique de la Suisse* (Bern, 1962), p. 530.

[jj] Europa Publications, Ltd., *The Middle East 1962* (London, 1962), p. 361.

[kk] D. E. Butler, *Elections Abroad* (London, 1959), pp. 74, 269.

[ll] *The Europa Yearbook, 1961* (London, 1961), *2,* 995.

[mm] Institute of Electoral Research, *Parliaments and Electoral Systems* (London, 1962). In a few cases (e.g., Pakistan) there have been elections for local but not for national offices.

25-28. PARTY BREAKDOWN OF VOTES IN NATIONAL ELECTIONS

Tables 25-28 present breakdowns of the vote by four major party group-ings—communist, religious-oriented, socialist, and noncommunist secular parties. Where data are available we give the percentage of votes for the lower house of the national legislature. In parliamentary systems there is of course little choice; in presidential systems the choice of votes for legislators maximizes in most cases the influence of party rather than of personality. Also where possible we have used the average percentage received in the two most recent elections, so as to minimize the effects of year-to-year fluctuations.[1] And for a few countries where the communist party is illegal we went back to the most recent vote in which communists were openly on the ballot. Where the communist party was illegal in all the elections for which data were readily available we have simply not re-corded any percentage, since zero in such situations would almost cer-tainly understate the communists' true strength. Finally, note that in the following tables zero sometimes indicates some very small percentage (under .5%).

Obviously there are serious problems involved in properly identifying a party—it is not always easy to know what parties should be labeled commu-nist or socialist. The category "religious-oriented" parties is even more difficult to make comparable. It includes such diverse groups as the Jan Sangh in India and the very broadly based Christian Democratic Union in West Germany. But despite the problems it does seem that, if used with care, meaningful comparisons can be drawn with these figures. The table excludes the states of Africa, where either the franchise is so restricted as to make voting percentages unrepresentative or, as in the new states, the party structure is simply not comparable with that in other areas. "Noncommunist secular parties" includes all but communist votes and votes for religious parties; it also includes independents.

---

1. Except in cases like the Dominican Republic where a major change of regime made the most recent election totals entirely noncomparable with preceding ballots.

TABLE 25

Votes for Communist Party as a Percentage of Total Vote

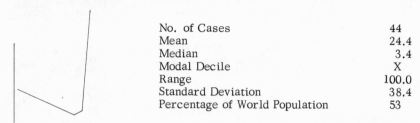

No. of Cases	44
Mean	24.4
Median	3.4
Modal Decile	X
Range	100.0
Standard Deviation	38.4
Percentage of World Population	53

% of Table Population	Case Deciles	Rank	Country	Comm. % of Total Vote	Range Deciles	Avg. of Years
	I	2	Albania	100.0[a]	I–VII	1958
		2	U. S. S. R.	100.0[a]		1958
		2	Bulgaria	100.0[a]		1957
		4	Czechoslovakia	99.9[a]		1960
	II	5	East Germany	99.7[a]		1954,58
		6	Hungary	99.6[a]		1958
		7	Romania	99.3[a,b]		1957,61
		8	Poland	98.4[a]		1957
	III	9	Yugoslavia	96.7[a]		1958
		10	Italy	24.0[c]	VIII	1958,63
		11	Finland	22.7[a,b]		1958,62
26.5		12	France	21.0[a,b]		1958,62
		13	Indonesia	17.0[d]	IX	1955
	IV	14	Iceland	15.7[a]		1959
		15	Chile	12.0[b]		1961
63.8		16	India	10.1[a,d]		1957,62
		17	Luxembourg	7.1[a]	X	1954
	V	18	Venezuela	6.0[e]		1958
		19	Sweden	4.0[a]		1958,60
		20	Netherlands	3.9[a]		1956,59
		21	Ceylon	3.7[a]		1960
		22	Israel	3.5[d]		1959,61
	VI	23	Uruguay	3.3[b,f]		1958,62
		24	Norway	3.2[g]		1957,61
		25	Austria	3.0[a,b]		1959,62
		26.5	Brazil	2.8[f]		1958
	VII	26.5	Japan	2.8[h]		1958,60
		28	Switzerland	2.6[a]		1955
75.0		29	Belgium	2.5[a,b]		1958,61
		30.5	Denmark	2.2[a]		1957,60
	VIII	30.5	West Germany	2.2[a,b]		1953
		32.5	Bolivia	2.0[b]		1962
		32.5	Peru	2.0[b]		1962
		34	Australia	.5[a]		1958
		35.5	New Zealand	.1[i]		1957,60
	IX	35.5	United Kingdom	.1[d]		1955,59
		40.5	Canada	.0[a,b]		1958,63
		40.5	Ecuador	.0[b]		1960

TABLE 25 (continued)

% of Table Population	Case Deciles	Rank	Country	Comm. % of Total Vote	Range Deciles	Avg. of Years
		40.5	El Salvador	.0[f]		1961
	X	40.5	Honduras	.0[f]		1957
		40.5	Ireland	.0[a, b]		1957,61
		40.5	Jamaica	.0[b]		1962
		40.5	Turkey	.0[b, e]		1957,61
		40.5	United States	.0[j]		1952

[a] Institute of Electoral Research, *Review of Elections, 1954-1958* (London, 1960); *1959* (London, 1961); *1960* (London, 1962).

[b] *The Europa Yearbook, 1963* (London, 1963), *1-2*.

[c] The Italian Information Center, *Italy's General Elections* (New York, 1963).

[d] *Keesing's Archives, 1955-56* (London, 1957); *1961-62* (London, 1963).

[e] S. H. Steinberg, ed., *Statesman's Yearbook, 1959* (New York, 1960).

[f] *Hispanic American Report,* October 1957–October 1963.

[g] Central Bureau of Statistics of Norway, *Statistical Yearbook of Norway* (Oslo, 1962), p. 288.

[h] Robert Scalapino and Junnosuke Masumi, *Parties and Politics in Contemporary Japan* (Berkeley, Cal., 1962).

[i] Department of Statistics, *New Zealand Official Yearbook 1961* (Wellington, 1961), p. 1110.

[j] U. S. Bureau of the Census, *Statistical Abstract of the U.S. 1962* (Washington, 1962), p. 376.

TABLE 26

Votes for Religious Parties as a Percentage of Total Vote

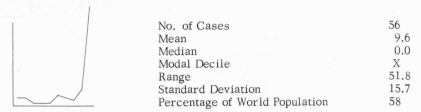

No. of Cases		56
Mean		9.6
Median		0.0
Modal Decile		X
Range		51.8
Standard Deviation		15.7
Percentage of World Population		58

% of Table Population	Case Deciles	Rank	Country	Religious % of Total Vote	Range Deciles	Avg. of Years
	I	1	Netherlands	51.8	I	1956,59
		2	Indonesia	50.0		1955
		3	West Germany	47.8		1957,61
		4	Luxembourg	45.0	II	1954
		5	Belgium	44.1		1958,61
	II	6	Austria	43.7		1959,62
		7	Italy	40.3	III,IV	1958,63
		8	Chile	30.0	V	1961
		9	Switzerland	24.3	VI,VII	1955
		10	Colombia	23.0[a,b]		1958,62
		11	Ecuador	22.5		1960
	III	12	Malaya	21.2[a]		1959
		13	Israel	15.0	VIII	1959,61
		14	Venezuela	14.6		1958
		15.5	Mexico	10.6[b]	IX	1958,61
		15.5	Turkey	10.6		1957,61
19.3	IV	17	Norway	9.8		1957,61
		18	India	8.0		1957,62
		19	Puerto Rico	6.5[a]		1960
		20	France	6.4		1958,62
		21	Uruguay	3.5	X	1958,62
51.9	V	22	Brazil	3.3		1958
		23	Peru	2.9		1962
		24	Bolivia	2.0		1962
53.9		25	Argentina	.1[b]		1957,60
		40.5	Albania	.0		1958
		40.5	Australia	.0		1955,58
	VI	40.5	Bulgaria	.0		1957
		40.5	Canada	.0		1958,63
		40.5	Ceylon	.0		1960
		40.5	Costa Rica	.0[a,b]		1958,62
		40.5	Czechoslovakia	.0		1960
		40.5	Denmark	.0		1957,60
	VII	40.5	Dominican Republic	.0[a]		1962
		40.5	East Germany	.0		1954,58
		40.5	Finland	.0		1958,62
		40.5	Greece	.0[a,c]		1958,61
		40.5	Honduras	.0		1957
		40.5	Hungary	.0		1958
	VIII	40.5	Iceland	.0		1959

TABLE 26 (continued)

% of Table Population	Case Deciles	Rank	Country	Religious % of Total Vote	Range Deciles	Avg. of Years
		40.5	Ireland	.0		1957,61
		40.5	Jamaica	.0		1962
		40.5	Japan	.0		1958,60
		40.5	New Zealand	.0		1957,60
	IX	40.5	Panama	.0[a]		1960
		40.5	Paraguay	.0[b]		1963
		40.5	Philippines	.0[a]		1957,61
		40.5	Poland	.0		1957
		40.5	Romania	.0		1957,61
		40.5	Singapore	.0[a]		1959
	X	40.5	South Korea	.0		1960
		40.5	Sweden	.0		1958,62
		40.5	United Kingdom	.0		1955,59
		40.5	United States	.0		1950,62
		40.5	U. S. S. R.	.0		1958
		40.5	Yugoslavia	.0		1958

Sources: Same as those listed for communist votes in preceding table, with the exceptions noted.

[a] *The Europa Yearbook, 1963,* vols. 1–2 (London, 1963).

[b] *Hispanic American Report,* October 1957–October 1963.

[c] Institute of Electoral Research, *Review of Elections, 1954-58* (London, 1960); *1959* (London, 1961); *1960* (London, 1962).

TABLE 27

Votes for Socialist Parties as a Percentage of Total Vote

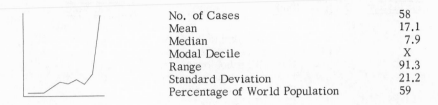

No. of Cases	58
Mean	17.1
Median	7.9
Modal Decile	X
Range	91.3
Standard Deviation	21.2
Percentage of World Population	59

% of Table Population	Case Deciles	Rank	Country	Socialist as % of Total Vote	Range Deciles	Avg. of Years
	I	1	Singapore	91.3	I, II	1959
		2	Burma	70.0[a,b]	III, IV	1956,60
		3	Australia	51.9	V	1955,58
		4	Jamaica	49.0		1962
		5	Norway	48.8		1957,61
	II	6	Sweden	47.4		1958,60
		7	New Zealand	45.9		1957,60
		8.5	Austria	45.0	VI	1959,62
		8.5	United Kingdom	45.0		1955,59
		10	Ceylon	43.8		1960
		11	Denmark	43.7		1957,60
	III	12	Belgium	36.3	VII	1958,61
		13	Japan	34.7		1958,60
		14	West Germany	34.0		1957,61
		15	Luxembourg	32.6		1954
		16	Netherlands	31.6		1956,59
		17	Switzerland	29.1		1955
	IV	18	Indonesia	26.0	VIII	1955
		19	Finland	24.5		1958,62
		20	Greece[1]	19.6		1958,61
		21	Iceland	18.8		1959
		22	Chile	17.8	IX	1961
25.8	V	23	Italy[2]	17.5		1958,63
		24	France	15.2		1958,62
		25	Israel[3]	13.6		1959,61
		26	Malaya	13.0		1959
		27	Canada	11.4		1958,63
		28	Ireland	10.6		1957,61
55.3	VI	29	India	10.0		1957,62
		30	Ecuador	5.8	X	1960
		31	Uruguay	3.2		1958,62
		32	South Korea	1.5		1960
		33	Mexico	1.3		1958,61
		34	Peru	1.0		1962
60.9	VII	35	Argentina	.8		1957,60
		47	Albania	.0		1958
		47	Bolivia	.0		1962
		47	Brazil	.0		1958
		47	Bulgaria	.0		1957

TABLE 27 (continued)

% of Table Population	Case Deciles	Rank	Country	Socialist as % of Total Vote	Range Deciles	Avg. of Years
		47	Colombia	.0		1958,62
	VIII	47	Costa Rica	.0		1958,62
		47	Czechoslovakia	.0		1960
		47	Dominican Republic	.0		1962
		47	East Germany	.0		1954,58
		47	El Salvador	.0		1961
		47	Honduras	.0		1957
	IX	47	Hungary	.0		1958
		47	Panama	.0		1960
		47	Paraguay	.0		1963
		47	Philippines	.0		1957,61
		47	Poland	.0		1957
		47	Puerto Rico	.0		1960
	X	47	Romania	.0		1957,61
		47	Turkey	.0		1957,61
		47	U.S.S.R.	.0		1958
		47	United States	.0		1960,62
		47	Venezuela	.0		1958
		47	Yugoslavia	.0		1958

[1] The Union of the Democratic Left (EDA) has been included among the socialist parties because it represents various shades of "Left" opinion, in part Communist and pro-Communist, and in part non-Communist.

[2] Includes the Socialist Party of Pietro Nenni and the Social Democratic Party.

[3] Israel's major party, the Labor Party (Mapai), has headed every government since the country's founding and has avoided implementing the socialist attitudes of some of its members in order to act as the party of national unity. In this role, it has at different times formed coalitions with parties ranging from doctrinaire socialists (Mapam) to conservatives (General Zionists). Hence, it is not included among the socialist parties.

Sources: Same as those listed for communist votes and for religious votes in tables 25 and 26, with the exceptions noted.

[a] *The Europa Yearbook, 1963,* vol. 1 (London, 1963).

[b] *Far Eastern Survey,* May 1960.

TABLE 28

Votes for Noncommunist Secular Parties as a Percentage of Total Vote

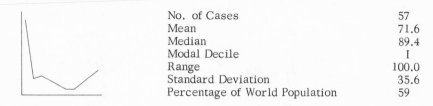

No. of Cases	57
Mean	71.6
Median	89.4
Modal Decile	I
Range	100.0
Standard Deviation	35.6
Percentage of World Population	59

% of Table Population	Case Deciles	Rank	Country	Noncom. Sec. % of Total Vote	Range Deciles	Avg. of Years
	I	8.5	Argentina	100.0	I	1957,60
		8.5	Canada	100.0		1958,63
		8.5	Costa Rica	100.0		1958,62
		8.5	Dominican Republic	100.0		1962
		8.5	El Salvador	100.0		1961
	II	8.5	Greece	100.0		1958,61
		8.5	Honduras	100.0		1957
		8.5	Ireland	100.0		1957,61
		8.5	Jamaica	100.0		1962
		8.5	New Zealand	100.0		1957,60
		8.5	Panama	100.0		1960
	III	8.5	Paraguay	100.0		1963
		8.5	Philippines	100.0		1957,61
		8.5	Singapore	100.0		1959
		8.5	South Korea	100.0		1960
		8.5	United States	100.0		1960,62
		17	United Kingdom	99.9		1955,59
	IV	18	Australia	99.5		1955,58
		19	Denmark	97.8		1957,60
26.8 ------------		20	Japan	97.2		1958,60
		21	Ceylon	96.3		1960
		22.5	Bolivia	96.0		1962
	V	22.5	Sweden	96.0		1958,62
		24	Peru	95.1		1962
		25	Brazil	93.9		1958
		26	Puerto Rico	93.5		1960
		27	Uruguay	93.2		1958,62
		28.5	Mexico	89.4	II	1958,61
	VI	28.5	Turkey	89.4		1957,61
		30	Norway	87.0		1957,61
		31	Iceland	84.3		1959
62.5 ------------		32	India	81.9		1957,62
		33	Israel	81.5		1959,61
		34	Venezuela	79.4	III, IV	1958
	VII	35	Malaya	78.8		1959
		36	Ecuador	77.5		1960
		37	Finland	77.3		1958,62
		38	Colombia	77.0		1958,62
		39	Switzerland	73.1		1955
	VIII	40	France	72.6		1958,62

TABLE 28 (continued)

% of Table Population	Case Deciles	Rank	Country	Noncom. Sec. % of Total Vote	Range Deciles	Avg. of Years
		41	Chile	58.0	V	1961
		42	Belgium	53.4		1958,61
		43	Austria	53.3		1959,62
		44	West Germany	52.2		1957,61
		45	Luxembourg	47.9	VI	1954
	IX	46	Netherlands	44.3		1956,59
75.3		47	Italy	35.7	VII–IX	1958,63
		48	Indonesia	33.0		1955
		53.5	Albania	.0	X	1958
		53.5	Bulgaria	.0		1957
		53.5	Czechoslovakia	.0		1960
	X	53.5	East Germany	.0		1954,58
		53.5	Hungary	.0		1958
		53.5	Poland	.0		1957
		53.5	Romania	.0		1957,61
		53.5	U. S. S. R.	.0		1958
		53.5	Yugoslavia	.0		1958

Sources: Same as those listed for communist votes, for religious votes, and for socialist votes in tables 25–27.

29. DEATHS FROM DOMESTIC GROUP VIOLENCE PER 1,000,000 POPU-LATION, 1950–1962

One of the most widely used concepts in political analysis is stability. It is, however, often used imprecisely or is used by different authors to mean different things. To some "stability" means maintenance of a parti-cular system of government, a particular constitutional order. To others "stability" may mean the continuance of a particular leader, or party, or coalition in power. By the first definition the French Third Republic was "stable" over a long period of time; by the second it most certainly was not. Yet another definition might be concerned with the frequency of poli-tical violence; an unstable system would be one marked by frequent riots, coups, assassinations, or rebellions. Another might be concerned with the basic economic relationships of the country; an unstable state would be one in which ownership of the means of production changed sharply. Still other definitions have appeared in the literature.

Faced with a conceptual problem of this nature there is little point in trying to isolate a single meaning of "stability" so as to use it exclusively. We have used here two quite distinct indices to measure different aspects of stability. Neither is by itself adequate as a means to tap the complex of events often covered by this broad term, but they do to some extent tap particular aspects of the concept. They are best used together, or even with still other measures the reader may devise. We emphasize that each is a *partial* measure, and furthermore that the two indices are not highly correlated. We do not imply that because a country is high on one of these indices it is necessarily high on another. On the contrary, overemphasis on either of the indices will produce some striking anomalies.

One index measures, for the period 1950 through 1962, "the number of people killed in all forms of domestic violence: any deaths resulting di-rectly from violence of an intergroup nature, thus excluding deaths by murder and execution." The forerunner of this series was compiled, for the 1955–57 period only, by Rudolph J. Rummel.[1] To reduce the effect of unique events, such as the Hungarian revolution of 1956, we have extended Rummel's series both backward and forward to a total of 13 years. We have limited ourselves to independent states so as to avoid the distorting effects of violence directed against a colonial power; in the interests of retaining a substantial number of Asian states in the series we have there-fore not been able to extend it back before 1950. To control for country size we have transformed the absolute data on deaths into deaths per 1,000,000 population.

The basic sources used include *The New York Times Index, New Inter-national Yearbook, Facts on File,* and *Brittanica Book of the Year.* Occa-sionally we have resorted to specialized works to remove ambiguities. The most likely source of error is systematic under-reporting of deaths in

---

1. Rudolph J. Rummel, "Dimensions of Conflict Behavior Within and Between Nations," *General Systems*, Yearbook of the Society for the Advancement of General Systems Theory, Ann Arbor, Mich., 1963.

some countries, due either to press censorship or to lack of world interest. In his original study Rummel attempted to control for these factors,
using a "censorship scale" and an index of world interest based on the
number of resident embassies and legations in a country. Neither showed
a significant correlation with the violence data, indicating that censorship
and world interest, *as tapped by these measures,* had little effect on the
results.[2] Nevertheless we have found quite a number of instances where,
though violence was reported, the number of deaths was not known with any
precision. We were forced in these cases to make very rough estimates.
The most approximate figures are footnoted, and must be assigned a very
wide error range, usually not less than ±50%. The coder's judgment might
also be thought to bias the results, but an independent check of our data by
a second coder showed less than .1% disagreement on the number of deaths.
The chief source of error remains inadequate information.

Several other imaginative efforts have been made to measure violent
change, and should be mentioned. Ivo Feierabend and associates have
compiled a seven-point index of political stability.[3] Various possible
events are assigned scores of from zero to seven, with an orderly general
election scored zero and civil war scored six. The time period is 1955 to
1961. This would appear to be a fruitful approach, but at the moment the
time span employed is fairly short, and, more serious, the stability score
has not been thoroughly validated. There is some question as to whether
the kinds of events in any one scoring group are not too heterogenous, and
even as to the relative degree of violence attributed to events assigned
different scores.

Another attempt to grapple with this difficult problem is represented by
Harry Eckstein's data on internal war.[4] Eckstein has recorded, from the
New York Times Index, the number of violent events occurring in the period
1946-59. All recorded events, from rioting to civil and guerilla warfare,
are counted. He gives for each country both the overall total number of
events and the subtotals for each of seven categories such as "turmoil,"
"terrorism," and "mutiny." The overall number of events probably does
not make a good index, as it weights equally events of very different magnitude. Probably a scale like Feierabend's could be constructed, but that
would not be entirely satisfactory. Furthermore, Eckstein mentions some
significant omissions which diminish the data's usefulness. And finally,
the dependence on a single source, the *Times Index,* also introduces some
distortions.

While these two approaches are valuable, and while we are aware of de-
ficiencies in our own index, it nevertheless seems to us that the violent
deaths index is the most satisfactory.

---

2. Ibid.
3. Ivo K. Feierabend, Rosalind L. Feierabend, and Betty A. Nesvold, "Correlates of Political
Stability," Paper Presented at the 1963 Annual Meeting of the American Political Science Association, Sept. 4-7, 1963.
4. Harry Eckstein, *Internal War: The Problem of Anticipation,* a report submitted to the Research Group in Psychology and the Social Sciences, Smithsonian Institution, Washington, D.C.,
1962.

TABLE 29

Deaths from Domestic Group Violence per
1,000,000 Population, 1950–1962

No. of Cases	74
Mean	107
Median	3
Modal Decile	X
Range	2,900
Standard Deviation	387
Percentage of World Population	90

% of Table Population	Case Deciles	Rank	Country	Deaths from Domestic Group Violence per 1,000,000 Population 1950–62	Range Deciles
	I	1	Cuba[1]	2,900	I–V
		2	Hungary	1,335	VI,VII
		3	Indonesia[1]	860	VIII
		4	Bolivia	663	
		5	Iraq[1]	344	IX
		6	Colombia	316	
		7	Philippines	292	
	II	8	Argentina	217	X
		9	Burma[1]	152	
		10.5	Honduras	111	
		10.5	Venezuela	111	
		12	Paraguay	60	
		13	Guatemala	57	
		14	South Korea	49	
	III	15	Syria	44	
		16	Ceylon	42	
		17	Iran	36	
		18	South Africa	33	
		19	Dominican Republic	31	
		20	Peru	26	
		21	Panama	25	
		22	Costa Rica	24	
12.4	IV	23	Afghanistan[1]	21	
		24	China (Mainland)[1]	20	
		25	Ecuador	18	
		27	Haiti	16	
		27	Lebanon	16	
		27	Nicaragua	16	
55.3		29	India[1]	14	
	V	30	Ethiopia	10	
		31	Pakistan	9	
		32	Yemen	8	
		33.5	Jordan	7	
		33.5	Nepal	7	
		35	Poland	5	
		36	Mexico	4	
		38.5	Bulgaria	3	

TABLE 29 (continued)

% of Table Population	Case Deciles	Rank	Country	Deaths from Domestic Group Violence per 1,000,000 Population 1950–62	Range Deciles
	VI	38.5	East Germany	3	
		38.5	Israel	3	
		38.5	Thailand	3	
		42	Chile	2	
		42	El Salvador	2	
		42	Greece	2	
		44	Egypt	1.6	
	VII	45.5	Brazil	1.0	
		45.5	Portugal	1.0	
		47.5	Belgium	.9	
75.5		47.5	Turkey	.9	
		49.5	Czechoslovakia	.7	
		49.5	U.S.S.R.	.7	
		51.5	France	.3	
	VIII	51.5	Uruguay	.3	
		54	Italy	.2	
		54	Saudi Arabia	.2	
		54	Spain	.2	
		56	Japan	.1	
		57	West Germany	.02	
		58	United States	.01	
		66.5	Australia	.0	
	IX	66.5	Austria	.0	
		66.5	Canada	.0	
		66.5	Denmark	.0	
		66.5	Finland	.0	
		66.5	Ireland	.0	
		66.5	Liberia	.0	
		66.5	Netherlands	.0	
	X	66.5	New Zealand	.0	
		66.5	Norway	.0	
		66.5	Romania	.0	
		66.5	Sweden	.0	
		66.5	Switzerland	.0	
		66.5	Taiwan	.0	
		66.5	United Kingdom	.0	
		66.5	Yugoslavia	.0	

[1] Based on rough approximation. Precise data unavailable.

Sources: *Facts on File* (New York, 1950–62); Wyatt MacGaffey and Clifford Bar-nett, *Cuba: Its People, Its Society, Its Culture* (New Haven, Conn., 1962); *New York Times Index* (New York, 1950–62); *The Britannica Yearbook* (Chicago, 1950–62); *The New International Yearbook* (New York, 1950–62); *The Times* (London) *Index* (London, 1950–62).

30. EXECUTIVE STABILITY: NUMBER OF YEARS INDEPENDENT/ NUMBER OF CHIEF EXECUTIVES, 1945-1961

Table 30 represents an effort to measure a second kind of political stability. It gives the rate of turnover in office of the legally designated chief executive. "Chief executive" of course means, in a presidential system, the president; in a parliamentary system it means the premier or prime minister. In a monarchy the designation of chief executive depends upon whether the prime minister is responsible to a legislative body or to the king. When a country is ruled by a junta we have considered the junta collectively as the "chief executive" unless at some point it appears that collective leadership has clearly been replaced by the predominance of a single individual. Such a change is considered a change in the chief executive. On the other hand there is considered to be no change in the chief executive if the form of the system is changed while the same individual continues to hold the principal post. Thus Yugoslavia's constitutional shift from a parliamentary to a presidential system is not recorded because Marshal Tito held the top post, without interruption, under both systems.

Revolutionary coups, even if they were in turn soon overthrown, were considered changes if it seemed that the revolutionary regime did indeed have effective control of the government, though perhaps only for a matter of days. In a very few cases where the original regime returned to power almost immediately with little difficulty, and it appeared that the revolutionary regime did not have effective control (e.g. the abortive overthrow of Ethiopia's Haile Selassie in 1961), the changes were not recorded.

Information was sufficiently complete for us to be sure that, in virtually all cases, our index was free from error in the sense of inaccuracy. But in terms of its definition—of what it is measuring—it is far from perfect. One could quarrel with the decision to deal with the legally defined heads of state (except in the case of successful revolution) in communist countries, where the party secretary, not the constitutional chief of state, often wields actual power. The measure does not distinguish the cause of turnover—orderly succession following death is really quite different from a coup. Nor does it distinguish between succession from within the same party and replacement from a quite different group. Nor is it always easy to decide what to do in the case of a parliamentary system with an extraordinarily strong president (France).

On the other hand, most attempts to meet these objections raise more problems than they solve. If one does not count orderly succession after death as a change, one must then fairly arbitrarily say how long the former chief would have continued in office had he lived. Or if one chooses to deal only with party change, what does one do with coalitions? What if one party drops out but the rest of the coalition remains unchanged? Or if the coalition remains but a new prime minister is chosen from one of the other governing parties?

In the final analysis it would make little difference for most countries whether our measure were replaced with a slightly different one. For example, the decision to treat France as still a parliamentary rather than

a presidential system has meant the designation of one more chief of state
(M. Debré, who replaced Gen. De Gaulle, the last premier of the Fourth
Republic) than if we considered President De Gaulle as the only chief of
state since the end of the Fourth Republic. But given the previous instability of French governments (25 heads of state since 1945) the decision
does not affect France's instability score much. A determination contrary
to the one made here about any single case would have little effect on most
countries' positions on the scale.

Again we emphasize that this concept taps only one dimension of political
stability. Another effort is represented by Seymour Martin Lipset's work
on the stability of democracy. Lipset established two groupings of national
political systems: stable and unstable democracies, and popular and elite-
based dictatorships. The criteria were essentially the presence or absence
of free elections and the presence or absence of a totalitarian movement,
either fascist or communist, which at any point over the past 30 years received as much as 20% of the vote.[1]

Clearly this is a different dimension from the one measured in Table
30, but it is nonetheless an important one. Yet, as Lipset is well aware,
the index is imprecise. It requires a substantial amount of subjective
judgment. Furthermore, instead of giving us a fairly detailed ranking, it
makes at most four basic distinctions.

Russell Fitzgibbon and Kenneth Johnson asked expert judges to score the
20 Latin American states on such supposed elements of democracy as
political freedoms, the role of the military, the condition of the press,
etc., and compiled a composite index.[2] While helpful, it is difficult not to
agree with Phillips Cutright's criticism of

the lack of agreement among raters concerning the rank order and, with
larger numbers of nations, the necessity to abandon subjective evaluations and turn to objective indicators—what expert can be in intimate
contact with the political histories of all the nations of the world and
also be willing or able to order them on simple scales, let alone multiple
dimensions? We can devise statistical and objective methods of measuring political development, just as the economist does when he asks
about energy consumption per capita and not what an expert believes the
whole economy of a nation has been doing over the past year. This implies that we can also remove ourselves from the world of ethnocentric
judgments about the goodness or evil of political systems and turn to
other aspects of political systems in order to understand them.[3]

Cutright's answer is to construct an index not of democracy, but of political development—an index of the complexity and specialization of political
institutions. As developed the index weights heavily the role of political
parties, and is in fact not unlike many Western conceptions of democracy.[4]
We have not included it here because it seemed to us that the system of
assigning points and scaling might appear rather arbitrary to some readers, and we have tried to confine this book to direct measures of quantities
rather than composite scores and scales. Cutright's method, however, is
an original and promising one.

1. Seymour Martin Lipset, "Some Social Requisites of Democracy: Economic Development and
Political Legitimacy," *American Political Science Review*, 53 (March 1959), 69–105.
2. Russell Fitzgibbon and Kenneth Johnson, "The Measurement of Latin American Political
Change," *American Political Science Review*, 55 (September 1961), 515–26.
3. Phillips Cutright, "National Political Development: Measurement and Analysis," *American
Sociological Review*, 28 (April 1963), 253–64.
4. Ibid., 255–56.

TABLE 30

Executive Stability: Number of Years Independent/Number of
Chief Executives, 1945–1961

No. of Cases	87
Mean	4.38
Median	3.00
Modal Decile	X
Range	16.46
Standard Deviation	4.20
Percentage of World Population	70

% of Table Population	Case Deciles	Rank	Country	Stability Index	Range Deciles
	I	3.5	Ethiopia	17.00	I
		3.5	Liberia	17.00	
		3.5	Portugal	17.00	
		3.5	Spain	17.00	
		3.5	Taiwan	17.00	
		3.5	Yugoslavia	17.00	
24.8		7	India	14.00	II, III
		8	West Germany	12.00	IV, V
	II	11	Albania	8.50	VI
		11	Poland	8.50	
		11	Sweden	8.50	
		11	Switzerland	8.50	
		11	Yemen	8.50	
		14	South Vietnam	7.00	VII
		15	East Germany	6.00	
		18.5	Afghanistan	5.67	
		18.5	Australia	5.67	
	III	18.5	Canada	5.67	
		18.5	Dominican Republic	5.67	
		18.5	Mongolian People's Republic	5.67	
		18.5	Saudi Arabia	5.67	
		22	Ghana	5.00	
		27.5	Austria	4.25	VIII
		27.5	Czechoslovakia	4.25	
		27.5	Luxembourg	4.25	
		27.5	Mexico	4.25	
	IV	27.5	New Zealand	4.25	
		27.5	Nicaragua	4.25	
		27.5	Norway	4.25	
		27.5	South Africa	4.25	
		27.5	U.S.S.R.	4.25	
		27.5	United States	4.25	
56.6		33	Malaya	4.00	
		37	Argentina	3.40	IX
	V	37	Bulgaria	3.40	
		37	Cuba	3.40	
		37	Honduras	3.40	
		37	Netherlands	3.40	

TABLE 30 (continued)

% of Table Population	Case Deciles	Rank	Country	Stability Index	Range Deciles
		37	Romania	3.40	
		37	United Kingdom	3.40	
		41	South Korea	3.25	
		43.5	Guinea	3.00	
		43.5	Morocco	3.00	
	VI	43.5	Philippines	3.00	
		43.5	Tunisia	3.00	
		46.5	Chile	2.83	
		46.5	Ireland	2.83	
		49	Burma	2.80	
		49	Ceylon	2.80	
74.6		49	Israel	2.80	
		54	Colombia	2.43	
		54	Costa Rica	2.43	
	VII	54	Denmark	2.43	
		54	Paraguay	2.43	
		54	Peru	2.43	
		54	Turkey	2.43	
		54	Uruguay	2.43	
		58	Libya	2.20	
		60	Guatemala	2.13	X
		60	Iceland	2.13	
	VIII	60	Venezuela	2.13	
		62	Sudan	2.00	
		63.5	Ecuador	1.89	
		63.5	El Salvador	1.89	
		65	Pakistan	1.75	
		66	Bolivia	1.70	
		68.5	Belgium	1.55	
		68.5	Brazil	1.55	
		68.5	Haiti	1.55	
	IX	68.5	Italy	1.55	
		72.5	Finland	1.42	
		72.5	Nepal	1.42	
		72.5	Panama	1.42	
		72.5	Thailand	1.42	
		75	Indonesia	1.33	
		76.5	Hungary	1.31	
		76.5	Japan	1.31	
		79	Egypt	1.21	
	X	79	Greece	1.21	
		79	Iran	1.21	
		81	Jordan	.84	
		82.5	Iraq	.81	
		82.5	Lebanon	.81	
		84	Laos	.78	
		85	France	.68	
		86.5	Cambodia	.54	
		86.5	Syria	.54	

Sources: *Americana Book of the Year, 1946-1962* (New York, 1946–62); *Britannica Book of the Year, 1946-1962* (Chicago, 1946–62); *The New York Times Index; 1945-1961* (New York, 1946–62).

Communications

The development of modern communications has immense effects on a country. The mass media are clearly a source of aspirations; the "revolution of rising expectations" occurs as people are brought into contact with images of the living habits of others.[1] The media may expand the market for many types of goods; by making mass production possible they may have profound economic effects. A high level of communications development represents a capability of a nation and of a government. Communications systems provide governments with the ability to mobilize their populations, to instill certain desires and goals. The media may also provide an opportunity for a government to control its populace; to the degree it can control the content of the media it can hope to control political attitudes. On the other hand, a government which cannot satisfactorily control the content of the media may not be in serious difficulty as long as the media are rudimentary, but it may be faced with increasing opposition as they develop. Finally, if the government can control the media it can use them to teach skills to the populace. Obviously newspapers can improve literacy, but all the media can be used to raise the level of technical competence.

Communications media may have major consequences for the political unity of a nation. A nation, in the sense of a people with shared values and aspirations, may not exist before modern communications become reasonably widespread. When radio, newspaper, and other media are introduced they may provide the means whereby the existence of common goals and values are recognized or created; equally they may point up underlying conflicts and inconsistencies. Modern communication may help to make a unified nation; on the other hand, if the mass media express themselves in a welter of local languages the effects may be extremely fissiparous.

Many series of data, often of reasonably high comparability, are available on communications. We have included here only a sample, but other possibilities include newsprint consumption per capita, telephones or telephone messages, book and film production, cinema seats, and other combinations of information on mail flows. To a degree they are closely correlated, and we tried to select a set of indices that would measure somewhat different aspects of the overall phenomenon. One distinct index that would have been desirable was for library books. Books represent accumulated knowledge in addition to current facilities; unfortunately the data on libraries and their contents suffer from such serious incomparabilities that we abandoned the effort for this edition.

For most of these indices a high value indicates a high level of technological advancement, but this is not uniformly true. Cinema attendance, for instance, tends not to be highest in the most developed states, where it

---

1. According to Daniel Lerner the impact of modern media on traditional cultures inevitably results in serious frustration. "The empathic individual imagination quickly (logarithmically it appears) outruns societal achievement." Cf. Lerner, "Toward a Communication Theory of Modernization," in Lucian Pye, ed., *Communications and Political Development* (Princeton, 1963), p. 335.

seems to be replaced by other forms of entertainment. In underdeveloped countries the cost of cinema attendance may be relatively low.[2] Television sets, on the other hand, imply both a reasonably advanced technology and a number of people with some surplus income. Newspaper readership implies at least the basic skill of literacy on the part of the consumer; this is not the case with radios. Egypt, for example, ranks in the middle of the series for radio sets, but well down in the list of newspapers per 1,000. In a number of countries radios have been used as a very cheap means of bringing information to most of the population. Wired speakers may be installed, or a central set placed in the village square. Not incidentally, these methods also carry exceptional possibilities for control by the government concerned.

Naturally most of these series do not directly measure the number of people exposed to a medium, but only relative ranks. The number of newspaper readers surely exceeds the number of newspapers sold in every country. In some underdeveloped states the number of people seeing each copy may be quite high. Similarly the number of radio listeners is almost always greater than the number of sets. This is especially true where central radios for a whole village are common.

---

2. Cf. Daniel Lerner, *The Passing of Traditional Society* (Glencoe, Ill., 1958), p. 120, who notes that while a cinema ticket costs a Turkish worker more labor than it does an American worker, the differential is much less than for most other consumer goods or means of access to the mass media.

31. DAILY NEWSPAPER CIRCULATION PER 1,000 POPULATION

The following data are for "general interest newspapers," defined as "any periodical publication which serves as an initial source of written news of current events in the fields of public affairs, international affairs, politics, government, etc."[1] To be considered a "daily" newspaper it must be issued four or more days a week. Circulation figures are seldom audited or certified; thus for most countries the figures given are estimates. It is not possible to assess any precise error margin, but the close correlation of the figures in this table with those for radio receivers per 1,000 population to be discussed below suggests that the values given are not seriously distorted reflections of the actual communications situation in most countries. Errors in population estimates of course apply as previously discussed.

---

1. UNESCO, *Basic Facts and Figures*, *1960* (Paris, 1961), p. 106.

TABLE 31

Daily Newspaper Circulation per 1,000 Population

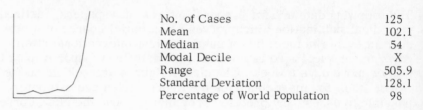

No. of Cases	125
Mean	102.1
Median	54
Modal Decile	X
Range	505.9
Standard Deviation	128.1
Percentage of World Population	98

% of Table Population	Case Deciles	Rank	Country	Circ. per 1,000 Pop.	Range Deciles	Year
	I	1	United Kingdom	506	I	1961
		2	Sweden	477		1961
		3	East Germany	456		1959
		4	Iceland	450	II	1961
		5	Luxembourg	445		1960
		6	Japan	416		1961
		7	Norway	384	III	1961
		8	New Zealand	383		1961
		9	Australia	376		1961
		10	Switzerland	374		1961
		11	Finland	358		1960
		12	Denmark	345	IV	1961
	II	13	United States	326		1960
		14	West Germany	307		1960
		15	Belgium	285	V	1961
		16	Netherlands	278		1961
		17	Czechoslovakia	269		1961
		18	Uruguay[1]	260		1960
		19	France	252	VI	1960
		20	Canada	231		1960
		21	Ireland	225		1961
		22	Hong Kong	223		1961
		23	Israel	210		1957
		24	Austria	208		1960
	III	25	Bulgaria	200	VII	1961
25.6 ------------		26	U.S.S.R.	172		1960
		27	Romania	161		1961
		28	Argentina	155		1959
		29	Hungary	152		1961
		30	Poland	150	VIII	1961
		31	Singapore	140		1961
		32	Chile[2]	134		1961
		33.5	Cuba	129		1956
		33.5	Netherlands Antilles	129		1961
		35	Greece	125		1959
		36	Malta & Gozo	124		1956
		37	Cyprus	123		1960
	IV	38	Panama	104		1959
		39	Mongolian People's Republic	103		1956
		40	Italy	101	IX	1961

TABLE 31 (continued)

% of Table Population	Case Deciles	Rank	Country	Circ. per 1,000 Pop.	Range Deciles	Year
		41	Lebanon	97		1959
		42	Venezuela[3]	96		1960
		43	Costa Rica	94		1961
		44	Mauritius	89		1961
		45	Trinidad & Tobago	86		1960
		46	Barbados	85		1961
		47	Mexico	83		1961
		48	Portugal	81		1961
		49	British Guiana	79		1961
	V	50	Peru[2]	76		1957
		51	Spain	70		1960
		52	South Korea	69		1961
		53.5	Malaya	67		1960
		53.5	Surinam	67		1957
		56	Nicaragua	66		1959
		56	Taiwan	66		1961
		56	Yugoslavia	66		1961
		58	Jamaica	63		1961
		59.5	Puerto Rico	61		1961
		59.5	South Africa	61		1959
		61.5	Colombia	56		1961
		61.5	Ecuador	56		1961
	VI	63	Brazil	54		1960
		64	Albania	47	X	1961
		65.5	El Salvador	45		1960
		65.5	Turkey	45		1961
		67.5	Ceylon	37		1960
		67.5	Paraguay	37		1959
		69	Bolivia	34		1959
		70.5	Ghana	32		1961
		70.5	Southern Rhodesia	32		1959
		72	South Vietnam	28		1958
		73	Dominican Republic	27		1960
		74.5	Honduras	25		1959
	VII	74.5	Sarawak	25		1961
		76	Guatemala	23		1961
		77.5	Algeria	22		1961
43.9		77.5	Morocco[3]	22		1960
		79.5	China (Mainland)	20		1955
		79.5	Egypt	20		1958
		81	Syria	19		1958
		82.5	Jordan[3]	18		1960
		82.5	Philippines	18		1960
		84	Iran	15		1961
		86.5	Kenya	14		1961
		86.5	South West Africa	14		1960
		86.5	Thailand	14		1960
	VIII	86.5	Tunisia	14		1960
		89	Burma	12		1960
72.0		91	Haiti	11		1960
		91	India[1]	11		1960

TABLE 31 (continued)

% of Table Population	Case Deciles	Rank	Country	Circ. per 1,000 Pop.	Range Deciles	Year
		91	Indonesia	11		1959
		93	Iraq	10		1957
		94.5	Angola[1]	9		1961
		94.5	Madagascar	9		1961
		97	Nigeria[3]	8		1961
		97	Sierra Leone	8		1961
		97	Uganda	8		1960
		100	Libya[1]	7		1960
	IX	100	Northern Rhodesia	7		1959
		100	Pakistan	7		1960
		102.5	Cambodia	6		1960
		102.5	Senegal	6		1960
		104	Afghanistan	5		1960
		107	Kuwait	4		1960
		107	Saudi Arabia	4		1960
		107	Sudan	4		1961
		107	Tanganyika	4		1961
		107	Togo	4		1961
		110.5	Ivory Coast	3		1961
		110.5	Mozambique	3		1960
		113.5	Cameroun	2		1961
	X	113.5	Congo (Leopoldville)	2		1959
		113.5	Dahomey	2		1961
		113.5	Ethiopia[1]	2		1960
		116.5	Congo (Brazzaville)	1		1960
		116.5	Mali	1		1959
		118.5	Liberia	.8		1961
		118.5	Nepal	.8		1960
		120	Laos	.6		1957
		121.5	Central African Republic	.4		1960
		121.5	Niger	.4		1960
		123	Chad	.3		1961
		124	Guinea	.2		1959
		125	Upper Volta	.1		1957

[1] Circulation figures for some newspapers (one-third or less of all papers, certainly much less than one-third of total circulation) not available.

[2] Circulation figures for some newspapers (less than 10% of all papers, certainly much less than 10% of total circulation) not available.

[3] Circulation figures for some newspapers (less than 20% of all papers, certainly much less than 20% of total circulation) not available.

Source: U. N., *Statistical Yearbook, 1962* (New York, 1963).

32–34. ITEMS OF DOMESTIC MAIL PER CAPITA; ITEMS OF FOREIGN MAIL SENT PER CAPITA; FOREIGN ITEMS SENT AS A PROPORTION OF FOREIGN ITEMS RECEIVED

The data in Tables 32–34, based as they are on government statistics of postage handled, are likely to be of a high level of reliability and comparability. They cover "letters (airmail, ordinary mail, and registered), postcards, printed matter, business papers, small merchandise samples, small packets, and phonopost packets. They include mail carried without charge, but exclude ordinary packages, and letters and packages with a declared value."[1] While different national definitions and regulations undoubtedly decrease comparability to some extent, it is probable that their effect is less than that of errors in the estimation of total population.

These figures are useful for the examination of a number of problems. Obviously the domestic mail per capita data form another measure of complex internal communication and interaction; they also provide an excellent check on official statistics of literacy. The foreign mail per capita series can test a number of hypotheses about the involvement of a state in international affairs. It would seem plausible that foreign mail should be greater the smaller the geographic area of a country, the smaller its population, and the higher its level of economic, social, and cultural activity. All these hypotheses are supported by examination of the appropriate tables; a careful analysis of the degree and nature of the relationship, perhaps by the technique of multiple regression, would bring out more information.[2] Colonies tend to rank somewhat higher than one would expect from their area, population, and development. Inferences about this series can profitably be checked against another series on international transactions, such as that of the ratio of foreign trade to G. N. P.

It is clear from Table 34, for the ratio of foreign mail sent to foreign mail received, that there is much variation. Former colonial powers are almost without exception near the top; also, a high ratio of mail sent to mail received is associated with economic development. A number of advanced states with few or no colonies, however, are near the middle of the list. Six of the nine Latin American states for which we have data are in the last case decile; this may suggest something about the balance of their economies. Whatever the causes of an imbalance between foreign mail sent and received, it may have important consequences for decision making, indicating as it does one measure of the relative importance of incoming and outgoing information.

---

1. U. N., *Statistical Yearbook, 1962* (New York, 1963), p. 405.
2. Cf. Karl W. Deutsch, "International Communication: The Media and Flows," *Public Opinion Quarterly, 20* (Spring 1956), 143–60, and the discussion in Part B of this book.

TABLE 32

Items of Domestic Mail per Capita

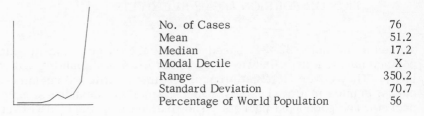

No. of Cases	76
Mean	51.2
Median	17.2
Modal Decile	X
Range	350.2
Standard Deviation	70.7
Percentage of World Population	56

% of Table Population	Case Deciles	Rank	Country	Items per Capita	Range Deciles	Year
	I	1	United States	350.3	I, II	1961
		2	Switzerland	261.4	III	1961
		3	Belgium	228.5	IV	1960
		4	New Zealand	206.3	V	1961
		5	United Kingdom	190.6		1961
		6	Australia	170.3	VI	1961
		7	France	166.7		1961
	II	8	Netherlands	162.4		1961
		9	Sweden	154.3		1961
		10	West Germany	152.5		1961
		11	Luxembourg	131.5	VII	1960
		12	Norway	109.0		1961
		13	Denmark	106.7		1960
		14	Austria	104.6	VIII	1961
26.0		15	Italy	97.6		1961
	III	16	Ireland	94.1		1961
		17	British Guiana	84.2		1960
		18	East Germany	83.3		1960
		19	Iceland	69.1	IX	1960
		20	Finland	68.1		1961
		21	Argentina	65.2		1960
		22	Spain	62.6		1961
	IV	23	Brazil	62.0		1960
		24	Israel	56.8		1961
		25	South Africa	56.7		1961
		26	Hungary	55.7		1961
		27	Yugoslavia	47.4		1961
		28	Portugal	38.8		1960
		29	Taiwan	33.4		1960
		30	Ceylon	30.0	X	1961
	V	31	Poland	29.8		1960
		32	Malta & Gozo	29.5		1960
		33	Cyprus	24.3		1960
		34	Greece	23.0		1961
		35.5	Mexico	18.8		1961
		35.5	Uruguay	18.8		1959
		37	Singapore	18.6		1961
	VI	38	Jamaica	18.2		1960
		39	Netherlands Antilles	16.2		1960
		40	Trinidad & Tobago	15.9		1957

TABLE 32 (continued)

% of Table Population	Case Deciles	Rank	Country	Items per Capita	Range Deciles	Year
		41	Hong Kong	14.1		1961
		42	Chile	13.1		1961
		43	Rhodesia & Nyasaland	12.7		1960
		44	Ghana	11.8		1960
		45	Malaya	11.4		1960
47.5	VII	46	Egypt	8.5		1960
		47	India	8.3		1960
		48	Lebanon	7.3		1960
		49	Sarawak	6.8		1960
		50	Iran	6.7		1956
75.0		51	Mauritius	6.5		1960
		52	Turkey	6.2		1960
		53	South Korea	5.9		1961
	VIII	54	Pakistan	5.8		1960
		55	Madagascar	5.1		1960
		56	Morocco	4.3		1956
		57	Colombia	4.1		1960
		58	Aden	3.2		1961
		59	Libya	3.0		1960
		61	Jordan	2.6		1958
	IX	61	Sierra Leone	2.6		1960
		61	Nigeria	2.6		1961
		63.5	El Salvador	2.5		1961
		63.5	South Vietnam	2.5		1960
		65	Angola	2.4		1960
		66	Congo (Leopoldville)	2.2		1961
		67	Indonesia	2.1		1961
		68	Mozambique	1.9		1960
	X	69.5	Paraguay	1.4		1961
		69.5	Thailand	1.4		1961
		71	French Equatorial Africa	1.3		1960
		72	Togo	1.2		1961
		73	French Cameroons	1.1		1957
		74	French West Africa	1.0		1957
		75	Burma	.6		1961
		76	Laos	.1		1959

Sources: U.N., *Statistical Yearbook, 1962* (New York, 1963); U.S. Department of Commerce, *Statistical Abstract of the United States, 1962* (Washington, D.C., 1962), p. 513.

TABLE 33

Items of Foreign Mail Sent per Capita

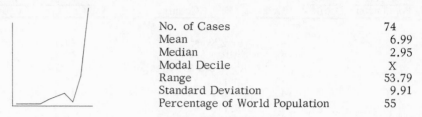

No. of Cases	74
Mean	6.99
Median	2.95
Modal Decile	X
Range	53.79
Standard Deviation	9.91
Percentage of World Population	55

% of Table Population	Case Deciles	Rank	Country	Foreign Mail Sent per Cap.	Range Deciles	Year
	I	1	British Guiana	53.80	I–III	1960
		2	Malta & Gozo	37.01	IV	1960
		3	Switzerland	31.81	V,VI	1961
		4	Luxembourg	31.53		1961
		5	Ireland	31.35		1960
		6	Hong Kong	21.49	VII	1961
		7	Singapore	18.45		1961
	II	8	Netherlands Antilles	17.98		1960
		9	Austria	17.17		1961
		10	Cyprus	17.06		1960
		11	New Zealand	16.96		1961
		12	Belgium	15.95	VIII	1960
		13	Netherlands	14.78		1961
		14	Israel	10.36	IX	1961
	III	15	United Kingdom	9.73		1961
		16	Jamaica	9.25		1960
		17	Lebanon	8.78		1960
		18	France	8.36		1961
		19	Portugal	8.32		1960
		20	Sweden	8.31		1961
		21	West Germany	8.10		1961
		22	Denmark	7.60		1960
	IV	23	Norway	7.55		1961
		24	Trinidad & Tobago	7.47		1957
		25	Australia	7.04		1961
		26	Iceland	6.35		1960
		27	Italy	6.32		1961
		28	Libya	5.08	X	1960
		29	Spain	4.58		1961
	V	30	Aden	4.38		1961
		31	Finland	4.25		1961
		32	Mexico	3.85		1961
		33	South Africa	3.62		1961
		34	East Germany	3.50		1961
		35	Greece	3.37		1961
		36	Malaya	3.26		1960
24.3	VI	37	Rhodesia & Nyasaland	2.96		1960
		38	United States	2.94		1960
		39	Mauritius	2.88		1960
		40	Jordan	2.47		1958

TABLE 33 (continued)

% of Table Population	Case Deciles	Rank	Country	Foreign Mail Sent per Cap.	Range Deciles	Year
		41	Argentina	2.45		1960
		42	Madagascar	2.03		1961
		43	Sarawak	1.89		1960
	VII	44.5	Morocco	1.63		1961
		44.5	Mozambique	1.63		1960
		46	Sierra Leone	1.61		1960
		47	Egypt	1.48		1960
		48	Yugoslavia	1.46		1961
		49	Ghana	1.45		1960
		50	Chile	1.33		1961
		51	Togo	1.32		1961
	VIII	52	Brazil	1.29		1957
		53	Poland	1.27		1960
		54	French Equatorial Africa	1.18		1960
		55	El Salvador	.92		1961
		56	Paraguay	.87		1961
		57	South Vietnam	.78		1960
49.7		58	Ceylon	.77		1959
		59	Taiwan	.75		1960
	IX	60	Iran	.74		1956
		61	Pakistan	.72		1960
		62.5	Congo (Leopoldville)	.59		1958
		62.5	French West Africa	.59		1957
		64.5	Nigeria	.50		1961
		64.5	Turkey	.50		1960
		66	Colombia	.39		1960
64.6	X	67	South Korea	.20		1961
		68	India	.17		1960
		69	Angola	.15		1960
		70	Thailand	.13		1961
		71	Burma	.10		1961
		72	Indonesia	.06		1961
		73	Laos	.03		1959
		74	Uruguay	.01		1959

Sources: U. N., *Demographic Yearbook, 1961* (New York, 1962); U. N., *Statistical Yearbook, 1962* (New York, 1963).

TABLE 34

Foreign Items Sent/Foreign Items Received

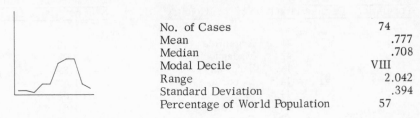

No. of Cases	74
Mean	.777
Median	.708
Modal Decile	VIII
Range	2.042
Standard Deviation	.394
Percentage of World Population	57

% of Table Population	Case Deciles	Rank	Country	For. Items Sent/Rec.	Range Deciles	Year
	I	1	East Germany	2.050	I	1961
		2	Mauritius	2.024		1961
		3	Jordan	1.751	II	1958
		4	Netherlands	1.703		1961
		5	Singapore	1.441	III	1961
		6	West Germany	1.325	IV	1961
		7	United Kingdom	1.321		1961
	II	8	Belgium	1.270		1961
		9	Poland	1.261		1960
		10	Malta & Gozo	1.242		1960
		11	Switzerland	1.169	V	1958
		12	Chile	1.148		1959
		13	Portugal	1.143		1961
		14	Italy	1.102		1961
		15	Nigeria	1.060		1961
	III	16	Hong Kong	1.028	VI	1961
		17	Austria	.973		1961
		18	Turkey	.895		1961
		19.5	Aden	.882		1961
		19.5	Japan	.882		1961
25.5		21	Spain	.870		1961
		22	Malaya	.869		1961
	IV	23.5	Israel	.857		1961
		23.5	Mexico	.857		1961
		25	Brazil	.849		1957
		26	Denmark	.847		1961
		27.5	Cyprus	.841		1960
		27.5	Morocco	.841		1961
60.5		29	India	.831		1960
	V	30	South Korea	.830		1961
		31	Sweden	.816	VII	1961
		32	Yugoslavia	.800		1961
		33	Ireland	.770		1961
		34	Norway	.756		1961
		35	Rhodesia & Nyasaland	.742		1960
		36	South Vietnam	.721		1961
	VI	37	Egypt	.711		1961
		38	Libya	.704		1960
		39	South Africa	.702		1961
		40	French Cameroons	.681		1961
		41	Taiwan	.667		1960

TABLE 34 (continued)

% of Table Population	Case Deciles	Rank	Country	For. Items Sent/Rec.	Range Deciles	Year
		42.5	Ceylon	.639		1961
		42.5	Pakistan	.639		1960
		44	Algeria	.636		1957
75.6	VII	45	Netherlands Antilles	.630		1960
		46	French Equatorial Africa	.627		1960
		47	Laos	.622		1959
		48	Sierra Leone	.620	VIII	1961
		49	Sarawak	.613		1961
		50	Lebanon	.607		1961
		51	Jamaica	.588		1961
	VIII	52	Finland	.570		1961
		53	Togo	.564		1961
		54	Indonesia	.534		1961
		55	United States	.531		1960
		56	Madagascar	.519		1961
		57	Congo (Leopoldville)	.502		1961
		58	Luxembourg	.499		1961
		59.5	French West Africa	.493		1957
	IX	59.5	Mozambique	.493		1961
		61	Australia	.474		1961
		62	Angola	.473		1961
		63	Iceland	.467		1961
		64	Greece	.439		1956
		65	Ghana	.438		1960
		66	Trinidad & Tobago	.423		1957
	X	67	El Salvador	.372	IX	1961
		68	Paraguay	.359		1961
		69	Iran	.339		1956
		70	Thailand	.318		1961
		71	Colombia	.212		1960
		72	Argentina	.167	X	1961
		73	Burma	.133		1961
		74	Uruguay	.008		1959

Source: U. N., *Statistical Yearbook, 1962* (New York, 1963), pp. 405–10.

35-37. RADIOS PER 1,000 POPULATION; RADIOS PER 1,000 POPULA-
TION—AVERAGE ANNUAL INCREASE; TELEVISION SETS PER
1,000 POPULATION

The data in Tables 35-37 are based either on national estimates of receivers in use (R) or on the number of licenses granted (L). The estimates
are usually more reliable than the license figures, which understate the
total to varying degrees. In some cases a single license may suffice for
more than one radio in a household; in all countries a certain amount of
evasion of license fees exists. Data on average annual change are not
likely to be affected by the estimation method as long as it is constant.

It is impossible to devise any adequate measure for the degree of understatement in these cases; to provide a general estimate we repeated the
procedure attempted for military personnel and expenditure ratios. The
logarithms of radios per 1,000 and newspapers per 1,000 were plotted on
Figure A.2 and the regression line was drawn. The correlation around

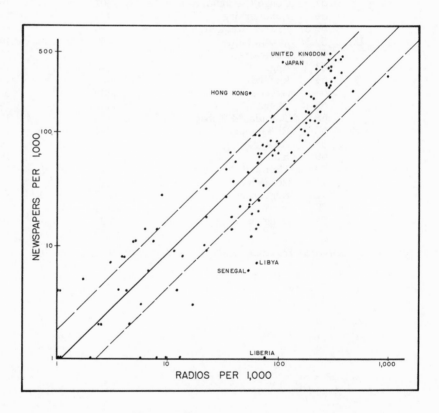

Figure A.2   Reliability Check for Newspapers per 1,000 Population and Radios per 1,000 Population

118

the regression line is quite high (r = .87), again suggesting that with these data measurement error is not as great as one might expect. Virtually all the important deviations from the "predicted" position (the regression line) are for countries whose radio data are based on licenses and which are above the line (e.g., Hong Kong, Japan, and the United Kingdom). There are also a few African countries where radios are more common than newspapers. As in Figure A.1, the dashed lines indicate values that differ by a factor of two from the "predicted" level.

TABLE 35

Radios per 1,000 Population

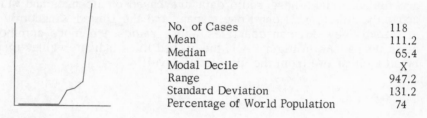

No. of Cases	118
Mean	111.2
Median	65.4
Modal Decile	X
Range	947.2
Standard Deviation	131.2
Percentage of World Population	74

% of Table Population	Case Deciles	Rank	Country	Radios per 1,000 Pop.	Range Deciles	Year
	I	1	United States (R)	948.0	I–V	1959
		2	Canada (R)	451.0	VI	1960
		3	Sweden (L)	378.0	VII	1961
		4	Denmark (L)	365.0		1961
		5	East Germany (R)	348.0		1961
		6.5	Luxembourg (L)	319.0		1961
		6.5	West Germany (L)	319.0		1961
		8	Belgium (L)	298.0		1961
		9.5	Finland (L)	289.0		1961
		9.5	United Kingdom (L)	289.0		1961
		11	Austria (L)	288.0		1961
	II	12.5	Norway (L)	286.0		1961
		12.5	Uruguay (R)	286.0		1959
		14	France (L)	282.0	VIII	1961
		15	Iceland (L)	279.0		1961
		16	Switzerland (L)	272.0		1961
		17.5	Czechoslovakia (L)	263.0		1961
		17.5	Netherlands (L)	263.0		1961
		19	New Zealand (L)	242.0		1961
		20	Hungary (L)	231.0		1961
		21	Malta & Gozo (L)	222.0		1961
		22	Australia (L)	215.0		1961
20.3		23	Netherlands Antilles (R)	207.5		1959
	III	24	U.S.S.R. (R)	205.0		1960
		25	Bulgaria (R)	202.0		1961
		26	Israel (L)	194.0		1959
		27	Cuba (R)	187.0	IX	1961
		28	Venezuela (R)	186.0		1960
		29	Poland (L)	183.0		1961
		30	Cyprus (L)	178.0		1960
		31	Ireland (L)	176.0		1961
		32	Argentina (R)	175.0		1960
		33	Italy (L)	170.0		1961
		34	Barbados (L)	161.0		1961
		35	Panama (R)	159.0		1959
	IV	36	Colombia (R)	139.5		1960
		37	Chile (R)	130.2		1961
		38	Surinam (R)	129.9		1960
		39	Romania (L)	117.0		1961
		40	Japan (L)	106.7		1961

TABLE 35 (continued)

% of Table Population	Case Deciles	Rank	Country	Radios per 1,000 Pop.	Range Deciles	Year
		41	Yugoslavia (L)	98.6		1961
		42	Portugal (L)	98.1		1961
		43	Mexico (R)	96.9		1961
		44	El Salvador (R)	92.0	X	1961
		45	Spain (L)	90.0		1960
		46	Greece (L)	89.9		1959
		47	Singapore (L)	88.3		1961
	V	48	Jamaica (R)	87.9		1959
		49	Trinidad & Tobago (L)	84.1		1960
		50	Peru (R)	77.9		1959
		51	Liberia (R)	77.5		1960
		52	Bolivia (R)	72.7		1961
		53	British Guiana (L)	72.2		1961
		54	Taiwan (L)	69.5		1961
		55	South Africa (L)	66.2		1961
		56.5	Costa Rica (R)	66.1		1961
		56.5	Honduras (L)	66.1		1961
		58	Egypt (L)	65.8		1961
		59	Nicaragua (R)	65.5		1961
49.9	VI	60	Iran (R)	65.3		1961
		61	Brazil (R)	64.3		1961
		62	Tunisia (L)	63.5		1961
		63	Libya (L)	63.1		1959
		64.5	Lebanon (L)	60.8		1960
		64.5	Paraguay (R)	60.8		1959
		66	Syria (L)	57.3		1959
		67.5	Hong Kong (L)	55.3		1961
		67.5	Sarawak (R)	55.3		1961
		69.5	Guatemala (L)	54.3		1961
		69.5	Senegal (R)	54.3		1959
	VII	71	Algeria (L)	54.1		1960
		72	Turkey (L)	52.5		1961
		73	Aden (L)	49.6		1961
		74	Gabon (L)	48.0		1959
		75	Morocco (L)	45.5		1961
		76	Ecuador (R)	40.6		1959
		77	Ceylon (L)	38.4		1961
		78	Jordan (L)	37.7		1960
		79	South West Africa (L)	37.2		1959
		80	Malaya (L)	36.5		1960
		81	Dominican Republic (R)	33.8		1960
		82	Albania (L)	33.6		1960
	VIII	83	Madagascar (R)	22.4		1961
		84	Philippines (L)	22.3		1959
		85	Ghana (L)	22.2		1959
		86	Iraq (L)	21.2		1960
		87	Rhodesia & Nyasaland (L)	17.6		1961
		88	Ivory Coast (L)	16.0		1960
		89	Uganda (R)	13.8		1959
		90	Congo (Brazzaville) (L)	13.0		1950
		91	Saudi Arabia (R)	12.1		1959

TABLE 35 (continued)

% of Table Population	Case Deciles	Rank	Country	Radios per 1,000 Pop.	Range Deciles	Year
		92	Angola (L)	11.4		1960
		93	Central African Republic (L)	9.8		1960
		94	South Vietnam (L)	8.9		1960
	IX	95.5	Kenya (L)	8.0		1960
		95.5	Laos (L)	8.0		1961
		97	Indonesia (L)	7.4		1959
		98	Cambodia (R)	6.5		1960
		99	Thailand (L)	6.2		1960
		100	Mozambique (L)	5.7		1960
		101.5	Burma (L)	5.6		1960
70.6 -----------		101.5	Chad (L)	5.6		1961
		103	India (L)	5.0		1960
		104	Haiti (L)	4.9		1961
		105	Ethiopia (R)	4.5		1961
		106	Togo (R)	4.3		1961
	X	107	Nigeria (R)	4.0		1960
		108	Sierra Leone (L)	3.9		1961
		109	Tanganyika (R)	3.6		1961
		110	Pakistan (L)	3.0		1960
		111.5	Cameroun (R)	2.5		1959
		111.5	Congo (Leopoldville) (L)	2.5		1959
		113	Dahomey (L)	2.4		1961
		114	Mali (L)	2.0		1960
		115	Afghanistan (R)	1.7		1960
		116.5	Niger (L)	.9		1959
		116.5	Sudan (L)	.9		1960
		118	Upper Volta (R)	.8		1959

Source: U. N., *Statistical Yearbook, 1962* (New York, 1963).

TABLE 36

Radios per 1,000 Population—Average Annual Increase

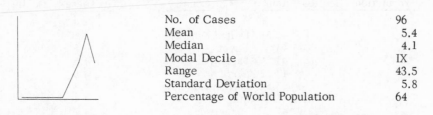

No. of Cases	96
Mean	5.4
Median	4.1
Modal Decile	IX
Range	43.5
Standard Deviation	5.8
Percentage of World Population	64

% of Table Population	Case Deciles	Rank	Country	Avg. Ann. Increase	Range Deciles	Years
	I	1	United States	40.5	I–III	1948–59
		2	Canada	25.3	IV,V	1948–60
		3	East Germany	14.6	VI	1948–61
		4	Uruguay	14.3	VII	1948–60
		5	Hungary	13.8		1948–61
		6.5	Belgium	13.4		1948–61
		6.5	Cyprus	13.4		1948–60
		8	Bulgaria	13.3		1948–61
		9	Venezuela	12.8		1948–60
	II	10	West Germany	12.4		1948–61
		11	Luxembourg	11.6		1948–61
		12	Poland	11.2		1948–61
		13	Barbados	10.8		1948–61
		14	France	10.2		1948–61
		15.5	Austria	9.9	VIII	1948–61
		15.5	Finland	9.9		1948–61
		17	Surinam	9.6		1949–60
		18	Colombia	9.5		1950–60
		19	Italy	9.4		1948–61
	III	20	Malta & Gozo	9.3		1948–61
		21.5	Denmark	8.7		1948–61
		21.5	Israel	8.7		1950–59
24.7		23	Romania	7.8		1948–61
		24.5	Cuba	7.5		1950–61
		24.5	Netherlands	7.5		1948–61
		26	Ireland	7.4		1949–61
		27	Greece	7.3		1949–59
		28	Czechoslovakia	7.1		1948–61
	IV	30	Spain	6.5		1948–60
		30	Sweden	6.5		1948–61
		30	Switzerland	6.5		1948–61
		32.5	Jamaica	6.4		1948–59
		32.5	Yugoslavia	6.4		1948–61
		34	Norway	6.3		1948–61
		35	Taiwan	6.2		1950–61
		36	Portugal	5.9		1948–61
		37	Panama	5.5	IX	1949–59
		38	Mexico	5.3		1948–61
	V	39	Argentina	4.7		1950–60
		40.5	Iran	4.6		1948–61

TABLE 36 (continued)

% of Table Population	Case Deciles	Rank	Country	Avg. Ann. Increase	Range Deciles	Years
		40.5	United Kingdom	4.6		1948–61
		43	Egypt	4.5		1949–61
		43	Sarawak	4.5		1949–61
		43	Syria	4.5		1949–59
		45.5	British Guiana	4.4		1948–61
		45.5	Singapore	4.4		1950–61
		47.5	Nicaragua	4.2		1950–61
		47.5	Trinidad & Tobago	4.2		1948–60
	VI	49	Aden	4.0		1949–61
		50.5	Honduras	3.9		1948–61
		50.5	Tunisia	3.9		1948–61
		52	Guatemala	3.7		1949–61
		53.5	Costa Rica	3.4		1950–61
		53.5	Jordan	3.4		1950–60
		55	Chile	3.2		1949–61
		56.5	Algeria	3.1		1950–60
		56.5	Turkey	3.1		1948–61
	VII	58	Hong Kong	3.0		1948–61
		59.5	Lebanon	2.9		1948–60
		59.5	Morocco	2.9		1948–61
		61	Ecuador	2.8		1948–59
		62.5	Ceylon	2.7		1948–61
		62.5	Malaya	2.7		1948–60
		64	Albania	2.6		1950–60
		65	Iceland	2.4		1949–61
		66.5	Bolivia	2.1		1950–61
		66.5	Peru	2.1		1950–59
	VIII	68	South West Africa	2.0		1950–59
		69	South Africa	1.9		1948–61
		70.5	Ghana	1.8		1948–59
		70.5	Philippines	1.8		1949–59
		72.5	Dominican Republic	1.6		1948–60
		72.5	Iraq	1.6		1950–60
49.6		74	Uganda	1.5		1950–59
		75	Brazil	1.4		1950–61
		76	Rhodesia & Nyasaland	1.2	X	1950–61
	IX	77	Paraguay	1.0		1949–59
		78.5	Angola	.9		1949–60
		78.5	Japan	.9		1948–61
		80	New Zealand	.8		1948–61
		81	Indonesia	.6		1949–59
64.6		82	Kenya	.5		1948–60
		84	Burma	.4		1948–60
		84	India	.4		1948–60
		84	Mozambique	.4		1948–60
		87.5	Haiti	.3		1950–61
	X	87.5	Nigeria	.3		1950–60
		87.5	Sierra Leone	.3		1948–61
		87.5	Tanganyika	.3		1948–61
		90.5	Congo (Leopoldville)	.2		1948–59
		90.5	Pakistan	.2		1950–60

TABLE 36 (continued)

% of Table Population	Case Deciles	Rank	Country	Avg. Ann. Increase	Range Deciles	Years
		92.5	Afghanistan	.1		1950–60
		92.5	Thailand	.1		1950–60
		94.5	Laos	– .3		1957–61
		94.5	Netherlands Antilles	– .3		1950–59
		96	Australia	– 3.0		1949–61

Sources: U. N., *Demographic Yearbook, 1961* (New York, 1962); U. N., *Statistical Yearbook, 1962* (New York, 1963).

TABLE 37

Television Sets per 1,000 Population
(1961)

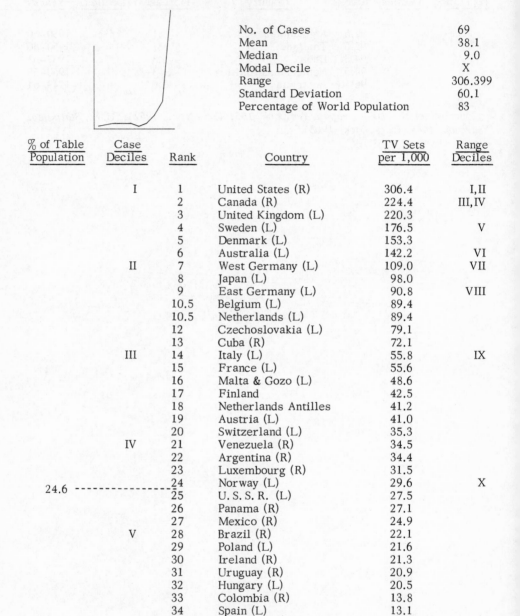

No. of Cases	69
Mean	38.1
Median	9.0
Modal Decile	X
Range	306.399
Standard Deviation	60.1
Percentage of World Population	83

% of Table Population	Case Deciles	Rank	Country	TV Sets per 1,000	Range Deciles
	I	1	United States (R)	306.4	I,II
		2	Canada (R)	224.4	III,IV
		3	United Kingdom (L)	220.3	
		4	Sweden (L)	176.5	V
		5	Denmark (L)	153.3	
		6	Australia (L)	142.2	VI
	II	7	West Germany (L)	109.0	VII
		8	Japan (L)	98.0	
		9	East Germany (L)	90.8	VIII
		10.5	Belgium (L)	89.4	
		10.5	Netherlands (L)	89.4	
		12	Czechoslovakia (L)	79.1	
		13	Cuba (R)	72.1	
	III	14	Italy (L)	55.8	IX
		15	France (L)	55.6	
		16	Malta & Gozo (L)	48.6	
		17	Finland	42.5	
		18	Netherlands Antilles	41.2	
		19	Austria (L)	41.0	
		20	Switzerland (L)	35.3	
	IV	21	Venezuela (R)	34.5	
		22	Argentina (R)	34.4	
		23	Luxembourg (R)	31.5	
24.6 -----------------		24	Norway (L)	29.6	X
		25	U.S.S.R. (L)	27.5	
		26	Panama (R)	27.1	
		27	Mexico (R)	24.9	
	V	28	Brazil (R)	22.1	
		29	Poland (L)	21.6	
		30	Ireland (R)	21.3	
		31	Uruguay (R)	20.9	
		32	Hungary (L)	20.5	
		33	Colombia (R)	13.8	
		34	Spain (L)	13.1	
	VI	35	Guatemala (R)	9.0	
		36	El Salvador (R)	8.0	
		37	New Zealand (L)	7.9	
		38.5	Peru (R)	7.6	
		38.5	Portugal (L)	7.6	

TABLE 37 (continued)

% of Table Population	Case Deciles	Rank	Country	TV Sets per 1,000	Range Deciles
		40	Kuwait (R)	6.2	
		41	Algeria (L)	6.1	
	VII	42	Dominican Republic (R)[1]	6.0	
		43	Costa Rica (R)	5.9	
		44	Cyprus (L)	5.5	
		45	Lebanon (R)[1]	4.9	
		46	Iraq (R)[1]	4.8	
		47	Romania (L)	4.7	
		48	Egypt (L)	3.4	
	VIII	49.5	Nicaragua (R)	3.3	
		49.5	Yugoslavia (L)	3.3	
		51	Hong Kong (L)	3.0	
		52	Thailand (R)	2.9	
		53	Honduras (R)	2.1	
		54	Iran (R)	1.9	
		55.5	Philippines (R)	1.6	
	IX	55.5	Rhodesia & Nyasaland (R)	1.6	
		57.5	Bulgaria (R)	1.4	
50.1		57.5	Saudi Arabia (R)	1.4	
		59	Ecuador (R)	1.1	
		60	South Korea (R)	.8	
		61.5	Haiti (R)	.5	
		61.5	Tunisia	.5	
	X	63	Chile (R)	.4	
		64.5	Nigeria (R)	.2	
		64.5	Syria (R)	.2	
		66	Cambodia	.1	
		67.5	China (Mainland) (R)	.03	
82.4		67.5	Turkey (R)	.03	
		69	India (L)	.001	

[1] Year is 1960.

Source: U. N., *Statistical Yearbook, 1962* (New York, 1963).

38. CINEMA ATTENDANCE PER CAPITA

Of the data available on cinema seats and cinema attendance, the following seem the most accurate and comparable. They are for the number of paid admissions to film performances, whether of 35 mm. or 16 mm. films, and for permanent establishments, mobile units, and drive-ins. As cinema admissions are subject to tax in most countries the data are likely to be quite accurate, probably as good as the population estimates used for the denominator.

TABLE 38

Cinema Attendance per Capita

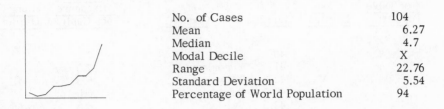

No. of Cases	104
Mean	6.27
Median	4.7
Modal Decile	X
Range	22.76
Standard Deviation	5.54
Percentage of World Population	94

% of Table Population	Case Deciles	Rank	Country	Cinema Attendance per Capita	Range Deciles	Year
	I	1	Hong Kong	22.8	I	1959
		2	Lebanon	22.5		1960
		3	Australia	21.3		1958
		4	Israel	18.5	II	1959
		5	U.S.S.R.	17.7	III	1960
		6	New Zealand	16.6		1961
		7	Sarawak	15.7	IV	1960
		8	Italy	15.1		1959
		9	Bulgaria	14.8		1961
		10	Luxembourg	14.3		1960
	II	11	Austria	14.2		1961
		12.5	East Germany	13.8		1960
		12.5	Singapore	13.8		1960
		14.5	Hungary	13.5	V	1961
		14.5	Ireland	13.5		1961
		16	Malta & Gozo	13.1		1961
		17	Czechoslovakia	12.9		1960
		18	Spain	12.2		1959
		19	United States	11.8		1961
		20	Mauritius	11.4		1961
	III	21	Mexico	10.4	VI	1961
		22.5	Denmark	9.6		1960
		22.5	United Kingdom	9.6		1960
22.9		24	Norway	9.4		1961
		26	Japan	9.2		1961
		26	Venezuela	9.2		1959
		26	West Germany	9.2		1961
		28	Uruguay	9.1		1958
		29	Trinidad & Tobago	9.0	VII	1958
		30	Malaya	8.9		1960
		32	Belgium	8.8		1960
	IV	32	Netherlands Antilles	8.8		1955
		32	Romania	8.8		1961
		34	Cyprus	8.5		1960
		35	Argentina	7.9		1959
		36	Barbados	7.8		1961
		37	British Guiana	7.7		1960
		38	Switzerland	7.3		1961
		39	Cuba	7.2		1961

TABLE 38 (continued)

% of Table Population	Case Deciles	Rank	Country	Cinema Attendance per Capita	Range Deciles	Year
		40	France	7.1		1961
		41	Yugoslavia	7.0		1960
	V	42	Taiwan	6.8	VIII	1958
		43.5	Peru	6.6		1958
		43.5	Sweden	6.6		1961
		45	Canada	6.5		1960
		46.5	Finland	6.3		1960
		46.5	Greece	6.3		1958
		48	Poland	6.2		1961
		49	Burma	5.5		1960
		50	Surinam	5.4		1960
		51.5	Colombia	4.8		1960
	VI	51.5	Jamaica	4.8		1957
		53.5	Albania	4.6		1961
		53.5	Nicaragua	4.6		1952
		55.5	Brazil	4.5	IX	1960
		55.5	El Salvador	4.5		1958
		57.5	Netherlands	4.4		1961
		57.5	South Africa	4.4		1950
		59	South Korea	4.3		1959
		60	Chile	3.8		1958
57.4		61	India	3.6		1960
		62	Puerto Rico	3.4		1959
	VII	63	Jordan	3.2		1961
		64.5	Indonesia	3.0		1957
		64.5	Libya	3.0		1955
		66.5	Ceylon	2.9		1958
		66.5	Portugal	2.9		1961
		69	Algeria	2.6		1960
		69	Egypt	2.6		1961
		69	Guatemala	2.6		1961
		71	Iran	2.5		1961
63.8		72	Ecuador	2.4		1952
	VIII	73	China (Mainland)	2.2	X	1956
		74.5	Dominican Republic	2.1		1955
		74.5	Syria	2.1		1959
		76	Mali	1.9		1960
		77	Ghana	1.6		1961
		78.5	Morocco	1.5		1961
		78.5	Tunisia	1.5		1960
		80.5	South Vietnam	1.4		1958
		80.5	Sudan	1.4		1957
		82.5	Aden	1.1		1960
	IX	82.5	Turkey	1.1		1959
		84	Pakistan	1.0		1959
		85	Kuwait	.9		1959
		87	Cambodia[1]	.6		1960
		87	Liberia	.6		1960
		87	Philippines	.6		1958

TABLE 38 (continued)

% of Table Population	Case Deciles	Rank	Country	Cinema Attendance per Capita	Range Deciles	Year
		90	Kenya	.5		1961
		90	Madagascar	.5		1960
		90	Tanganyika	.5		1960
		92.5	Angola	.4		1960
		92.5	Somalia[2]	.4		1958
	X	95.5	Haiti	.3		1958
		95.5	Mozambique	.3		1960
		95.5	Ruanda-Urundi	.3		1959
		95.5	Uganda	.3		1959
		99	Dahomey	.2		1961
		99	Sierra Leone	.2		1961
		99	Togo	.2		1957
		102	Chad	.1		1959
		102	Congo (Leopoldville)	.1		1955
		102	Nigeria	.1		1955
		104	Laos	.04		1959

[1] For only 15 of 33 cinemas.
[2] For only 20 of 24 cinemas.

Source: U. N., *Statistical Yearbook, 1962* (New York, 1963).

39. SPEAKERS OF DOMINANT LANGUAGE AS A PERCENTAGE OF POPULATION

These data are presented as a preliminary attempt to compare the size of a certain kind of group that may be actually or potentially relevant politically. Obviously the mere existence of a minority language group will have varying effects in different countries.

Three definitions have been used:

A. "Mother tongue" (the language spoken by the individual, or in his home, in early childhood).

B. "Language currently or usually spoken in the home."

C. "Ability to speak a language."[1]

Clearly these definitions affect comparability, particularly as each reflects to a different degree the process of assimilation (or lack of it) to the dominant language. The first, "mother tongue," gives no information about the degree of assimilation that has occurred since childhood. The second indicates, in addition to native speakers of the language, those who have become assimilated to the extent that the dominant language is their principal tongue even in private life. The third of course identifies all those who have learned the dominant language at all. (It is to be expected that rather wide differences in facility with the dominant language exist both within and between countries. This is in itself a source of some incomparability.)

It is impossible to make these data fully comparable. In the case of the first two definitions we cannot know, from the published information, how many individuals *also* speak the dominant language to some degree. On the other hand, where data are given according to the third definition it is not possible to know which of two languages a person speaks is actually his mother tongue or the language he speaks at home. Sometimes, but by no means always, it is possible to guess.

Though these differences certainly do affect comparability, in most cases the effect is not too serious. In the great majority of countries for which we have information, persons who speak both the dominant language and another are less than 15% of the population, usually much less.[2] We have recorded in Table 39 the percentage of the population speaking the dominant language, whatever the definition used. Where definitions B or C are used we give in parentheses, if possible, the percentage speaking both the dominant language and some other tongue used within the country. Where the definition is known we have of course identified it by the appropriate code letter. Some other incomparabilities may have been introduced by the distinction between a language and a dialect. But as we have identified the dominant language by name in each case, any such incomparabilities will be apparent to the reader.

---

1. Definitions from U. N., *Demographic Yearbook, 1956* (New York, 1957), p. 34.

2. This does not include second languages clearly not spoken by a group indigenous to the country (e. g., English in Sweden). Even so, one or two exceptions to the statement noted above are major. In Paraguay the majority of the population is reported as speaking both Spanish and Guarani.

"Dominant" language in this context refers simply to the language spoken by the largest number of people, not necessarily by a majority. It does not refer to a minority language which may be politically dominant, or most frequently used in commerce. Finally, note that data for a number of European countries are omitted. In quite a number of cases it is clear that the overwhelming majority of the population—virtually 100%—speaks the dominant language. But unless we were able to find some authoritative evidence for a fairly reliable figure we decided not to dignify our estimates with an apparent precision. The reader who wishes to supply the appropriate estimate can easily do so.

TABLE 39

Speakers of Dominant Language as a Percentage of Population

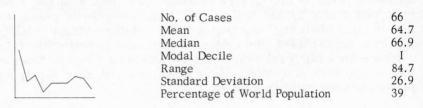

No. of Cases	66
Mean	64.7
Median	66.9
Modal Decile	I
Range	84.7
Standard Deviation	26.9
Percentage of World Population	39

% of Table Population	Case Deciles	Rank	Country	Speakers as % Pop.	Range Deciles	Year
I	I	1	Norway (Norwegian, C)	99.7	I	1950
		2.5	East Germany (German, B)	99.5		1946
		2.5	West Germany (German, B)	99.5		1950
		4	Madagascar (Malagasy, C)	99.0[a]		1942
		5	Austria (German, B)	98.7		1951
		6.5	Dominican Republic (Spanish, A)	98.0		1950
	II	6.5	Egypt (Arabic, C)	98.0[a]		1942
		8	Greece (Greek, B)	97.7		1951
		9	Costa Rica (Spanish, A)	97.4		1950
		10	Brazil[1] (Portuguese, B)	97.2		1950
		11	Nicaragua (Spanish, B)	96.2		1950
		12	Mexico (Spanish, C) (7.6)	95.9		1950
		13	Paraguay (Guarani, C) (53.8)	93.9		1950
	III	14	Ecuador (Spanish, B) (7.3)	93.0		1950
		15	Somalia (Somali, C)	92.7[a]		1942
		16	Syria (Arabic, A)	92.1[b]		1956
		17	Panama (Spanish, A)	91.8		1950
		18	Finland (Finnish, B)	91.1	II	1950
		19	Tunisia (Arabic, C)	90.5[a]		1942
		20	Libya (Arabic, C)	90.0[a]		1942

TABLE 39 (continued)

% of Table Population	Case Deciles	Rank	Country	Speakers as % Pop.	Range Deciles	Year
	IV	21	Poland (Polish, B)	87.5		1946
24.7 ------------		22	Turkey (Turkish, B)	87.1		1950
		23	Romania (Romanian, A)	85.7		1948
		24	Cyprus (Greek, B)	80.8	III	1946
		25	Canada (English, C) (12.2)	79.6[e]		1961
		26	Ruanda-Urundi (Ruanda, C)	79.4[a]		1942
	V	27	Algeria (Arabic, B) (10.5)	78.1		1948
		28	Morocco (Arabic, C)	77.4[a]		1942
		29	Mauritania (Arabic, C)	76.7[a]		1942
		30	Ceylon (Sinhalese, C) (14.1)	75.5		1946
		31	Mongolian People's Republic (Khalkha Mongolian, A)	75.0[d]		1956
		32	Yugoslavia (Serbo-Croatian, A)	73.2	IV	1953
	VI	33	Switzerland (German, B)	72.1		1950
		34	Ghana (Twi-Fante, C)	61.6[a]	V	1942
		35	Israel (Hebrew, B)	60.9[e]		1954
		36	Ethiopia (Amharic, C)	60.8[a]		1942
		37	Belgium (Flemish, C) (18.4)	60.1		1947
		38	Guatemala (Spanish, B)	59.5		1950
		39	Afghanistan (Pushtu, A)	56.0[f]	VI	1961
	VII	40	Pakistan (Bengali, A)	54.4		1951
		41	Sudan (Arabic, C)	53.8[a]		1942
		42	Tanganyika (Swahili, C)	51.9[a]		1942
		43	Dahomey (Fon, C)	50.8[a]		1942
		44	French Cameroons (Pongwe Dialects, C)	48.0[a]	VII	1942
		45	Sierra Leone (Mende, C)	45.0[a]		1942

TABLE 39 (continued)

% of Table Population	Case Deciles	Rank	Country	Speakers as % Pop.	Range Deciles	Year
	VIII	46	Mauritius (Creole French, B)	44.2		1952
48.9 - - - - - - - - - - - -		47	India (Hindi, A)	42.0		1951
92.5 - - - - - - - - - - - -		48	South Africa (Nguni Group, B)	40.4		1946
		49	Guinea (Fula, C)	39.0[a]	VIII	1942
		50	Angola (Umbundu, C)	38.9[a]		1942
		51	Senegal (Wolof, C)	37.7[a]		1942
		52	Philippines (English, C)	37.2[g]		1948
	IX	53	Bolivia (Quecha, B)	36.5		1950
		54	Nigeria (Hausa, C)	36.3[a]		1942
		55	Niger (Hausa, C)	33.7[a]		1942
		56	Togo (Ewe, C)	32.0[a]		1942
		57	Mali (Mandingo, C)	31.3[a]	IX	1942
		58	Ivory Coast (Mossi, C)	30.2[a]		1942
		59.5	French Equatorial Africa (Arabic, C)	28.6[a]		1942
	X	59.5	Uganda (Ganda, C)	28.6[a]		1942
		61	Liberia (Kru, C)	26.3[a]		1942
		62	Congo (Leopoldville) (Swahili, C)[2]	24.0[a]		1942
		63	Rhodesia & Nyasaland (Shona Dialects, C)	23.5[a]		1942
		64	Mozambique (Mali, C)	21.8[a]	X	1942
		65	Kenya (Kikuyu, C)	20.8[a]		1942
		66	British Cameroons (Bafundum-Bansaw, C)	15.0[a]		1942

[1] Population adjusted to include Indian jungle population, assumed not to speak Portuguese.

[2] Luba-Lulua also 24.0%.

Source: Unless otherwise noted, U. N., *Demographic Yearbook, 1956* (New York, 1957).

[a] Duncan MacDougald, Jr., *The Languages and Press of Africa* (Philadelphia, 1944).

[b] Subcontractor's Monograph, HRAF-40, Patoi-4, *The Republic of Syria, 1* (New Haven, 1956), 130.

TABLE 39 (continued)

    ᶜ Dominion Bureau of Statistics, *Canada Yearbook, 1962* (Ottawa, 1962), p. 1204.

    ᵈ Subcontractor's Monograph, HRAF-39, Wash.-1, *Mongolian People's Republic, 1* (New Haven, 1956), c 163.

    ᵉ Central Bureau of Statistics, Government Printer,   *The Statistical Abstract of Israel, 1959–60* (Jerusalem, 1960), p. 395.

    ᶠ Donald Wilber, *Afghanistan* (New Haven, 1962).

    ᵍ Subcontractor's Monograph, HRAF-16, Chicago-5, *The Philippines*, *1*(New Haven, 1955), 332.

Wealth

40-41. AREA

The data in Tables 40-41 apply to total area, including inland water and uninhabited stretches of land lying within the boundaries. Wholly uninhabited areas, such as the polar regions and a few small islands, are usually excluded. The total area data are almost certainly the most reliable in this book, and in virtually all cases the error margin of the estimates must be within ±2%. It is unlikely that there is any consistent bias toward either overstatement or understatement. What error there is stems from:

1. The quality of surveys. Some figures are based on geodetic surveys carried out by modern scientific methods; others are merely approximations based on incomplete information.

2. The definition of "inland water." This term "may vary in meaning from one country to another; in one, it may comprise only major rivers and lakes (in accord with the standard), while in others, it may include, in addition, coastal bays, inlets, and gulfs. Variations of this type between countries with long coastlines can jeopardize comparability."[1]

In Table 41, population per square kilometer, virtually all important error is attributable to the population data.

Population density is obviously one measure of relative wealth in natural resources, but it is not by itself a good indicator. A nation with limited physical lebensraum may be blessed with other resources of a physical or human nature. Many of the economically most advanced states are among the most densely populated. Nor does an overall figure measure intra-country variations, which may be especially significant. Egypt, for example, shows a very moderate density, but virtually all its population is concentrated along the Nile, with vast regions uninhabited.

In many ways population sparseness might be considered a handicap to economic development. A thinly spread population clearly requires a greater investment in transportation and communication facilities per capita. But one must distinguish between density with and without urbanization. Daniel Lerner has suggested, on the basis of data for 73 countries, that density makes no contribution to economic development unless it is accompanied by the growth of cities.[2] Literacy, for example, tended in Lerner's findings to be lowest where density was high but urbanization was low.

------

1. U. N., *Demographic Yearbook, 1960* (New York, 1961), p. 15.
2. Daniel Lerner, *The Passing of Traditional Society* (Glencoe, Ill., 1958), p. 66.

TABLE 40

Area (Square Kilometers)

No. of Cases	133
Mean	979,754
Median	245,857
Modal Decile	X
Range	22,402,684
Standard Deviation	2,558,036
Percentage of World Population	99

% of Table Population	Case Deciles	Rank	Country	Area (sq. km.)	Range Deciles
	I	1	U. S. S. R.	22,403,000	I–V
		2	Canada	9,974,375	VI
30.7		3	China (Mainland)	9,761,012	
		4	United States	9,363,387	
		5	Brazil	8,513,844	VII,VIII
		6	Australia	7,704,159	
54.2		7	India[1]	3,267,567	IX
		8	Argentina	2,778,412	
		9	Sudan	2,505,823	
		10	Algeria	2,381,741	
		11	Congo (Leopoldville)	2,344,932	
		12	Mexico	1,969,269	X
		13	Libya	1,759,540	
	II	14	Iran	1,630,000	
		15	Saudi Arabia	1,600,000	
		16	Mongolian People's Republic	1,531,000	
		17	Indonesia	1,491,562	
		18	Peru	1,285,215	
		19	Chad	1,284,000	
		20	Rhodesia & Nyasaland	1,253,116	
		21	Angola	1,246,700	
		22	South Africa	1,224,378	
		23	Mali	1,204,021	
		24	Niger	1,188,794	
		25	Ethiopia	1,184,320	
		26	Colombia	1,138,355	
	III	27	Bolivia	1,098,581	
		28	Mauritania	1,085,805	
		29	Egypt	1,000,000	
		30	Pakistan	944,824	
		31	Tanganyika	937,061	
		32	Nigeria	923,772	
		33	Venezuela	912,050	
		34	South West Africa	822,907	
		35	Mozambique	783,030	
		36	Turkey	780,576	
		37	Chile	741,767	
		38	Burma	677,950	

TABLE 40 (continued)

% of Table Population	Case Deciles	Rank	Country	Area (sq. km.)	Range Deciles
		39	Afghanistan	650,000	
	IV	40	Somalia	637,661	
		41	Central African Republic	617,000	
		42	Madagascar	590,000	
74.6 -------------		43	Kenya	582,646	
		44	France	551,208	
		45	Thailand	514,000	
		46	Spain²	503,486	
		47	Cameroun	475,444	
		48	Sweden	449,682	
		49	Iraq	444,442	
		50	Morocco	443,680	
		51	Paraguay	406,752	
		52	Japan	369,661	
	V	53	Congo (Brazzaville)	342,000	
		54	Finland	337,009	
		55	Norway	323,917	
		56	Ivory Coast	322,463	
		57	Poland	311,730	
		58	Italy	301,226	
		59	Philippines	299,404	
		60	Aden	290,374	
		61	Upper Volta	274,122	
		62	Ecuador	270,670	
		63	New Zealand²	268,676	
		64	Gabon	267,000	
		65	Yugoslavia	255,804	
	VI	66	West Germany	247,960	
		67	Guinea	245,857	
		68	United Kingdom	244,016	
		69	Uganda	243,410	
		70	Ghana	237,873	
		71	Romania	237,500	
		72	Laos	236,800	
		73	British Guiana	214,970	
		74	Senegal	197,161	
		75	Yemen	195,000	
		76	Uruguay	186,926	
		77	Syria	184,479	
		78	Cambodia	172,511	
		79	South Vietnam	170,831	
	VII	80	North Vietnam	155,203	
		81	Nicaragua	148,000	
		82	Surinam	142,822	
		83	Nepal	140,798	
		84	Greece	132,562	
		85	Malaya	131,287	
		86	Czechoslovakia	127,859	
		87	Tunisia	125,180	
		88	North Korea	123,962	
		89	Sarawak	123,025	

TABLE 40 (continued)

% of Table Population	Case Deciles	Rank	Country	Area (sq. km.)	Range Deciles
		90	Dahomey	115,762	
		91	Cuba	114,524	
		92	Honduras	112,088	
	VIII	93	Bulgaria	111,493	
		94	Liberia	111,370	
		95	Guatemala	108,889	
		96	East Germany	107,431	
		97	Iceland	103,000	
		98	South Korea	96,929	
		99	Jordan	96,610	
		100	Hungary	93,030	
		101	Portugal[2]	92,200	
		102	Austria	83,849	
		103	Panama	74,470	
		104	Sierra Leone	72,326	
		105	Ireland	70,283	
	IX	106	Ceylon	65,610	
		107	Togo	57,000	
		108	Costa Rica	50,000	
		109	Dominican Republic	48,734	
		110	Denmark	43,042	
		111	Switzerland	41,288	
		112	Taiwan	35,961	
		113	Netherlands	32,450	
		114	Belgium	30,507	
		115	Albania	28,748	
		116	Burundi	27,834	
		117	Haiti	27,750	
		118	Rwanda	26,338	
	X	119	Israel	20,700	
		120	El Salvador	20,000	
		121	Kuwait	15,540	
		122	Jamaica	11,424	
		123	Lebanon	10,400	
		124	Cyprus	9,251	
		125	Puerto Rico	8,897	
		126	Trinidad & Tobago	5,128	
		127	Luxembourg	2,586	
		128	Mauritius[2]	2,096	
		129	Hong Kong	1,013	
		130	Netherlands Antilles	961	
		131	Singapore	581	
		132	Barbados	431	
		133	Malta & Gozo	316	

[1] Includes Kashmir-Jammu.
[2] Includes island dependencies.

Source: U. N., *Statistical Yearbook, 1959* (New York, 1960); *1962* (New York, 1963).

TABLE 41

Population per Square Kilometer

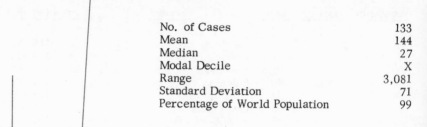

No. of Cases	133
Mean	144
Median	27
Modal Decile	X
Range	3,081
Standard Deviation	71
Percentage of World Population	99

% of Table Population	Case Deciles	Rank	Country	Pop. per sq. km.	Range Deciles
	I	1	Hong Kong	3,082	I–VI
		2	Singapore	2,904	
		3	Malta & Gozo	1,041	VII,VIII
		4	Barbados	548	IX
		5	Mauritius	352	
		6	Netherlands	346	
		7	Taiwan	305	X
		8	Belgium	301	
		9	Puerto Rico	271	
		10	South Korea	258	
		11	Japan	254	
		12.5	West Germany	217	
		12.5	United Kingdom	217	
	II	14	Netherlands Antilles	202	
		15	Lebanon	175	
		16	Trinidad & Tobago	168	
		17	Italy	164	
		18	Ceylon	155	
		19	Haiti	153	
		20	East Germany	149	
		21	Jamaica	143	
25.9		22	India	138	
		23	Switzerland	133	
		24	El Salvador	127	
		25	Luxembourg	123	
		26.5	Czechoslovakia	108	
	III	26.5	Hungary	108	
		28	Denmark	107	
		29	Israel	106	
		30	North Vietnam	105	
		31	Rwanda	104	
		32.5	Pakistan	100	
		32.5	Portugal	100	
		34.5	Philippines	96	
		34.5	Poland	96	
		36	South Vietnam	85	
		37	Austria	84	

TABLE 41 (continued)

% of Table Population	Case Deciles	Rank	Country	Pop. per sq. km.	Range Deciles
		38	France	83	
		39	Burundi	81	
	IV	40	Romania	78	
		41	Yugoslavia	73	
		42.5	Bulgaria	72	
60.4 --------------		42.5	China (Mainland)	72	
		44	North Korea	69	
		45	Nepal	67	
		47	Dominican Republic	64	
		47	Greece	64	
		47	Indonesia	64	
		49	Cyprus	62	
		50.5	Cuba	61	
		50.5	Spain	61	
		52	Malaya	54	
		53	Thailand	53	
	V	54	Albania	50	
		55	Ireland	40	
		56	Nigeria	39	
		57	Turkey	37	
		58	Guatemala	36	
		59.5	Sierra Leone	34	
		59.5	Tunisia	34	
		61	Burma	32	
		62	Cambodia	31	
		63.5	Ghana	29	
		63.5	Uganda	29	
		66	Egypt	27	
		66	Morocco	27	
	VI	66	Syria	27	
		68.5	Togo	26	
		68.5	Yemen	26	
		70	Costa Rica	24	
		71.5	Afghanistan	21	
73.8 ---------------		71.5	Kuwait	21	
		73	United States	20	
		74.5	Dahomey	18	
		74.5	Mexico	18	
		77.5	Ethiopia	17	
		77.5	Honduras	17	
		77.5	Jordan	17	
		77.5	Sweden	17	
	VII	81	Ecuador	16	
		81	Iraq	16	
		81	Upper Volta	16	
		84	Panama	15	
		84	Senegal	15	
		84	Uruguay	15	
		88	Colombia	13	
		88	Finland	13	
		88	Iran	13	

TABLE 41 (continued)

% of Table Population	Case Deciles	Rank	Country	Pop. per sq. km.	Range Deciles
		88	Kenya	13	
		88	South Africa	13	
		91.5	Guinea	12	
		91.5	Liberia	12	
		93.5	Chile	11	
	VIII	93.5	Norway	11	
		96.5	Ivory Coast	10	
		96.5	Nicaragua	10	
		96.5	Tanganyika	10	
		96.5	U. S. S. R.	10	
		100.5	Brazil	9	
		100.5	Cameroun	9	
		100.5	Madagascar	9	
		100.5	New Zealand	9	
		105	Argentina	8	
		105	Laos	8	
		105	Mozambique	8	
		105	Peru	8	
	IX	105	Venezuela	8	
		108	Rhodesia & Nyasaland	7	
		109.5	Congo (Leopoldville)	6	
		109.5	Sarawak	6	
		111.5	Algeria	5	
		111.5	Sudan	5	
		114.5	Aden	4	
		114.5	Angola	4	
		114.5	Paraguay	4	
		114.5	Saudi Arabia	4	
		119	Bolivia	3	
		119	British Guiana	3	
		119	Congo (Brazzaville)	3	
	X	119	Mali	3	
		119	Somalia	3	
		125	Canada	2	
		125	Central African Republic	2	
		125	Chad	2	
		125	Gabon	2	
		125	Iceland	2	
		125	Niger	2	
		125	Surinam	2	
		131	Australia	1	
		131	Libya	1	
		131	Mauritania	1	
		131	Mongolian People's Republic	1	
		131	South West Africa	1	

Source: U. N., *Statistical Yearbook, 1962* (New York, 1963).

Agricultural land here combines the categories described by the Food and Agriculture Organization as "arable land and land under tree crops" and "permanent meadows and pastures." These are defined as "land planted to crops, land temporarily fallow, temporary meadows or pasture, garden land, area under fruit trees, vines, fruit-bearing shrubs, rubber planta-tions . . . land under herbaceous forage crops."[1] The line between "per-manent meadows and pastures" and "forests and woodlands" often varies because of the doubtful classification of pastures producing some wood from scattered trees and forests.

It is impossible to be very precise in assessing an error margin, but a few general observations may help. Data may be unreliable because na-tional governments simply do not have adequate information, whatever the definitions. The major remaining source of incomparability stems from the definitional line, not always applied uniformly, between meadows and pastures on the one hand and forests and woodlands on the other. Though for some countries the proportion exceeds one-half, on the average about 30% of a nation's land is classified as forests and woodlands, with about an equal amount classified as agricultural land. It would seem very unlikely that area covered by scattered trees, and therefore miscategorized, would exceed 20% of either the agricultural or the forest land of a country. Thus ±20% can perhaps be taken, in most cases, as a very approximate error margin. Given the wide range of data in Table 42, even this much error would not cause a country to be too seriously misplaced from its proper ranking.

---

1. F.A.O., *Production Yearbook, 1959* (Rome, 1960).

TABLE 42

Population per 1,000 Hectares of Agricultural Land

No. of Cases				115		
Mean				2,941		
Median				1,103		
Modal Decile				X		
Range				108,211		
Standard Deviation				712		
Percentage of World Population				96		

% of Table Population	Case Deciles	Rank	Country	Pop. per 1,000 Hectares	Range Deciles	Year
	I	1	Singapore	108,214	I–VI	1958
		2	Hong Kong	98,143		1958
		3	Netherlands Antilles	33,400	VII,VIII	1951
		4	South Korea	11,185	IX	1958
		5	Taiwan	10,446	X	1958
		6	Egypt	9,282		1957
		7	Malta & Gozo	8,050		1958
		8	Japan	7,563		1958
		9	Barbados	7,121		1958
		10	Ceylon	6,434		1960
		11	Lebanon	6,000		1958
	II	12	Belgium	5,257		1958
		13	Netherlands	4,855		1958
		14	Mauritius	4,711		1958
		15	Trinidad & Tobago	4,383		1958
		16	Puerto Rico	4,030		1958
		17	West Germany	3,631		1958
		18	Norway	3,420		1958
		19	Jamaica	3,410		1958
		20	North Vietnam	3,184		1960
		21	Malaya	2,980		1958
		22	Philippines	2,753		1957
	III	23	United Kingdom	2,677		1958
		24	East Germany	2,521		1958
		25	Kenya	2,367		1957
		26	Italy	2,323		1958
		27	Switzerland	2,320		1956
		28	South Vietnam	2,298		1959
		29	Luxembourg	2,286		1958
32.9 -----------		30	India	2,279		1957
		31	Indonesia	2,276		1954
		32	Cambodia	2,180		1956
57.2 -----------		33	China (Mainland)	2,070		1954
		34	Czechoslovakia	1,821		1957
	IV	35	Austria	1,720		1958
		36	Pakistan	1,708		1957
		37	Sweden	1,705		1958
		38	Israel	1,649		1958

TABLE 42 (continued)

% of Table Population	Case Deciles	Rank	Country	Pop. per 1,000 Hectares	Range Deciles	Year
		39	Dominican Republic	1,536		1946
		40	Finland	1,512		1958
		41	El Salvador	1,497		1950
		42	Denmark	1,434		1958
		43	Poland	1,411		1958
		44	Bulgaria	1,380		1957
		45	Hungary	1,370		1958
	V	46	Guatemala	1,365		1950
		47	Thailand	1,352		1957
		48	Spain	1,347		1958
		49	France	1,288		1958
		50	Paraguay	1,252		1954
		51.5	Albania	1,248		1959
		51.5	Romania	1,248		1957
		53	Yugoslavia	1,215		1958
		54	Ruanda-Urundi	1,176		1958
		55	Chile	1,164		1956
		56	Ecuador	1,145		1956
		57	Nepal	1,131		1957
	VI	58	Uganda	1,103		1958
		59	Portugal	1,087		1958
		60	Cyprus	1,042		1958
		61	Haiti	1,014		1950
		62	Afghanistan	981		1955
		63	Iraq	972		1955
		64	Costa Rica	948		1955
		65	Greece	930		1957
		66	Cuba	859		1946
		67	Jordan	854		1954
		68	Panama	838		1952
	VII	69	Nicaragua	824		1960
		70	Laos	816		1956
		71	Tunisia	760		1957
		72	Peru	723		1957
75.3 -------------		73	Colombia	714		1956
		74	Nigeria	713		1956
		75	Morocco	644		1960
		76	Togo	610		1960
		77	Iran	608		1950
		78	Ireland	598		1958
		79	Honduras	554		1955
		80	Turkey	483		1958
	VIII	81	French West Africa	431		1950
		82	Brazil	410		1950
		83	United States	399		1959
		84	Syria	387		1957
		85	Sierra Leone	385		1958
		86	Southern Rhodesia	377		1955
		87	U. S. S. R.	339		1956
		88	Mexico	296		1950
		89	Venezuela	287		1956

TABLE 42 (continued)

% of Table Population	Case Deciles	Rank	Country	Pop. per 1,000 Hectares	Range Deciles	Year
		90	Congo (Leopoldville)	263		1958
		91	Canada	257		1956
	IX	92	Bolivia	228		1956
		93	Tanganyika	220		1960
		94	Algeria	215		1957
		95	British Guiana	192		1958
		96	Uruguay	187		1957
		97	New Zealand	170		1957
		98	Angola	152		1953
		99	South Africa	148		1958
		100	Madagascar	140		1960
		101	Mozambique	121		1948
		102	Yemen	115		1949
		103	Libya	106		1959
	X	104	Argentina	102		1957
		105	Somalia	90		1957
		106	Sudan	88		1956
		107	Sarawak	86		1952
		108	Iceland	79		1956
		109	Saudi Arabia	75		1952
		110	Kuwait	55		1949
		111	French Equatorial Africa	54		1950
		112	Northern Rhodesia	38		1958
		113	Australia	21		1957
		114	South West Africa	10		1955
		115	Mongolian People's Republic	3		1945

Sources: F.A.O., *Production Yearbook, 1959* (New York, 1960); *1960* (New York, 1961); *1961* (New York, 1962); U.N., *Demographic Yearbook, 1949–50* (New York, 1951); *1956* (New York, 1957); *1957* (New York, 1958); *1959* (New York, 1960); *1961* (New York, 1962).

Estimates of Gross National Product are subject to substantial variation in accuracy. In most countries the individual components are based on a combination of reliable reported figures, estimates reliable within $\pm 5\%$, rough estimates, and guesses. The mix varies substantially from one country to another. Due to the canceling of errors, the resultant combined estimate for any country can be expected to be accurate within a narrower error margin than may be true of some of the components. Agriculture, and especially the subsistence sector in underdeveloped economies, is likely to be underestimated in national income accounts.[1]

No precise calculation of error margins is available, but some rough estimates can be made. Paul Studenski has divided G. N. P. estimates into three groups, A, B, and C, ranging from highest to lowest reliability, but he does not attempt precise error margins.[2] An official evaluation of the United Kingdom's reported G. N. P. rated it as accurate within $\pm 3\%$—this is surely among the best available. An evaluation of the Malayan data, which Studenski regards as in the least reliable class, appraised them as accurate within $\pm 10\%$. This is perhaps optimistic, and is surely so for most underdeveloped countries.[3]

From this we have derived the following code, which must be regarded as approximate only:

I. Accurate within $\pm 5\%$. Countries in Studenski's group A.

II. Accurate within $\pm 10\%$. Countries in Studenski's group B.

III. Accurate within $\pm 20\%$. Countries in Studenski's group C, plus all others except for

IV. Estimates made "by subjective judgment of the relation of per capita income to other countries, or on some very general basis."[4] The error margin here should be under $\pm 50\%$, but it is impossible to say how much under.

All this applies to estimates prepared in the national currency of the country in question; converting them into U. S. dollars raises additional difficulties. In principle, the conversion should be made in terms of the purchasing power of the local currency with regard to items commonly consumed. For example, a man would surely starve on an annual income of $100 in the United States, but given the price of staple foods in Burma the same amount, converted into Burmese *kyat,* keeps him alive at least at the subsistence level.

---

1. Cf. A. R. Prest, *The Investigation of National Income in British Tropical Dependencies*, University of London, Institute of Commonwealth Studies, Commonwealth Papers, no. IV (London, 1957), on some of the problems.

2. Paul Studenski, *The Income of Nations, Part Two: Theory and Methodology* (New York, 1961), p. 103.

3. Ibid., pp. 102–03. Cf. Oskar Morgenstern, *On the Accuracy of Economic Observations* (Princeton, 1963), for a more skeptical evaluation of national income data.

4. Mikoto Usui and E. E. Hagen, *World Income, 1957* (Cambridge, Mass., 1959), p. 6.

A further difficulty arises in comparing socialist and capitalist economies. Comparison is difficult between free-market economies and systems where prices are not set by market forces. Though methods of
adjustment have been developed, no thoroughly satisfactory solution exists.
And of course comparison between Soviet-type and other economies is
made even more hazardous by the different accounting methods employed,
as expressed in the terms gross national product and gross material product (in communist countries). The following data include a factor for converting the latter figure to the former one, but some accuracy clearly is
lost.

Several attempts at converting G. N. P. at local currencies into equivalent
U. S. dollar purchasing power have been made; the only satisfactory ones
apply to just a few countries, or to aggregates for large geographical
areas.[5] We have therefore not attempted to improve on the published results of estimates converted at current exchange rates. The result of
using exchange rates is that the poverty of the underdeveloped countries is
exaggerated, perhaps by a factor of as much as four for the least developed
areas. Nevertheless the *rankings* should not be significantly affected.

The problem of choosing the appropriate "current exchange rate" still
remains for those countries where there are two or more official rates, or
where the official rate differs substantially from the free market rate.
Here we have not attempted to improve on the rates used by the compilers
of the following estimates; the reader is referred to the original source
for details. This is, of course, an additional source of possible error.

One further problem of comparability might be discussed under the heading "costs of civilization." A substantial part of an industrialized country's
G. N. P. is devoted not directly to the comfort of the population, but to
making the high level of production and industrialization possible. Urbanization brings its own special costs in terms of crowding, air and water
pollution, need for mass transit facilities, etc. A worker in the city earn-
ing the same wage as a rural laborer probably has a lower standard of
living—unless he attaches significant value to the real cultural or other
advantages of city life. In other words, this kind of cost or gain is not easy
to measure, and it is not all one-sided. Again we can feel much surer
about the accuracy of our rankings than about the absolute difference between two countries.

The preceding discussion suggests that G. N. P. and G. N. P. per capita
are used as indicators of many different values. Most often total G. N. P.
is employed as a measure of production, of the total wealth or resources
of a country. The comparability problems referred to above limit its
applicability in this respect, but it is probably as good an indicator as we
have. Not uncommonly G. N. P. is also used as a measure of power, of the

----

5. Colin Clark's country-by-country estimates are probably the most detailed, but leave much
to be desired. Cf. his *Conditions of Economic Progress* (3d ed. New York, 1957); also earlier
editions. Milton Gilbert and Associates (*Comparative National Products and Price Levels, A Study
of Western Europe and the United States*, Paris, 1958) have produced better estimates for the
North Atlantic countries. Cf. Everett E. Hagen, "Some Facts About Income Levels and Economic
Growth," *The Review of Economics and Statistics, 42* (February 1960), 62-67.

resources available to a country to enforce its will upon others.[6] Examination of the G. N. P. table indicates a reasonably good fit between intuitive judgments of power and rankings by total G. N. P. Nevertheless the rankings are better than the absolute level. Power in the modern world depends heavily on industrial production and scientific and technological capabilities. While these are correlated with G. N. P. the correlation is not perfect; such data as the proportion of G. N. P. spent on private consumption are also relevant. Or some aspects of power may be associated with G. N. P. but in a highly discontinuous fashion. Space exploration and the equipment for nuclear warfare are expensive and require a substantial economic base, but a nation with such capabilities almost surely is very significantly more "powerful" than a nation without them but with nearly as great a G. N. P. Or on the other side of the coin, a high G. N. P. brings expenses—troops, for instance, must be provided with more comforts.[7] Once more, the rankings are more solid power indices than are the absolute values.

G. N. P. per capita is frequently employed as a measure of comfort or well-being. For some purposes this is useful, but it too has its hazards. As with total G. N. P. as a measure of power one would want to know the relative proportion of expenditure on private consumption. A combination of these two items of data might provide a better measure. Even so, one must also consider the internal distribution of income. If concentrated in the hands of a wealthy minority a relatively high average income will not properly reflect the welfare of a majority of the populace. Or such factors as climate may distort income as a well-being indicator. A Mediterranean dweller has free a climate that a Scandinavian can provide only indoors, and only at great expense. In this situation G. N. P. is a far better measure of *production* than of *welfare*. Finally, in addition to these difficulties, per capita G. N. P. is rather clearly not a good measure of health, particularly as more direct indices exist. The United States, though at the top of the per capita G. N. P. list, has neither the highest life expectancy nor the lowest infant mortality rate. Either of the latter measures is probably a better index of average health than is per capita G. N. P.

---

6. Cf. A. F. K. Organski, *World Politics* (New York, 1958), chs. 5–8.

7. On these and similar problems cf. Klaus Knorr, *The War Potential of Nations* (Princeton, 1956). Charles Hitch and Dayton McKean (*The Economics of Defense in the Nuclear Age*, Cambridge, Mass., 1961, ch. 1) defend the use of G. N. P. as a power index on the grounds that it measures the total productive capacity of the economy and in time the end use of that capacity can be shifted from one good to another.

TABLE 43

Gross National Product, 1957, $U.S.

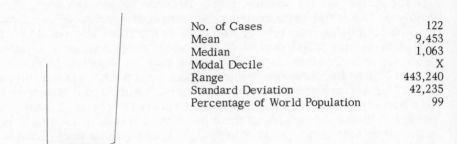

	No. of Cases	122
	Mean	9,453
	Median	1,063
	Modal Decile	X
	Range	443,240
	Standard Deviation	42,235
	Percentage of World Population	99

% of Table Population	Case Deciles	Rank	Country	G. N. P. (million $)	Range Deciles
	I	1	United States (I)	443,270	I–VII
		2	U. S. S. R. (III)	121,920	VIII
		3	United Kingdom (I)	61,379	IX
17.0		4	West Germany (II)	49,906	
		5	China (Mainland) (III)	46,256	
		6	France (II)	41,563	X
		7	Canada (I)	32,291	
57.2		8	India (III)	28,648	
		9	Japan (III)	27,844	
		10	Italy (II)	25,003	
		11	Brazil (III)	17,950	
		12	Poland (III)	13,442	
	II	13	Australia (I)	12,750	
		14	Indonesia (III)	11,148	
		15	Belgium (II)	10,748	
		16	Sweden (I)	10,166	
		17	East Germany (III)	9,841	
		18	Argentina (III)	9,744	
		19	Netherlands (I)	9,216	
		20	Czechoslovakia (II)	9,080	
		21	Spain (III)	8,639	
		22	Mexico (III)	8,240	
		23	Switzerland (I)	7,305	
		24	Romania (III)	6,508	
74.5	III	25	Pakistan (III)	6,001	
		26	Turkey (III)	5,621	
		27	South Africa (III)	5,606	
		28	Philippines (III)	4,995	
		29	Hungary (III)	4,809	
		30	Yugoslavia (III)	4,771	
		31	Denmark (I)	4,756	
		32	Austria (II)	4,685	
		33	Venezuela (III)	4,013	
		34	Norway (I)	3,950	
		35	Colombia (I)	3,479	
		36	Finland (II)	3,441	
	IV	37	Egypt (III)	3,423	
		38	South Korea (III)	3,213	

TABLE 43 (continued)

% of Table Population	Case Deciles	Rank	Country	G. N. P. (million $)	Range Deciles
		39	New Zealand (I)	2,923	
		40	Bulgaria (III)	2,798	
		41	Cuba (III)	2,764	
		42	Greece (III)	2,750	
		43	Chile (III)	2,697	
		44	Nigeria (III)	2,519	
		45	Malaya (III)	2,235	
		46	Iran (IV)	2,079	
		47	Thailand (III)	2,062	
		48	Portugal (III)	1,997	
	V	49	French West Africa (III)	1,896	
		50	Algeria (III)	1,807	
		51	Peru (III)	1,787	
		52	Ireland (II)	1,588	
		53	Taiwan (III)	1,533	
		54	Morocco (III)	1,441	
		55	Israel (II)	1,407	
		56	Puerto Rico (II)	1,286	
		57	Uruguay (III)	1,281	
		58	Congo (Leopoldville) (III)	1,240	
		59	Ceylon (III)	1,178	
		60	Burma (III)	1,134	
	VI	61	Ethiopia (IV)	1,100	
		62	Saudi Arabia (IV)	1,026	
		63	Iraq (IV)	1,015	
		64	Rhodesia & Nyasaland (III)	1,003	
		65	South Vietnam (III)	941	
		66	Ghana (III)	818	
		67	North Vietnam (IV)	798	
		68	Ecuador (III)	736	
		69	Syria (III)	725	
		70	Tunisia (III)	662	
		71	North Korea (IV)	655	
		72	Guatemala (III)	652	
		73	Afghanistan (IV)	650	
	VII	74	Dominican Republic (III)	645	
		75	Sudan (IV)	642	
		76	Hong Kong (III)	640	
		77	Kuwait (IV)	603	
		78	Lebanon (III)	591	
		79	Singapore (IV)	584	
		80	Kenya (III)	546	
		81	Tanganyika (III)	534	
		82	El Salvador (III)	515	
		83	Jamaica (III)	504	
		84	French Equatorial Africa (III)	458	
		85	Cambodia (III)	456	
	VIII	86	Luxembourg (III)	439	
		87	Madagascar (III)	433	
		88	Mozambique (IV)	432	
		89	Nepal (IV)	395	

TABLE 43 (continued)

% of Table Population	Case Deciles	Rank	Country	G. N. P. (million $)	Range Deciles
		90	Costa Rica (III)	369	
		91	Uganda (III)	364	
		92	Haiti (III)	355	
		93	Honduras (III)	344	
		94	French Cameroons (III)	334	
		95.5	Bolivia (III)	324	
		95.5	Trinidad & Tobago (III)	324	
		97	Ruanda-Urundi (IV)	320	
	IX	98	Panama (III)	318	
		99	Angola (IV)	261	
		100	Albania (IV)	256	
		101	Cyprus (III)	250	
		102	Yemen (IV)	225	
		103	Nicaragua (III)	213	
		104	Jordan (III)	198	
		105	Paraguay (III)	187	
		106	Mauritius (III)	150	
		107	Liberia (IV)	127	
		108	British Guiana (III)	121	
		109	Malta & Gozo (IV)	120	
	X	110	Somalia (IV)	105	
		111	Aden (IV)	95	
		112.5	British Cameroons (IV)	94	
		112.5	Iceland (III)	94	
		114	Laos (IV)	83	
		115	Libya (IV)	68	
		116	Sarawak (IV)	64	
		117	Togo (IV)	55	
		118.5	Mongolian People's Republic (IV)	52	
		118.5	South West Africa (IV)	52	
		120	Barbados (IV)[1]	46	
		121	Surinam (III)	33	
		122	Netherlands Antilles (IV)	30	

[1] Estimated from Usui and Hagen's data for West Indies.

Source: Mikoto Usui and E. E. Hagen, *World Income, 1957* (Cambridge, Mass., 1959).

TABLE 44

Gross National Product per Capita, 1957, $U.S.

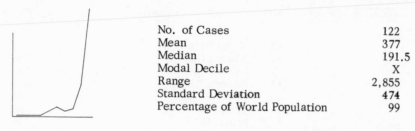

No. of Cases	122
Mean	377
Median	191.5
Modal Decile	X
Range	2,855
Standard Deviation	474
Percentage of World Population	99

% of Table Population	Case Deciles	Rank	Country	G.N.P. per Capita	Range Deciles
	I	1	Kuwait (IV)	2,900	I
		2	United States (I)	2,577	II, III
		3	Canada (I)	1,947	IV, V
		4	Switzerland (I)	1,428	VI
		5	Luxembourg (III)	1,388	
		6	Sweden (I)	1,380	
		7	Australia (I)	1,316	
		8	New Zealand (I)	1,310	
		9	Belgium (II)	1,196	
		10	United Kingdom (I)	1,189	
		11	Norway (I)	1,130	VII
		12	Denmark (I)	1,057	
	II	13	France (II)	943	
		14	West Germany (II)	927	
		15	Netherlands (I)	836	VIII
		16	Finland (II)	794	
		17	Israel (II)	726	
		18	Czechoslovakia (II)	680	
		19	Austria (II)	670	
		20	Venezuela (III)	648	
		21.5	U.S.S.R. (III)	600	IX
		21.5	East Germany (III)	600	
		23	Iceland (III)	572	
		24	Puerto Rico (II)	563	
	III	25	Ireland (II)	550	
		26	Italy (II)	516	
		27.5	Argentina (III)	490	
25.4		27.5	Hungary (III)	490	
		29	Uruguay (III)	478	
		30	Poland (III)	475	
		31	Cyprus (III)	467	
		32	Cuba (III)	431	
		33	Trinidad & Tobago (III)	423	
		34	Singapore (IV)	400	
		35	South Africa (III)	395	
		36	Chile (III)	379	
	IV	37	Malta & Gozo (IV)	377	
		38	Bulgaria (III)	365	
		39	Lebanon (III)	362	
		40	Romania (III)	360	

TABLE 44 (continued)

% of Table Population	Case Deciles	Rank	Country	G. N. P. per Capita	Range Deciles
		41	Costa Rica (III)	357	
		42	Malaya (III)	356	
		43	Greece (III)	340	
		44	Panama (III)	329	X
		45	Jamaica (III)	316	
		46	Japan (III)	306	
		47.5	Brazil (III)	293	
		47.5	Spain (III)	293	
	V	49	Hong Kong (III)	272	
		50	Yugoslavia (III)	265	
		51	Colombia (III)	263	
		52	Mexico (III)	262	
		53	Dominican Republic (III)	239	
		54	British Guiana (III)	235	
		55	Mauritius (III)	225	
		56	Portugal (III)	224	
		57.5	Philippines (III)	220	
		57.5	Turkey (III)	220	
		59	El Salvador (III)	219	
		60	Barbados (IV)[1]	200	
	VI	61	Honduras (III)	194	
		62.5	Ecuador (III)	189	
		62.5	Guatemala (III)	189	
		64	Peru (III)	179	
		65	Algeria (III)	178	
		66	Albania (IV)	175	
		67.5	Syria (III)	173	
		67.5	Tunisia (III)	173	
		69	Ghana (III)	172	
		70	Saudi Arabia (IV)	170	
		71	Taiwan (III)	161	
		72.5	Nicaragua (III)	160	
		72.5	Netherlands Antilles (IV)	160	
	VII	74	Iraq (IV)	156	
		75	South Korea (III)	144	
		77	Egypt (III)	142	
		77	Morocco (III)	142	
		77	Surinam (III)	142	
		79	Rhodesia & Nyasaland (III)	135	
		80	Indonesia (III)	131	
		81.5	Ceylon (III)	129	
		81.5	Jordan (III)	129	
		83	Aden (IV)	120	
		84	Paraguay (III)	114	
		85	Iran (IV)	108	
50.0	VIII	86.5	French Cameroons (III)	105	
		86.5	Haiti (III)	105	
		89	Liberia (IV)	100	
		89	Sarawak (IV)	100	
		89	South West Africa (IV)	100	
		91.5	Bolivia (III)	99	

TABLE 44 (continued)

% of Table Population	Case Deciles	Rank	Country	G. N. P. per Capita	Range Deciles
		91.5	Cambodia (III)	99	
		93	French West Africa (III)	98	
		94	Thailand (III)	96	
		95	French Equatorial Africa (III)	94	
		96	Congo (Leopoldville) (III)	92	
		97	Madagascar (III)	88	
	IX	98	Kenya (III)	87	
		99	Nigeria (III)	78	
		100	South Vietnam (III)	76	
		101.5	China (Mainland) (III)	73	
92.4		101.5	India (III)	73	
		104	Mozambique (IV)	70	
		104	Pakistan (III)	70	
		104	Ruanda-Urundi (IV)	70	
		106	North Korea (IV)	68	
		107	Uganda (III)	64	
		108	Tanganyika (III)	61	
		110.5	Angola (IV)	60	
	X	110.5	British Cameroons (IV)	60	
		110.5	Libya (IV)	60	
		110.5	Sudan (IV)	60	
		113.5	Burma (III)	57	
		113.5	Somalia (IV)	57	
		115.5	Ethiopia (IV)	55	
		115.5	North Vietnam (IV)	55	
		119	Afghanistan (IV)	50	
		119	Laos (IV)	50	
		119	Mongolian People's Republic (IV)	50	
		119	Togo (IV)	50	
		119	Yemen (IV)	50	
		122	Nepal (IV)	45	

[1] Estimated from Usui and Hagen's data for West Indies.

Source: Mikoto Usui and E. E. Hagen, *World Income, 1957* (Cambridge, Mass., 1959).

45. ANNUAL GROWTH OF G. N. P. PER CAPITA

At least four sources of error, some of which have been discussed previously, affect estimates of G. N. P. growth rates.

1. Change in G. N. P. Growth rates are in one sense more accurate than G. N. P. totals, since sectors of the economy whose production is over- or underestimated are likely to be erroneously estimated in a consistent fashion. Such errors thus should not seriously affect the growth rates unless the sectors are growing at a substantially different rate from the rest of the economy. But unfortunately this is precisely what happens in some underdeveloped countries. Agriculture is under-reported and also grows more slowly than industry. The result is an overall growth rate exaggerated because of the rapid growth of industry.

2. Real change in G. N. P. This introduces the problem of a price index. No general statement on reliability can be very precise; a rough guess is that the error margins correspond roughly to those applied to the G. N. P. data for three groups of countries: $\pm 5\%$, $\pm 10\%$, $\pm 20\%$.[1]

3. Population growth. Error ranges for population growth rates were discussed earlier; for most of the countries here the error margins do not exceed 10%.

4. National differences in calculating procedure, or even deliberate distortion. Most of these figures are based on official data, unrevised. This can lead to major incomparabilities. The growth rate reported in U. N. publications for the Soviet Union is about 40% higher than that cited in the unofficial study used below. Except for China (Mainland) we have been forced to use the official figures for other communist countries. They should be treated with caution.

Any comprehensive estimate of error must be very approximate. At least the individual items of error are not likely to cumulate. It may be useful to treat the estimates for countries in groups I and II (as labeled in Table 43) as accurate within $\pm 15\%$. Data for other countries are perhaps comparable within $\pm 25\%$.[2]

Though it should not be considered as *error,* one final source of incomparability stems from the years to which the indices apply. While Table 45 applies to a fairly long period (averaging about nine years, though sometimes much shorter) this is not long enough to eliminate all the effects of

---

1. No data for countries in the $\pm 50\%$ group are included in Table 45. For details on the price index used for particular countries see U. N., *Monthly Bulletin of Statistics*, *Supplement, 1959,* pp. 137–55.

2. Oskar Morgenstern (*On the Accuracy of Economic Observations*, Princeton, 1963) is highly critical of growth rate comparisons. Most of his ire, however, is directed against trying to measure year-to-year changes, not growth over periods of a decade. It may be noted that both E. E. Hagen and Jacob Viner (National Bureau of Economic Research, *Problems in the International Comparison of Economic Accounts, Studies in Income and Wealth,* 20, Princeton, 1957, pp. 377ff. attribute greater accuracy to the comparison of growth rates than of absolute levels of G. N. P. Hagen is co-author of the G. N. P. estimates in tables 43–44.

business cycles, war, or recovery from war. Other base years would make some difference, as would common base years for all countries.

G. N. P. growth rates obviously can be used as indices of change in whatever G. N. P. is supposed to measure. But in addition the growth rate itself has important political and social effects. It represents one measure (in conjunction with such others as urbanization or literacy trends) of social change. As an indicator of increasing capabilities it may be set against increasing expectations. It has important consequences for a society's ability to meet the demands of various groups; social change may involve less conflict if total wealth is growing rapidly enough so that no major group need suffer a diminution in at least its absolute income level, or, even better, if all groups can in some degree experience improvement. A rapid rate of growth may serve as a source of pride and accomplishment for the politically relevant sectors of an underdeveloped country; its absence may be taken as a wider symbol of inefficiency and unprogressiveness.

TABLE 45

Annual Growth of G. N. P. per Capita

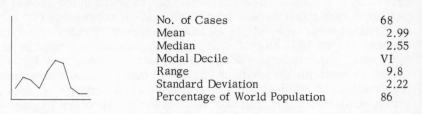

	No. of Cases	68
	Mean	2.99
	Median	2.55
	Modal Decile	VI
	Range	9.8
	Standard Deviation	2.22
	Percentage of World Population	86

% of Table Population	Case Deciles	Rank	Country	G. N. P. per Cap. % Annual Change	Range Deciles	Years
	I	1	Japan	7.6	I	1953–60
		2.5	Austria	7.2		1948–60
		2.5	Yugoslavia[1]	7.2		1953–60
		4	Romania[1]	6.9[a]		1953–60
		5	Bulgaria[1]	6.5	II	1953–60
		6.5	Jamaica	6.3[a]		1954–59
		6.5	West Germany	6.3		1950–60
	II	8.5	Czechoslovakia[1]	6.0[a]		1952–60
		8.5	Trinidad & Tobago	6.0[a]		1952–60
		10.5	Israel	5.8[a]		1952–60
		10.5	Poland[1]	5.8		1953–60
18.0		12	U. S. S. R.	5.7[b]		1950–60
		13	China (Mainland)[1]	5.5[c]	III	1952–61
	III	14	Italy	5.4		1948–60
		15	Greece	5.3		1950–60
		16	Puerto Rico	5.0		1948–60
		17	Spain[2]	4.9		1950–59
		18	Hungary[1]	4.8[a]		1952–60
		19	Algeria	4.7		1950–58
		20	Venezuela[3]	4.4	IV	1950–60
	IV	21	Albania[1]	4.0[d]		1955–58
50.2		22	Burma[3]	3.9		1955–58
		23	Finland[4]	3.7		1948–60
		24	France	3.5	V	1950–60
		25	Switzerland[5]	3.4		1950–59
		27	Portugal	3.2		1948–60
		27	Netherlands	3.2		1948–60
	V	27	Taiwan	3.2		1953–60
		29.5	Brazil[6]	3.1		1948–60
		29.5	Denmark	3.1		1948–60
		31	Sweden	3.0		1948–60
		32.5	Congo (Leopoldville)[3]	2.8		1950–59
		32.5	Rhodesia & Nyasaland	2.8		1954–60
	VI	34	Norway	2.6	VI	1948–60
		35	Belgium	2.5		1948–60
		36.5	Philippines	2.4[a]		1952–60
		36.5	South Korea	2.4		1953–60
		38.5	Mexico	2.3		1948–59
		38.5	United Kingdom	2.3		1948–60
		40	Colombia	2.2		1950–59

TABLE 45 (continued)

% of Table Population	Case Deciles	Rank	Country	G. N. P. per Cap. % Annual Change	Range Deciles	Years
	VII	41	Tunisia	2.0[d]		1950–58
		44.5	Ecuador	1.8		1950–60
		44.5	El Salvador	1.8[e]		1953–59
		44.5	Ireland	1.8		1953–60
		44.5	Luxembourg	1.8		1953–59
		44.5	Turkey[4]	1.8[a]		1952–60
		44.5	United States	1.8		1948–60
	VIII	48 .	Thailand	1.7[a]	VII	1952–60
		50	Canada	1.6		1948–60
74.5		50	Iceland	1.6		1954–60
		50	Panama	1.6[e]		1950–58
		52.5 .	Indonesia[6]	1.5[e]		1951–59
		52.5	Peru	1.5		1950–58
		54	Cyprus	1.4		1950–60
		55	Chile	1.3		1950–60
	IX	57 .	Ceylon[3]	1.2		1950–60
		57	Guatemala	1.2		1948–60
		57	Nigeria	1.2		1953–57
		59.5 .	Cambodia[4]	1.0		1953–59
		59.5 .	India[6]	1.0		1948–59
		61	Malaya	0.6	VIII	1955–60
		62	Honduras	0.4[a]		1952–59
	X	63 .	Pakistan[2]	0.3		1953–60
		64	Bolivia	−0.2[d]		1950–55
		65	Argentina	−0.4	IX	1950–60
		66	Paraguay[6]	−1.0		1950–60
		67	Morocco	−1.9[a]	X	1952–60
		68	Syria[6]	−2.2[a]		1954–60

[1] Net material product.
[2] Net national product at factor cost.
[3] Gross domestic product at market prices.
[4] Gross domestic product at factor cost.
[5] Net national product at market prices.
[6] Net domestic product at factor cost.

Sources: Unless otherwise noted, U. N., *Statistical Yearbook, 1961* (New York, 1962).

[a] U. N., *Yearbook of National Accounts Statistics, 1962* (New York, 1963).

[b] Stanley H. Cohn, "The Gross National Product in the Soviet Union: Comparative Growth Rates," Joint Economic Committee, *Dimensions of Soviet Economic Power,* 87th Congress, 2d Session (Washington, D.C., 1962), p. 75. I am indebted to Professor Abram Bergson of Harvard University for the reference.

[c] U. N. E. C. A. F. E., *Economic Survey of Asia and the Far East, 1961* (Bangkok, 1962), p. 92.

[d] U. N., *Yearbook of National Accounts Statistics, 1960* (New York, 1961).

[e] U. N., *Compendium of Social Statistics, 1963* (New York, 1963).

46. FOREIGN TRADE AS A PERCENTAGE OF G. N. P.

Most data on foreign trade (merchandise only) are subject to various incomparabilities due to differences in exchange rates, valuation systems (f.o.b. or c.i.f.), treatment of re-exports, and the inclusion or exclusion of items such as gold. The trade figures on which the following tables are based, however, have in most cases been specially adjusted by the United Nations Statistical Office and should be accurate and comparable within quite narrow limits, perhaps $\pm 5\%$. They are not always identical with the totals in the national accounts. In a few cases imports are listed c.i.f. rather than f.o.b. This results in the overvaluation of imports by about 10%, or the exaggeration of total trade by 5%.[1]

The only serious sources of error in these data seem to be in the estimates of G. N. P., and the ratios should be considered accurate within approximately the same limits as the G. N. P. data. To avoid difficulties with exchange rates we have kept the figures in local currencies. Occasionally the United Nations, in the *Yearbook of International Trade Statistics*, lists two rates—one for comparison with the external transactions of other states and one appropriate to the valuation of the country's internal trade. Since we want to compare foreign trade *ratios* (not total value) we of course use the latter.

The proportion of foreign trade in a nation's economy is likely to have a major effect on that nation's orientation toward the external world.[2] Specifically, a nation is likely to treat messages from other countries, or concerning other countries, as more salient the greater the proportion foreign trade is to its G. N. P. and hence the greater the economic power base of foreign trade interest groups in that nation's political processes. The salience of a message, of course, only determines the attention given to it, and not the actual response. Countries with high trade–G. N. P. ratios might be expected, *ceteris paribus,* to give relatively more attention to one or more foreign countries and to allocate relatively more of their resources in response to events abroad. Their responses may however be friendly or hostile. They may cooperate more fully with certain foreign powers or with some international organization, or they may be unusually preoccupied with nationalism, anticolonialism, or similar responses.

One may ask not only what are the possible consequences of a high trade–G. N. P. ratio, but what factors may account for that high ratio. A not inconsiderable amount of empirical work has been done on this question, indicating a positive relationship between the foreign trade ratio and colo-

---

1. On the comparison of international trade statistics see R. G. D. Allen and J. Edward Ely, eds., *International Trade Statistics* (New York, 1953), and U. N., *Monthly Bulletin of Statistics, Supplement, 1959*, ch. 9.
2. Cf. K. W. Deutsch, C. I. Bliss, and Alexander Eckstein, "Population, Sovereignty, and the Share of Foreign Trade," *Economic Development and Cultural Change, 10* (July 1962), 353-56; K. W. Deutsch and Alexander Eckstein, "National Industrialization and the Declining Share of the International Economic Sector, 1890-1959," *World Politics, 13* (January 1961), 267-99; and Bruce M. Russett, *Community and Contention: Britain and America in the Twentieth Century* (Cambridge, Mass., 1963), chs. 2, 3.

nial status and negative relationships between it and both economic development and population. Thus the current achievement of political independence by former colonies, coupled with economic development, may tend to diminish the role of foreign trade in their economies and likewise diminish that of international trade in the world economy. And a frequently hypothesized trend—the political integration of smaller units, particularly ex-colonies—may also have the effect of diminishing their trade with the rest of the world. "Internationalist," as contrasted with "nationalist," political pressures in the emerging nations are unlikely to receive greater support from international economic interests during the forthcoming years than in the past. Of course these statements are derived merely from a cross-sectional analysis of a single point in time and should be supplemented by trend studies, but they are nevertheless provocative.[3]

------

3. Some trend studies have been done for individual countries, with modest support for these conclusions. For theory and data on cross-national comparisons of this variable see Hollis B. Chenery, "Patterns of Industrial Growth," *American Economic Review*, *50* (September 1950), 624–54; Deutsch, Bliss, and Eckstein, op. cit.; Deutsch and Eckstein, op. cit.; Charles P. Kindleberger, *Foreign Trade and the National Economy* (New Haven, 1962); and Simon Kuznets, *Six Lectures on Economic Growth* (Glencoe, Ill., 1959).

TABLE 46

Foreign Trade (Exports + Imports) as a Percentage of G. N. P.

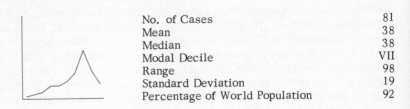

No. of Cases	81
Mean	38
Median	38
Modal Decile	VII
Range	98
Standard Deviation	19
Percentage of World Population	92

% of Table Population	Case Deciles	Rank	Country	Trade as % G. N. P.	Range Deciles	Year
	I	1	Barbados	103	I,II	1959
		2	Libya	79	III	1959
		3	Mauritius	77		1959
		4	Netherlands	74		1959
		5	Cyprus	72	IV	1959
		6	Liberia	71		1959
		8	Bolivia	66		1959
		8	Malta & Gozo	66		1959
	II	8	Rhodesia & Nyasaland	66		1959
		10	Congo (Leopoldville)	65		1959
		11.5	Cameroun	63	V	1960
		11.5	Ceylon	63		1959
		13	Cuba	60		1958
		14	Belgium−Luxembourg	57		1959
		15.5	Denmark	55		1959
		15.5	Ireland	55		1959
	III	17	Jordan	53	VI	1959
		18	Venezuela	52		1959
		19	Norway	51		1959
		20	Lebanon	50		1959
		21.5	El Salvador	49		1960
		21.5	Jamaica	49		1959
		23	Tunisia	48		1959
		24	Switzerland	46		1959
	IV	25.5	Ghana	44	VII	1960
		25.5	Tanganyika	44		1957
		27.5	Finland	43		1959
		27.5	New Zealand	43		1959
		29.5	Costa Rica	42		1959
		29.5	Uganda	42		1957
		33	Austria	41		1959
		33	Iceland	41		1959
	V	33	Nicaragua	41		1960
		33	Sweden	41		1959
		33	Syria	41		1957
		36	Peru	40		1959
		39	Burma	38		1959
		39	Dominican Republic	38		1959
		39	Egypt	38		1959
		39	Honduras	38		1958

TABLE 46 (continued)

% of Table Population	Case Deciles	Rank	Country	Trade as % G. N. P.	Range Deciles	Year
	VI	39	South Africa	38		1959
		42	Guatemala	37		1959
		43.5	Portugal	35		1959
		43.5	Thailand	35		1959
		45	Nigeria	34	VIII	1959
		47	Morocco	33		1959
		47	Panama	33		1959
		47	Sudan	33		1959
	VII	49.5	Canada	31		1959
		49.5	West Germany	31		1959
		51	United Kingdom	30		1959
		53	Ecuador	29		1959
		53	Paraguay	29		1959
		53	Uruguay	29		1959
		55.5	Cambodia	28		1959
		55.5	Haiti	28		1960
	VIII	57	Israel	27		1959
		58.5	Australia	26		1959
		58.5	Greece	26		1959
		60	Argentina	25		1959
		61	Colombia	23	IX	1959
		62.5	Chile	22		1960
		62.5	Italy	22		1959
		64.5	Indonesia[1]	21		1959
28.3	IX	64.5	Japan	21		1959
		67	Ethiopia	20		1959
		67	France	20		1959
		67	Taiwan	20		1959
		69	Philippines	19		1959
		70	Mexico	18		1959
		71	Spain	17		1959
		72.5	Brazil	15		1959
	X	72.5	South Vietnam	15		1959
		74	Turkey	14	X	1959
		75	Yugoslavia[2]	13		1959
42.9		76	Pakistan	12		1959
		77.5	India	11		1959
		77.5	South Korea	11		1959
88.4		79	China (Mainland)	9[a]		1952
		80	United States	7		1959
		81	U. S. S. R.	5[b]		1955

[1] Exchange rate for imports estimated; total trade subject to error of $\pm 20\%$ as a result.

[2] G. N. P. assumed equal to 110% of net material product.

Sources, except where noted:

Trade: *International Financial Statistics, 16* (May 1963); U. N., *Yearbook of International Trade Statistics, 1958* (New York, 1960).

G. N. P.: A. I. D., *Economic Data Book* (Washington, D. C., 1962, loose-leaf); U. N., *Yearbook of National Accounts Statistics, 1961* (New York, 1962).

[a] Alexander Eckstein, *The National Income of Communist China* (New York, 1961), pp. 54, 56.

[b] Abram Bergson, *The Real National Income of Soviet Russia Since 1928* (Cambridge, Mass., 1961).

47-48. GROSS DOMESTIC CAPITAL FORMATION AS A PERCENTAGE OF G. N. P.; PRIVATE CONSUMPTION AS A PERCENTAGE OF G. N. P.

Obviously the accuracy of these series depends heavily upon the quality of the final estimates of G. N. P., as discussed previously. Estimation of the individual components can, however, lead to additional inaccuracy.

In the developed countries, at least, these errors are not likely to be too serious with regard to private consumption. The United Kingdom Central Statistical Office estimated that its figures for consumption were accurate within $\pm 3\%$—the same estimate it applied to its total for G. N. P.[1] Precise attempts at assessing error margins are rarely made, but it would seem plausible to suggest that the error for consumption expenditures is approximately that for G. N. P. Furthermore, it is somewhat more likely that the errors are compensatory (e.g., an underestimate of G. N. P. coupled with a roughly equal underestimate of consumption) than that they are cumulative (errors in the opposite direction, resulting in a doubling of error when the component is expressed as a total of G. N. P.). Thus it should not be unrealistic to propose that the error margins for consumption as a percentage of G. N. P. are no wider than those for G. N. P. itself. Since no data are presented for consumption in countries in G. N. P. accuracy class IV (see introduction to Table 43), the error margins therefore remain at about $\pm 5\%$, $\pm 10\%$, and $\pm 20\%$ for classes I, II, and III.

Error is probably greater for the estimation of gross capital formation. The United Kingdom study previously referred to assigned an error margin of between $\pm 3\%$ and $\pm 10\%$ to its figures for fixed capital formation, and of greater than $\pm 10\%$ to figures for increase in stocks. Since changes in stocks typically amount to only about 15% of capital formation the greater error there can be disregarded without too much harm; even so the figures for capital formation are likely to be fully twice as inaccurate as those for G. N. P. or consumption. Though some of the inaccuracies may be compensatory, our error margins for capital formation as a percentage of G. N. P. should nevertheless be wider than those applying only to the latter.

Differences in national price structure raise an additional problem of comparability, if not strictly speaking of accuracy. In underdeveloped countries the prices of capital goods are typically higher, relative to those for consumer goods, than are those applying in the United States or Western Europe. Simon Kuznets suggests that this may mean that the share of consumption is underestimated by as much as perhaps 10% in underdeveloped countries (i.e., a percentage given as 70% might actually be as high as 77% allowing for price differences).[2] Since this underestimate of consumption is at the expense of an overestimate of capital formation, and the latter is a much smaller fraction of total expenditure, capital formation may possibly, in some instances, be exaggerated by 75%. Except where noted, the percentages are given in current prices.

1. *National Income Statistics, Sources and Methods* (London, 1956), p. 36.
2. "Quantitative Aspects of the Economic Growth of Nations: VII. The Share and Structure of Consumption," *Economic Development and Cultural Change, 10* (January 1962) 11-16.

166

On the other hand, in less-developed countries nonmonetary capital formation may be substantial and often not recorded in the estimates.[3] To the extent this occurs it is a partial corrective to the overestimate resulting from different prices.

Three elements reducing the seriousness of these errors should be noted:

1. Though the price problem materially affects cross-national comparison of capital formation in *real* terms it does not alter comparison of *savings* fractions. Savings must be measured as nonexpenditures for consumption; that is, they must be measured in the currency of the individual country. Conversion to some international price index would be distorting.

2. The errors tend to increase regularly as they deal with progressively lower levels of economic development and, at least for price differences, the errors tend to be in the same direction. Thus they may not significantly change the rankings of countries, either throughout the entire range or within various subgroups defined by income levels.

3. Excluding the communist countries, the range of estimates of consumption as a percentage of G. N. P. is less than 30% (86.0% to 58.1%), suggesting that the error margins indicated above may actually be too wide.

These data might be used to investigate a great number of propositions. One would be about the alleged alternative between guns and butter, using the earlier series on military expenditures. Do consumption and military expenditure often come into conflict, or is there a tendency for investment to be slighted instead? Is a high degree of income inequality essential to make substantial savings available for investment? Using the series on government revenue and expenditure, is it true that a large public sector mitigates against high rates of investment? Or, with the religion series, are predominantly Protestant countries more frugal or industrious (as in the famous Weberian theory) than Catholic countries?

---

3. Cf. Simon Kuznets, "Quantitative Proportions: International Comparisons for Recent Years," *Economic Development and Cultural Change*, 8 (July 1960), 24–25.

TABLE 47

Gross Domestic Capital Formation as a Percentage of G. N. P.

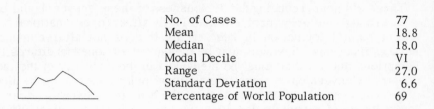

No. of Cases	77
Mean	18.8
Median	18.0
Modal Decile	VI
Range	27.0
Standard Deviation	6.6
Percentage of World Population	69

% of Table Population	Case Deciles	Rank	Country	Capital Formation as % of G. N. P.	Range Deciles	Years
	I	1	Rhodesia & Nyasaland	32.0	I	1954–59
		2	Yugoslavia	31.2		1952–58
		3	East Germany[1]	31.1		1954–58
		4	Venezuela	30.4		1950–59
		5	Norway	29.9		1950–59
		6	Japan	29.2	II	1950–59
		7	Australia	28.6		1950–59
	II	8	Trinidad & Tobago	28.1[a]		1951–60
		9	Congo (Leopoldville)	27.8		1950–59
		10	Luxembourg	27.6[a]		1952–60
		11.5	Israel	26.2	III	1955–59
		11.5	Peru	26.2		1950–58
		13	Barbados	26.1[a]		1948–59
		14	Finland	25.9		1950–59
		15	Bulgaria	25.7		1952–59
	III	16	Canada	25.1		1950–59
		17	Poland	24.8		1952–59
		18	Netherlands	24.3		1950–59
		19	South Africa	24.2		1950–59
		20	U. S. S. R.	24.1		1955
26.2 ------------		21	West Germany	23.8	IV	1950–59
		22	British Guiana	23.6[a]		1952–60
		23	New Zealand	23.2		1950–59
	IV	24	Switzerland	22.9		1954–59
		25	Algeria	22.5		1950–58
		26	Austria	22.0		1950–59
		27	Kenya[1]	21.3[a]		1954–60
		28	Sweden	21.2		1950–59
		29	Italy	20.9	V	1950–59
		30.5	Hungary	20.3		1954–59
	V	30.5	Jamaica	20.3		1950–59
		32	Costa Rica	20.0		1950–59
		33	Malta & Gozo	19.8[a]		1954–60
		34	Puerto Rico	19.4		1950–59
		35	Argentina	19.3		1950–59
		36	Denmark	18.9		1950–59
		37	France	18.8		1950–59
		38	Burma	18.1	VI	1950–59
	VI	39	Dominican Republic	18.0		1952–59

TABLE 47 (continued)

% of Table Population	Case Deciles	Rank	Country	Capital Formation as % of G. N. P.	Range Deciles	Years
		40.5	Colombia	17.8		1950–59
		40.5	United States	17.8		1950–59
		42	Spain	17.6		1954–57
		43.5	Greece	17.5		1950–59
		43.5	Taiwan	17.5		1951–59
		45	Iraq	17.2		1950–59
		46	Tanganyika[1]	16.9		1954–59
50.2	VII	47	Mexico	16.6		1952–58
		48	Belgium	16.2		1950–59
		49.5	Morocco	16.1		1951–58
		49.5	Portugal	16.1		1952–59
		51	Brazil	15.5	VII	1950–58
		52	Ireland	15.4		1953–59
		53	United Kingdom	15.2		1950–59
	VIII	55	Cuba	15.1		1950–57
		55	Honduras	15.1		1950–58
		55	Mauritius[2]	15.1[a]		1953–60
		57	Bolivia[1]	14.6[b]		1950–55
		58	Ecuador	14.5		1950–59
		59	Thailand	14.3		1952–57
		60.5	Turkey	13.7		1950–59
		60.5	Uganda[2]	13.7[a]		1954–60
	IX	62	South Korea	12.6	VIII	1953–59
		63	Panama	12.5		1950–58
		64	Egypt[1]	12.2		1951–56
		65.5	Ghana	11.9		1955–59
		65.5	Guatemala	11.9		1950–59
64.7		67	Ceylon	11.4		1950–59
		68.5	India[1]	10.8[b]		1950–56
		68.5	Malaya	10.8		1955–57
	X	70	Sudan	10.3[a]	IX	1955–60
		71	Chile	10.1		1950–59
		72	Paraguay	10.0[a]		1951–60
		73	Nigeria	9.4		1950–56
		74	Philippines	8.7		1950–59
		75	Haiti[1]	8.2[b]		1953–55
		76	Pakistan[2]	6.7[a]	X	1951–60
		77	Indonesia[1]	5.0		1951–52

[1] Gross domestic product.
[2] Fixed capital only.

Sources: Unless otherwise noted, Simon Kuznets, "Quantitative Aspects of the Economic Growth of Nations: VII. The Share and Structure of Consumption," *Economic Development and Cultural Change, 10* (January 1962), part II.

[a] Calculations by Miss Helen Stone of the Yale Economic Growth Center.

[b] Simon Kuznets, "Quantitative Aspects of the Economic Growth of Nations: V. Capital Formation Proportions: International Comparisons for Recent Years," *Economic Development and Cultural Change, 8* (July 1960), part II.

TABLE 48

Private Consumption as a Percentage of G. N. P.

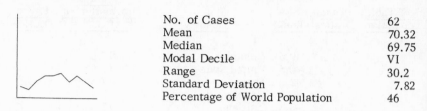

No. of Cases	62
Mean	70.32
Median	69.75
Modal Decile	VI
Range	30.2
Standard Deviation	7.82
Percentage of World Population	46

% of Table Population	Case Deciles	Rank	Country	Consumption as % of G. N. P.	Range Deciles	Years
	I	1	Nigeria	86.0	I	1950–56
		2	Philippines	84.8		1950–59
		3	Puerto Rico	84.5		1950–59
		4	South Korea	83.5		1953–59
		5	Chile	82.4	II	1950–59
		6	Panama	82.1		1950–58
	II	7	Ghana	81.5		1955–59
		8	Jamaica	79.9	III	1950–59
		9	Mexico	79.4		1952–58
		10.5	Guatemala	78.5		1950–59
		10.5	Honduras	78.5		1950–58
		12.5	Greece	77.8		1950–59
	III	12.5	Portugal	77.8		1952–59
		14	Turkey	76.9	IV	1950–59
		15	Thailand	76.8		1952–57
		16.5	Egypt[1]	75.9		1951–56
		16.5	Ireland	75.9		1953–59
		18	Colombia	75.7		1950–59
	IV	19	Ceylon	74.9		1950–59
		20	Morocco	74.5		1951–58
		21	Spain	74.1		1954–57
		23	Costa Rica	73.6	V	1950–59
		23	Cuba	73.6		1950–57
23.6	V	23	Ecuador	73.6		1950–59
		25	Brazil	73.4		1950–59
		26	Hungary	72.9		1954–59
		27	Tanganyika[1]	72.5		1954–59
		28	Israel	72.0		1955–59
		29	Belgium	71.1		1950–59
		30	Taiwan	70.8	VI	1951–59
	VI	31	Poland[2]	69.8		1952–59
		32	Bulgaria[2]	69.7		1952–57
		33.5	Peru	68.8		1950–58
		33.5	Rhodesia & Nyasaland	68.8		1954–59
		35.5	Argentina	68.6		1950–59
		35.5	Denmark	68.6		1950–59
	VII	37	Italy	68.2		1950–59
		38	Dominican Republic	67.8		1952–59
		39	Burma	67.5	VII	1950–59
		40	France	67.0		1950–59

TABLE 48 (continued)

% of Table Population	Case Deciles	Rank	Country	Consumption as % of G. N. P.	Range Deciles	Years
		41	United Kingdom	66.7		1950–59
50.3	VIII	42	South Africa	66.6		1950–59
		43	New Zealand	65.8		1950–59
		44	Austria	65.2		1950–59
		45	Malaya	64.7	VIII	1955–57
		46	Australia	63.9		1950–59
		47	United States	63.7		1950–59
		48	Algeria	63.6		1950–58
	IX	49	Canada	63.5		1950–59
		50	Switzerland	63.2		1954–59
		51	Iraq	62.0		1950–59
		52	Sweden	61.9		1950–59
		53	Congo (Leopoldville)	60.6	IX	1950–59
		54	Finland	60.5		1950–59
	X	56	East Germany[2]	60.0		1954–58
		56	Netherlands	60.0		1950–59
72.3		56	Norway	60.0		1950–59
		58	Japan	59.5		1950–59
		59	West Germany	58.7	X	1950–59
		60	Venezuela	58.1		1950–59
		61	Yugoslavia	55.9		1952–58
		62	U. S. S. R.	55.8		1955

[1] Gross domestic product.
[2] Constant prices.

Source: Simon Kuznets, "Quantitative Aspects of the Economic Growth of Nations: VII. The Share and Structure of Consumption," *Economic Development and Cultural Change, 10* (January 1962), part II.

49. PERCENTAGE OF GROSS DOMESTIC PRODUCT ORIGINATING IN AGRICULTURE

This series attempts to compare the proportionate contribution of agriculture to the national economy. It supplements, but is by no means equivalent to, data presented below on labor force distribution.

In most countries, particularly underdeveloped ones, agricultural production is likely to be underreported in totals for G. N. P. or Gross Domestic Product (G. D. P.).[1] But it is in just these countries where such a large proportion of G. D. P. is derived from agriculture.

Thus underestimation of agricultural production produces underestimation of G. D. P., and the errors are to a large degree compensatory when one refers to agriculture as a proportion of G. D. P. It would seem probable, therefore, that the error margins earlier applied to G. N. P. are appropriate here.

---

1. Simon Kuznets, however, regarded his data on agricultural production in the United States as among the more reliable items. (Cf. his *National Income and Its Composition, 1919-1938*, New York, 1941, pp. 512-13.)

TABLE 49

Percentage of Gross Domestic Product Originating in Agriculture

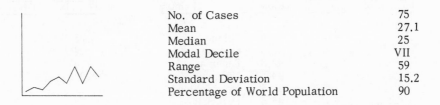

No. of Cases	75
Mean	27.1
Median	25
Modal Decile	VII
Range	59
Standard Deviation	15.2
Percentage of World Population	90

% of Table Population	Case Deciles	Rank	Country	Ag. as % G.D.P.	Range Deciles	Year
	I	1	Nigeria	63	I	1957
		2	Uganda	62		1961
		3.5	Sudan	57	II	1960
		3.5	Tanganyika	57		1961
		5.5	Indonesia	56		1959
		5.5	Pakistan	56		1961
9.2		7	Ceylon	49	III	1960
	II	8.5	China (Mainland)	48		1956
		8.5	India	48		1960
		10	Malaya	45	IV	1960
51.0		11	Honduras	44		1960
		12.5	Albania	43		1958
		12.5	Burma	43		1961
		15	Cambodia	41		1959
		15	South Korea	41		1961
	III	15	Turkey	41		1960
		17	Kenya	39	V	1961
		18.5	Paraguay	38		1961
		18.5	Thailand	38		1961
		20.5	Costa Rica	37		1961
		20.5	Ecuador	37		1961
		22	El Salvador	36		1960
	IV	24	Colombia	34		1960
		24	Philippines	34		1960
		24	Taiwan	34		1960
		26.5	Romania	33	VI	1959
		26.5	Egypt	33		1956
		28.5	Guatemala	32		1961
		28.5	Syria	32		1959
		30.5	Congo (Leopoldville)	30		1959
	VI	30.5	Greece	30		1961
		33.5	Brazil	27	VII	1959
		33.5	Mauritius	27		1961
		33.5	Morocco	27		1961
		33.5	Yugoslavia	27		1961
		36.5	Portugal	26		1960
		36.5	Spain	26		1960
	VI	39.5	British Guiana	25		1960
		39.5	Ireland	25		1961
		39.5	Peru	25		1959

TABLE 49 (continued)

% of Table Population	Case Deciles	Rank	Country	Ag. as % G.D.P.	Range Deciles	Year
		39.5	Poland	25		1960
		42.5	Cyprus	24		1961
		42.5	Panama	24		1960
		44	Hungary	23		1960
		45.5	New Zealand	22		1954
75.7	VII	45.5	U. S. S. R.[1]	22		1958
		47.5	Algeria	21	VIII	1958
		47.5	Finland	21		1961
		49.5	Argentina	20		1961
		49.5	Rhodesia & Nyasaland	20		1961
		51.5	Italy	17		1961
		51.5	Lebanon	17		1958
	VIII	53	Japan	15	IX	1960
		55.5	Chile	14		1960
		55.5	Czechoslovakia	14		1961
		55.5	Denmark	14		1961
		55.5	Jordan	14		1959
		58.5	Jamaica	13		1960
		58.5	Trinidad & Tobago	13		1960
		61.5	East Germany	12		1960
	IX	61.5	Israel	12		1960
		61.5	Norway	12		1960
		61.5	Puerto Rico	12		1961
		64.5	Austria	11		1960
		64.5	South Africa	11		1960
		66	Netherlands	10		1961
		67	France	9	X	1961
	X	68	Luxembourg	8		1960
		69.5	Belgium	7		1960
		69.5	Malta & Gozo	7		1961
		72	Canada	6		1961
		72	Venezuela	6		1959
		72	West Germany	6		1961
		74.5	United Kingdom	4		1961
		74.5	United States	4		1961

[1] Excludes fishing and forestry, which are included for other states.   Net national product.

Sources: U. N., *Statistical Yearbook, 1962* (New York, 1963);   Simon Kuznets, "A Comparative Appraisal," in Abram Bergson and Simon Kuznets, eds., *Economic Trends in the Soviet Union* (Cambridge, Mass., 1963), p. 342.

50-52. PERCENTAGE OF LABOR FORCE EMPLOYED IN AGRICULTURE

According to the definition employed by the International Labor Office, the economically active population refers to "the total of employed persons (including employers, persons working on their own account, salaried employees and wage earners, and, so far as data are available, unpaid family workers) and of persons unemployed at the time of the census. The economically active population does not include students, women occupied solely in domestic duties, retired persons, persons living entirely on their own means, and persons dependent upon others."[1]

Like all population statistics, reliability is dependent upon the quality of the basic census or estimate. In addition, two major sources of incomparability arise. Many countries include in the "economically active population" only persons who have reached a certain minimum age, and the minimum age used may vary from country to country. Other nations make no such age provision. Also, it is often not clear to what extent unpaid family workers—usually women—who assist in family enterprises are included among the enumerated economically active population. Since many of these family enterprises are farms, this difficulty is most serious in measuring agricultural employment. Nevertheless it is highly probable that the percentages given are comparable with a range of $\pm 10\%$ for the advanced countries and $\pm 15\%$ for the underdeveloped states.

Using this kind of information, Table 51 gives the average annual change in the percentage of the labor force employed in agriculture. Though many nations may use different definitions of labor force or of agricultural employees, these definitions do not, in most instances, change seriously from one census to the next. For this reason the error margins in Table 51 are likely to be narrower than those in Table 50. In addition, most of the countries with less reliable data had to be dropped from this series simply because no information was available for earlier years. This series follows the method used for change in the percentage of the population in cities: the change is the percentage of the labor force in agriculture in the later year, minus the percentage in the early year, with the remainder divided by the number of years elapsed.

Table 52, using the datum "nonagricultural employment as a percentage of working-age population," avoids many of the difficulties of Tables 50–51. Because the information necessary to compile this table is often lacking, the series is much shorter. And there is the additional difficulty of error introduced by the estimates of working-age population, which frequently must be projected several years forward from a census year. But partly because we largely avoid such problems as those arising from the classification of unpaid family workers, and partly because the countries eliminated from Table 50 tend to be those for which employment data are most approximate, it seems possible that these figures are comparable within $\pm 10\%$, or even less for the industrial countries.

---

1. I.L.O., *Yearbook of Labour Statistics, 1962* (Geneva, 1962), p. 1.

"Agricultural employment" designates all individuals employed in fishing, hunting, and forestry, as well as agriculture. These series are useful as supplements and checks on other measures of economic development. Most developed states, even "agricultural" ones like Uruguay and New Zealand, have only a minority of the economically active population employed in agriculture. Still, the variations may be important. Rural people, especially owner–cultivators, are often alleged to be more conservative than city-dwellers.[2] They tend to have less contact with modern communications media. The change series provides a good indicator of the rate of modernization and/or social mobilization in a society. And the agricultural labor force series may be used with the data on the percentage of G. D. P. originating in agriculture to form a measure of one kind of imbalance in the economy. If the agricultural labor force percentage is considerably higher than the agricultural percentage of G. D. P., serious social and political tensions may be indicated.

---

2. There is some evidence, however, that very isolated groups, such as lumbermen or some fishermen, may be more radical than most in the population. See Seymour Martin Lipset, *Political Man* (Garden City, N.Y., 1960), p. 231.

TABLE 50

Percentage of Labor Force Employed in Agriculture

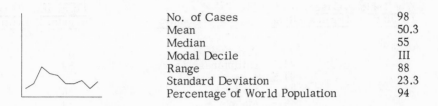

No. of Cases	98
Mean	50.3
Median	55
Modal Decile	III
Range	88
Standard Deviation	23.3
Percentage of World Population	94

% of Table Population	Case Deciles	Rank	Country	% Labor Force in Agric.	Range Deciles	Year
	I	1	Nepal	93	I	1953
		3	Laos	90[a]		1953
		3	Sierra Leone	90[a]		1950
		3	Nyasaland	90[a]		1949
		5	Afghanistan	85[a]		1954
		6	Congo (Leopoldville)	84	II	1955
		7	Haiti	83		1950
		8	Thailand	82		1960
		9	Iraq	81[a]		1950
	II	11	South West Africa	80[a]		1946
		11	Iran	80[a]		1953
		11	Cambodia	80[a]		1955
		13	Turkey	77		1954
		14	Algeria	75	III	1954
		15	Mozambique	74		1950
		16.5	Bolivia[1,2]	72		1950
		16.5	Albania	72[a]		1955
		19	India	71[b]		1961
		19	Mongolian People's Republic	71[a]		1955
	III	19	Morocco	71		1952
		23	Ghana	70[a]		1950
24.2		23	Romania	70		1956
		23	South Korea	70[c]		1955
		23	Syria	70[a]		1952
		23	Burma	70[c]		1955
		26	China (Mainland)	69[a]		1950
		28	Guatemala	68		1950
		28	Nicaragua	68		1950
		28	Tunisia	68		1956
	IV	30.5	Yugoslavia	67		1953
		30.5	Northern Rhodesia	67[a]		1950
49.7		32	Honduras	66	IV	1961
		33.5	Pakistan	65		1955
		33.5	Surinam	65[a]		1950
		35.5	Bulgaria	64		1956
		35.5	Egypt	64		1947
		37	El Salvador	63		1950
		38.5	Indonesia	61[d]		1960
		38.5	Brazil	61		1950

TABLE 50 (continued)

% of Table Population	Case Deciles	Rank	Country	% Labor Force in Agric.	Range Deciles	Year
	V	40	Peru	60[e]		1950
		41.5	Philippines[3]	59		1959
		41.5	Nigeria	59[a]		1950
		44	Sarawak	58[a]		1947
		44	Malaya	58		1957
		44	Mexico	58		1958
		46	Poland	57	V	1950
		47	Dominican Republic	56[f]		1950
		49	Paraguay[1]	55		1950
	VI	49	Costa Rica	55		1950
		49	Colombia[1]	55		1951
		51	Panama[1]	54		1950
		52.5	Ecuador	53		1961
		52.5	Ceylon[4]	53		1953
		55.5	Taiwan	50		1956
		55.5	Spain	50		1958
		55.5	Lebanon	50[e]		1955
		55.5	Cyprus	50[g]		1957
		58	Jamaica	49		1953
	VII	60	Greece	48	VI	1951
		60	Portugal	48		1950
75.5 -------------		60	U. S. S. R.	48[h]		1959
		62	British Guiana[1]	47		1946
		63	Finland	46		1950
		64	Mauritius	44		1952
		65.5	Venezuela[1]	42		1950
		65.5	Cuba	42		1953
		68	Japan	40	VII	1959
		68	Iceland	40		1950
	VIII	68	Ireland	40		1951
		70.5	Hungary	38		1960
		70.5	Czechoslovakia	38		1950
		72	Uruguay	37[a]		1950
		73	South Africa	33		1951
		74	Austria	32		1951
		75	Chile	30	VIII	1952
		76.5	Italy	29		1960
		76.5	Barbados	29		1946
		78.5	France	26		1957
	IX	78.5	Norway	26		1950
		80.5	Trinidad & Tobago	25		1956
		80.5	Argentina	25[e]		1950
		82	Puerto Rico	24		1961
		83.5	Denmark	23		1955
		83.5	Luxembourg	23[g]		1956
		85	East Germany	19[i]	IX	1958
		86	New Zealand	16		1956

TABLE 50 (continued)

% of Table Population	Case Deciles	Rank	Country	% Labor Force in Agric.	Range Deciles	Year
		87	Israel	15		1960
		88.5	West Germany[3]	14		1959
	X	88.5	Australia	14		1954
		90.5	Malta & Gozo	13	X	1948
		90.5	Sweden	13		1960
		92.5	Canada[1,3]	12		1961
		92.5	Switzerland	12		1960
		94	Netherlands	11[j]		1959
		95.5	Belgium	10[f]		1958
		95.5	United States	10[k]		1957
		97	Singapore	8		1957
		98	United Kingdom	5		1951

[1] Adjusted to include tribal Indians.
[2] Adjusted to include colonos and communarios.
[3] Adjusted to include military personnel.
[4] Not including unpaid family workers.

Sources: Unless otherwise noted, I. L. O., *Yearbook of Labour Statistics, 1962* (Geneva, 1963); *1959* (Geneva, 1960).

[a] Norton Ginsburg, *Atlas of Economic Development* (Chicago, 1961), pp. 32, 34.

[b] Y. S. Yegnaraman, "Estimates of Employment and Underemployment at the Beginning of the Third Plan," *AICC Economic Review, 14* (June 22, 1962), 32.

[c] U. S. Senate, Special Committee to Study the Foreign Aid Program, *Foreign Aid Program,* 86th Congress, 1st Session (Washington, D. C., 1957), p. 243.

[d] U. S. Economic Survey Team to Indonesia, *Indonesia* (New Haven, 1963), p. 30.

[e] U. N., *Economic Bulletin for Latin America, 2,* no. 1 (1956), p. 21; *6,* no. 2 (1960), p. 43.

[f] U. N., *Demographic Yearbook, 1956* (New York, 1957), 356.

[g] *Worldmark Encyclopedia of the Nations* (New York, 1960).

[h] Warren W. Eason, "Labor Force," in Abram Bergson and Simon Kuznets, eds., *Economic Trends in the Soviet Union* (Cambridge, Mass., 1963), p. 77.

[i] Wolfgang F. Stolper, *The Structure of the East German Economy* (Cambridge, Mass., 1960), p. 37.

[j] Statistical Office of European Communities, *Basic Statistics for Fifteen European Countries* (Brussels, 1961), p. 21.

[k] Donald J. Bogue, *Population of the United States* (Glencoe, Ill., 1959), p. 446.

TABLE 51

Percentage of Labor Force Employed in Agriculture—
Average Annual Change

No. of Cases	49
Mean	− .56
Median	− .48
Modal Decile	III
Range	2.24
Standard Deviation	.42
Percentage of World Population	57

% of Table Population	Case Deciles	Rank	Country	Annual Change in % Emp. in Agriculture	Range Deciles	Years
27.4	I	1	India	.17	I	1931–61
		2	Czechoslovakia	.05		1930–50
		3	United Kingdom	− .06	II	1931–51
		4	Portugal	− .10		1940–50
	II	5	Malaya	− .12		1931–57
		6	Morocco	− .19		1936–52
		7.5	Panama	− .20		1940–50
		7.5	Trinidad & Tobago	− .20		1946–56
		9	Austria	− .24		1934–51
	III	10.5	Belgium	− .25		1930–58
		10.5	Turkey	− .25		1935–55
		12	Australia	− .29	III	1933–54
		14	Guatemala	− .30		1940–50
		14	Switzerland	− .30		1930–60
	IV	14	Thailand	− .30		1937–60
		16	British Guiana	− .33		1931–46
		17	Netherlands	− .34		1930–59
		18	New Zealand	− .35		1936–56
		19	Poland	− .37		1931–50
	V	20	Mexico	− .39		1940–58
		21	Denmark	− .40		1940–55
		22.5	Chile	− .42		1940–52
		22.5	Japan	− .42		1930–59
50.2		24	Norway	− .45		1930–50
	VI	25	France	− .48		1936–57
		27	Hungary	− .50		1930–60
		27	Nicaragua	− .50		1940–50
		27	Yugoslavia	− .50		1931–53
		29	United States	− .51	IV	1940–57
	VII	31	Brazil	− .60		1940–50
		31	El Salvador	− .60		1930–50
		31	Ireland	− .60		1936–51
		33	West Germany	− .65		1939–59
		34	Sweden	− .67		1930–60
75.2	VIII	36	Canada	− .70		1941–61
		36	Egypt	− .70		1937–47
		36	Philippines	− .70		1939–59
		38	Bulgaria	− .74	V	1934–56

TABLE 51 (continued)

% of Table Population	Case Deciles	Rank	Country	Annual Change in % Emp. in Agriculture	Range Deciles	Years
		39	Italy	− .79		1936–60
	IX	40	Iceland	− .85		1930–50
		41	Cyprus	− .87		1931–46
		42	Puerto Rico	− .90		1930–61
		43	Venezuela	−1.00	VI	1941–50
		44	U.S.S.R.	−1.08		1930–59
	X	45	Finland	−1.10		1940–50
		46	Colombia	−1.31	VII	1938–51
		47	Dominican Republic	−1.40	VIII	1935–50
		48	Honduras	−1.55		1950–61
		49	South Africa	−2.07	IX,X	1936–51

Sources: For early years, F.A.O., *Production Yearbook, 1961* (Rome, 1962). Later years as in Table 50. U.S.S.R., both years as in Table 50.

TABLE 52

Nonagricultural Employment as a Percentage of Working-Age Population

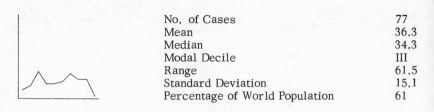

	No. of Cases	77
	Mean	36.3
	Median	34.3
	Modal Decile	III
	Range	61.5
	Standard Deviation	15.1
	Percentage of World Population	61

% of Table Population	Case Deciles	Rank	Country	Nonag. Emp. %	Range Deciles	Year
	I	1	United Kingdom	66.6[a]	I	1960
		2	Hong Kong	65.5		1961
		3	Switzerland	62.8		1960
		4	West Germany	60.7		1960
		5	Sweden	58.9	II	1960
		6	Denmark	57.8		1955
		7	Barbados	57.2		1946
	II	8	United States	56.3		1960
		9	Australia	56.0		1954
		10	Singapore	55.4		1957
		11	Luxembourg	53.4	III	1959
		12	Belgium	53.0		1960
		13	New Zealand	52.5		1956
		14	Netherlands	52.0		1947
		15.5	Canada	51.8		1962
	III	15.5	France	51.8		1957
		17	Czechoslovakia	51.4		1960
		18.5	Israel	49.8		1961
		18.5	Trinidad & Tobago	49.8		1956
27.3		20	Japan	49.6		1960
		21	Austria	49.2		1951
		22	Finland	48.9		1960
	IV	23	Norway	48.2		1960
		24	Malta & Gozo	47.8	IV	1948
		25.5	Italy	46.8		1961
		25.5	U.S.S.R.	46.8[b]		1959
		27	Argentina	46.3		1947
		28	Iceland	46.1		1950
		29	Hungary	45.7		1960
		30	South Africa	42.1		1951
	V	31	Chile	41.9	V	1952
		32	Ireland	41.3		1960
		33	Puerto Rico	41.2		1962
		34	British Guiana	40.6		1946
		35	Cyprus	39.1		1946
		36	Jamaica	36.5		1953
		37	Venezuela	36.4		1950
		38	Poland	34.3	VI	1950
	VI	39	Cuba	33.0		1953
		40	Panama	32.9		1950

TABLE 52 (continued)

% of Table Population	Case Deciles	Rank	Country	Nonag. Emp. %	Range Deciles	Year
		41	Ecuador	32.7		1950
		42	Mauritius	32.4		1952
		43	Portugal	31.9		1950
		44	Greece	30.9		1961
49.9		45	Taiwan	30.0		1956
		46	Spain	29.8		1950
	VII	47.5	Bulgaria	29.6	VII	1956
		47.5	Ceylon	29.6		1953
		49	Costa Rica	28.8		1950
		50	Colombia	27.5		1951
		51	Malaya	27.4		1957
		52	Romania	27.3		1956
		53	Iran	27.2		1956
	VIII	54	Philippines	26.2		1960
		55	Paraguay	25.7		1950
		56	Peru	25.0		1940
		57	Mexico	24.8		1950
		58	Yugoslavia	24.5		1953
		59	El Salvador	23.1	VIII	1950
		60	Bolivia	22.8		1950
		61	Honduras	21.3		1961
	IX	62	Pakistan	20.7		1955
		63	Egypt	20.6		1947
		64	Turkey	20.1		1955
		65	Guatemala	19.9		1950
		66	Tunisia	19.6		1956
		67	Nicaragua	18.8		1950
		68.5	India	17.2[c]	IX	1961
		68.5	Thailand	17.2		1960
	X	70	Algeria	16.8		1954
		71	Haiti	16.3		1950
70.9		72	Morocco	16.1		1952
		73	Chad	13.9		1960
		74	South Korea	13.7		1955
		75	Congo (Leopoldville)	13.5		1955
		76	Mozambique	12.6		1950
		77	Nepal	5.1	X	1953

Sources: Unless otherwise noted: I.L.O., *Yearbook of Labour Statistics, 1962* (Geneva, 1963); *1961* (Geneva, 1962).

[a] Central Statistical Office, *Statistical Abstract of the United Kingdom, 1961*(London, 1961), pp. 103, 107.

[b] Warren W. Eason, "Labor Force," in Abram Bergson and Simon Kuznets, eds., *Economic Trends in the Soviet Union* (Cambridge, Mass., 1963), p. 77.

[c] Y. S. Yegnaraman, "Estimates of Employment and Underemployment at the Beginning of the Third Plan," *AICC Economic Review, 14* (June 22, 1962), 32.

53. EMPLOYMENT IN INDUSTRY AS A PERCENTAGE OF WORKING-AGE POPULATION

"Industry" is here defined as manufacturing, mining, and transportation. Some incomparabilities of definition surely exist, but most data are based on the international standard classification. Major known deviations are noted.

These percentages can be no more accurate than the base estimates of working-age population, and the reader is again referred to the discussion introducing Table 2. Some additional error, of a magnitude difficult to measure, is attributable to the estimates of employment in various sectors. In his early study of the American economy, Simon Kuznets assigned an error margin of approximately 10% to his totals of employment in most of the subsectors making up the industrial segment.[1] These error margins applied, however, largely to years in which there were no censuses or sample surveys—his totals had to be built from much less accurate sources. Our figures apply only to years of censuses or reasonably reliable sample surveys. Furthermore, his 10% error margin was a *maximum* error; a "high average" would undoubtedly have been lower. Though our sector estimates undoubtedly do contain some fairly serious inaccuracies, it would seem reasonable to consider the following data as subject mainly to error in estimating working-age population.

------

1. *National Income and Its Composition, 1919-1938* (New York, 1941), pp. 514–19.

184

TABLE 53

Employment in Industry as a Percentage of Working-Age Population

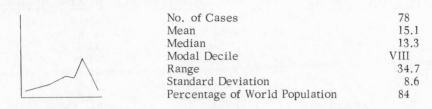

No. of Cases	78
Mean	15.1
Median	13.3
Modal Decile	VIII
Range	34.7
Standard Deviation	8.6
Percentage of World Population	84

% of Table Population	Case Deciles	Rank	Country	% Emp. in Ind.	Range Deciles	Year
	I	1	United Kingdom	35.2[a]	I	1959
		2	Switzerland	35.1		1960
		3	Hong Kong	33.3		1961
		4	West Germany	31.9		1960
		5	Czechoslovakia[1]	30.4	II	1960
		6	East Germany	30.1		1946
		7	Luxembourg	29.4		1959
	II	8	Sweden	28.1	III	1960
		9	Austria	27.5		1951
		10	Belgium	26.1		1960
		11	Hungary	25.5		1960
		12	Australia	25.2		1954
		13	Denmark	24.2	IV	1955
		14	U.S.S.R.	23.9[b]		1959
		15	Norway	23.7		1960
	III	16	France	23.4		1957
		17	Finland[1]	22.2		1960
		18	New Zealand	21.8		1956
		19	Iceland	21.3	V	1950
		20	Japan	20.4		1960
		21	Netherlands	20.3		1947
		22	Trinidad & Tobago	20.1		1956
22.9		23	Canada	20.0		1961
	IV	24	United States[1,2]	19.2		1961
		25	Barbados	19.0		1946
		26	Israel	18.0		1961
		27	Italy	17.8	VI	1951
		28	Argentina	17.7		1947
		29	British Guiana	16.9		1946
		30	South Africa	16.6		1951
		31	Chile	16.5		1952
	V	32.5	Bulgaria[1]	15.7		1956
		32.5	Cyprus	15.7		1946
		34.5	Ecuador	15.4		1950
		34.5	Ireland	15.4		1960
		36	Poland	15.3		1950
		37	Singapore	14.9		1957
		38	Portugal	14.2	VII	1950
		39	Spain	13.5		1950
	VI	40	Malta & Gozo	13.1		1948
		41.5	Cuba	12.6		1953

TABLE 53 (continued)

% of Table Population	Case Deciles	Rank	Country	% Emp. in Ind.	Range Deciles	Year
		41.5	Peru	12.6		1940
		43	Greece	12.0		1961
		44	Jamaica	11.4		1953
		45	Puerto Rico	11.2		1950
		46	Mauritius	11.1		1952
	VII	47	Yugoslavia	10.5	VIII	1953
		48	Colombia	10.4		1951
		49	Bolivia	10.3		1950
		50	Iran	10.2		1956
		51	Paraguay	10.0		1950
		52	Venezuela	9.8		1950
		53	Philippines	9.7		1960
		54	Taiwan	9.6		1956
	VIII	55.5	Costa Rica	9.4		1950
		55.5	Mexico	9.4		1958
		57	Ceylon	8.9		1953
45.8		58	Morocco	8.8		1952
		60.5	El Salvador	8.3		1950
		60.5	Guatemala	8.3		1950
		60.5	India	8.3[c]		1961
		60.5	Nicaragua	8.3		1950
	IX	63	Malaya	8.0		1957
		64	Egypt	7.6		1947
		65	Pakistan	7.4	IX	1956
		66	Turkey	7.2		1955
		67	Panama	6.2		1950
		68	Honduras	5.9		1961
		69	South Korea	5.8		1955
		70	Tunisia	5.7		1956
69.2	X	71	China (Mainland)	5.4[d]		1952
		72	Congo (Leopoldville)	5.2		1955
		73	Haiti	5.1		1950
		74	Thailand	4.6		1960
		75	Algeria	4.4		1954
		76	Mozambique	2.9	X	1950
		77	Nepal	2.4		1953
		78	Chad	.5		1960

[1] Includes construction; excludes transportation.
[2] Includes some public utilities—error does not exceed 1%.
[3] Agricultural wage and salary earners estimated.

Sources: Unless otherwise noted: I. L. O., *Yearbook of Labour Statistics, 1962* (Geneva, 1963); *1961* (Geneva, 1962).
[a] Central Statistical Office, *Statistical Abstract of the United Kingdom, 1961*(London, 1961) pp. 103, 107.
[b] Warren W. Eason, "Labor Force," in Abram Bergson and Simon Kuznets, eds., *Economic Trends in the Soviet Union* (Cambridge, Mass., 1963), pp. 77, 82.
[c] Y. S. Yegnaraman, "Estimates of Employment and Underemployment at the Beginning of the Third Plan," *AICC Economic Review, 14* (June 22, 1962), 32.
[d] Alexander Eckstein, *The National Income of Communist China* (New York, 1961), p. 37.

Unemployment data suffer from the same problems of reliability and comparability as do labor force statistics. In addition there are problems both of definition and of compilation. The basic definition applies to "persons out of work and seeking employment . . . Loss of working time through sickness, accident, and industrial disputes is usually excluded."[1]

The system of compiling statistics varies substantially in various countries. The International Labor Office has grouped them into six types, roughly in order of reliability:

1. Sample surveys of the labor force.
2. Employment office statistics showing registrations for work.
3. Employment office statistics of registered unemployed.
4. Compulsory unemployment insurance statistics.
5. Unemployment relief statistics.
6. Trade union statistics of unemployment.

The inclusiveness of these systems varies significantly. Sample surveys are probably, for most purposes, the most satisfactory, but *not* the most inclusive.[2] Unemployment insurance, unemployment relief, and trade union statistics tend seriously to understate the level of unemployment if any substantial segment of the working population is ineligible for coverage. Trade union statistics are particularly inadequate due to their exclusion of new entrants into the labor force and, of course, nonunion labor. Employment office statistics of registrations tend to be more complete, but again they underestimate the number seeking jobs for the first time, skilled workers who may not register if jobs calling for their skills are known to be unavailable, and persons who are not eligible for any benefits. Also, in many countries women fail to register as fully as men. On the other hand, employment office registrations may substantially overstate the level of unemployment as compared with the results that would be obtained by the sample survey method. This is particularly the case in Italy, where registrations produce a total of unemployed over 50% greater than that shown by competent surveys. Employment office statistics there include, "registrations by persons already employed, registrations by elderly persons who do not want to work but only wish to maintain eligibility for family allowances, and failure of registrants to cancel their registrations after obtaining jobs."[3] Known serious limitations to comparability are noted.

Another source of noncomparability is the denominator usually used—unemployment as a percentage of the "labor force." National definitions of "labor force" vary substantially, and it is impossible without very detailed study to make them comparable. The solution attempted here is to use two different denominators: working-age population and wage and salary earners.

---

1. I. L. O., *Yearbook of Labour Statistics, 1962* (Geneva, 1963), p. 192.

2. President's Committee to Appraise Employment and Unemployment Statistics, *Measuring Employment and Unemployment* (Washington, D. C., 1962), pp. 233-70. Cf. the excellent discussion of comparability for cross-national comparisons.

3. Ibid., p. 244.

A comparison of our totals for unemployment with the figures for eight countries adjusted by the President's Committee[4] suggests that the totals, and thus the percentages, may only be comparable within an error margin as wide as $\pm 100\%$, although in most cases the error margin should not exceed $\pm 50\%$. Though very high, the effects are not as serious as might first appear. The extremely low unemployment figures are much more likely to be significantly noncomparable than the higher ones. Thus an unemployment rate given as 1% might, if computed on a fully comparable basis, be double that, or 2%. But an unemployment rate given as 6% is almost certain to be, however computed, well under 10%. Yet it must be noted that even these error margins apply only to the better statistics—those gathered by methods 1, 2, or 3 above, and applying to advanced industrial countries. Other rates must be interpreted with extreme caution, and no adequate estimate of their error margin can be given.

To measure the social and economic impact of unemployment we have computed the number of unemployed as a percentage of wage and salary earners (including unemployed), and as a percentage of the working-age population. As noted above, both of these seem more comparable, each for somewhat different purposes, than the commonly used unemployment as a percentage of the labor force. One point should of course be clear: unemployment figures cannot measure underemployment. In many underdeveloped countries underemployment is a major social and economic problem. Many laborers have jobs that occupy them for only a small fraction of the day or year. Many men in agriculture work on jobs that could be done equally well by far fewer laborers, with no addition of capital equipment. In these countries unemployment may be low, concealing a substantial amount of underemployment. Unfortunately, adequate data for cross-national comparisons of the latter do not exist.

Unemployment percentages are of great interest to the economist as indices of activity. A high unemployment rate clearly indicates important unused resources and an economy operating at a lower level of production than that of which it is capable. Unemployment rates are of obvious relevance to theories of social stability. High unemployment may have magnified effects on certain subgroups within a population (e.g., Negroes in the United States). High unemployment may make it virtually impossible successfully to integrate such subgroups more fully into the society. Even moderate-appearing overall unemployment rates may, in underdeveloped countries, conceal a high rate of urban unemployment, and consequent social tension. On the other hand, in a developed country a very low rate of unemployment, "over-full" employment, may indicate a lack of flexibility in the economy. It may indicate a low rate of job turnover (usually reflected in at least short periods of unemployment for those concerned), or an inability to meet further demands upon the economy. Potential or actual inflation is frequently associated with very low unemployment. The presence of many alternative employment opportunities may, it is alleged, contribute to a weakening of incentives and labor discipline.

---

4. Ibid.

TABLE 54

Unemployed as a Percentage of Working-Age Population,
Average 1958–1960

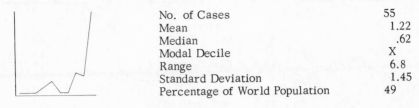

No. of Cases	55
Mean	1.22
Median	.62
Modal Decile	X
Range	6.8
Standard Deviation	1.45
Percentage of World Population	49

% of Table Population	Case Deciles	Rank	Country	Unemp. as % Wrkng-Age Pop.	Range Deciles
	I	1	Puerto Rico (1)	6.81	I,II
		2	Philippines (1)	5.31	III,IV
		3	Canada (1)	4.05	V
		4	United States (1)	3.88	
		5	Ireland (2)	3.57	
	II	6	Singapore (2)	3.56	
		7	Italy (1)	3.41	
		8	Belgium (4)[1]	3.04	VI
		9	Ceylon (2)	2.26	VII
		10	Austria (3)	2.19	
	III	11	Egypt (1)	1.92	VIII
		12	Malta & Gozo (3)	1.78	
		13	Finland (1)	1.73	
		14	Greece (3)	1.72	
		15	British Guiana (3)	1.68	
	IV	16	Denmark (6)	1.65	
23.8		17	Chile (1)[2]	1.60	
		18	United Kingdom (3)	1.38	
		19.5	West Germany (3)	1.31	IX
		19.5	Yugoslavia (3)[1]	1.31	
		21	Cyprus (2)	1.29	
	V	22	Norway (3)	.94	
		23	Netherlands (3)	.90	
		24	Japan (1)	.89	
		25	Mauritius (2)	.81	
		26	South Africa (3)[3]	.67	X
	VI	27	Israel (3)[4]	.63	
		28	Malaya (2)[5]	.61	
		29	Sierra Leone (3)	.55	
		30	Morocco (2)	.53	
42.6		31	Sweden (3)	.52	
		32	India (2)	.51	
73.9	VII	33	Spain (3)	.46	
		34	France (3)	.43	
		35	French Cameroons (3)[6]	.39	
		36	Australia (6)	.37	
		37	Turkey (2)	.35	
		38	Ghana (2)	.33	
	VIII	39	Pakistan (2)[7]	.31	

TABLE 54 (continued)

% of Table Population	Case Deciles	Rank	Country	Unemp. as % Wrkng-Age Pop.	Range Deciles
		40	Northern Rhodesia (2)[8]	.22	
		41	Kenya (2)[5,6]	.20	
		42	Indonesia (2)	.19	
		43.5	East Germany (2)	.11	
	IX	43.5	Southern Rhodesia (3)[5]	.11	
		45	Algeria (3)	.09	
		46.5	New Zealand (3)	.07	
		46.5	Switzerland (3)	.07	
		48	Haiti (2)	.05	
		49.5	Iraq (2)	.04	
	X	49.5	Togo (2)	.04	
		51.5	Ivory Coast (2)	.03	
		51.5	Nigeria (2)	.03	
		54	Chad (2)	.01	
		54	Luxembourg (5)	.01	
		54	Upper Volta (2)	.01	

[1] Including partially unemployed.
[2] Year is 1959.
[3] Unemployed indigenous females not included.
[4] Excluding registrations at Youth Employment Offices during 1959–60.
[5] Average of years 1959–60.
[6] Unemployed males only.
[7] Average of years 1956–58.
[8] Unemployed Africans only.

Sources: I. L. O., *Yearbook of Labour Statistics, 1962* (Geneva, 1963); *1961* (Geneva, 1962); U. N., *Report on the World Social Situation* (New York, 1961), p. 13.

TABLE 55

Unemployed as a Percentage of Wage and Salary Earners

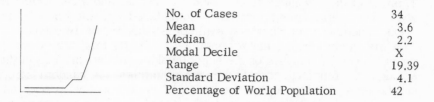

No. of Cases	34
Mean	3.6
Median	2.2
Modal Decile	X
Range	19.39
Standard Deviation	4.1
Percentage of World Population	42

% of Table Population	Case Deciles	Rank	Country	Unemp. as % W. & S.E.	Range Deciles	Year
	I	1	Philippines (1)	19.4	I–III	1960
		2	Puerto Rico (1)	13.0	IV	1960
		3	Egypt (1)	11.0	V	1960
	II	4	Canada (1)	9.0	VI	1961
		5	Ireland (2)	7.1	VII	1951
		6	United States (1)	7.0		1960
	III	7	Italy (1)	6.3		1960
25.3		8	Yugoslavia (3)[1]	5.5	VIII	1960
		9	Austria (3)	4.9		1959
		10	Denmark (5)	4.2		1955
	IV	11	Spain (3)	3.8	IX	1960
62.2		12	India (2)	3.5		1961
		13	Ghana (2)	3.4		1960
	V	14	Ceylon (2)	2.9		1953
		15	Japan (1)	2.8		1959
74.9		16	West Germany (3)	2.5		1959
	VI	17	Turkey (2)	2.4		1955
		18	Singapore (2)	2.0		1957
		19.5	Finland (1)	1.7	X	1950
		19.5	Norway (3)	1.7		1960
	VII	21.5	Kenya (2)[2]	1.4		1960
		21.5	United Kingdom (3)	1.4		1951
		23.5	Israel (3)	1.3		1960
	VIII	23.5	Pakistan (2)	1.3		1956
		25	Nigeria (2)	1.1		1959
		26	Northern Rhodesia (2)	1.0		1960
		27	Sweden (3)	.9		1950
	IX	28	Mauritius (3)	.8		1952
		29.5	France (3)	.6		1957
		29.5	Switzerland (3)	.6		1950
	X	31	Australia (3)	.5		1960
		32	Algeria (3)	.3		1954
		33	New Zealand (3)	.04		1956
		34	Chad (2)	.01		1960

[1] Includes partially unemployed.
[2] Unemployed males only.

Sources: I. L. O., *Yearbook of Labour Statistics, 1962* (Geneva, 1963); 1961 (Geneva, 1962).

56. INDEX OF ACHIEVEMENT MOTIVATION

This set of data is taken from David C. McClelland's *The Achieving Society*.[1] The achievement motive is considered evident when an individual seeks "success in competition with some standard of excellence."

In his study McClelland attempted to identify this achievement motive through content analysis of the schoolbooks used by children in the second through the fourth grades of various countries. A random sample of 21 stories was selected from the books of each country, proper names and other national identifications were disguised, and then each story was coded for presence of the achievement motive. The procedures are described at some length by McClelland.

In a few instances the indices were derived from books in only one or two of several languages used in a given country. The most important such instances are Algeria, Tunisia, South Africa, and Switzerland. In the first two countries only French readers were used. This does not, however, seem too serious a limitation, since French has been until very recently the language of the politically and economically dominant groups in these countries—in the 1950s literate Algerians (Europeans and Moslems combined) were more likely to be literate in French than in Arabic. Only English readers were used in South Africa, but the English-speaking minority has tended to predominate in commerce and the professions in South Africa, and at least until the 1950s most Negro education was in English or the vernacular, not Afrikaans (though the books used in African education are not the same as those used in white classes). Thus the concentration of attention on a single language group, while regrettable, probably does not bias the results too severely. For Switzerland both German and French readers were analyzed, and in the composite score the German readers were weighted double to correspond roughly to the preponderance of German speakers in the population. The relatively small Italian-speaking minority was not represented.

Measures of achievement motivation have been widely tested and refined. The analysis of schoolbooks usually produced findings which closely approximated other measures, such as direct interviewing, of the strength of the achievement motive in a culture.[2] Furthermore, there was good evidence that the sampled stories were reliable indicators of differences that would have shown up in other randomly selected stories for the same countries. The stories were divided into two separate groups, each containing half the stories for each country. The countries' scores were then computed for each half separately, and then the scores for the two groups were correlated. The result was a correlation of $r = .59$. Finally, the scores of various countries seemed associated not only with attitudes, but with performance. McClelland reports predicting growth in electrical output by means of several physical and economic variables widely believed to play

---

1. Princeton, 1961.
2. David C. McClelland, *The Achieving Society* (Princeton, 1961), ch. 3.

an important causal role in economic development, finding the deviations from the predicted results of this model, and then correlating the deviations with the indices of achievement motivation. The result was a correlation of $r = .43$, suggesting that the achievement motive, as measured, plays a significant role in influencing development.[3] Even so it must be recognized that the following table contains a number of apparent anomalies, such as the relatively low rank of the U. S. S. R., and should be treated as typifying a still experimental rather than definitive approach.

---

3. Ibid., pp. 97–103.

TABLE 56

Index of Achievement Motivation—Children's Readers, 1950

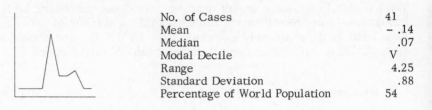

No. of Cases	41
Mean	− .14
Median	.07
Modal Decile	V
Range	4.25
Standard Deviation	.88
Percentage of World Population	54

% of Table Population	Case Deciles	Rank	Country	Achievement Motivation Index	Range Deciles
	I	1	Turkey	2.16	I, II
		2	Argentina	1.84	
		3.5	India	.95	III
28.9		3.5	Lebanon	.95	
	II	5.5	Australia	.51	IV
		5.5	France	.51	
		8	Israel	.44	V
		8	South Africa[1]	.44	
	III	8	Spain	.44	
		11.5	Canada	.39	
		11.5	Greece	.39	
		11.5	Ireland	.39	
	IV	11.5	Pakistan	.39	
		14.5	Bulgaria	.32	
52.7		14.5	United States	.32	
		16.5	West Germany	.19	
	V	16.5	Tunisia[2]	.19	
		19	Portugal	.13	
		19	Syria	.13	
		19	U. S. S. R.	.13	
	VI	21	New Zealand	.07	
		22	Iraq	− .07	VI
		23.5	Austria	− .19	
		23.5	Uruguay	− .19	
	VII	25	Hungary	− .25	
		26	Norway	− .39	
75.9		27	United Kingdom	− .44	VII
		28	Sweden	− .51	
	VIII	29	Mexico	− .57	
		30	Finland	− .64	
		31	Netherlands	− .69	
		32	Italy	− .89	VIII
	IX	33	Japan	− .95	
		34	Switzerland[3]	−1.06	
		35.5	Chile	−1.08	
		35.5	Iran	−1.08	
	X	37	Brazil	−1.15	
		38	Denmark	−1.27	IX
		39	Poland	−1.52	
		40	Algeria[2]	−1.91	X
		41	Belgium	−2.09	

TABLE 56 (continued)

[1] English-language readers only.

[2] French-language readers only.

[3] Mean of French- and German-language readers, with German readers weighted double.

Source: David C. McClelland, *The Achieving Society* (Princeton, 1961), pp. 461–62, Copyright 1961, D. Van Nostrand Company, Inc.

Health

57. LIFE EXPECTANCY: FEMALES AT AGE ZERO

Table 57 gives data only for countries where the data appeared to be reliable within an error margin of $\pm 10\%$, on the same principles applied to the earlier estimates of birth and death rates. Data are given for females since in many underdeveloped countries they tend to live only as long as males, whereas in developed countries their average life span may exceed males' by up to 10%; using data for females thus permits a wider range and clearer distinctions. In some cases, however, information was given only for the average life expectancy of both sexes. These countries are identified by a (B) following the country name, and the data underestimate the life expectancy of females by something less than 5%.

Life expectancy data for age zero obviously represent an averaging of the risks confronting an individual at various ages. They do not, for example, identify a society in which childhood mortality is unusually high but once the child has reached a certain age he stands quite a good chance of attaining middle age. Nor of course do gross data distinguish among the rates for various regional, occupational, or ethnic subgroups. But applied to the overall population they provide a useful measure of health and well-being.

TABLE 57

Life Expectancy: Females at Age Zero

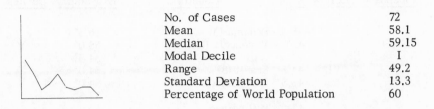

No. of Cases	72
Mean	58.1
Median	59.15
Modal Decile	I
Range	49.2
Standard Deviation	13.3
Percentage of World Population	60

% of Table Population	Case Deciles	Rank	Country	Life Expectancy	Range Deciles	Years
	I	1	Sweden	75.2	I	1959
		2	Norway	74.7		1951–55
		3	Netherlands	73.9		1953–55
		4	France	73.8		1960
		5	United Kingdom	73.6		1958–60
		6	Israel[1]	73.5		1960
		7.5	New Zealand	73.0		1955–57
	II	7.5	United States	73.0		1959
		9	Canada	72.9		1955–57
		10	Australia	72.8		1953–55
		11	Denmark	72.6		1951–55
19.5		12	Czechoslovakia	72.3		1958
		13	U. S. S. R.	72.0		1958–59
		14	West Germany	71.9		1959–60
	III	15	East Germany	71.0		1956–57
		16	Switzerland	70.9		1948–53
		17.5	Iceland	70.3		1941–50
		17.5	Malta & Gozo	70.3		1957–59
		19	Italy	70.0	II	1954–57
		20	Japan	69.9		1959
		21	Finland	69.8		1951–55
	IV	22	Hungary	69.4		1958
		23	Poland	68.9		1958
		24	Cyprus	68.8		1948–50
		25	Belgium	67.3		1946–49
		26	Ireland	67.1		1950–52
		27	Austria	67.0		1949–51
		28	Uruguay (B)	66.5[a]		1955–60
	V	29	Luxembourg	65.8		1946–48
		30	Taiwan	65.6		1959–60
		31.5	Argentina (B)	65.0[a]	III	1955–60
		31.5	Portugal	65.0		1957–58
50.3		33	Spain	63.5		1950
		34	Trinidad & Tobago	63.4		1957
		35	Ceylon	59.4	IV	1954
	VI	36	Yugoslavia	59.3		1952–54
		37.5	Costa Rica (B)	59.0[a]		1955–60
		37.5	Cuba (B)	59.0[a]		1955–60
		39	Jamaica	58.9		1950–52
		40	Malaya	58.2		1956–58

TABLE 57 (continued)

% of Table Population	Case Deciles	Rank	Country	Life Expectancy	Range Deciles	Years
		41	Panama (B)	56.5^a		1955–60
		42	Venezuela (B)	55.0^a	V	1955–60
		43	Chile (B)	54.5^a		1955–60
	VII	44.5	Brazil (B)	54.0^a		1955–60
		44.5	Paraguay (B)	54.0^a		1955–60
		46	Mexico (B)	53.5^a		1955–60
		47	Philippines	53.4		1946–49
		48	Nicaragua (B)	52.5^a		1955–60
		49	Mauritius	52.3		1951–53
		50	British Guiana	52.1		1945–47
	VIII	51	Thailand	51.9		1947–48
		52	Peru (B)	51.5^a		1955–60
		53	Colombia (B)	50.5^a	VI	1955–60
		54	Turkey[2]	50.4		1950–51
		55	El Salvador (B)	50.0^a		1955–60
		56	Honduras (B)	47.5^a		1955–60
		57	Dominican Republic (B)	47.0^a		1955–60
	IX	58	Ecuador (B)	45.5^a	VII	1955–60
		59	Cambodia	43.3		1958–59
		60	Guatemala (B)	43.0^a		1955–60
		61	Haiti (B)	42.5^a		1955–60
		62	Bolivia (B)	40.5^a	VIII	1955–60
		63	Congo (Leopoldville)	40.0		1950–52
		64	Ghana (B)	38.0		1948
	X	65.5	Northern Rhodesia[3]	37.0		1950
		65.5	Senegal (B)	37.0		1957
		68	Burma (B)	35.0^b	IX	1950–55
		68	Ivory Coast (B)	35.0		1956–58
73.5		68	Pakistan (B)	35.0^b		1950–55
		70	India (B)	32.2^c		1951
		71	Central African Republic (B)	32.0		1959
		72	Mali (B)	26.0	X	1957

[1] Jewish population only.
[2] Provincial capitals only.
[3] Indigenous population only.

Sources: Unless otherwise noted, U. N., *Demographic Yearbook, 1961* (New York, 1962).
   ^{a} U. N. E. C. L. A., *Economic Bulletin for Latin America, Suplemento Estadistico,* October, 1962, p. 8.
   ^{b} U. N., *Report on the World Social Situation* (New York, 1957), p. 20.
   ^{c} A. Coale and E. Hoover, *Population Growth and Economic Development in Low Income Countries* (Princeton, 1958), ch. 5.

These data apply to deaths of live-born infants under one year of age. Possibilities for under-registration are obvious. Though inaccuracies are almost exclusively on the side of under-registration, it may be live births, infant deaths, or both that are under-registered. In some cases infant deaths are recorded without the live births ever having been registered; in such cases the infant mortality rate is overstated. If both the deaths and the births of such infants go unrecorded, the rate is understated.

As with live births, we have included only those registered rates regarded by the United Nations as at least 90% complete. But because of the problems just described this means an error margin of $\pm 10\%$. We also have included estimated rates (E) that seemed likely to be accurate within the same error margin.

In addition to problems of completeness, there are some difficulties in making comparable the definitions used in various countries. As with live births, there are the criteria for "live"—breathing or simply any signs of life. There are also the cases in which infants dying within 24 hours of birth or before registration are not counted. These incomparabilities should not, however, increase the error margins of the data by more than about another $\pm 1\%$.[1]

Quite possibly the infant mortality rate gives the best overall measure of national health that we have. Almost certainly these data are more reliable, and more comparable, than for example the series on physicians or hospitals per 100,000. Of course they measure directly only the facilities available to the very young, but they seem to be highly correlated with the general level of medical care and well-being, especially as distributed throughout subsectors of the population. Part of the reason is that a relatively modest expenditure on medical care can reduce a very high infant mortality rate (over 200 per 1,000) to a moderate one (around 75). Quite substantial additional expenditure may be necessary, however, to reduce the rate from 50 to 30. Thus a moderate amount of medical care, spread fairly evenly throughout a population, may be expected to result in a moderate infant mortality rate. But the same amount of money, heavily concentrated, will produce a low rate for a small minority of the population and leave a high infant mortality rate for the great majority—and consequently a rather high mean rate.

Infant mortality rates are directly relevant to factors affecting fertility and human reproduction. The mores of some cultures are closely tied to a high "wastage" of births. A couple may plan or hope to give birth to twice as many children as it would want in a completed family, simply because it cannot expect all the infants to live to adolescence. A man who wants an heir, or children to care for him in his old age, must have many as a form of insurance. But as infant mortality rates come down because of modern health measures, mores and individual expectations may change much more slowly. Even couples who are made aware of the possibility of family planning may not see its desirability if they think in terms of high, or recently high, infant mortality.

---

1. Cf. U.N., *Handbook of Vital Statistics Methods* (New York, 1954), pp. 53–59.

TABLE 58

Infant Deaths per 1,000 Live Births

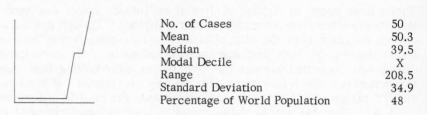

No. of Cases	50
Mean	50.3
Median	39.5
Modal Decile	X
Range	208.5
Standard Deviation	34.9
Percentage of World Population	48

% of Table Population	Case Deciles	Rank	Country	Infant Mortality Rate	Range Deciles	Year
30.7 -------------	I -----	1	India (E)	225.0	I—IV	1951
		2	Chile (E)	127.9	V	1960
		3	Yugoslavia	100.0	VI	1958
		4	Guatemala	91.9	VII	1960
		5	Costa Rica	78.9	VIII	1959
	II	6	Mexico	77.7		1959
		7	Portugal	77.5		1960
		8	El Salvador	76.3		1960
		9	Romania	75.7		1960
		10	Poland	74.7		1959
	III	11	Nicaragua	71.7		1956
		12	Mauritius	69.5		1960
		13	Malaya	68.9		1960
		14	British Guiana[1]	67.1		1958
		15	Barbados	60.4		1960
	IV	16	Jamaica	58.7		1958
		17	Panama	54.8	IX	1956
		18	Puerto Rico	52.4		1959
		19	Italy	48.7		1959
		20	Hungary	47.6		1960
	V	21	Trinidad & Tobago	45.4		1960
		22	Bulgaria	45.1		1960
		23	Spain	43.5		1960
		24	Hong Kong	41.5		1960
		25	Surinam[2]	40.7		1957
47.7 -------------	VI -----	26	Malta & Gozo	38.3		1960
		27	Japan	37.7		1959
		28	Austria	37.5		1960
		29	Belgium	35.4	X	1959
		30	U. S. S. R.	35.0		1960
	VII	31	West Germany	33.8		1960
		32	Singapore	32.3		1961
		33	Luxembourg	31.5		1960
74.6 -------------		34	Czechoslovakia	31.0		1959
		35.5	Ireland	30.5		1961
	VIII	35.5	Taiwan	30.5		1960
		37	Cyprus (E)	29.9		1960
		38	France	27.4		1960
		39	Canada	27.3		1960

TABLE 58 (continued)

% of Table Population	Case Deciles	Rank	Country	Infant Mortality Rate	Range Deciles	Year
		40	United States	26.4		1959
	IX	41	United Kingdom	24.1		1959
		42	Denmark	23.7		1959
		43	New Zealand	22.8		1961
		44	Iceland	22.4		1955
		45	Switzerland	21.1		1960
	X	46	Finland	21.0		1960
		47	Norway	20.2		1959
		48	Australia	19.5		1961
		49	Sweden	16.6		1960
		50	Netherlands	16.5		1960

[1] Excludes Amerindians.
[2] Excludes Indians and Negroes living in tribes.

Sources: A. Coale and E. Hoover, *Population Growth and Economic Development in Low Income Countries* (Princeton, 1958); U. N., *Demographic Yearbook, 1961* (New York, 1962); U. N. E. C. L. A., *Human Resources of Central America, Panama, and Mexico, 1950–1980* (New York, 1960), p. 32.

59. INHABITANTS PER PHYSICIAN

These data are for the total number of qualified physicians working in a country, either privately or in hospitals, laboratories, or public health services.[1] Since in virtually every country physicians must be licensed, the data are likely to be quite complete and reliable. Some differences of definition do nevertheless arise. Where possible physicians registered but not resident in a country have been excluded, as have physicians no longer active and practicing. While this adjustment could not satisfactorily be made for many countries, available information suggests that the failure to exclude such persons rarely adds as much as 15% to the total for any nation.[2] Differences in the definition of a qualified physician undoubtedly exist, but it is clear that the following data do not include such individuals as medical assistants or indigenous medical practitioners.

As a check on the reliability of the index we again employed the technique of graphing it against a related index, in this case inhabitants per hospital bed. The results, in Figure A.3, showed a fairly high correlation around the regression line of r = .67. As before, the dashed lines show the values that deviate from the regression line by 100% above the line or 50% below it. Again, all deviation is not error. On the contrary, most can be explained by the peculiarities of particular countries. In the Congo (Leopold-ville) for instance, there were good hospitals but most foreign doctors fled the country during the prolonged civil unrest.

It should be obvious that the quality of medical personnel varies very substantially from one country to another, even where the overall number may be similar. This may result merely from differences in available resources; it may also be the consequence of deliberate public policy. Some underdeveloped countries have tried to maintain high standards even at the expense of drastically limiting the total number of physicians. Others have consciously relaxed standards on the grounds that the public good would be better served by quantity. Such countries will be at quite different positions in Table 59, and the consequences of their policies will not be the same. Another problem of comparability stems from the concentration of medical personnel in many states. The disproportion between urban and rural services varies widely. In some countries a relatively modest ratio of inhabitants per physician may conceal a heavy concentration on the minority of the population involved in the modern sector. Or in other countries medical personnel may be concentrated on certain great estates. Plantation workers may be well cared for, but other members of the native population neglected.

For these reasons the overall inhabitant–physician ratio is less satisfactory, in terms of comparability, than life expectancy data or, especially, infant mortality rates. But it nevertheless seemed important to have some measure of well-being for those countries, a substantial number, where

---

1. W.H.O., *Annual Epidemiological and Vital Statistics, 1959* (Geneva, 1962), p. 650.
2. Cf. ibid., notes 12 and 13, p. 662.

we had no better data. This series provides a means of comparing, albeit rather crudely, the worldwide distribution of health facilities with the distribution of such other values as education or income.

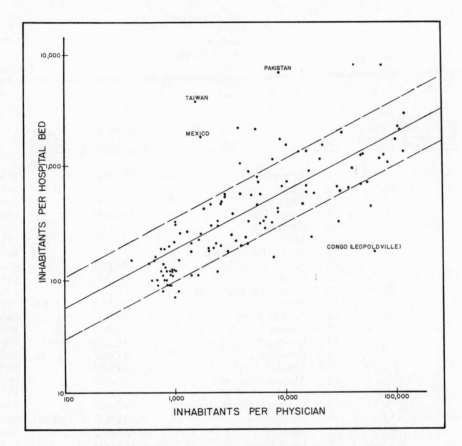

Figure A.3 Reliability Check for Inhabitants per Hospital Bed
and Inhabitants per Physician

TABLE 59

Inhabitants per Physician

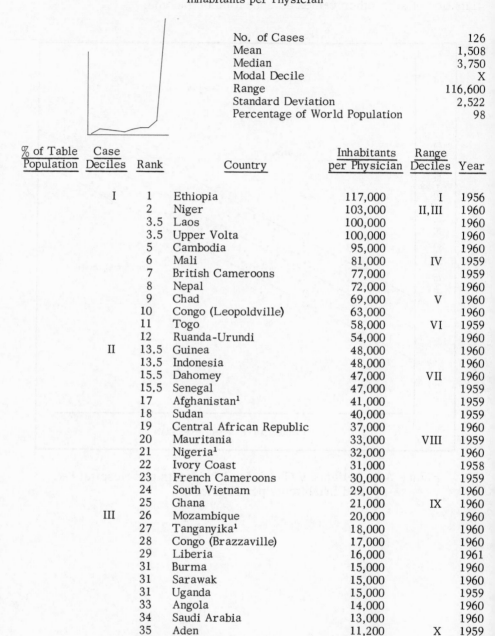

			No. of Cases	126
			Mean	1,508
			Median	3,750
			Modal Decile	X
			Range	116,600
			Standard Deviation	2,522
			Percentage of World Population	98

% of Table Population	Case Deciles	Rank	Country	Inhabitants per Physician	Range Deciles	Year
	I	1	Ethiopia	117,000	I	1956
		2	Niger	103,000	II, III	1960
		3.5	Laos	100,000		1960
		3.5	Upper Volta	100,000		1960
		5	Cambodia	95,000		1960
		6	Mali	81,000	IV	1959
		7	British Cameroons	77,000		1959
		8	Nepal	72,000		1960
		9	Chad	69,000	V	1960
		10	Congo (Leopoldville)	63,000		1960
		11	Togo	58,000	VI	1959
		12	Ruanda-Urundi	54,000		1960
	II	13.5	Guinea	48,000		1960
		13.5	Indonesia	48,000		1960
		15.5	Dahomey	47,000	VII	1960
		15.5	Senegal	47,000		1959
		17	Afghanistan[1]	41,000		1959
		18	Sudan	40,000		1959
		19	Central African Republic	37,000		1960
		20	Mauritania	33,000	VIII	1959
		21	Nigeria[1]	32,000		1960
		22	Ivory Coast	31,000		1958
		23	French Cameroons	30,000		1959
		24	South Vietnam	29,000		1960
		25	Ghana	21,000	IX	1960
	III	26	Mozambique	20,000		1960
		27	Tanganyika[1]	18,000		1960
		28	Congo (Brazzaville)	17,000		1960
		29	Liberia	16,000		1961
		31	Burma	15,000		1960
		31	Sarawak	15,000		1960
		31	Uganda	15,000		1959
		33	Angola	14,000		1960
		34	Saudi Arabia	13,000		1960
		35	Aden	11,200	X	1959
		36.5	Haiti	10,000		1958
		36.5	Kenya	10,000		1959
	IV	38	Morocco	9,400		1960
34.9		39	China (Mainland)	8,700		1957
		40	Pakistan	8,670		1960

TABLE 59 (continued)

% of Table Population	Case Deciles	Rank	Country	Inhabitants per Physician	Range Deciles	Year
		41	Madagascar	8,427		1958
		42	Tunisia	8,200		1959
		43	Gabon	7,700		1960
		44	Thailand	7,500		1960
		45	Rhodesia & Nyasaland[1]	7,400		1960
		46	North Korea	6,700		1956
		47.5	Guatemala	6,400		1957
		47.5	Malaya	6,400		1960
		49	Algeria	6,096		1959
		50.5	Jordan	5,800		1960
	V	50.5	Libya	5,800		1960
		52	Iraq	5,600		1959
		53	Philippines	5,555		1958
		54	El Salvador	5,400		1960
56.8		55	India	5,200		1956
		56	Honduras	4,800		1957
		57	Syria	4,600		1959
		58.5	Ceylon	4,500		1960
		58.5	Mauritius	4,500		1960
		60	Jamaica	4,300		1959
		61.5	Bolivia	3,900		1957
		61.5	British Guiana	3,900		1960
	VI	63	Iran	3,800		1960
		64	South Korea[1]	3,700		1958
		65	Albania	3,500		1960
		66	Hong Kong[1]	3,300		1960
		67	Panama	3,200		1960
		68	Barbados	3,000		1960
		69.5	Nicaragua	2,800		1960
		69.5	Turkey	2,800		1960
		72	Costa Rica	2,600		1960
		72	Ecuador	2,600		1960
		72	Egypt[1]	2,600		1960
		75	Colombia	2,400		1960
		75	Mongolian People's Republic	2,400		1960
	VII	75	Singapore	2,400		1959
		77	Trinidad & Tobago	2,300		1960
		78	Puerto Rico[2]	2,200		1959
		79.5	Brazil	2,100		1958
		79.5	Peru[1]	2,100		1960
		81.5	South Africa[1]	2,000		1960
		81.5	Surinam	2,000		1959
		83	Paraguay	1,800		1960
		84.5	Chile	1,700		1960
		84.5	Mexico	1,700		1960
		86	Yugoslavia	1,637		1960
		87	Finland	1,600		1959
	VIII	88	Taiwan	1,500		1960
		89.5	Cyprus	1,400		1960
		89.5	Netherlands Antilles	1,400		1960
		91	Portugal	1,394		1959

TABLE 59 (continued)

% of Table Population	Case Deciles	Rank	Country	Inhabitants per Physician	Range Deciles	Year
		92	Venezuela	1,300		1960
		93.5	Lebanon[1]	1,100		1960
		93.5	Poland	1,100		1960
		95	Sweden	1,089		1959
		96	France	1,014		1956
		98	Cuba	1,000		1960
		98	Ireland	1,000		1951
		98	Spain	1,000		1960
		100	Malta & Gozo	980		1960
	IX	101	Norway	946		1959
		102	United Kingdom	935		1960
		103.5	Japan	930		1959
75.1		103.5	Kuwait	930		1960
		105	Luxembourg	910		1960
		106.5	Canada	900		1960
		106.5	Netherlands	900		1959
		108	Uruguay	870		1957
		109	Australia	860		1960
		110	Iceland	840		1958
		111	Denmark	830		1959
		112	Belgium	819		1959
		113	Greece	800		1960
	X	114	West Germany	798		1959
		115	Romania	788		1960
		116	United States	780		1961
		117	Switzerland	765		1960
		118	Italy	746		1960
		119	Bulgaria	740		1959
		120	New Zealand[1]	700		1960
		121	Austria	695		1960
		122	Argentina	660		1960
		123	Hungary	650		1959
		124	Czechoslovakia	620		1960
		125	U. S. S. R.	578		1959
		126	Israel	400		1960

[1] Registered physicians, not necessarily practicing in the country.
[2] Excluding federal personnel.

Sources: W. H. O., *Annual Epidemiological and Vital Statistics, 1959* (Geneva, 1962); *Worldmark Encyclopedia of the Nations* (New York, 1960).

Some significant problems of completeness and comparability arise with these data. "A census of hospitals and of their bed capacity is not taken every year in all countries. Moreover, the figures may be incomplete because the respective data are not always communicated by all establishments . . . In the absence of precise definitions of the terms 'hospital,' 'establishment,' etc., and of the exact equivalents . . . for such terms as 'clinique,' 'nursing home,' it has not always been possible to make an absolutely clear distinction between hospitals proper and 'other establishments.'"[1]

The data given here ostensibly refer only to hospitals, and thus exclude establishments such as homes for the aged or leprosaria. *Hospitals* for geriatrics, and *hospitals* for the treatment of lepers are nevertheless included, and undoubtedly differences exist as to precisely where the distinction is drawn. And inclusion of all types of hospitals for tuberculosis or the aged means that countries with much tuberculosis or many old people may appear to have higher bed ratios than would otherwise be true.[2] Furthermore, the quality of establishments indicated by a hospital bed obviously varies greatly. One final difficulty stems from unutilized capacity. In some countries with very low inhabitant–bed ratios a portion of the total facilities are not utilized because of nursing shortages. Occasionally a country's actual capacity is overstated by as much as 15% for this reason.

These difficulties must be borne in mind when comparing countries. No precise error margin can realistically be assessed, but the high correlation in Figure A.3 between the logarithms for the data in this table and those in the one for inhabitants per physician would indicate that the inaccuracies are not usually too serious. One would expect, with perfect data, quite a high correlation between physicians and hospital beds. The most striking departures from the regression line are identified on the graph.

Table 61, presenting trend data, where the definitions are presumably more nearly constant from year to year within the same country, avoids some but not all of the difficulties discussed above. Whatever their faults the tables for hospital beds and rates of change do give us some means for comparing trends in world health. In the trend table a *negative* rate indicates an *increase of well-being;* i.e., better health is associated with a decline in the number of inhabitants per hospital bed. A positive rate thus indicates that population has been increasing faster than the number of beds. In a number of cases the rate of growth in inhabitants per bed has been more rapid than the rate of population increase. Clearly in some of these instances hospitals have gone out of use without being replaced or in some instances perhaps the definition of "hospital bed" has changed.

---

1. W.H.O., *Annual Epidemiological and Vital Statistics, 1959* (Geneva, 1962), p. 683.
2. Only, of course, if special facilities for the aged or the tubercular exist. Nevertheless statistics for *general* hospitals might, if available in comparable form, be preferred.

TABLE 60

Inhabitants per Hospital Bed

No. of Cases	129
Mean	789
Median	330
Modal Decile	X
Range	8030
Standard Deviation	1281
Percentage of World Population	98

% of Table Population	Case Deciles	Rank	Country	Inhab. per Hosp. Bed	Range Deciles	Year
	I	1.5	Afghanistan	8100	I	1960
		1.5	Nepal	8100		1960
		3	Pakistan	7000	II–V	1960
		4	Taiwan	3900	VI	1960
		5	Mauritania	3600		1960
		6	Yemen	3300		1959
		7	Ethiopia	3000	VII	1960
		8.5	Laos	2300	VIII	1960
		8.5	South Korea	2300		1959
		10.5	India	2200		1959
		10.5	Niger	2200		1960
		12	Nigeria	2100		1960
23.2	II	13	Mexico	1900		1960
		14.5	Cambodia	1800		1960
		14.5	China (Mainland)	1800		1959
		16.5	Ghana[1]	1600	IX	1960
		16.5	Haiti	1600		1959
		19	Aden	1400		1959
		19	Burma	1400		1960
		19	Saudi Arabia	1400		1960
		23	British Cameroons	1300		1959
		23	Guinea	1300		1960
		23	Indonesia	1300		1960
		23	Senegal	1300		1959
48.3	III	23	Sierra Leone	1300		1959
		27	Chad[1]	1200		1960
		27	Mozambique	1200		1960
		27	Thailand	1200		1960
		29.5	Iran	1100		1960
		29.5	Mali	1100		1960
		31	Sudan	1000		1960
		32	Liberia	940		1960
		33	Syria	920		1959
		34	Philippines	810	X	1960
		35.5	Kenya	740		1959
		35.5	Ruanda-Urundi	740		1960
		37	Iraq	730		1959
		38	Dahomey	710		1960
	IV	39.5	Somalia	690		1959
		39.5	Uganda	690		1960

TABLE 60 (continued)

% of Table Population	Case Deciles	Rank	Country	Inhab. per Hosp. Bed	Range Deciles	Year
		41.5	Morocco	680		1960
		41.5	South Vietnam	680		1960
		43	Central African Republic	660		1960
		44	Ivory Coast[1]	610		1959
		45	Sarawak[1]	600		1960
		46	Tanganyika	590		1959
		47	Bolivia	580		1960
		48.5	Jordan	570		1960
		48.5	Nicaragua	570		1960
		50	Honduras	560		1960
		51.5	Togo	550		1960
	V	51.5	Turkey	550		1960
		53	Ecuador	490		1959
		54.5	Angola	480		1960
		54.5	Egypt	480		1960
		56	Peru	470		1960
		57.5	El Salvador	460		1960
		57.5	Tunisia	460		1959
		59	Paraguay	430		1960
		60.5	Dominican Republic	400		1960
		60.5	Madagascar	400		1959
		62	Hong Kong	390		1960
		63	Guatemala	360		1959
		66	Algeria	330		1960
	VI	66	Ceylon	330		1960
		66	Colombia	330		1960
		66	Cuba	330		1960
		66	French Cameroons	330		1959
		69	Rhodesia & Nyasaland	325		1959
		70	Libya	320		1960
		71	Spain	310		1959
		72.5	Brazil	300		1959
		72.5	Singapore	300		1960
		74	Malaya	290		1960
		75	Venezuela	270		1960
		76.5	Chile	260		1960
		76.5	Lebanon	260		1960
	VII	78	Panama	250		1960
		79.5	Congo (Brazzaville)	240		1960
		79.5	Jamaica[1]	240		1960
		81	Yugoslavia	230		1959
		82	Albania	220		1959
		84	Cyprus	210		1959
		84	Mauritius	210		1960
		84	Trinidad & Tobago	210		1960
		87	British Guiana	200		1959
		87	Costa Rica	200		1959
		87	Uruguay[1]	200		1959
		90.5	Bulgaria	190		1959
		90.5	Greece	190		1959
	VIII	90.5	Puerto Rico	190		1959

TABLE 60 (continued)

% of Table Population	Case Deciles	Rank	Country	Inhab. per Hosp. Bed	Range Deciles	Year
		90.5	Surinam	190		1960
		94.5	Barbados	180		1960
		94.5	Congo (Leopoldville)	180		1960
		94.5	Portugal	180		1960
		94.5	South Africa	180		1959
		97.5	Argentina	160		1960
		97.5	Gabon	160		1960
		100	Hungary	150		1960
		100	Israel	150		1960
72.2		100	Poland	150		1960
		102.5	Romania	140		1960
		102.5	U. S. S. R.	140		1960
	IX	104	Belgium	130		1959
		108	Denmark	120		1959
		108	France	120		1959
		108	Italy	120		1959
		108	Japan	120		1959
		108	Kuwait	120		1960
		108	Mongolian People's Republic	120		1956
		108	Netherlands	120		1958
		114.5	Finland	110		1960
		114.5	Malta & Gozo	110		1959
		114.5	Netherlands Antilles	110		1960
		114.5	Norway	110		1959
		114.5	United Kingdom	110		1960
	X	114.5	United States	110		1959
		119.5	Austria	100		1960
		119.5	Czechoslovakia	100		1960
		119.5	Iceland	100		1959
		119.5	West Germany	100		1959
		124	Australia	90		1960
		124	Canada	90		1959
		124	East Germany	90		1959
		124	Luxembourg	90		1960
		124	New Zealand	90		1959
		127.5	Sweden	80		1959
		127.5	Switzerland	80		1956
		129	Ireland	70		1959

[1] Government establishments only.

Source: U. N., *Compendium of Social Statistics, 1963* (New York, 1963).

TABLE 61

Inhabitants per Hospital Bed—Annual Percentage Rate of Change

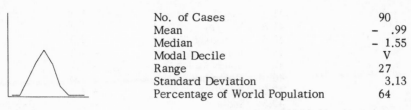

	No. of Cases	90
	Mean	− .99
	Median	− 1.55
	Modal Decile	V
	Range	27
	Standard Deviation	3.13
	Percentage of World Population	64

% of Table Population	Case Deciles	Rank	Country	% Annual Change	Range Deciles	Years
	I	1	British Guiana	+10.4	I	1951–58
		2	Lebanon	5.5	II	1951–60
		3	Surinam	4.3	III	1951–60
		4	France	4.2		1951–58
		5	Taiwan	3.3		1951–60
		6	Aden[1]	3.1		1951–59
		7	El Salvador	2.8		1955–60
		8	Switzerland	2.7		1951–56
		10	Denmark	2.6		1951–58
	II	10	Ecuador	2.6		1953–58
		10	Malaya	2.6		1951–60
		12	Chile	2.4		1951–60
		13	Madagascar	2.3		1951–58
		14	Costa Rica	2.1	IV	1953–58
		15	Singapore	2.0		1951–60
		16	United Kingdom	1.8		1951–60
		17.5	Uruguay	1.5		1951–58
		17.5	West Germany	1.5		1951–58
	III	19.5	Honduras	1.4		1951–58
		19.5	United States	1.4		1951–58
		21	Nicaragua	1.0		1951–60
		22	Haiti	.9		1951–58
		27.5	Argentina	.0		1951–60
		27.5	Australia	.0		1951–60
		27.5	Dominican Republic	.0		1951–60
		27.5	Hungary	.0		1955–60
		27.5	Iceland	.0		1951–58
	IV	27.5	Ireland	.0		1951–58
		27.5	Israel	.0		1951–60
		27.5	New Zealand	.0		1951–58
		27.5	Panama	.0		1951–60
		27.5	Sweden	.0		1951–58
		33	Kenya	− .2		1951–58
		34	Algeria	− .3		1951–60
25.4		35	Canada	− .5	V	1949–58
		36	Barbados	− .6		1951–60
	V	37	Peru	− .9		1951–60
		38	Finland	− 1.0		1951–60
		39.5	Austria	− 1.1		1951–60
		39.5	Belgium	− 1.1		1951–58

TABLE 61 (continued)

% of Table Population	Case Deciles	Rank	Country	% Annual Change	Range Deciles	Years
		41.5	Egypt	− 1.2		1955–60
		41.5	Norway	− 1.2		1951–58
		43.5	Paraguay	− 1.3		1955–60
		43.5	Poland	− 1.3		1955–60
		45	South Africa	− 1.5		1951–58
	VI	46	Colombia	− 1.6		1951–60
		47.5	Brazil	− 1.8		1951–58
57.6		47.5	India	− 1.8		1951–58
		49.5	Czechoslovakia	− 1.9		1955–60
		49.5	Ceylon	− 1.9		1954–56
		51	Venezuela	− 2.0		1953–60
		52	Congo (Leopoldville)	− 2.2		1951–60
		53.5	Afghanistan	− 2.3		1951–60
		53.5	Indonesia	− 2.3		1951–60
	VII	55	Netherlands Antilles	− 2.4		1953–60
		56	Portugal	− 2.5		1954–60
		57.5	Guatemala	− 2.8		1951–58
		57.5	Nigeria	− 2.8		1951–60
		59.5	Jordan	− 2.9		1951–60
		59.5	Uganda	− 2.9		1951–60
		61	Ruanda-Urundi	− 3.0		1951–60
		62	Luxembourg	− 3.1		1951–60
		63.5	South Vietnam	− 3.2	VI	1951–60
	VIII	63.5	Tanganyika	− 3.2		1951–58
		65	Laos	− 3.3		1951–60
		66	Somalia	− 3.6		1951–58
		67	Hong Kong	− 3.7		1954–60
		68	Sierra Leone	− 3.8		1951–58
		69	Burma	− 3.9		1951–60
		70	Yugoslavia	− 4.2		1951–58
		72.5	Italy	− 4.4		1951–58
		72.5	Puerto Rico	− 4.4		1951–58
	IX	72.5	Tunisia	− 4.4		1951–58
86.3		72.5	U.S.S.R.	− 4.4		1950–58
		75	Rhodesia & Nyasaland	− 4.7		1951–58
		76	Cyprus	− 5.0		1951–58
		77.5	Netherlands	− 5.3		1950–58
		77.5	Togo	− 5.3		1951–58
		79.5	Cambodia	− 5.4		1952–60
		79.5	Greece	− 5.4		1951–58
		81	Iraq	− 5.7		1951–58
	X	82	Syria	− 5.8		1951–58
		83	Turkey	− 6.0	VII	1951–60
		84	Iran	− 6.9		1951–60
		85	Japan	− 7.0		1951–58
		86.5	Philippines	− 7.4		1951–58
		86.5	Thailand	− 7.4		1954–60
		88	Romania	− 7.6		1954–60
		89	Albania	− 9.4	VIII, IX	1953–58
		90	Liberia	−16.6	X	1952–60

[1] Combined from Aden Colony (1951–60) and Aden Protectorate (1951–58).

Sources: U.N., *Compendium of Social Statistics, 1963* (New York, 1963); U.N., *Report on the World Social Situation* (New York, 1957).

Education

62. STUDENTS ENROLLED IN HIGHER EDUCATION PER 100,000 POPULATION

Higher education here includes universities and post-secondary professional schools, including higher teacher-training. Despite efforts to standardize definitions some incomparabilities, especially with regard to technical schools, undoubtedly still exist. Adult education, apprenticeship courses, and correspondence courses are generally excluded.[1] In a number of cases we have adjusted the published figures to remove major known incomparabilities. It is impossible to know the amount of residual error or the degree of error inherent in our adjustments, but it seems likely that the figures are usually accurate within perhaps $\pm 10\%$.

As the age range of students at this level is more flexible than at the lower level of education, we have not attempted to relate the enrollment figures to a certain age group in the population. This nevertheless introduces a further element of incomparability, if not of inaccuracy.

One further limitation on the conclusions that should be drawn from Table 62 is the problem of "wastage." Some school systems, such as those of the United Kingdom and Italy, concentrate on educating a carefully preselected student body; most of those admitted to universities graduate. But in countries like the United States and France only half, or even less, of those admitted actually earn degrees. This means that if one is interested in the output of trained individuals the enrollment rates should be deflated by quite different amounts in different countries. Where we have been able to obtain figures for degrees granted as a percentage of admissions we have given this information in parentheses after the country name.[2]

Obviously there may be immense differences in the quality of higher education, both between countries and within a single country. Higher education in some nations may be equivalent only to secondary education in others.

---

1. Cf. John Vaisey, "A Note on Comparative Statistics," in A. H. Halsey, ed., *Ability and Educational Opportunity*, Organization for Economic Cooperation and Development (n.p., 1961), p. 181, who notes that part-time education is, at least in Britain, a relatively inefficient system and partly for this reason excludes it from his tables.

2. Our source is Halsey, ed., *Ability and Educational Opportunity*, pp. 190–93. The figures are for 1957–58.

213

TABLE 62

Students Enrolled in Higher Education per 100,000 Population

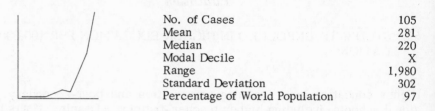

No. of Cases	105
Mean	281
Median	220
Modal Decile	X
Range	1,980
Standard Deviation	302
Percentage of World Population	97

% of Table Population	Case Deciles	Rank	Country	Enrollment per 100,000	Range Deciles	Year
	I	1	United States (45)	1,983	I–III	1960
		2	Puerto Rico	1,192	IV,V	1961
		3	Philippines[1]	976	VI	1960
		4	Netherlands (49)	923		1960
		5	Australia	856		1960
		6	New Zealand	839		1960
		7	Argentina	827		1960
		8	Japan	750	VII	1960
		9	Israel	668		1960
		10	France (38)	667		1959
	II	11	Canada (51)	645		1960
		12	Denmark	570	VIII	1960
		13	Austria (41)	546		1960
		14	Uruguay	541		1960
		15	U. S. S. R.[2]	539		1960
		16	Belgium (67)	536		1959
		17	Finland	529		1960
		18	West Germany (46)	528		1960
		19	Yugoslavia	524		1960
24.8	III	20	Malaya	475		1960
		21	United Kingdom (65)	460		1959
		22	Bulgaria	456		1959
		23	Iceland	445		1960
		24	Singapore	437		1960
		25	Sweden (32)	401		1960
		26	Egypt	399		1960
		27.5	Czechoslovakia	398	IX	1959
		27.5	Switzerland	398		1960
		29	South Korea	397		1960
		30	East Germany	395		1959
		31	Panama	371		1960
	IV	32.5	Ireland (79)	362		1959
		32.5	Italy (71)	362		1959
		34	Venezuela	355		1959
		35	Poland	351		1960
		36	Lebanon	345		1959
		37	Taiwan	329		1960
		38	Costa Rica	326		1960
		39	Greece (58)	320		1959
		40	Colombia	296		1960

TABLE 62 (continued)

% of Table Population	Case Deciles	Rank	Country	Enrollment per 100,000	Range Deciles	Year
		41	Portugal	272		1960
	V	44	Cuba	258		1960
		44	Hungary	258		1959
		44	Mexico	258		1960
		44	Norway	258		1960
		44	Spain (49)	258		1960
		47	Chile	257		1960
		48	Turkey	255		1961
		49	Peru	253		1959
		50	Thailand	251		1960
		51	Romania[2]	226		1960
		52	Syria	223		1959
55.8	VI	53	India	220		1959
		54	Ecuador	193	X	1960
		55	South Africa	189		1960
		56	Paraguay	188		1960
		57	Hong Kong	176		1959
		58	Iraq	173		1960
		59	Bolivia	166		1950
		60	Pakistan	165		1960
		61	Dominican Republic[3]	149		1957
		62	Albania	145		1959
	VII	63	Malta & Gozo	142		1960
		64	Guatemala	135		1960
		65	Brazil	132		1960
		66	Nicaragua	110		1961
		67	Surinam	109		1959
		68	Iran	90		1960
		69	El Salvador	89		1960
		70	South Vietnam	83		1960
		71.5	Cyprus	78		1958
		71.5	Honduras	78		1960
64.9	VIII	73	Algeria	70		1960
		74	China (Mainland)	69		1959
		75	Tunisia	64		1960
		76	Burma	63		1958
		77	Indonesia	62		1959
		78	Trinidad & Tobago	61		1959
		79.5	Ceylon	56		1960
		79.5	Nepal	56		1961
		81	Senegal	55		1959
		82	Libya	49		1959
		83	Jamaica	42		1959
	IX	84	Morocco	40		1960
		85	Luxembourg	36		1960
		86	Sudan	34		1960
		87.5	Haiti	29		1959
		87.5	Ghana	29		1959
		89	British Guiana	27		1960
		90	Barbados	24		1959
		91	Madagascar	21		1960

TABLE 62 (continued)

% of Table Population	Case Deciles	Rank	Country	Enrollment per 100,000	Range Deciles	Year
		92	Sierra Leone	19		1959
		93	Cambodia	18		1960
		94.5	Mauritius	14		1960
	X	94.5	Uganda	14		1960
		96	Afghanistan	12		1960
		97	Tanganyika	9		1960
		98	Saudi Arabia	6		1960
		99.5	Ethiopia	5		1960
		99.5	Kenya	5		1960
		102.5	Congo (Leopoldville)	4		1959
		102.5	Ivory Coast	4		1959
		102.5	Laos	4		1960
		102.5	Nigeria	4		1960
		105	Rhodesia & Nyasaland	3		1959

[1] Includes private non-degree-granting colleges.
[2] Adjusted to exclude estimated number of evening and correspondence students. Excludes higher teacher-training.

Sources: Nicholas DeWitt, *Education and Professional Employment in the U.S.S.R.* (Washington, D.C., 1961), pp. 231, 634; U.N., *Compendium of Social Statistics, 1963* (New York, 1963); UNESCO, *International Yearbook of Education, 1960* (Paris, 1962).

63. PRIMARY AND SECONDARY SCHOOL PUPILS AS A PERCENTAGE OF POPULATION AGED 5–19

Except where otherwise noted the data in Table 63 are believed to include both public and private schools. Enrollment figures, however, do not "always correspond to the number of pupils who really go to school. This is particularly important with regard to the primary education. In many regions where primary schools have been set up recently, and where many people have not yet attained a cultural level sufficient to make them understand the value of schooling, one may find that the actual attendance is far below enrollments, even though primary education might be obligatory according to law."[1] And of course data on school enrollments cannot accurately reflect the quality of education offered.

Another difficulty arises with the age groups chosen as the denominator in the following ratios. In few countries do the age levels of the pupils enrolled correspond exactly to the arbitrary age group 5–19.[2] Thus these figures are inadequate as measures of the proportion of children at any particular age level, such as age 10, receiving education. But they do, in a more useful way, indicate the amount of schooling received by children. A country that provides virtually all its children with only four years of education would rank quite low in the table. So would a country that provides half its children with eight years of schooling and the rest with none. This is regrettable, since the two systems may have rather different effects. Nevertheless, given the nature of the data now available it cannot be avoided, and for many purposes useful comparison is still possible.[3] Accuracy of the denominator, population aged 5–19, is subject to the same qualifications as discussed previously for working-age population.

---

1. U. N., *Statistical Papers, Series K, No. 1, Survey of Social Statistics* (New York, 1954), p. 29.
2. By combining primary and secondary education we avoid many problems of incomparability as to the distinctions actually drawn in various countries.
3. Detailed information on the school systems of each country can be found in UNESCO, *World Survey of Education* (Paris, 1958). But while this provides data on the nature of the school system and the customary or legal levels of education, it still is not sufficient. Population age-structure data are not adequate for enough countries to permit matching customary education levels with appropriate numbers of potential pupils. Even if they were, this procedure would not take account of pupils who fell short of or exceeded the customary level.

TABLE 63

Primary and Secondary School Pupils as a Percentage of
Population Aged 5–19

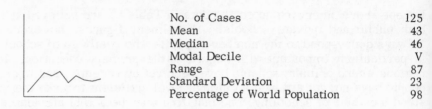

	No. of Cases	125
	Mean	43
	Median	46
	Modal Decile	V
	Range	87
	Standard Deviation	23
	Percentage of World Population	98

% of Table Population	Case Deciles	Rank	Country	Prim. & Sec. School Pupils as a % of Pop. Aged 5–19	Range Deciles	Year
	I	1	Iceland	89	I	1960
		2	Malta & Gozo	82		1960
		3	United States	81		1960
		5	Canada	80	II	1959
		5	New Zealand	80		1960
		5	United Kingdom	80		1959
		7	Australia[1]	77		1960
		8.5	France	76		1960
		8.5	Ireland	76		1959
		10.5	Japan	73		1960
		10.5	West Germany	73		1960
		12.5	Belgium	72		1959
	II	12.5	Denmark	72		1960
		14.5	Czechoslovakia	71	III	1960
		14.5	Sweden	71		1959
		17	Barbados	70		1960
		17	Finland	70		1959
		17	Norway[2]	70		1960
		19.5	Israel	69		1959
		19.5	Poland	69		1960
		21.5	British Guiana	68		1960
		21.5	Netherlands	68		1960
		24	Bulgaria	66		1960
		24	Hungary	66		1960
	III	24	Puerto Rico	66		1950
		27	Mauritius	64		1960
		27	Surinam	64		1959
		27	Trinidad & Tobago	64		1959
		29.5	Singapore	63		1960
		29.5	Yugoslavia	63		1960
		31	Cuba	61	IV	1960
		32.5	Ceylon	60		1959
		32.5	Spain	60		1960
		34.5	Austria	59		1960
		34.5	Taiwan	59		1960
		36.5	Chile	58		1960
		36.5	Romania	58		1960
22.9	IV	39.5	Argentina	57		1960

TABLE 63 (continued)

% of Table Population	Case Deciles	Rank	Country	Prim. & Sec. School Pupils as a % of Pop. Aged 5–19	Range Deciles	Year
		39.5	Netherlands Antilles	57		1950
		39.5	Switzerland[2]	57		1959
		39.5	U.S.S.R.	57		1960
		43	Albania	56		1959
		43	Costa Rica	56		1960
		43	Uruguay	56		1959
		45	Cyprus	55		1958
		46.5	East Germany	54	V	1960
		46.5	Jamaica	54		1960
		49	Greece	53		1959
		49	Lebanon	53		1960
	V	49	Panama	53		1960
		51.5	Luxembourg	52		1960
		51.5	South Korea	52		1960
		53	Venezuela	51		1959
		55	Malaya	50		1960
		55	Italy	50		1959
		55	Paraguay[1]	50		1960
		57.5	Dominican Republic	49		1960
		57.5	Hong Kong	49		1960
		59.5	Kuwait	47		1960
		59.5	Philippines	47		1960
		62	Jordan	46		1960
		62	Portugal	46		1960
	VI	62	Thailand	46		1960
39.0		64	Mexico	42	VI	1960
		65	China (Mainland)	41		1959
		66.5	Ecuador	40		1960
		66.5	Sarawak	40		1960
		68.5	Peru	39		1959
		68.5	South Africa	39		1950
		71	Brazil	38		1960
		71	El Salvador	38		1960
		71	Turkey	38		1961
		73.5	Colombia	37		1960
		73.5	Iraq	37		1960
	VII	75.5	Gabon	36	VII	1960
		75.5	Rhodesia & Nyasaland	36		1960
		77.5	Kenya	35		1960
		77.5	Libya	35		1959
		79.5	Egypt	33		1960
		79.5	Congo (Brazzaville)	33		1960
		81.5	Honduras	32		1960
		81.5	Indonesia	32		1959
		85	Cambodia[2]	31		1960
		85	Cameroun	31		1959
		85	Congo (Leopoldville)	31		1959
		85	Syria	31		1959
		85	Tunisia	31		1960

TABLE 63 (continued)

% of Table Population	Case Deciles	Rank	Country	Prim. & Sec. School Pupils as a % of Pop. Aged 5–19	Range Deciles	Year
73.9	VIII	88	Bolivia	30		1960
		89	India	29		1959
		90	Ghana	28	VIII	1959
		91	Burma	27		1958
		92	Madagascar	26		1960
		94	Guatemala	25		1960
		94	Nicaragua	25		1960
		94	Nigeria	25		1960
		96.5	Iran	24		1960
		96.5	South West Africa	24		1950
		98	Algeria	23		1960
		99.5	Haiti	21		1959
	IX	99.5	Morocco	21		1960
		101	Pakistan	20		1960
		102.5	Ivory Coast	19	IX	1959
		102.5	Mozambique	19		1959
		104	Ruanda-Urundi	17		1960
		106	Central African Republic	16		1960
		106	Laos	16		1960
		106	Togo	16		1960
		108.5	Tanganyika	14		1960
		108.5	Uganda	14		1960
		110.5	Dahomey	13		1960
		110.5	Senegal	13		1959
		112	Liberia	12		1959
	X	113.5	Guinea	10	X	1960
		113.5	Sierra Leone	10		1959
		115	Sudan	9		1960
		116	Angola	7		1959
		117	Chad	6		1960
		119	Mauritania	5		1960
		119	Saudi Arabia	5		1960
		119	Upper Volta	5		1960
		122	Afghanistan	4		1960
		122	Mali	4		1959
		122	Somalia	4		1960
		124.5	Ethiopia	2		1960
		124.5	Niger	2		1959

[1] Excludes vocational training.
[2] Public schools only.

Sources: John S. Aird, *The Size, Composition, and Growth of the Population of Communist China* (Washington, D.C., 1961), p. 82; Leo A. Orleans, *Professional Manpower and Education in Communist China* (Washington, D.C., 1961); U.N., *Compendium of Social Statistics, 1963* (New York, 1963).

Comparability is affected by at least five factors[1]:

1. Classification of persons of unknown literacy. In most cases persons of unknown literacy were classified by the data-gathering nation as literate. Obviously this is not always accurate.

2. Semi-literates. "Literate" individuals are supposed to be only those who can both read *and* write. In a few cases, however, it is known that individuals who could *either* read or write were included.

3. Language of literacy. In most cases ability to read and write any language signifies literacy; in a few a particular language or languages were specified.

4. The degree of literacy. The ability to read and write a simple message is supposed to be the criterion, but obviously the stringency with which the test is applied will vary.

5. Minimum age. In most of the following instances data were given as the percentage literate of those 15 and over, but a few countries either gave a lower minimum age or none at all. When this is the case literacy is likely to appear higher because primary school pupils, excluded in other countries, are here included. We have attempted to correct the literacy figure to what it might be for the 15 and over age group, but the effort can give only an approximation.

The first two factors are likely to produce an overestimate of literacy in some countries, the third an underestimate, and the fourth and fifth, as corrected, should be without systematic bias. The effect varies greatly with the overall level of literacy. Literacy percentages at the high end of the scale (95%) should be accurate within an error margin of less than 5%; it would not be surprising if a few of those at the lower end of the scale were off by as much as 50%.

Our second table on literacy, Table 65, lists average annual changes. These data are based exclusively on census or sample survey data, rather than mere estimates. For this reason, and because repeated national censuses, even if biased, are likely to retain the same bias, the error margins for the changes should be narrower than those in the longer series for literacy at a single point in time. Again the change is calculated simply as the percentage literate in the later year, minus the percentage in the early year, divided by the number of years elapsed.

Literacy is, without question, a basic element in a country's capability for economic development. It is a prerequisite to learning virtually any modern technical skill. But though it may be essential to economic change, it may also be a potent force in social change and the building of social tensions. Men who are literate but disaffected may have the means for political protest, not always of a peaceful sort. Literacy may help to create a feeling of national identity or it may provide the means for underlying conflicts to make themselves felt. Finally, literacy may also serve as a means for a government to mobilize and control a population.

---

1. See UNESCO, *Manual of Educational Statistics* (Paris, 1961), ch. 3, for a discussion.

TABLE 64

Percentage Literate of Population Aged 15 and Over

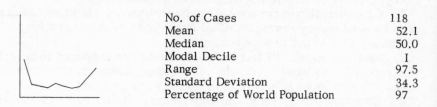

		No. of Cases	118
		Mean	52.1
		Median	50.0
		Modal Decile	I
		Range	97.5
		Standard Deviation	34.3
		Percentage of World Population	97

% of Table Population	Case Deciles	Rank	Country	% of Pop. Literate	Range Deciles	Year
	I	7.5	Australia	98.5	I	1950
		7.5	Austria	98.5		1950
		7.5	Denmark	98.5		1950
		7.5	East Germany	98.5		1950
		7.5	Finland	98.5		1950
		7.5	Iceland	98.5		1950
		7.5	Ireland	98.5		1950
		7.5	Netherlands	98.5		1950
		7.5	New Zealand	98.5		1950
		7.5	Norway	98.5		1950
		7.5	Sweden	98.5		1950
	II	7.5	Switzerland	98.5		1950
		7.5	United Kingdom	98.5		1950
		7.5	West Germany	98.5		1950
		15.5	Japan[1]	98.0		1960
		15.5	United States	98.0		1959
		17.5	Canada	97.5		1950
		17.5	Czechoslovakia	97.5		1950
		19	Hungary	97.0		1960
		20	Belgium	96.7		1947
		21	Luxembourg	96.5		1950
		22	France	96.4		1946
		23.5	Poland	95.0		1960
26.8	III	23.5	U. S. S. R.[2]	95.0		1959
		25	Israel[3]	93.7		1948
		26	Barbados	91.1		1946
		27	Romania	89.0		1956
		28	Italy	87.5	II	1950
		29	Spain	87.0		1960
		30	Argentina	86.4		1947
		31	Bulgaria	85.0		1956
		32	Puerto Rico	81.0		1960
		33	Uruguay	80.9		1950
		34	Chile	80.1		1952
		35	Greece	80.0		1961
	IV	36	Costa Rica	79.4		1950
		37	Cuba	77.5	III	1950
		39	Jamaica	77.0		1953
		39	South Korea	77.0		1955
		39	Yugoslavia	77.0		1961

TABLE 64 (continued)

% of Table Population	Case Deciles	Rank	Country	% of Pop. Literate	Range Deciles	Year
		41	Philippines	75.0		1958
		42	British Guiana	74.0		1946
		43	Trinidad & Tobago	73.8		1946
		44	Surinam	72.5		1950
		45	Thailand	68.0	IV	1960
		46	Paraguay	65.8		1950
		47	Panama[4]	65.7		1950
	V	48	Ceylon	63.0		1946
		49	Colombia	62.0		1951
		50	Cyprus	60.5		1946
		51	Albania[5]	60.0		1955
		52	Dominican Republic	59.9		1956
		53	Malta & Gozo	57.6	V	1948
		54.5	Hong Kong	57.5		1950
		54.5	Mongolian People's Republic	57.5		1950
		56	Portugal	55.9		1950
		57	Ecuador	55.7		1950
		58	Taiwan[6]	54.0		1956
		59	Venezuela	52.2		1950
		60	Mauritius	51.8		1952
	VI	61.5	Mexico[7]	50.0		1950
		61.5	Singapore	50.0		1957
41.8		63	Brazil	49.4	VI	1950
		65.5	Burma	47.5		1950
		65.5	China (Mainland)	47.5		1950
		65.5	Lebanon	47.5		1950
		65.5	Peru	47.5		1950
		68	Honduras[1]	44.0		1960
		69	South Africa	42.5		1950
		70	El Salvador	39.4	VII	1950
		71	Turkey	39.0		1955
	VII	72.5	Malaya	38.4		1947
		72.5	Nicaragua	38.4		1950
		74	Congo (Leopoldville)	37.5		1950
		75	Madagascar	33.5		1953
		76	Bolivia	32.1		1950
		77	Kuwait[8]	30.0	VIII	1957
		78	Guatemala	29.4		1950
		79.5	Syria	27.5		1950
		79.5	Uganda[1]	27.5		1959
		82	Ghana	22.5		1950
		82	Kenya	22.5		1950
		82	South West Africa	22.5		1950
	VIII	84	Sarawak	21.0		1960
71.1		85	Egypt	19.9	IX	1947
		86	India	19.3		1951
		87	Algeria	19.0		1954
		90.5	Cambodia	17.5		1950
		90.5	Indonesia	17.5		1950
		90.5	Jordan	17.5		1950
		90.5	Laos	17.5		1950

TABLE 64 (continued)

% of Table Population	Case Deciles	Rank	Country	% of Pop. Literate	Range Deciles	Year
		90.5	Tunisia	17.5		1950
		90.5	Vietnam	17.5		1950
		94	Rhodesia & Nyasaland	16.1		1950
		95	Iran	15.0		1956
	IX	96.5	Libya	13.0		1954
		96.5	Pakistan[8]	13.0		1951
		98	Morocco	12.5		1950
		99	Haiti	10.5	X	1950
		100.5	Iraq[9]	10.0		1947
		100.5	Nigeria[6]	10.0		1952
		102	Sudan[9]	9.0		1956
		105	Liberia	7.5		1950
		105	Ruanda-Urundi	7.5		1950
		105	Sierra Leone	7.5		1950
		105	Tanganyika	7.5		1950
		105	Togo	7.5		1950
	X	108	French Cameroons	7.0		1952
		109.5	Aden	5.0		1950
		109.5	Nepal	5.0		1953
		114	Afghanistan	2.5		1950
		114	Angola	2.5		1950
		114	Ethiopia	2.5		1950
		114	French Equatorial Africa	2.5		1950
		114	French West Africa	2.5		1950
		114	Saudi Arabia	2.5		1950
		114	Yemen	2.5		1950
		118	Mozambique	1.0		1950

[1] Illiteracy defined as "never attended school."
[2] Adjusted from population aged 9–49.
[3] Jewish population only.
[4] Adjusted to include tribal Indians.
[5] Adjusted from population aged 9 and over.
[6] Adjusted from population aged 7 and over.
[7] Adjusted from population aged 6 and over.
[8] Adjusted from population of all ages.
[9] Adjusted from population aged 5 and over.

Sources: U. N., *Compendium of Social Statistics, 1963* (New York, 1963); U. N., *Report on the World Social Situation* (New York, 1959); UNESCO, *Basic Facts and Figures, 1959* (Paris, 1960).

TABLE 65

Percentage Literate of Population Aged 15 and Over—
Average Annual Increase

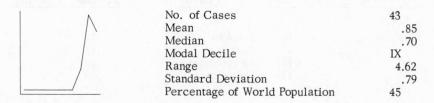

No. of Cases	43
Mean	.85
Median	.70
Modal Decile	IX
Range	4.62
Standard Deviation	.79
Percentage of World Population	45

% of Table Population	Case Deciles	Rank	Country	% Av. Ann. Increase	Range Deciles	Years
	I	1	Albania	4.71	I–III	1945–55
		2	Mauritius	3.01	IV–VI	1944–52
		3	Dominican Republic[1]	1.67	VII	1935–56
		4	U. S. S. R.[2]	1.46	VIII	1926–59
	II	5	Philippines	1.42		1948–58
		6	Romania[3]	1.30		1930–56
		7.5	Panama[4]	1.23		1940–50
		7.5	Thailand	1.23		1947–60
	III	9	British Guiana[5]	1.12		1921–46
		11	Cyprus	1.00	IX	1921–46
		11	Trinidad & Tobago[6]	1.00		1921–46
		11	Venezuela	1.00		1936–50
	IV	13	Turkey	.98		1935–55
25.0		14	Finland	.95		1920–50
		15	Bulgaria	.93		1934–56
		16	Malaya	.87		1947–57
		17	Puerto Rico	.78		1935–60
	V	18	Yugoslavia	.75		1931–61
		19	Spain	.73		1920–60
		20	Greece	.72		1928–61
		21	Portugal	.71		1920–50
	VI	22	Poland	.70		1931–60
		23.5	Ceylon	.67		1946–53
		23.5	El Salvador	.67		1930–50
		25	Mexico[7]	.65		1930–50
	VII	26.5	Guatemala[1]	.59		1921–50
		26.5	Jamaica[8]	.59		1921–53
		28	Costa Rica	.57		1927–50
		29	Chile	.53	X	1920–52
		30	Italy	.51		1931–51
	VIII	31	Brazil	.48		1920–50
		32	Colombia	.47		1938–51
50.0		33	Egypt	.46		1927–47
		34	Singapore	.41		1947–57
	IX	35	Honduras[9]	.37		1930–61
		36.5	Cuba	.27		1931–53
83.2		36.5	India	.27		1921–51
		38	Hungary	.26		1920–60
	X	39	Algeria	.20		1948–54

TABLE 65 (continued)

% of Table Population	Case Deciles	Rank	Country	% Av. Ann. Increase	Range Deciles	Years
		40	Belgium	.17		1920–47
		41	Canada	.11		1921–50
		42	Mozambique	.10		1940–50
		43	United States	.09		1930–59

[1] Data for early year adjusted from population aged 9 and over.
[2] Data for 1959 adjusted from population aged 9–49.
[3] Data for 1930 adjusted from population aged 13 and over.
[4] Adjusted to include Indian jungle population.
[5] Data for 1921 adjusted from population aged 5 and over.
[6] Data for 1921 adjusted from population of all ages.
[7] Data for 1930 adjusted from population aged 10 and over; data for 1950 adjusted from population aged 6 and over.
[8] Data for 1961 adjusted from population aged 10 and over.
[9] Data for 1921 adjusted from population aged 10 and over.

Sources: U. N., *Compendium of Social Statistics, 1963* (New York, 1963); U. N., *Demographic Yearbook, 1960* (New York, 1961); U. N., *Report on the World Social Situation* (New York, 1957).

Family and Social Relations

66. MARRIAGES PER 1,000 POPULATION AGED 15–44

There are substantial differences in the kinds of unions recognized as marriages in various countries. The formal definition used by the United Nations is "the legal union of persons of opposite sex. The legality of the union may be established by civil, religious, or other means as recognized by the laws of each country. Marriage statistics, therefore, include both first marriages and remarriages after divorce, widowhood, or annulment."[1]

Incomparabilities result in part from the difference between civil and religious marriages. Both are included wherever possible, but in some countries the only statistics compiled are for civil marriages, though religious marriages may be recognized. In other countries the only records available are church registers.

It is difficult properly to define "completeness," since in many countries the act of legalizing a marriage *is* the process of registration. In other countries, however, religious ceremonies may be recognized as legal even though they are never registered. Where this is the case and the United Nations regards the figures as less than 90% complete we have generally not recorded any figure. In one case, however, an estimate of the degree of completeness was available, and we adjusted the registered total accordingly.

The other problem of comparability arises from unions which are not legally recognized, but nevertheless are recognized as marriages by the local mores. These include marriages according to tribal or customary rites, and so-called "consensual marriages." No reliable data on tribal or customary rites are usually available, and in these cases a true element of incomparability is introduced. The problem is less serious, however, with consensual marriages. If what we are attempting to measure is the frequency of formal, permanent (in principle, at least) marriages, consensual marriages do not, in most cases, fit the definition. In many parts of Latin America, for example, the frequency of consensual marriages is very high, as is the frequency with which these unions are broken.

The problem of finding a suitable denominator for computing rates is not an easy one. One solution, the crude marriage rate, is simply the number of marriages in a year per 1,000 population. This, however, takes no account of differences in the age structure of various countries—one would expect a higher crude marriage rate in countries with relatively young populations (high birth rates, recently lowered death rates). The United Nations *Demographic Yearbook* has attempted to solve the problem by computing marriage rates per 1,000 "marriageable" people.[2] This solution is

---

1. U.N., *Demographic Yearbook, 1959* (New York, 1960), p. 17.
2. Ibid., Table 17.

made unsatisfactory by differences in national treatment of marriageable
population. In a ratio with broad uses for social comparison, consensually
married individuals should be included in the marriageable population. If
they are not, the marriageable population will appear lower, and the marriage rate thus will appear higher than otherwise. In some countries this
makes little difference; in a few states of Central America and the Ca-
ribbean where we have data it makes a difference of 50% or more in the
rate. Unfortunately only about 20% of the countries reporting data are
known to include consensually married couples in the marriageable population. The alternative, to exclude them in every case, is to hide the very
information we seek.

The solution chosen here has been to compute the number of marriages
per 1,000 people of "marriageable age," regardless of their marital status.
Marriageable age has been rather arbitrarily defined as 15–44. A few
marriages occur at earlier ages, quite a number at later ages. Yet for
those countries for which we have age-specific marriage rates, about 90%
of all marriages are entered into by individuals in the 15–44 bracket. Use
of this group as the denominator, then, provides a reasonably satisfactory
means of controlling for different age structures in various populations.
Most of the cross-national variation remaining can thus be traced to social
variables, though incompleteness of registration, errors in the total population estimate, and, of course, errors in estimating the age structure of
populations, cannot be disregarded. In Table 66, however, we are dealing
with countries whose population data are relatively accurate, so most
error, excluding marriage registration error, should be within a margin
of ±5%. Registration error should not exceed 10%, in virtually all cases
on the side of under-reporting.

Marriage rates may not seem directly relevant to politics, but they reflect important social characteristics. It is often asserted that the very
impermanence of family formation in some states of Latin America contributes to the high birth rate. Where marriage is rare but consensual or
casual relationships common, there may be little incentive to limit family
size. And the upbringing of children born to such unions will usually be
fundamentally different from that of children in stable families. Of course
mere knowledge that the marriage rate is low does not itself provide all
the information needed. As will be seen from Table 66 Latin American
marriage rates are generally low, but Ireland's is lower than that of several South and Central American states. Neither the causes nor the consequences are the same. Ireland and Latin America are at opposite ends
of the birth rate table.

TABLE 66

Marriages per 1,000 Population Aged 15–44

No. of Cases	50
Mean	174.16
Median	18.05
Modal Decile	V
Range	18.5
Standard Deviation	37.09
Percentage of World Population	33

% of Table Population	Case Deciles	Rank	Country	Marriages per 1,000 Pop. 15–44	Range Deciles	Years
	I	1	U. S. S. R.	26.6	I	1959–60
22.9		2	Romania	23.1	II	1959–60
		3	West Germany	22.6	III	1959–60
		4	Jordan (E)	22.5		1959–60
		5	Puerto Rico	22.0		1959–60
	II	6	Hungary	21.8		1959–60
		7	United States	21.5		1959–60
		8	Austria	20.6	IV	1959–60
49.9		9	Yugoslavia	20.5		1959–60
		10.5	New Zealand	20.2		1959–60
	III	10.5	Taiwan	20.2		1959–60
		12	Poland	20.1		1959–60
		14	Bulgaria	19.4		1959–60
		14	Czechoslovakia	19.4		1959–60
		14	Japan	19.4		1959–60
	IV	16.5	Iceland	19.2		1959–60
		16.5	Israel	19.2		1959–60
		18	Netherlands	19.1	V	1959–60
		19	United Kingdom	18.9		1959–60
		20	Denmark	18.7		1959–60
	V	21	Costa Rica	18.5		1959–60
		22.5	Switzerland	18.4		1959–60
73.4		22.5	Belgium	18.4		1959–60
		24	France	18.2		1959–60
		25	Portugal	18.1		1959–60
	VI	26	Canada	18.0		1959–60
		27.5	Australia	17.8		1959–60
		27.5	Italy	17.8		1959–60
		29	Finland	17.6		1959–60
		30	Trinidad & Tobago	17.0	VI	1959–60
	VII	31	Luxembourg	16.9		1959–60
		33	Cyprus	16.6		1959–60
		33	Norway	16.6		1959–60
		33	Spain	16.6		1959–60
		35	Sweden	16.5		1959–60
	VIII	36	Chile	16.1		1959–60
		37	Mexico	15.6		1959–60
		38	Malta & Gozo	15.3	VII	1959–60
		39	Argentina	14.7		1959–60

TABLE 66 (continued)

% of Table Population	Case Deciles	Rank	Country	Marriages per 1,000 Pop. 15–44	Range Deciles	Years
		40	Netherlands Antilles	14.3		1959–60
	IX	41	Ireland	14.1		1959–60
		42	Jamaica	12.8	VIII	1959–60
		43	Mauritius	12.5		1959–60
		44	Guatemala	10.9	IX	1959–60
		45.5	Barbados	10.6		1959–60
	X	45.5	Peru	10.6		1959–60
		47	Dominican Republic	9.6	X	1958–59
		48	British Guiana	9.3		1959–60
		49	Honduras[1]	8.7		1958,60
		50	El Salvador[1]	8.1		1958,60

[1] 1959 data not representative because of special missionary campaign to register consensual marriages.

Sources: U. N., *Demographic Yearbook, 1961* (New York, 1962); *1960* (New York, 1961); U. S., Department of Commerce, *Statistical Abstract of the United States, 1962* (Washington, D. C., 1962), p. 70. For sources of age breakdowns see Table 2.

Long-term immigrants are defined as those admitted for a stay of more than one year. In most cases short-term immigrants (one year or less), visitors in transit, excursionists (less than 24 hours), and cruise-ship visitors are excluded. Exceptions, where known, are noted.

Original sources of the data include frontier control, port statistics, and population registers. These differences introduce some problems of comparability. Two other problems affect reliability. The definitions of long-term immigration and emigration are based on intentions expressed by the travelers, who may later change their plans. Also, virtually all clandestine migration is unaccounted for in these tables.

There is no way of determining satisfactorily the degree of error involved. A general impression may be gained by comparing, where available, data on emigration by country of intended residence with data on immigration by country of last permanent residence. The difference between the two figures for any given pair of countries provides a rough measure of incomparability. Some sources of difference do not, of course, affect comparability—these sources include persons changing their destinations en route, births and deaths en route, and arrivals at the beginning of the calendar year.[1] Nevertheless these sources can account for only a small portion of the differences, often of the magnitude of ±50%, observed between the data for paired countries. Very roughly, then, national statistics on long-term migration should not be considered comparable within an error margin of less than ±50%. The failure in some instances to differentiate between long- and short-term visitors makes comparison still more difficult.

Migration data may identify various kinds of social tensions. High emigration rates usually indicate serious political or economic dissatisfactions.[2] Historically the emigrant's primary motive has probably been the desire to improve his material standard of living. Occasionally the main force is a pull from some prosperous country, but most often the pull is coupled with a push—serious economic deprivations in the home country. Not infrequently emigration also results from political or religious persecution, creating another kind of discontent.

But of course the absence of high emigration cannot be taken as itself an indication of an absence of discontent. Large-scale emigration implies a population with access to basic information about the external world and its attractions. It implies that there is a potential host country where many immigrants will be accepted. European migrants have an immensely easier task in finding a new home than do migrants from Asia or Africa. And naturally a very low rate of emigration may simply reflect the fact that the government does not permit emigration, or that evidencing any interest in emigration may be taken as proof of disloyalty.

---

1. U.N., *Demographic Yearbook, 1959* (New York, 1960), pp. 29–32.
2. Sometimes, however, high emigration may merely indicate the returnees from an even higher rate of immigration. See Israel in the following tables.

Immigration rates tell something about the potential stress resulting from the influx of great numbers of people. These stresses may apply both to the incoming peoples and to the society to which they are to be assimilated. The degree to which tension results depends upon the characteristics of the immigrants, the culture to which they come, and the kinds of opportunities they find. Gross immigration totals cannot provide this information, though they can at least identify potential tension points. Further examination would require country of origin and destination matrices and data on the educational, occupational, and other characteristics of the migrants.[3]

---

3. Some of these data are available, but not for many countries. Cf. U. N., *Demographic Yearbook, 1959* (New York, 1960). Table 35, for some country of origin and destination data, and U. N., *Economic Characteristics of International Migrants: Statistics for Selected Countries, 1918-1954* (New York, 1958), for data on occupation and status.

TABLE 67

Immigrants per 1,000 Population

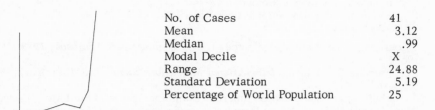

	No. of Cases	41
	Mean	3.12
	Median	.99
	Modal Decile	X
	Range	24.88
	Standard Deviation	5.19
	Percentage of World Population	25

% of Table Population	Case Deciles	Rank	Country	Immig. per 1,000 Pop.	Range Deciles	Years (Ann. Avg.)
	I	1	Israel	24.89	I, II	1957–58
		2	Venezuela	17.56[a]	III–V	1952–56
		3	Canada	12.17[b]	VI, VII	1957–58
		4	Australia	11.74		1957–58
	II	5	New Zealand	11.44		1957–58
		6	Belgium	6.43	VIII	1957–58
		7	Denmark	5.01		1957–58
		8	Netherlands	4.04	IX	1957–58
	III	9	Malta & Gozo[1]	4.02		1957–58
		10	Poland	3.20		1957–58
		11	Uruguay	3.04		1955–56
		12	Cyprus	2.95		1957–58
	IV	13	Trinidad & Tobago	2.59		1957–58
		14	Rhodesia & Nyasaland	2.18	X	1958
36.4		15	United States	1.68[c]		1957–58
		16	France	1.59[a]		1955–58
	V	17	United Kingdom	1.47[d]		1946–57
		18	Dominican Republic	1.27		1958
		19	Jamaica[2]	1.19		1957–58
50.0		20	Paraguay	1.13		1957–58
	VI	21	Argentina[3]	.99		1958
		22	Turkey[4]	.98		1957–58
		23	Brazil	.84		1957–58
		24	Morocco	.62		1957–58
	VII	25	Italy	.55[d]		1946–57
73.7		26	Panama[4]	.54		1957–58
		27.5	Sarawak	.48		1957–58
		27.5	Spain	.48[d]		1946–57
	VIII	29	Portugal	.42[d]		1946–57
		30	Colombia	.37		1957–58
		31	Ireland	.34[d]		1946–57
		32	Sweden	.28[d]		1946–57
	IX	33	Mauritius	.23		1957–58
		34.5	Austria[4]	.18		1957–58
		34.5	Yugoslavia	.18		1957–58
		36.5	Finland	.16		1957–58
	X	36.5	Mexico[4]	.16		1957–58
		38	Nigeria	.15		1957–58
		39	Czechoslovakia	.12		1957–58
		40	Haiti	.11[e]		1958
		41	Bulgaria	.01		1957–58

TABLE 67 (continued)

[1] Returning emigrants only.   Immigration not permitted.
[2] Intended stay over six months.
[3] Aliens immigrating for the first time.
[4] Aliens only.

Sources: Unless otherwise noted, U. N., *Demographic Yearbook, 1959* (New York, 1960).

[a] Anthony Bouscaren, *International Migrations Since 1945* (New York, 1963), pp. 80, 151.

[b] Ministry of Trade and Commerce, Dominion Bureau of Statistics, Canada Yearbook, Handbook and Library Division, *Canada Year Book 1962* (Ottawa, 1962), p. 163.

[c] U. S. Department of Commerce, Bureau of the Census, *Statistical Abstract of the United States, 1961* (Washington, D. C., 1961), p. 97.

[d] I. L. O., *International Migration, 1945–1957* (Geneva, 1959), p. 169.

[e] Institut Haitien de Statistique, Departement de la Coordination et de l'Information, Republique d'Haiti, *Bulletin Trimestriel de Statistique,* Nos. 30, 31, 32, March 1959 (Port-au-Prince, 1959), p. 152.

TABLE 68

Emigrants per 1,000 Population

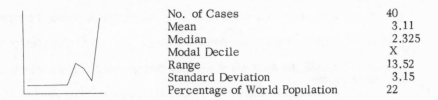

		No. of Cases	40
		Mean	3.11
		Median	2.325
		Modal Decile	X
		Range	13.52
		Standard Deviation	3.15
		Percentage of World Population	22

% of Table Population	Case Deciles	Rank	Country	Emig. per 1,000 Pop.	Range Deciles	Years (Ann. Avg.)
	I	1	Barbados	13.53	I,II	1957–58
		2	Ireland	13.40[a]		1951–56
		3	Malta & Gozo	10.05	III–V	1957–58
		4	Cyprus	9.60		1958
	II	5	Denmark	6.65	VI	1957–58
		6	Israel	5.88		1957–58
		7	Poland	5.08	VII	1957–58
		8	Morocco	4.63		1957–58
	III	9	Italy	4.47[b]		1956–57
		10	Australia	4.42		1957–58
		11	Netherlands	4.29		1957–58
		12	Belgium	4.26		1957–58
	IV	13	New Zealand	4.14		1957–58
		14	Portugal	3.88	VIII	1957–58
		15	Taiwan[1]	3.80		1957–58
23.2		16	Greece	3.38		1957–58
	V	17	United Kingdom	3.03[c]		1946–57
		18	Yugoslavia	2.73		1957–58
		19	Canada[2]	2.72[d]		1957–58
		20	Trinidad & Tobago	2.33	IX	1957–58
	VI	21	West Germany	2.32		1946–55
		22	Spain	1.68[e]		1946–47
50.2		23	Finland	1.24	X	1957–58
		24	Norway	.95[b]		1946–55
	VII	25	Switzerland	.87[b]		1946–55
		26	Colombia	.84		1957–58
		27	Kenya	.75		1957–58
		28	South Africa	.69		1957–58
	VIII	29	Sweden	.64[c]		1946–57
		30	Sarawak	.54		1957–58
		31	Austria	.35		1957–58
		32	Mauritius	.23		1957–58
	IX	33	Uganda	.22		1958
		34.5	Czechoslovakia	.16		1957–58
64.3		34.5	Tanganyika	.16		1957–58
		36	United States	.14[e]		1956–57
	X	37	South West Africa	.12		1956–57
		38.5	Bulgaria	.03		1957–58
		38.5	Ceylon	.03		1957–58
		40	Nigeria	.01		1956–57

TABLE 68 (continued)

[1] Including some short-term departures.
[2] Emigrants to United States only.

Sources: Unless otherwise noted, U. N., *Demographic Yearbook, 1961* (New York, 1962).

[a] Central Statistics Office, *Statistical Abstract of Ireland, 1960* (Dublin, 1960), p. 17.

[b] Paul A. Ladame, *Le Role des Migrations dans le Monde Libre* (Geneva and Paris, 1958), pp. 453, 466.

[c] I. L. O., *International Migration, 1945–1957* (Geneva, 1959), p. 169.

[d] Ministry of Trade and Commerce, Dominion Bureau of Statistics, Canada Year-book, Handbook and Library Division, *Canada Year Book 1962* (Ottawa, 1962), p. 163.

[e] U. S. Department of Commerce, Bureau of the Census, *Statistical Abstract of the United States, 1958* (Washington, D. C., 1958), p. 95.

69-70. LAND DISTRIBUTION

With a few exceptions, noted in each case, the data in Tables 69 and 70 refer to landholdings, any part of which is used for agriculture. Thus no distinction is made with regard to the portion of the holdings which is not arable, or pasture land only, or actually cultivated. Also, in a few cases the available data did not refer to the smallest holdings—usually holdings under one hectare in size. Such instances are noted. The indices calculated are likely in such cases to underestimate slightly the degree of inequality. In two instances (communist countries), allowance could not be made for farmers and acreage in state farms or collectives. Because in these cases most farmers still operate privately owned farms the omission did not seem serious, though it may slightly exaggerate the *inequality*. A few other countries, where cooperative holdings were more widespread, were excluded from the table because the omission of cooperatives seemed likely to have a serious biasing effect. With these exceptions the data seem accurate and comparable within a very narrow range. Because of the lack of distinction among different qualities of land they must nevertheless be compared with caution.

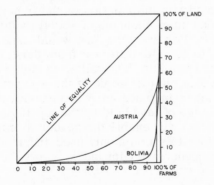

Figure A.4 Lorenz Curves of Land Distribution: Austria and Bolivia

The measure of inequality used is the Gini index of concentration, derived as follows. We begin with a Lorenz curve (Figure A.4) drawn by connecting the points given in a cumulative distribution, e.g. the proportion of land held by each decile of farmers. All farms are ranked in order from the smallest to the largest, so that one can say what proportion of the total *number* of farms accounts for a given proportion of the total *area* of agricultural land. In Figure A.4 the cumulated percentage of farms is given along the horizontal axis, and the cumulated percentage of the area along the vertical axis. The 45° line represents the condition of perfect equality, in which each percentile of farmers would make an equal contribution to the cumulated total of agricultural land. Thus, under complete equality, each 10 per cent of the population would have exactly 10 per cent of the land; any two-thirds of the population would have exactly two-thirds of the land. How far in fact the curve for a particular distribution departs from the "line of equality" gives us a visual measure of the inequality involved.

The Lorenz curve provides an extremely useful way of showing the complete pattern of a distribution, but it is impractical to try to compare whole Lorenz curves for any substantial number of countries. But if we measure the *area* between the cumulated distribution and the line of equality we have the Gini index, a simple summary measure of the total inequality of a distribution.[1] The Gini index calculates over the whole population the difference between an "ideal" cumulative distribution of land (where all farms are the same size) and the actual distribution. The higher the Gini index the greater the inequality.

Table 70 lists farm households which rent all their land as a percentage of the total number of farms. The relevance of these two series to theories of stable or democratic politics should be obvious. A large and prosperous middle class has long been considered by many theorists to be essential to the development of democracy or, in the long run, stability. Similarly, a "sturdy yeomanry" composed of prosperous farmers who own their own land has been thought to be a major source of opposition to violent change. Various countries' programs of land reform have been built on these premises. Some of these theories are too simplistic; at the very least they must be supplemented with information on the importance of agriculture in the economy, various other channels of social mobility, the overall wealth of the society, etc.[2] For example, one would expect the consequences of inequality in Egypt to be quite different from those in Austria, even though the Gini indices are identical. The following data can be used, in conjunction with earlier tables, to test some of these hypotheses.

In Table 69 we have included in parentheses, after the name of each country, the percentage of land held by the top 10% of all landowners. The inclusion of this datum will enable the reader to compare, for each country, the results from this commonly used index of inequality with those from the more comprehensive Gini index.

----

1. The Gini number for a Lorenz curve is actually twice the area mentioned divided by the area (10,000 for 100 by 100 axes) of the whole square. Formula:

$$G = \frac{2 \int_0^{100} (x - f(x))\ dx}{10,000}$$

where x is the cumulated population percentage and f(x) is the height of the Lorenz curve. Cf. Mary Jean Bowman, "A Graphical Analysis of Personal Income Distribution in the United States," *American Economic Review, 35* (September 1945), 607–28.

2. Cf. Bruce M. Russett, "Inequality and Instability: The Relation of Land Tenure to Politics," *World Politics, 16* (April 1964), 442–54.

TABLE 69

Distribution of Agricultural Land: Gini Index of Inequality

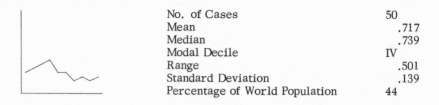

No. of Cases	50
Mean	.717
Median	.739
Modal Decile	IV
Range	.501
Standard Deviation	.139
Percentage of World Population	44

% of Table Population	Case Deciles	Rank	Country	Index of Inequality	Range Deciles	Year
	I	1.5	Bolivia (97)	.938[a]	I	1950
		1.5	Chile (92)	.938[b]		1936
		3	Australia (89)[1]	.929[c]		1948
		4	Venezuela	.909[d]		1956
		5	Costa Rica (82)	.892[a]		1950
	II	6	Iraq (83)	.881	II	1958
		7	Peru (87)	.875[e]		1950
		8	Ecuador (83)	.864[a]		1954
		9	Argentina (81)	.863[f]		1952
		10	Guatemala (85)	.860[a]		1950
	III	11	Colombia (80)	.849[a]		1954
		12	Brazil (79)	.837[a]	III	1950
		13	El Salvador (80)	.828[f]		1950
		14	Jamaica (82)	.820[g]		1943
		15	Uruguay (78)[2]	.817[a]		1950
	IV	16	Italy (76)	.803[c]		1946
		17	Dominican Republic (75)	.795[a]		1950
		18	Cuba (74)	.792[h]		1945
		19	Spain (79)	.780[i]	IV	1929
		20	New Zealand (71)	.773[c]		1949
	V	21.5	Honduras (70)	.757[a]		1952
		21.5	Nicaragua (67)[3]	.757[a]		1950
		23	Greece (76)	.747[j]		1930
		24.5	Austria (68)	.740		1951
		24.5	Egypt (73)	.740[c]		1949
	VI	26	Puerto Rico (70)	.738		1959
		27	Panama (62)	.737	V	1961
29.4		28	United Kingdom (62)	.710		1950
		29	Surinam (69)	.709[g]		1959
		30	United States (63)	.705		1950
	VII	31	Libya (54)	.700		1960
		32	West Germany	.674[k]	VI	1949
		33	South Vietnam (68)	.671[l]		1935
		34	Norway (49)[1]	.669		1959
		35	Taiwan (62)	.652[m]		1930
	VIII	36	Luxembourg (46)	.638		1950
		37	Netherlands (42)[4]	.605[k]	VII	1950
		38	Finland (48)[5]	.599[c]		1950
		39	Ireland (46)	.598		1960
		40	Belgium (46)	.587	VIII	1959

TABLE 69 (continued)

% of Table Population	Case Deciles	Rank	Country	Index of Inequality	Range Deciles	Year
	IX	41	France (50)	.583[n]		1948
49.3		42	Sweden (48)[6]	.577[c]		1944
		43	Philippines (50)	.564	IX	1948
		44	India (48)	.522[o]		1955
81.9		45	Switzerland (34)[7]	.498[c]		1939
	X	46	Canada (40)	.497[p]		1931
		47	Japan (37)	.470	X	1960
		48	Denmark (36)	.458		1959
		49	Poland (32)[8]	.450		1960
		50	Yugoslavia (34)[8]	.437[c]		1950

[1] Excludes holdings under 1 acre (.4 hectares). Not serious. 11.8% of all holdings are in 1–19.9 acre group, but the mean holding is 9 acres.

[2] Excludes holdings under 1 hectare. Probably not serious. Mean size of plot in 1–5 hectare group is 2.7 hectares. Only 13% of all holdings are in this group.

[3] Excludes holdings under .7 hectares. May be serious. Mean size of plot in .7–3.5 hectare group is 1.8 hectares, and 20% of all holdings are in this group.

[4] *Agricultural* area of holdings only.

[5] *Arable* area of holdings only.

[6] Excludes holdings under .26 hectares. Probably not serious. Mean size of plot in .26–2 hectare group is 1.25 hectares, though 28.5% of all holdings are in this group. *Arable* area of holdings only.

[7] *Cultivated* area of holdings only.

[8] Excludes collectives and state farms (less than 20% of farmers).

Sources: Unless otherwise noted, F. A. O., *Monthly Bulletin of Agricultural Statistics, 1–11* (1953–63).
[a] Center of Latin American Studies, U.C.L.A., *Statistical Abstract of Latin America, 1961* (Los Angeles, 1961), p. 38.
[b] *Estadistica Chilena,* December 1937, p. 681.
[c] U. N., Department of Economic Affairs, *Progress in Land Reform* (New York, 1954).
[d] Albert O. Hirschman, ed., *Latin American Issues* (New York, 1961), p. 187.
[e] Thomas R. Ford, *Man and Land in Peru* (Gainesville, Fla., 1955), pp. 63–68. Rough estimate—excludes *selva*.
[f] International Co-operation Administration, *Latin American USOM's Seminar on Agrarian Reform, February 21–24, 1961* (Washington, D.C., 1961).
[g] U. N., *Compendium of Social Statistics, 1963* (New York, 1963).
[h] IBRD, *Report on Cuba* (Washington, D.C., 1951), p. 88.
[i] E. Martinez de Bujanda, "Agrarian Reform in Spain," *International Review of Agriculture, 1933,* p. 116 E.
[j] W. S. Woytinsky and E. S. Woytinsky, *World Population and Production* (New York, 1955), pp. 490–91.
[k] F. A. O., *Report on the 1950 World Census of Agriculture, 1* (Rome, 1955).
[l] Jean de la Roche, *A Program of Social and Cultural Activity in Indo-China* (New York, 1945).
[m] Sidney Klein, *The Pattern of Land Tenure Reform in East Asia* (New York, 1958).
[n] K. Parsons et al., ed., *Land Tenure* (Madison, Wis., 1956).
[o] Central Statistical Organization, *Statistical Abstract, India, 1955–56* (New Delhi, 1957), pp. 510–11.
[p] Karl Pelzer, *Population and Land Utilization* (New York, 1941).

TABLE 70

Farms on Rented Land as a Percentage of Total Farms

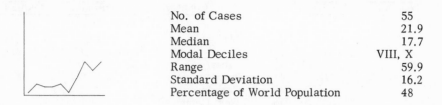

No. of Cases	55
Mean	21.9
Median	17.7
Modal Deciles	VIII, X
Range	59.9
Standard Deviation	16.2
Percentage of World Population	48

% of Table Population	Case Deciles	Rank	Country	% Farms Rented	Range Deciles	Year
	I	1	Belgium	62.3	I	1950
		2	Cuba	53.8	II	1945
		3	Netherlands	53.3		1948
32.0		4	India	53.0[a]		1931
		5	Surinam	52.2		1959
	II	6	Hong Kong	49.1	III	1961
		7	Trinidad & Tobago	47.8		1946
		8	United Kingdom	44.5		1950
		9	Spain	43.7[b]	IV	1950
		10	British Guiana	41.2		1952
	III	11	Taiwan	40.0[a]		1948
		12	Philippines	37.3[b]	V	1948
		13	Barbados	35.4		1946
		14	Uruguay	34.7		1951
		15	Argentina	32.8[c]		1952
		16	Portugal	27.1	VI	1952
	IV	17	France	26.0[a]	VII	1946
		18	Italy	23.8[a]		1930
		19	New Zealand	22.3		1950
		20	Dominican Republic	20.8[e]		1950
50.4		21	Venezuela	20.6[c]		1950
	V	22	United States	20.4		1959
		23.5	Bolivia	20.0[c]	VIII	1950
		23.5	South Vietnam[1]	20.0[d]		1950
		25.5	Sweden	18.9[a]		1944
		25.5	Switzerland	18.9[a]		1944
		27	Luxembourg	18.8		1950
	VI	28	Greece	17.7[a]		1939
		29	Thailand	17.2		1950
		30	Guatemala	17.0[e]		1950
		31.5	Pakistan	16.7		1960
		31.5	Honduras	16.7		1952
	VII	33	El Salvador	15.1		1950
		34	Ecuador	14.6[c]		1954
		35	Chile	13.4[c]	IX	1955
		36	Panama	12.3		1961
		37	Colombia[2]	12.1[e]		1960
74.9		38	Egypt	11.6[f]		1939
	VIII	39	Austria	10.7		1951
		40	Jamaica	10.3		1943

TABLE 70 (continued)

% of Table Population	Case Deciles	Rank	Country	% Farms Rented	Range Deciles	Year
		41	Malaya	10.0		1960
		42	Brazil	9.1[e]		1950
		43	Libya	8.5[g]		1960
	IX	44	Norway	7.5[b]	X	1950
		45	Canada	7.2		1951
		46	West Germany	5.7		1949
		47	Israel	5.5		1950
		48	Costa Rica	5.4[c]		1950
		49	Jordan	4.4		1953
	X	50	Puerto Rico	3.6		1959
		51	Denmark	3.5		1949
		52	Mexico	3.1		1950
		53	Japan	2.9		1960
		54	Ireland[2]	2.5[a]		1932
		55	Finland	2.4		1950

[1] Estimated.
[2] Farm land instead of farms.

Sources: Unless otherwise noted, U.N., *Compendium of Social Statistics, 1963* (New York, 1963).

[a] W. S. and E. S. Woytinsky, *World Population and Production* (New York, 1953), p. 495.

[b] U.N., Department of Economic Affairs, *Progress in Land Reform* (New York, 1954), p. 118.

[c] Center for Latin American Studies, U.C.L.A., *Statistical Abstract of Latin America, 1961* (Los Angeles, 1962), p. 38.

[d] Erich Jacoby. *Agrarian Unrest in South East Asia* (London, 1961), p. 157.

[e] F.A.O., *Monthly Bulletin of Agricultural Economics and Statistics,* September 1962.

[f] Charles P. Issawi, *Egypt at Mid-Century* (New York, 1954), pp. 125–26.

[g] F.A.O., *Monthly Bulletin of Agricultural Economics and Statistics,* December 1962.

The cross-national comparison of income distribution is made difficult by incompleteness of coverage and by conceptual differences as to what is actually being compared. Much income simply is not reported. This is particularly true of deliberate evasion in the higher income bracket, though nonmonetary income in the lower brackets is also often not reported. Income distributions derived from tax returns are more likely to be subject to error from deliberate evasion than are distributions derived from survey research.

Making comparable the series being compared is equally important; for example, before-tax distributions should not be compared with post-tax distributions, nor should distributions for individual income earners be compared with those for families including more than one income recipient. While serious, however, these differences are not as weighty as is often believed. Available data indicate that allowing for taxes may reduce the share of the upper tenth of income earners fairly substantially in developed countries—a reduction ranging from about 20% in Australia and the United Kingdom to around 7% in the United States and West Germany. But for underdeveloped countries such as Ceylon, El Salvador, and Guatemala, the effect is much less—a maximum reduction of about 4%. In all these countries allowance for benefits derived from government services removes, at the most, an additional 5% of the upper income earners' receipts.

Another problem is the difference between families, income-receiving units, consuming units, and individual income recipients. For social and political comparisons one of the former would be preferred, yet the difference probably is not major. Distributions by individual income earners probably tend to be more unequal, by about 5% at the top levels, than do distributions by consuming units.

For social or political purposes allowance should also be made for differences in the size of income-receiving units—large families in some sense need more than small ones. This adjustment, where possible, uniformly increases the degree of inequality apparent. It tends to increase, by about 10%, the share of the upper tenth. Though the effect is perhaps slightly greater in underdeveloped countries it is generally quite uniform and, relative to the factors previously discussed, not a significant source of bias in cross-national comparisons.[1]

According to Simon Kuznets, "while it is impossible to set specific limits on . . . errors, the general cast of a total size distribution, given clear indications of the recipient unit and of the income apportioned, is not sensitive to even large errors for some of the components."[2] We have nevertheless used only income distributions that seemed to account for nearly

---

1. On some of these problems see Simon Kuznets, "Quantitative Aspects of the Economic Growth of Nations: VIII, Distribution of Income by Size," *Economic Development and Cultural Change*, 11 (January 1963), part II. Cf. also Irving Kravis, *The Structure of Income* (Philadelphia, 1962), ch. 7.
2. Kuznets, p. 15.

all of the national income in question,[3] and the primary—though not the sole—cautions in interpreting the data are those referred to, with approximate error margins above.

Two series are given—one before taxes and one after. The unit is family or consuming unit unless otherwise noted. We have again used the Gini index as the measure, and included in parentheses the percentage of income earned by the top 10% of income earners in the nation.

Inequality has a long history as a central concept in political, social, and economic thought from Plato and Aristotle to Karl Marx and the present. It is alleged to have major effects on political stability, on the nature of political regimes, and, in economics, on incentives and on the availability of resources for investment.[4] While the following data are not perfect, nor are they given for a great many countries, they may nevertheless be used to explore these and other questions.

———

3. Because they failed to meet this criterion, available data for Japan, the Philippines, and Switzerland were not included. On the first two, cf. Kuznets. Two partial exceptions, Canada and Israel, are given in Table 71 but noted.

4. If references are needed, cf. Bruce M. Russett, "Inequality and Instability: The Relation of Land Tenure to Politics," *World Politics, 16* (April 1964), 442–54, and Hayward R. Alker, Jr., and Bruce M. Russett, "On Measuring Inequality," *Behavioral Science, 9,* No. 3 (July 1964).

TABLE 71

Income Distribution Before Taxes: Gini Index of Inequality

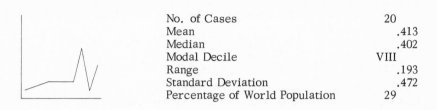

No. of Cases	20
Mean	.413
Median	.402
Modal Decile	VIII
Range	.193
Standard Deviation	.472
Percentage of World Population	29

% of Table Population	Rank	Country	Index of Inequality	Range Deciles	Year
	1	Mexico (47)	.540	I–III	1957
	2	West Germany (36)	.473[a]	IV	1950
	3	Ceylon (41)	.465		1953
	4	Guatemala (44)	.458	V	1948
	5	Barbados (34)	.454		1952
	6	Colombia (48)	.432	VI	1953
	7	Netherlands (38)	.431[b]		1950
	8	Denmark (31)	.421	VII	1952
	9	Puerto Rico (33)	.417		1953
	10	Italy (34)	.403[c]	VIII	1948
	11	El Salvador (44)	.400		1946
21.6	12	Sweden (30)	.399[d]		1960
	13	United States (30)	.397[e]		1956
	14	Canada (28)[1]	.390[f]		1955
	15	Norway (29)	.386		1950
49.9	16	United Kingdom (31)	.366	IX	1955
98.3	17	India (34)	.365[g]	X	1956
	18	New Zealand (30)[2]	.357[h]		1958
	19	Israel (24)[3]	.352[i]		1958
	20	Australia (28)	.347		1955

[1] Urban households only.
[2] Income recipients.
[3] Urban Jewish population only (about 75% of total).

Sources: Most of these data are derived from other analyses. Since the analyst has usually adjusted the data from his primary source we cite him rather than the latter. Unless otherwise noted, Simon Kuznets, "Quantitative Aspects of the Economic Growth of Nations: VIII. Distribution of Income by Size, *Economic Development and Cultural Change, 11* (January 1963).

[a] *Wirtschaft und Statistik, 6* (October 1954), 461. This figure seems high. An alternative calculation, based on "Die Schichtung der Privaten Haushaltseinhagen in der Bundesrepublik," *Wochenbericht* |(Berlin, May 11, 1962), p. 80, cited by Kuznets, gives a Gini index of .315 for 1959! Of the two, however, the index in the table seems the more soundly based.

[b] Robert M. Solow, "Income Inequality Since the War," in Ralph Freeman, *Postwar Economic Trends in the United States* (New York, 1960).

[c] U. N., *Statistical Papers,* Series E., No. 3 (New York, 1951).

[d] Statistika Centrallyran, *Statistisk Arsbok for Sverige, 1961* (Stockholm, 1961), p. 285.

TABLE 71 (continued)

[e] U. S. Department of Commerce, *Historical Statistics of the United States, Colonial Times to 1957* (Washington, D. C., 1960), p. 165.

[f] Irving B. Kravis, *The Structure of Income, Some Quantitative Essays* (Philadelphia, 1962), p. 246.

[g] H. F. Lydall, "The Inequality of Indian Incomes," *Economic Weekly* (Bombay) Special No., June 1960, pp. 873–74.

[h] Department of Statistics, *New Zealand Official Yearbook, 1961* (Wellington, 1961), p. 861.

[i] Giora Hanoch, "Income Differentials in Israel," in *Fifth Report, 1959 and 1960*, Falk Project for Economic Research in Israel (Jerusalem, 1961), p. 40.

TABLE 72

Income Distribution After Taxes: Gini Index of Inequality

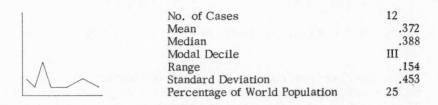

No. of Cases	12
Mean	.372
Median	.388
Modal Decile	III
Range	.154
Standard Deviation	.453
Percentage of World Population	25

% of Table Population	Rank	Country	Index of Inequality	Range Deciles	Year
	1	West Germany (34)	.432[a]	I	1950
	2	Guatemala (43)	.423		1948
	3	Ceylon (37)	.407	II	1953
	4	Denmark (29)[1]	.396	III	1952
	5	El Salvador (43)	.393		1946
	6.5	Netherlands (33)	.388[b]		1950
	6.5	Sweden (29)[1,2]	.388[b]		1948
35.3	8	United States (29)	.373[c]	IV,V	1956
98.2	9	India (33)	.350[d]	VI,VII	1956
	10	United Kingdom (26)	.318[b]	VIII,IX	1955
	11	Norway (26)[1]	.313		1950
	12	Australia (30)[1,3]	.277[e]	X	1956

[1] Income recipients.

[2] Not strictly comparable to data in Table 71. Comparable Gini index from the source cited there is .423 for *1948* incomes before tax.

[3] Not strictly comparable to data in Table 71. Comparable Gini index from the source cited there is .309 for *1956* incomes before tax.

Sources: Unless otherwise noted, Simon Kuznets, "Quantitative Aspects of the Economic Growth of Nations: VIII. Distribution of Income by Size," *Economic Development and Cultural Change, 11* (January 1963).

[a] *Wirtschaft und Statistik, 6* (October 1954), p. 461.

[b] Robert M. Solow, "Income Inequality Since the War," in Ralph Freeman, *Postwar Economic Trends in the United States* (New York, 1950).

[c] U. S. Department of Commerce, *Historical Statistics of the United States, Colonial Times to 1957* (Washington, D. C., 1960), p. 165.

[d] H. F. Lydall, "The Inequality of Indian Incomes," *Economic Weekly* (Bombay), Special No., June 1960, pp. 873–74.

[e] Commissioner of Taxation, *Thirty-Seventh Annual Report* (Canberra, 1957), p. 43.

Religion

73-75. RELIGIOUS COMPOSITION OF POPULATION

Tables 73-75 present country-by-country breakdowns for three major world religions—Roman Catholic, all Christian (including Catholics), and Moslem. They should be useful for examining a variety of hypotheses about the relation between religion and social and political practices.

Two of the series (Christian and Moslem) suffer from notable problems of comparability. The information is in most cases collected by agencies in the individual countries, not by any worldwide religious organization. The definition of an adherent to a particular sect thus varies from country to country. These series are most useful for identifying the general cultural characteristics of a country; in no case do the data imply current active participation in religious activities. Data built up from the files of religious organizations usually indicate some past or current association with the church—baptism for Catholics, Orthodox, and Anglicans; "joining the church" for many Protestants. Nominal adherence, as measured by responses to survey or census questions, is occasionally the basis in other countries. For many predominantly Moslem countries we lack adequate census data on this matter, and the percentages are merely more or less informed estimates. Nevertheless, the percentages do give a general order of magnitude that can be useful if an error of perhaps $\pm 10\%$ (more for the low values) is attributed to them. Some of the cases listed as zeroes (e.g. no Moslems, etc.) are undoubtedly not actually zero in fact, but rather some very low figure, usually under 1%.

The most rigorously comparable series is that for Roman Catholics, and it was precisely for this reason that data for Roman Catholics (and not data for Protestants or Orthodox) were included as a subcategory of "Christian." These data are built up from baptismal records, which are compiled with considerable care. In this case we can be sure that the same definition is used in every country. It seems likely that the data are as good as the basic population estimates in the denominator of the ratio, and can be used with the same error ranges. We repeat, however, that these are baptisms and not necessarily practicing Catholics. In much of Latin America and in some Western European states the ratio of practicing to baptized Catholics is very low; in other countries such as the United States the ratio is probably much higher.

TABLE 73

Roman Catholics as a Percentage of Total Population, 1958

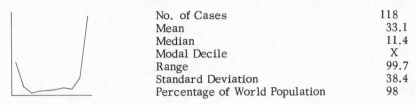

No. of Cases	118
Mean	33.1
Median	11.4
Modal Decile	X
Range	99.7
Standard Deviation	38.4
Percentage of World Population	98

% of Table Population	Case Deciles	Rank	Country	R.C. % of Total Pop.	Range Deciles
I		1	Spain	99.7	I
		2	Italy	99.5	
		3	El Salvador	98.9	
		4	Honduras	98.4	
		5	Colombia	97.5	
		6	Malta	96.9	
		7.5	Belgium	96.8	
		7.5	Luxembourg	96.8	
		9	Poland	96.1	
		10	Dominican Republic	95.5	
		11	Paraguay	95.3	
	II	12	Costa Rica	95.1	
		13.5	Mexico	95.0	
		13.5	Peru	95.0	
		15	Bolivia	94.7	
		16	Nicaragua	94.4	
		17	Venezuela	94.3	
		18	Ecuador	94.2	
		19	Ireland	94.0	
		20	Brazil	93.0	
		21	Guatemala	92.2	
		22	Portugal	92.1	
		23	Puerto Rico	91.9	
	III	24	Chile	90.0	
		25.5	Argentina	89.4	II
		25.5	Austria	89.4	
		27	Cuba	84.2	
		28	France	83.0	
		29	Philippines	81.7	
		30	Uruguay	80.0	
		31	Panama	75.8	III
		32	Haiti	69.9	
		33	Netherlands Antilles	68.3	IV,V
		34	Czechoslovakia	62.3	
		35	Hungary	60.9	
	IV	36	West Germany	48.4	VI
		37	Canada	44.0	
		38	Netherlands	40.4	
		39	Switzerland	39.7	
		40	Lebanon	38.6	VII

TABLE 73 (continued)

% of Table Population	Case Deciles	Rank	Country	R.C. % of Total Pop.	Range Deciles
		41	Ruanda-Urundi	35.8	
		42	Mauritius	35.7	
		43	Yugoslavia	32.0	
		44	Congo (Leopoldville)	31.5	
		45	Uganda	29.6	VIII
		46	Angola	26.4	
		47	United States	20.6	
25.5	V	48	Barbados	20.2	
		49	Australia	18.9	IX
		50	Madagascar	18.7	
		51	French Cameroons	17.2	
		52	Surinam	16.3	
		53	Togo	16.0	
		54	British Guiana	14.1	
		55.5	South West Africa	13.0	
		55.5	Tanganyika	13.0	
		57	Rhodesia & Nyasaland	12.9	
		58	New Zealand	12.3	
		59	French Equatorial Africa	11.6	
	VI	60	East Germany	11.1	
		61	Ghana	10.4	
		62	Algeria	9.5	X
		63	Kenya	8.7	
		64	United Kingdom	8.0	
		65	South Vietnam	7.7	
		66.5	Ceylon	7.5	
		66.5	Mozambique	7.5	
		68	Romania	7.3	
		69	Albania	6.8	
		70	South Africa	5.6	
	VII	71	Morocco	5.1	
		72	U.S.S.R.	5.0	
		73	British Cameroons	4.8	
		74	Tunisia	4.7	
		75	Syria	4.6	
		76	Hong Kong	4.3	
		77	Libya	4.1	
		78.5	Iraq	3.8	
		78.5	Nigeria	3.8	
		80.5	North Vietnam	3.7	
		80.5	Sarawak	3.7	
		82	French West Africa	3.5	
	VIII	83	Jordan	2.4	
		84	Malaya	2.3	
		85	Israel	1.9	
43.2		86	Sudan	1.7	
		87	India	1.4	
		89	Cyprus	1.3	
		89	Indonesia	1.3	
		89	Kuwait	1.3	
		91.5	Cambodia	1.2	

TABLE 73 (continued)

% of Table Population	Case Deciles	Rank	Country	R.C. % of Total Pop.	Range Deciles
		91.5	South Korea	1.2	
		93	Taiwan	1.1	
		94	Laos	1.0	
	IX	95	Burma	.9	
		96.5	Egypt	.8	
		96.5	Greece	.8	
		99	Bulgaria	.7	
		99	Liberia	.7	
		99	Sierra Leone	.7	
		101.5	Denmark	.6	
66.3		101.5	Ethiopia	.6	
		103.5	China (Mainland)	.5	
		103.5	Thailand	.5	
		105.5	Iceland	.4	
		105.5	North Korea	.4	
	X	108	Japan	.3	
		108	Pakistan	.3	
		108	Sweden	.3	
		110	Norway	.2	
		111.5	Iran	.1	
		111.5	Turkey	.1	
		115.5	Afghanistan	.0	
		115.5	Finland	.0	
		115.5	Mongolian People's Republic	.0	
		115.5	Nepal	.0	
		115.5	Saudi Arabia	.0	
		115.5	Yemen	.0	

Source: Catholic Students' Mission Crusade, *World Mission Map, 1958* (Cincinnati, Ohio, 1958).

TABLE 74

All Christians as a Percentage of Total Population

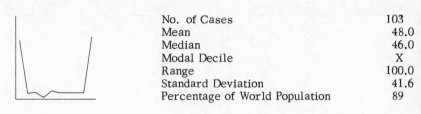

No. of Cases	103
Mean	48.0
Median	46.0
Modal Decile	X
Range	100.0
Standard Deviation	41.6
Percentage of World Population	89

% of Table Population	Case Deciles	Rank	Country	Christians as % Pop.	Range Deciles	Year
I		1	Ireland	100.0[a]	I	1960
		2	Nicaragua	99.9[b]		1950
		3.5	Dominican Republic	99.8[b]		1950
		3.5	Honduras	99.8[b]		1945
		5	Guatemala	99.7[b]		1950
		6	Mexico	99.6		1958
		7	Italy	99.2		1960
		9	Luxembourg	99.0		1960
		9	Panama	99.0		1940
		9	Sweden	99.0		1960
	II	12	Chile	98.0		1960
		12	Denmark	98.0		1960
		12	Switzerland	98.0		1950
		14	Portugal	97.7		1959
		15.5	France	97.5		1960
		15.5	Hungary	97.5		1960
		17.5	Bolivia	97.3		1942
		17.5	Poland	97.3[a]		1960
		19	Iceland	97.2[a]		1961
		20.5	Colombia	97.0		1957
	III	20.5	United Kingdom	97.0		1959
		22	Norway	96.3		1950
		23.5	Brazil	96.0		1950
		23.5	Spain	96.0[a]		1961
		25	Austria	95.9		1960
		26.5	Barbados	95.3[b]		1946
		26.5	Finland	95.3		1960
		28.5	Argentina	95.0[c]		1960
		28.5	Peru	95.0		1960
		30	West Germany	94.8		1950
	IV	31	Ecuador	94.3		1960
		32	East Germany	94.0		1960
		33	Philippines	93.0[c]		1961
		34	Greece	90.4		1951
		35	Romania	90.0[a]		1960
		36	Czechoslovakia	85.0[a]	II	1961
		37	Cyprus	82.0[c]		1961
		38.5	Canada	81.0		1951
		38.5	Netherlands	81.0		1960
		40	New Zealand	79.0	III	1956

TABLE 74 (continued)

% of Table Population	Case Deciles	Rank	Country	Christians as % Pop.	Range Deciles	Year
		41	Bulgaria	78.0[a]		1961
	V	42	Australia	75.0[a]		1962
		43	Yugoslavia	74.1[d]		1953
		44	Trinidad & Tobago	68.2[d]	IV	1960
		45	British Guiana	58.9[b]	V	1946
24.7		46	Gabon	57.0[c]		1957
		47	United States	55.8		1959
		48.5	Burundi	50.0[d]		1963
		48.5	Rwanda	50.0[d]		1963
		50.5	Congo (Brazzaville)	48.0[d]	VI	1962
		50.5	Ethiopia	48.0[c]		1961
	VI	52	Surinam	46.0[b]		1958
		53	Lebanon	44.0		1932
		54	Madagascar	36.0[c]	VII	1961
		55.5	Albania	35.0[a]		1961
		55.5	Congo (Leopoldville)	35.0		1958
		57	Kenya	33.0[d]		1962
		58	Cameroun	27.0[c]	VIII	1961
		59	Central African Republic	25.0[c]		1961
		60.5	Ghana	20.0[c]		1961
		60.5	Tanganyika	20.0[d]		1962
	VII	62	Togo	17.0[c]	IX	1962
		63	Syria	13.0[c]		1961
		64	Nigeria	12.0		1952
		65	Ivory Coast	11.0[a]		1962
		66.5	Algeria	9.0[d]	X	1961
		66.5	Ceylon	9.0[c]		1961
		68.5	Dahomey	8.0[c]		1961
		68.5	Liberia	8.0[c]		1961
		70	Egypt	7.0[c]		1961
		71	South Korea	6.2		1958
		73.5	Burma	5.0[a]		1962
	VIII	73.5	Chad	5.0[c]		1961
		73.5	Jordan	5.0[c]		1961
		73.5	Pakistan	5.0		1958
		77.5	Libya	4.0[c]		1961
		77.5	Mali	4.0		1959
		77.5	Morocco	4.0[c]		1961
		77.5	Tunisia	4.0[c]		1962
		80	Indonesia	3.3		1960
		82.5	Senegal	3.0[d]		1961
		82.5	Sudan	3.0[c]		1961
	IX	82.5	Taiwan	3.0[a]		1962
		82.5	Upper Volta	3.0[c]		1960
48.9		85	Iraq	2.5		1960
		86.5	India	2.0[c]		1961
		86.5	Israel	2.0[c]		1961
		88.5	Guinea	1.0[c]		1961
66.9		88.5	Turkey	1.0		1958
		90.5	China (Mainland)	.7		1959
		90.5	Japan	.7		1956

TABLE 74 (continued)

% of Table Population	Case Deciles	Rank	Country	Christians as % Pop.	Range Deciles	Year
		93.5	Aden	.5		1957
	X	93.5	Cambodia	.5		1958
		93.5	Iran	.5		1958
		93.5	Thailand	.5		1960
		99.5	Afghanistan	.0[c]		1961
		99.5	Laos	.0[d]		1961
		99.5	Mauritania	.0[c]		1961
		99.5	Nepal	.0[c]		1961
		99.5	Niger	.0[c]		1962
		99.5	Saudi Arabia	.0[c]		1961
		99.5	Somalia	.0[c]		1961
		99.5	Yemen	.0[c]		1961

Sources: Unless otherwise noted, *Worldmark Encyclopedia, 1960* (New York, 1960).
[a] *The Europa Yearbook, 1963* (London, 1963).
[b] Center for Latin American Studies, U. C. L. A., *Statistical Abstract of Latin America, 1962* (Los Angeles, 1962), p. 22.
[c] A. I. D., *Economic Data Book* (Washington, D. C., 1963, looseleaf).
[d] *Worldmark Encyclopedia, 1963* (New York, 1963).

TABLE 75

Moslems as a Percentage of Total Population

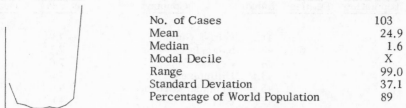

No. of Cases	103
Mean	24.9
Median	1.6
Modal Decile	X
Range	99.0
Standard Deviation	37.1
Percentage of World Population	89

% of Table Population	Case Deciles	Rank	Country	Moslems as % Pop.	Range Deciles	Year
	I	2.5	Afghanistan	99.0[a]	I	1961
		2.5	Mauritania	99.0[a]		1961
		2.5	Saudi Arabia	99.0[a]		1961
		2.5	Yemen	99.0[a]		1961
		6	Aden	98.0		1958
		6	Iran	98.0		1958
		6	Turkey	98.0		1958
		8	Iraq	96.0		1960
		10.5	Jordan	95.0[a]		1961
		10.5	Libya	95.0[a]		1961
	II	10.5	Somalia	95.0[a]		1961
		10.5	Tunisia	95.0[a]		1962
		13.5	Egypt	92.0[a]		1961
		13.5	Morocco	92.0[a]		1961
		15.5	Algeria	90.0[b]		1961
		15.5	Indonesia	90.0		1960
		17	Syria	87.0[a]	II	1961
		18	Pakistan	86.0		1958
		19.5	Niger	80.0[a]		1962
		19.5	Sudan	80.0[a]		1961
	III	21.5	Mali	75.0	III	1959
		21.5	Senegal	75.0[b]		1961
		23	Guinea	70.0[a]		1961
		24	Albania	65.0[c]	IV	1961
		25	Chad	52.0[a]	V	1961
		26	Ethiopia	43.0[a]	VI	1961
		27	Lebanon	42.0		1932
		28	Nigeria	33.0	VII	1952
		29	Surinam	26.7[d]	VIII	1958
		30	Ivory Coast	22.0[c]		1962
	IV	31	Tanganyika	20.0[b]		1962
		32.5	Cameroun	18.0[a]	IX	1961
		32.5	Cyprus	18.0[a]		1961
		34	Upper Volta	15.0[a]		1960
		35	Ghana	14.0[a]		1961
		36	Yugoslavia	12.3[b]		1953
17.4		37	Dahomey	12.0[a]		1961
		38	India	10.0[a]		1961
		39.5	Israel	9.0[a]	X	1961
		39.5	Madagascar	9.0[a]		1961

TABLE 75 (continued)

% of Table Population	Case Deciles	Rank	Country	Moslems as % Pop.	Range Deciles	Year
		41	British Guiana	7.9[d]		1946
	V	42	Bulgaria	7.5[c]		1961
		43.5	Ceylon	7.0[a]		1961
		43.5	Philippines	7.0[a]		1961
		45	Trinidad & Tobago	6.0[b]		1960
		47	Burma	4.0[c]		1962
		47	Central African Republic	4.0[a]		1961
		47	Kenya	4.0[b]		1962
		49	Togo	3.0[a]		1962
37.9		50	Cambodia	2.0		1958
		51	China (Mainland)	1.8		1953
	VI	52	Greece	1.6		1951
		55	Congo (Brazzaville)	1.0[b]		1962
		55	Congo (Leopoldville)	1.0		1958
		55	Gabon	1.0[a]		1957
		55	Liberia	1.0[a]		1961
		55	Spain	1.0[c]		1961
		58	France	.8		1960
67.7		59	Taiwan	.4[c]		1962
		81.5	Argentina	.0[a]		1960
		81.5	Australia	.0[c]		1962
	VII	81.5	Austria	.0		1960
		81.5	Barbados	.0[d]		1946
		81.5	Bolivia	.0		1942
		81.5	Brazil	.0		1950
		81.5	Burundi	.0[b]		1963
		81.5	Canada	.0		1951
		81.5	Chile	.0		1960
		81.5	Colombia	.0		1957
		81.5	Czechoslovakia	.0[c]		1961
		81.5	Denmark	.0		1960
		81.5	Dominican Republic	.0[d]		1950
	VIII	81.5	East Germany	.0		1960
		81.5	Ecuador	.0		1960
		81.5	Finland	.0		1960
		81.5	Guatemala	.0[d]		1950
		81.5	Honduras	.0[d]		1945
		81.5	Hungary	.0		1960
		81.5	Iceland	.0[c]		1961
		81.5	Ireland	.0[c]		1960
		81.5	Italy	.0		1960
		81.5	Japan	.0		1956
	IX	81.5	Laos	.0[b]		1961
		81.5	Luxembourg	.0		1960
		81.5	Mexico	.0		1958
		81.5	Nepal	.0[a]		1961
		81.5	Netherlands	.0		1960
		81.5	New Zealand	.0		1956
		81.5	Nicaragua	.0[d]		1950
		81.5	Norway	.0		1950
		81.5	Panama	.0		1940

TABLE 75 (continued)

% of Table Population	Case Deciles	Rank	Country	Moslems as % Pop.	Range Deciles	Year
		81.5	Peru	.0		1960
	X	81.5	Poland	.0[c]		1960
		81.5	Portugal	.0		1959
		81.5	Romania	.0[c]		1960
		81.5	Rwanda	.0[b]		1963
		81.5	South Korea	.0		1958
		81.5	Sweden	.0		1960
		81.5	Switzerland	.0		1950
		81.5	Thailand	.0		1960
		81.5	United Kingdom	.0		1959
		81.5	United States	.0		1959
		81.5	West Germany	.0		1950

Sources: Unless otherwise noted, *Worldmark Encyclopedia, 1960* (New York, 1960).
[a] A. I. D., *Economic Data Book* (Washington, D. C., 1963, looseleaf).
[b] *Worldmark Encyclopedia, 1963* (New York, 1963).
[c] *The Europa Yearbook, 1963* (London, 1963).
[d] Center for Latin American Studies, U. C. L. A., *Statistical Abstract of Latin America, 1962* (Los Angeles, 1962), p. 22.

Part B
The Analysis of Trends and Patterns

1. Correlations Among Political and Social Indices

Table B.1 represents a first-step analysis of our data, and gives the correlation coefficients (r) for each of 70 series with every other series. All of the series given in Part A of this volume are included, except for five that were given purely for illustrative purposes. (The first four series for government expenditure and revenue, Tables 11–14, are omitted, as is the series for military personnel as a percentage of total population, Table 21.)

Correlations with each variable are listed in separate sets below. Both the sets of correlations and the entries within each one are presented in the same order in which these variables appeared in Part A. The set of correlations with any particular variable should be read from left to right along each of five major rows. There are up to fourteen correlations in each of these rows. Above every coefficient is a four-letter code to identify the variable being correlated with the main variable of the set. Below it, in parentheses, is the number of cases for that correlation—the number of countries for which information was available for both variables. Thus the sixth cell from the left listed under "Variable 5: Live Births per 1,000 Population" is for its correlation with "Deaths per 1,000 Population." At the top is the abbreviation "DTHS," below it is the correlation coefficient, and below that is (56), the number of cases. Given this basic information about the strength of relationship and the N, the reader can judge for himself how "significant" (whether or not in a statistical sense) the correlation is. Note that in this section the decimal point has been left out; a correlation of unity is therefore given as 100.

A number of blanks exist in the table. The computer was instructed to print only those correlations that were 20 or higher in absolute value and based on an N of at least 12. The reader's attention is thus focused on the "significant" relationships rather than distracted by those where the correlation is very low or based on a deceptively small number of cases. In every instance, however, we have left the four-letter identification code so that the reader can immediately see which relationships were not "significant." Correlations with r = 50 or greater are underlined for emphasis.

The product-moment correlation coefficient is an adequate measure of the relationship between two variables when this relationship is approximately a linear one and when the data are distributed in an approximately "normal" (bell-shaped) fashion. The possibility of detecting higher correlations in the curvilinear case will be discussed in a later section of this book. With regard to the distribution of the variables being correlated below, it is well known that unequally distributed extreme data points in skewed distributions have too pronounced an effect on the calculation of the product-moment coefficient. The "bunching" of the data at one end of a distribution may also conceal relationships that would be revealed if data values for extreme cases were not so high.

As is clear from the graphs at the top of each table in Part A many social,

---

This section was written by Hayward R. Alker, Jr., and Bruce M. Russett.

economic, and political national attributes are not "normally" distributed, with most cases near some mean and fewer and fewer cases on either side the farther away from the mean one looks. To improve the chances of detecting relationships with the product-moment coefficient, those variables found from their graphs to have highly skewed distributions have been subjected to a logarithmic transformation before being correlated. Such series are labeled (L) following their headings in the table of correlations.

First, however, we present a table that shows the levels of statistical significance which might be attributed to the correlation coefficients. The level of significance in any case depends upon the strength of relationship (the correlation coefficient, r) and the number of cases (N). To find the level of significance appropriate to any particular value of r in the main table, find in the left-hand column of the significance table the N corre-

Minimum Values of r Which Are Statistically Significant at Various Levels[1]

	Significance Levels					
N =	.33	.10	.05	.02	.01	.001
12	31	41	50	60	65	78
15	27	36	45	54	59	72
20	23	31	38	47	52	65
25	21	27	34	42	46	58
30	—	25	31	38	42	54
40	—	21	27	33	38	47
50	—	—	24	29	33	43
60	—	—	22	27	30	39
70	—	—	20	25	28	37
80	—	—	—	23	26	34
90	—	—	—	22	25	32
100	—	—	—	21	24	31
110	—	—	—	20	23	29
120	—	—	—	—	22	28
133	—	—	—	—	21	27

---

1. This table is derived by use of the Z statistic. Cf. Hubert Blalock, *Social Statistics* (New York, 1960), pp. 305–07, 456–57.

sponding most closely to that in parentheses below the r. Read across to the same value of r or, if the r in question is between the values in two adjacent cells, to the lower of the two. Then read from the column heading the level of significance that can be assigned. Thus for a correlation coefficient of −34 for Votes for Noncommunist Secular Parties (Variable 28) and Gross Domestic Capital Formation as a Percentage of G. N. P. (Variable 47) one has an N of 50. It falls between 33 and 43 in the significance table. One takes the lower value, and finds from the column heading that it is significant at the .01 level. That is to say, a correlation in the direction indicated (in this case negative) would occur by chance only one time in one hundred in random samples of this size; all other times a negative correlation of this magnitude would indicate a negative correlation in the universe being sampled. (Levels of significance can be interpolated for N's not given in this table.) A dash in the significance table (—) indicates that an r of below 20 is significant at that level. A *correlation* must not, of course, be confused with a *causal* relationship.

Levels of significance should be attributed to these correlations, however, only with a clear understanding of the hazards and assumptions involved. A level of significance properly applies to a statistic obtained from a random sample of data from a larger universe with a particular distribution. The data in this *Handbook* are certainly not selected on a random basis, nor is it at all clear what the appropriate universe may be. For political entities in any given year the data in the *Handbook* are not a sample. In most cases they are the universe, or nearly the complete universe, being studied. One might perhaps consider them to be nevertheless a "sample" of a far greater number of units if one multiplies the number of political entities by the number of years in some time span. Thus the entities are, for the magnitudes and years assigned, a "sample" of units of analysis in the Western state system since, say, 1900. But obviously such a definition is highly arbitrary, the sample is anything but random, and the universe from which the sample is taken is probably not a "normal" population as the above significance calculation assumes.

Despite these glaring problems some social scientists nevertheless find it useful to employ the concept of statistical significance in this kind of context. It can be helpful, cautiously employed, if it is used primarily in a negative fashion; that is, to weed out those linear relationships that are misleading because based on a very small number of cases, a weak correlation coefficient, or both. Thus it is easy to say that a relationship between two variables is *not* statistically significant, that it could very easily have arisen by chance. But to turn the coin over and assert that a given relationship *is* significant is a riskier proposition, given the nature of the sampling and the doubt about the nature and shape of the universe. The reader who makes use of the significance table, then, should do so in full awareness of these problems. It may be helpful as a means of establishing some criteria as to which relationships may be treated seriously, as probably produced by something other than chance. But the table should not be used positively to attribute statistical significance to a given relationship, except in terms of a hypothetical universe with the appropriate characteristics from which the data are assumed to be randomly collected. A brief discussion follows the table.

TABLE B.1

Simple Correlations

VARIABLE 1   TPOP
TOTAL POPULATION, MID-YEAR 1961 (L)

TPOP	WAPC	WAGE	FEMW	BRTH	DTHS	NATR	POPR	PC20	20CH	GGEX	GGRV	CGEX	CGRV
100		-21		24	-35	-24						-29	
(133)		(78)		(56)	(60)	(111)						(41)	

GGEM	CGEM	MILP	DEFX	VOTE	COMV	RELV	SOCV	NCSV	VIOL	EXEC	NEWS	DOML	FOML
-31	-42		26					-21					-39
(18)	(21)		(82)					(57)					(72)

FS/R	RADS	RDCH	TELE	CINE	LANG	AREA	DENS	AGDS	GNP	GNPC	GPCH	TRDE	CAPF
					59			84				-69	
					(133)			(117)				(81)	

CONS	GPAG	LFAG	AGCH	NONA	INDY	UNWA	UNWS	ACHT	LIFE	INFD	PHYS	HOSP	HPCH
-24	21					28						21	
(62)	(75)					(33)						(126)	

HIED	PSED	LIT	LTCH	MARG	IMMG	EMIG	LNDG	RENT	YBFT	YAFT	CATH	CHRS	MOSL
		-32	50		-21	-26							
		(43)	(50)		(40)	(50)							

VARIABLE 2   WAPC
PERCENTAGE OF POPULATION OF WORKING AGE (15-64)

TPOP	WAPC	WAGE	FEMW	BRTH	DTHS	NATR	POPR	PC20	20CH	GGEX	GGRV	CGEX	CGRV
	100	48	28	-85		-91	-37	31		52	56	24	47
	(128)	(78)	(69)	(84)		(60)	(106)	(118)		(28)	(29)	(41)	(41)

GGEM	CGEM	MILP	DEFX	VOTE	COMV	RELV	SOCV	NCSV	VIOL	EXEC	NEWS	DOML	FOML
47	31	25		41	22	28	33	-42	-41		41	51	20
(18)	(21)	(85)		(96)	(44)	(56)	(58)	(57)	(74)		(119)	(72)	(70)

FS/R	RADS	RDCH	TELE	CINE	LANG	AREA	DENS	AGDS	GNP	GNPC	GPCH	TRDE	CAPF
39	40	47	35	30					43	48	45		38
(115)	(95)	(68)	(102)	(65)					(115)	(115)	(68)		(77)

CONS	GPAG	LFAG	AGCH	NONA	INDY	UNWA	UNWS	ACHT	LIFE	INFD	PHYS	HOSP	HPCH
-41	-36	-42	23	48	63				49	-30	-37	-48	
(62)	(75)	(95)	(48)	(77)	(78)				(71)	(50)	(123)	(127)	

HIED	PSED	LIT	LTCH	MARG	IMMG	EMIG	LNDG	RENT	YBFT	YAFT	CATH	CHRS	MOSL
35	31	49		30		21	-38		-25			36	-27
(104)	(122)	(114)		(49)		(39)	(49)		(20)			(100)	(100)

TABLE B.1 (continued)

VARIABLE 3   WAGE
WAGE AND SALARY EARNERS AS A PERCENTAGE OF WORKING AGE POPULATION

TPOP	WAPC	WAGE	FEMW	BRTH	DTHS	NATR	POPR	PC20	20CH	GGEX	GGRV	CGEX	CGRV
-21	48	100	43	-63	-39	-33	-31	69		40	45	42	43
(78)	(78)	(79)	(69)	(70)	(52)	(56)	(76)	(76)		(26)	(27)	(34)	(34)

GGEM	CGEM	MILP	DEFX	VOTE	COMV	RELV	SOCV	NCSV	VIOL	EXEC	NEWS	DOML	FOML
84	56		42			50		-35			74	75	73
(17)	(18)		(65)			(53)		(58)			(79)	(55)	(54)

FS/R	RADS	RDCH	TELE	CINE	LANG	AREA	DENS	AGDS	GNP	GNPC	GPCH	TRDE	CAPF
36	74	41	74	68	40	-23			21	76	27	28	41
(53)	(74)	(72)	(57)	(70)	(36)	(78)			(78)	(78)	(60)	(61)	(67)

CONS	GPAG	LFAG	AGCH	NONA	INDY	UNWA	UNWS	ACHT	LIFE	INFD	PHYS	HOSP	HPCH
-53	-68	-80		88	82	25		-20	76	-55	-64	-76	37
(55)	(61)	(77)		(73)	(73)	(45)		(36)	(63)	(48)	(77)	(78)	(62)

HIED	PSED	LIT	LTCH	MARG	IMMG	EMIG	LNDG	RENT	YBFT	YAFT	CATH	CHRS	MOSL
39	71	72		33	22							60	-38
(78)	(77)	(78)		(37)	(35)							(63)	(63)

VARIABLE 4   FEMW
FEMALE WAGE AND SALARY EARNERS AS A PERCENTAGE OF ALL EMPLOYEES

TPOP	WAPC	WAGE	FEMW	BRTH	DTHS	NATR	POPR	PC20	20CH	GGEX	GGRV	CGEX	CGRV
	28	43	100	-35		-38	-27	23	27	23	30		
	(69)	(69)	(69)	(63)		(53)	(68)	(67)	(42)	(24)	(25)		

GGEM	CGEM	MILP	DEFX	VOTE	COMV	RELV	SOCV	NCSV	VIOL	EXEC	NEWS	DOML	FOML
51	42		-21	41							32	53	42
(13)	(15)		(54)	(58)							(69)	(47)	(46)

FS/R	RADS	RDCH	TELE	CINE	LANG	AREA	DENS	AGDS	GNP	GNPC	GPCH	TRDE	CAPF
	27		31	23						31	32		25
	(65)		(52)	(62)						(69)	(54)		(59)

CONS	GPAG	LFAG	AGCH	NONA	INDY	UNWA	UNWS	ACHT	LIFE	INFD	PHYS	HOSP	HPCH
-23	-33	-24		41	43				26		-21	-36	
(50)	(54)	(68)		(68)	(67)				(55)		(69)	(69)	

HIED	PSED	LIT	LTCH	MARG	IMMG	EMIG	LNDG	RENT	YBFT	YAFT	CATH	CHRS	MOSL
40	51	24					-27	-21	34			59	-73
(68)	(69)	(36)					(42)	(46)	(17)			(55)	(55)

VARIABLE 5   BRTH
LIVE BIRTHS PER 1,000 POPULATION

TPOP	WAPC	WAGE	FEMW	BRTH	DTHS	NATR	POPR	PC20	20CH	GGEX	GGRV	CGEX	CGRV
	-85	-63	-35	100	39	92	76	-50	26	-63	-70	-29	-58
	(84)	(70)	(63)	(86)	(56)	(60)	(77)	(80)	(42)	(24)	(25)	(30)	(30)

GGEM	CGEM	MILP	DEFX	VOTE	COMV	RELV	SOCV	NCSV	VIOL	EXEC	NEWS	DOML	FOML
-47	-39	-41		-45	-23	-22	-35	42	55	-23	-73	-80	-46
(14)	(18)	(63)		(65)	(40)	(49)	(50)	(50)	(56)	(64)	(85)	(52)	(51)

FS/R	RADS	RDCH	TELE	CINE	LANG	AREA	DENS	AGDS	GNP	GNPC	GPCH	TRDE	CAPF
-23	-69	-43	-56	-52	-32		-31			-52	-76	-49	-45
(50)	(79)	(70)	(56)	(72)	(37)		(83)			(79)	(79)	(55)	(61)

CONS	GPAG	LFAG	AGCH	NONA	INDY	UNWA	UNWS	ACHT	LIFE	INFD	PHYS	HOSP	HPCH
45	59	65	-21	-72	-78	-28			-87	60	73	74	
(50)	(56)	(74)	(44)	(69)	(68)	(40)			(65)	(50)	(83)	(84)	

HIED	PSED	LIT	LTCH	MARG	IMMG	EMIG	LNDG	RENT	YBFT	YAFT	CATH	CHRS	MOSL
-56	-74	-81		-52			54		38	31		-53	46
(78)	(83)	(79)		(49)			(45)		(20)	(12)		(66)	(66)

TABLE B.1 (continued)

VARIABLE 6   DTHS
DEATHS PER 1,000 POPULATION (L)

TPOP	WAPC	WAGE	FEMW	BRTH	DTHS	NATR	POPR	PC20	20CH	GGEX	GGRV	CGEX	CGRV
24		-39		39	100			-33		-23	-32		
(56)		(52)		(56)	(56)			(54)		(22)	(23)		
GGEM	CGEM	MILP	DEFX	VOTE	COMV	RELV	SOCV	NCSV	VIOL	EXEC	NEWS	DOML	FOML
-33		-34		-46	-25		-24		42		-51	-30	-49
(13)		(44)		(47)	(34)		(42)		(42)		(56)	(42)	(41)
FS/R	RADS	RDCH	TELE	CINE	LANG	AREA	DENS	AGDS	GNP	GNPC	GPCH	TRDE	CAPF
	-50	-21	-41	-41	-43	21				-41	-35		-49
	(54)	(52)	(42)	(52)	(20)	(56)				(56)	(43)		(47)
CONS	GPAG	LFAG	AGCH	NONA	INDY	UNWA	UNWS	ACHT	LIFE	INFD	PHYS	HOSP	HPCH
39	38	41		-49	-33				-77	55	45	43	
(39)	(44)	(54)		(53)	(52)				(47)	(48)	(55)	(56)	
HIED	PSED	LIT	LTCH	MARG	IMMG	EMIG	LNDG	RENT	YBFT	YAFT	CATH	CHRS	MOSL
-61	-50			-41	-22	-21	20		22	27	29		
(56)	(56)			(47)	(29)	(30)	(37)		(19)	(12)	(53)		

VARIABLE 7   NATR
NATURAL INCREASE OF POPULATION--ANNUAL RATE

TPOP	WAPC	WAGE	FEMW	BRTH	DTHS	NATR	POPR	PC20	20CH	GGEX	GGRV	CGEX	CGRV
-35	-91	-33	-38	92		100	87		26	-63	-59		-41
(60)	(60)	(56)	(53)	(60)		(60)	(59)		(39)	(23)	(24)		(28)
GGEM	CGEM	MILP	DEFX	VOTE	COMV	RELV	SOCV	NCSV	VIOL	EXEC	NEWS	DOML	FOML
-26	-24	-27	-20	-42		-26	-22	38	39		-58	-75	-33
(13)	(15)	(48)	(44)	(51)		(44)	(45)	(45)	(46)		(60)	(44)	(43)
FS/R	RADS	RDCH	TELE	CINE	LANG	AREA	DENS	AGDS	GNP	GNPC	GPCH	TRDE	CAPF
	-57	-25	-35	-27					-54	-59	-27		-30
	(58)	(56)	(45)	(56)					(60)	(60)	(46)		(51)
CONS	GPAG	LFAG	AGCH	NONA	INDY	UNWA	UNWS	ACHT	LIFE	INFD	PHYS	HOSP	HPCH
43	42	43	-33	-48	-66	30			-59	39	70	60	23
(43)	(47)	(58)	(41)	(56)	(55)	(33)			(51)	(48)	(59)	(60)	(51)
HIED	PSED	LIT	LTCH	MARG	IMMG	EMIG	LNDG	RENT	YBFT	YAFT	CATH	CHRS	MOSL
-38	-42	-67	27	-36	20		51		41	33		-40	41
(59)	(60)	(60)	(35)	(48)	(32)		(40)		(20)	(12)		(47)	(47)

VARIABLE 8   POPR
ANNUAL PERCENTAGE RATE OF INCREASE OF POPULATION

TPOP	WAPC	WAGE	FEMW	BRTH	DTHS	NATR	POPR	PC20	20CH	GGEX	GGRV	CGEX	CGRV
-24	-37	-31	-27	76		87	100			-37	-49	-36	-42
(111)	(106)	(76)	(68)	(77)		(59)	(111)			(27)	(28)	(41)	(41)
GGEM	CGEM	MILP	DEFX	VOTE	COMV	RELV	SOCV	NCSV	VIOL	EXEC	NEWS	DOML	FOML
-35	-38	-20		-41	-25			38	38		-33	-51	-40
(17)	(20)	(80)		(83)	(43)			(56)	(68)		(107)	(68)	(67)
FS/R	RADS	RDCH	TELE	CINE	LANG	AREA	DENS	AGDS	GNP	GNPC	GPCH	TRDE	CAPF
-24	-39	-32	-30						-28		-44		-28
(66)	(101)	(92)	(66)						(107)		(68)		(75)
CONS	GPAG	LFAG	AGCH	NONA	INDY	UNWA	UNWS	ACHT	LIFE	INFD	PHYS	HOSP	HPCH
29	42	42		-35	-45				-52	35		21	
(61)	(74)	(92)		(76)	(77)				(67)	(49)		(108)	
HIED	PSED	LIT	LTCH	MARG	IMMG	EMIG	LNDG	RENT	YBFT	YAFT	CATH	CHRS	MOSL
-24	-20	-37	21	-36		-21	41		21	22		-36	22
(98)	(106)	(104)	(43)	(49)		(39)	(49)		(19)	(12)		(82)	(82)

TABLE B.1 (continued)

VARIABLE 9   PC20
PERCENTAGE OF POPULATION IN LOCALITIES OF OVER 20,000 POPULATION

TPOP	WAPC	WAGE	FEMW	BRTH	DTHS	NATR	POPR	PC20	20CH	GGEX	GGRV	CGEX	CGRV
	31	69	23	-50	-33			100	26	34	47	47	49
	(118)	(76)	(67)	(80)	(54)			(120)	(50)	(27)	(28)	(41)	(41)

SGEM	CGEM	MILP	DEFX	VOTE	COMV	RELV	SOCV	NCSV	VIOL	EXEC	NEWS	DOML	FOML
82	56	27	38	-23		38		-31		69	65	54	
(18)	(21)	(84)	(90)	(41)		(54)		(73)		(115)	(68)	(66)	

S/R	RADS	RDCH	TELE	CINE	LANG	AREA	DENS	AGDS	GNP	GNPC	GPCH	TRDE	CAPF
26	68	37	54	62	54	-22	27	23	35	71	27		42
(66)	(109)	(91)	(67)	(96)	(61)	(119)	(119)	(103)	(110)	(110)	(66)		(76)

CONS	GPAG	LFAG	AGCH	NONA	INDY	UNWA	UNWS	ACHT	LIFE	INFD	PHYS	HOSP	HPCH
-36	-67	-72		78	67	36			71	-43	-69	-62	24
(61)	(73)	(92)		(75)	(76)	(52)			(69)	(48)	(114)	(117)	(81)

MIED	PSED	LIT	LTCH	MARG	IMMG	EMIG	LNDG	RENT	YBFT	YAFT	CATH	CHRS	MOSL
56	72	66		28	50	44			-39	-35		50	-30
(100)	(115)	(109)		(48)	(39)	(40)			(20)	(12)		(95)	(95)

VARIABLE 10   20CH   PERCENTAGE OF POPULATION IN LOCALITIES OF OVER 20,000 POPULATION--AVERAGE ANNUAL INCREASE (L)

TPOP	WAPC	WAGE	FEMW	BRTH	DTHS	NATR	POPR	PC20	20CH	GGEX	GGRV	CGEX	CGRV
	27	26		26				26	100				
	(42)	(42)		(39)				(50)	(50)				

SGEM	CGEM	MILP	DEFX	VOTE	COMV	RELV	SOCV	NCSV	VIOL	EXEC	NEWS	DOML	FOML
						-54	-43	20					-27
						(36)	(36)	(38)					(36)

S/R	RADS	RDCH	TELE	CINE	LANG	AREA	DENS	AGDS	GNP	GNPC	GPCH	TRDE	CAPF
						21					26		
						(50)					(38)		

CONS	GPAG	LFAG	AGCH	NONA	INDY	UNWA	UNWS	ACHT	LIFE	INFD	PHYS	HOSP	HPCH
			-33										-27
			(36)										(40)

MIED	PSED	LIT	LTCH	MARG	IMMG	EMIG	LNDG	RENT	YBFT	YAFT	CATH	CHRS	MOSL
		22	41					-35	50			25	-42
		(50)	(27)					(34)	(13)			(39)	(39)

VARIABLE 15   GGEX   EXPENDITURE OF GENERAL GOVERNMENT, SOCIAL SECURITY, AND PUBLIC ENTERPRISES AS A PERCENTAGE OF G.N.P.

TPOP	WAPC	WAGE	FEMW	BRTH	DTHS	NATR	POPR	PC20	20CH	GGEX	GGRV	CGEX	CGRV
	52	40	23	-63	-23	-63	-37	34		100	95	89	89
	(28)	(26)	(24)	(24)	(22)	(23)	(27)	(27)		(28)	(28)	(25)	(25)

SGEM	CGEM	MILP	DEFX	VOTE	COMV	RELV	SOCV	NCSV	VIOL	EXEC	NEWS	DOML	FOML
79		37	63	25	31	-27	-25			55	41	41	
(13)		(26)	(26)	(21)	(22)	(21)	(25)			(28)	(25)	(25)	

S/R	RADS	RDCH	TELE	CINE	LANG	AREA	DENS	AGDS	GNP	GNPC	GPCH	TRDE	CAPF
31	42		53	29					34	53			41
(24)	(28)		(21)	(12)					(28)	(28)			(28)

CONS	GPAG	LFAG	AGCH	NONA	INDY	UNWA	UNWS	ACHT	LIFE	INFD	PHYS	HOSP	HPCH
-70	-61	-52		57	66		-26	-27	55	-65	-36	-56	
(25)	(25)	(28)		(26)	(26)		(18)	(24)	(25)	(22)	(28)	(28)	

MIED	PSED	LIT	LTCH	MARG	IMMG	EMIG	LNDG	RENT	YBFT	YAFT	CATH	CHRS	MOSL
42	45	50		54		-28	-29						-34
(28)	(28)	(28)		(21)		(20)	(22)						(25)

TABLE B.1 (continued)

VARIABLE 16   GGRV   REVENUE OF GENERAL GOVERNMENT,
SOCIAL SECURITY, AND PUBLIC ENTERPRISES AS A PERCENTAGE OF G.N.P.

TPOP	WAPC	WAGE	FEMW	BRTH	DTHS	NATR	POPR	PC20	20CH	GGEX	GGRV	CGEX	CGR
	56	45	30	-70	-32	-59	-49	47		95	100	86	9
	(29)	(27)	(25)	(25)	(23)	(24)	(28)	(28)		(28)	(29)	(26)	(26
GGEM	CGEM	MILP	DEFX	VOTE	COMV	RELV	SOCV	NCSV	VIOL	EXEC	NEWS	DOML	FON
	71	29	30	64		20	29	-23	-40		65	52	5
	(13)	(26)	(27)	(27)		(22)	(23)	(22)	(26)		(29)	(26)	(26
FS/R	RADS	RDCH	TELE	CINE	LANG	AREA	DENS	AGDS		GNP	GNPC	GPCH	TRDE	CAP
36	55		54	35	51					30	58	31		4
(25)	(29)		(22)	(29)	(13)					(29)	(29)	(25)		(29
CONS	GPAG	LFAG	AGCH	NONA	INDY	UNWA	UNWS	ACHT	LIFE	INFD	PHYS	HOSP	HPC
-67	-64	-55		60	56			-23	67	-65	-49	-63	
(26)	(25)	(29)		(27)	(27)			(25)	(26)	(23)	(29)	(29)	
HIED	PSED	LIT	LTCH	MARG	IMMG	EMIG	LNDG	RENT	YBFT	YAFT	CATH	CHRS	MOS
50	59	64		51		-23	-22	-22				31	-4
(29)	(29)	(29)		(22)		(21)	(23)	(25)				(26)	(26

VARIABLE 17   CGEX   EXPENDITURE OF CENTRAL GOVERNMENT,
SOCIAL SECURITY, AND PUBLIC ENTERPRISES AS A PERCENTAGE OF G.N.P.

TPOP	WAPC	WAGE	FEMW	BRTH	DTHS	NATR	POPR	PC20	20CH	GGEX	GGRV	CGEX	CGR
-29	24	42		-29			-36	47		89	86	100	8
(41)	(41)	(34)		(30)			(41)	(41)		(25)	(26)	(41)	(4]
GGEM	CGEM	MILP	DEFX	VOTE	COMV	RELV	SOCV	NCSV	VIOL	EXEC	NEWS	DOML	FON
35	75	44	35	44	22	35	48	-40	-32	-31	42		4
(12)	(15)	(38)	(40)	(38)	(25)	(28)	(29)	(28)	(38)	(38)	(41)		(30
FS/R	RADS	RDCH	TELE	CINE	LANG	AREA	DENS	AGDS		GNP	GNPC	GPCH	TRDE	CAP
51	44		33	28	35	-44	23	27			37	53	31	1
(29)	(41)		(30)	(37)	(21)	(41)	(41)	(40)			(41)	(31)	(38)	(39
CONS	GPAG	LFAG	AGCH	NONA	INDY	UNWA	UNWS	ACHT	LIFE	INFD	PHYS	HOSP	HPC
-39	-55	-47		52	40		-28	-25	56	-36	-39	-49	
(34)	(35)	(37)		(33)	(33)		(24)	(29)	(32)	(21)	(41)	(41)	
HIED	PSED	LIT	LTCH	MARG	IMMG	EMIG	LNDG	RENT	YBFT	YAFT	CATH	CHRS	MOS
31	46	30		38		29		-22					
(40)	(41)	(41)		(23)		(24)		(31)					

VARIABLE 18   CGRV   REVENUE OF CENTRAL GOVERNMENT,
SOCIAL SECURITY, AND PUBLIC ENTERPRISES AS A PERCENTAGE OF G.N.P.

TPOP	WAPC	WAGE	FEMW	BRTH	DTHS	NATR	POPR	PC20	20CH	GGEX	GGRV	CGEX	CGR
	47	43		-58		-41	-42	49		89	91	82	1(
	(41)	(34)		(30)		(28)	(41)	(41)		(25)	(26)	(41)	(41
GGEM	CGEM	MILP	DEFX	VOTE	COMV	RELV	SOCV	NCSV	VIOL	EXEC	NEWS	DOML	FON
34	69	30		40	21	33	54	-39	-45		53	39	4
(12)	(15)	(38)		(38)	(25)	(28)	(29)	(28)	(38)		(41)	(30)	(30
FS/R	RADS	RDCH	TELE	CINE	LANG	AREA	DENS	AGDS		GNP	GNPC	GPCH	TRDE	CAP
28	51		30	32	49	-38	33	36		27	47	60		3
(29)	(41)		(30)	(37)	(21)	(41)	(41)	(40)		(41)	(41)	(31)		(39
CONS	GPAG	LFAG	AGCH	NONA	INDY	UNWA	UNWS	ACHT	LIFE	INFD	PHYS	HOSP	HPC
-39	-47	-43		52	44		-26	-30	61	-42	-49	-58	
(34)	(35)	(37)		(33)	(33)		(24)	(29)	(32)	(21)	(41)	(41)	
HIED	PSED	LIT	LTCH	MARG	IMMG	EMIG	LNDG	RENT	YBFT	YAFT	CATH	CHRS	MOS
33	53	47				31	-22						
(40)	(41)	(41)				(24)	(29)						

TABLE B.1 (continued)

VARIABLE 19   GGEM   EMPLOYED BY GENERAL GOVERNMENT, SOCIAL
SECURITY, AND PUBLIC ENTERPRISES AS PERCENT OF WORKING AGE POPULATION

TPOP	WAPC	WAGE	FEMW	BRTH	DTHS	NATR	POPR	PC20	20CH	GGEX	GGRV	CGEX	CGRV
-31	47	84	51	-47	-33	-26	-35	82				35	34
(18)	(18)	(17)	(13)	(14)	(13)	(13)	(17)	(18)				(12)	(12)

GGEM	CGEM	MILP	DEFX	VOTE	COMV	RELV	SOCV	NCSV	VIOL	EXEC	NEWS	DOML	FOML
100	72			78			65	25	-63	-21	74	78	87
(18)	(12)			(16)			(12)	(12)	(12)	(14)	(18)	(15)	(15)

FS/R	RADS	RDCH	TELE	CINE	LANG	AREA	DENS	AGDS	GNP	GNPC	GPCH	TRDE	CAPF
	74		70	68			-38	-58	27	83	25	30	51
	(17)		(12)	(18)			(18)	(17)	(18)	(18)	(13)	(15)	(18)

CONS	GPAG	LFAG	AGCH	NONA	INDY	UNWA	UNWS	ACHT	LIFE	INFD	PHYS	HOSP	HPCH
-53	-75	-82	-21	79	72	21	-46		56	-63	-67	-79	40
(14)	(16)	(16)	(12)	(14)	(14)	(14)	(13)		(14)	(13)	(18)	(18)	(15)

HIED	PSED	LIT	LTCH	MARG	IMMG	EMIG	LNDG	RENT	YBFT	YAFT	CATH	CHRS	MOSL
52	74	68				67					23	77	-48
(18)	(18)	(18)				(12)					(17)	(16)	(16)

VARIABLE 20   CGEM   EMPLOYED BY CENTRAL GOVERNMENT, SOCIAL
SECURITY, AND PUBLIC ENTERPRISES AS PERCENT OF WORKING AGE POPULATION

TPOP	WAPC	WAGE	FEMW	BRTH	DTHS	NATR	POPR	PC20	20CH	GGEX	GGRV	CGEX	CGRV
-42	31	56	42	-39		-24	-38	56		79	71	75	69
(21)	(21)	(18)	(15)	(18)		(15)	(20)	(21)		(13)	(13)	(15)	(15)

GGEM	CGEM	MILP	DEFX	VOTE	COMV	RELV	SOCV	NCSV	VIOL	EXEC	NEWS	DOML	FOML
72	100			25		-24	60		-30		52	41	64
(12)	(21)			(18)		(14)	(14)		(17)		(21)	(17)	(17)

FS/R	RADS	RDCH	TELE	CINE	LANG	AREA	DENS	AGDS	GNP	GNPC	GPCH	TRDE	CAPF
	45		41	22		-24				50		42	29
	(20)		(15)	(19)		(21)				(20)		(19)	(20)

CONS	GPAG	LFAG	AGCH	NONA	INDY	UNWA	UNWS	ACHT	LIFE	INFD	PHYS	HOSP	HPCH
-31	-54	-51		59	59		-57		43	-50	-34	-52	35
(18)	(16)	(19)		(18)	(18)		(12)		(18)	(15)	(21)	(21)	(16)

HIED	PSED	LIT	LTCH	MARG	IMMG	EMIG	LNDG	RENT	YBFT	YAFT	CATH	CHRS	MOSL
42	35			-39				20				63	-23
(21)	(20)			(14)				(15)				(19)	(19)

VARIABLE 22   MILP
MILITARY PERSONNEL AS A PERCENTAGE OF POPULATION AGED 15-64 (L)

TPOP	WAPC	WAGE	FEMW	BRTH	DTHS	NATR	POPR	PC20	20CH	GGEX	GGRV	CGEX	CGRV
	25			-41	-34	-27	-20	27			29	44	30
	(85)			(63)	(44)	(48)	(80)	(84)			(26)	(38)	(38)

GGEM	CGEM	MILP	DEFX	VOTE	COMV	RELV	SOCV	NCSV	VIOL	EXEC	NEWS	DOML	FOML
		100	68	29	43			-35	-35				
		(88)	(75)	(73)	(42)			(53)	(74)				

FS/R	RADS	RDCH	TELE	CINE	LANG	AREA	DENS	AGDS	GNP	GNPC	GPCH	TRDE	CAPF
25	23	24									30	-22	26
(51)	(82)	(72)									(59)	(69)	(63)

CONS	GPAG	LFAG	AGCH	NONA	INDY	UNWA	UNWS	ACHT	LIFE	INFD	PHYS	HOSP	HPCH
-24	-24			20	24				43	-30	-23		-22
(55)	(61)			(62)	(63)				(60)	(38)	(84)		(65)

HIED	PSED	LIT	LTCH	MARG	IMMG	EMIG	LNDG	RENT	YBFT	YAFT	CATH	CHRS	MOSL
21	30	20		32		31	-25		-26	-25			
(83)	(83)	(85)		(40)		(29)	(47)		(12)	(87)			

TABLE B.1 (continued)

VARIABLE 23   DEFX
EXPENDITURE ON DEFENSE AS A PERCENTAGE OF G.N.P. (L)

TPOP	WAPC	WAGE	FEMW	BRTH	DTHS	NATR	POPR	PC20	20CH	GGEX	GGRV	CGEX	CGRV
26			-21			-20				37	30	35	
(82)			(54)			(44)				(26)	(27)	(40)	

GGEM	CGEM	MILP	DEFX	VOTE	COMV	RELV	SOCV	NCSV	VIOL	EXEC	NEWS	DOML	FOML
	68	100		34				-34					
	(75)	(82)		(35)				(46)					

FS/R	RADS	RDCH	TELE	CINE	LANG	AREA	DENS	AGDS	GNP	GNPC	GPCH	TRDE	CAPF
21					38					27		-26	
(52)					(40)					(81)		(74)	

CONS	GPAG	LFAG	AGCH	NONA	INDY	UNWA	UNWS	ACHT	LIFE	INFD	PHYS	HOSP	HPCH
-41					21					-30			
(55)					(59)					(34)			

HIED	PSED	LIT	LTCH	MARG	IMMG	EMIG	LNDG	RENT	YBFT	YAFT	CATH	CHRS	MOSL
29				50		45	-24		-57	-27	-21		21
(79)				(36)		(30)	(46)		(18)	(12)	(79)		(68)

VARIABLE 24   VOTE
VOTES IN NATIONAL ELECTIONS AS A PERCENTAGE OF VOTING AGE POPULATION

TPOP	WAPC	WAGE	FEMW	BRTH	DTHS	NATR	POPR	PC20	20CH	GGEX	GGRV	CGEX	CGRV
	41	42	41	-45	-46	-42	-41	38		63	64	44	40
	(96)	(65)	(58)	(65)	(47)	(51)	(83)	(90)		(26)	(27)	(38)	(38)

GGEM	CGEM	MILP	DEFX	VOTE	COMV	RELV	SOCV	NCSV	VIOL	EXEC	NEWS	DOML	FOML
78	25	29		100	54		21	-59	-22		52	42	26
(16)	(18)	(73)		(100)	(44)		(58)	(57)	(66)		(93)	(55)	(53)

FS/R	RADS	RDCH	TELE	CINE	LANG	AREA	DENS	AGDS	GNP	GNPC	GPCH	TRDE	CAPF
26	51	35	40	45	29	-22	29	27	28	46	55		38
(52)	(92)	(77)	(61)	(78)	(50)	(99)	(99)	(83)	(87)	(87)	(59)		(68)

CONS	GPAG	LFAG	AGCH	NONA	INDY	UNWA	UNWS	ACHT	LIFE	INFD	PHYS	HOSP	HPCH
-41	-50	-43		47	43				55	-37	-37	-48	
(57)	(63)	(76)		(62)	(62)				(63)	(42)	(93)	(96)	

HIED	PSED	LIT	LTCH	MARG	IMMG	EMIG	LNDG	RENT	YBFT	YAFT	CATH	CHRS	MOSL
37	53	63		57		29	-39		-45	-30		34	-43
(84)	(96)	(87)		(43)		(32)	(46)		(19)	(12)		(79)	(79)

VARIABLE 25   COMV
VOTES FOR COMMUNIST PARTY AS A PERCENTAGE OF TOTAL VOTE

TPOP	WAPC	WAGE	FEMW	BRTH	DTHS	NATR	POPR	PC20	20CH	GGEX	GGRV	CGEX	CGRV
	22			-23	-25		-25	-23				22	21
	(44)			(40)	(34)		(43)	(41)				(25)	(25)

GGEM	CGEM	MILP	DEFX	VOTE	COMV	RELV	SOCV	NCSV	VIOL	EXEC	NEWS	DOML	FOML
	43	34	54	100	-29	-50	-90		26				
	(42)	(35)	(44)	(44)	(43)	(44)	(44)		(43)				

FS/R	RADS	RDCH	TELE	CINE	LANG	AREA	DENS	AGDS	GNP	GNPC	GPCH	TRDE	CAPF
39				21							55	-42	32
(30)				(41)							(40)	(36)	(38)

CONS	GPAG	LFAG	AGCH	NONA	INDY	UNWA	UNWS	ACHT	LIFE	INFD	PHYS	HOSP	HPCH
-22		32								34			-45
(34)		(44)								(31)			(38)

HIED	PSED	LIT	LTCH	MARG	IMMG	EMIG	LNDG	RENT	YBFT	YAFT	CATH	CHRS	MOSL
			50	53	-55	-29	-41						
			(21)	(33)	(24)	(22)	(32)						

TABLE B.1 (continued)

```
VARIABLE 26      RELV
VOTES FOR RELIGIOUS PARTIES AS A PERCENTAGE OF TOTAL VOTE

TPOP WAPC WAGE FEMW BRTH DTHS NATR POPR PC20 20CH GGEX GGRV CGEX CGRV
     28             -22       -26            -54   25   20   35   33
     (56)           (49)      (44)           (36) (21) (22) (28) (28)
GGEM CGEM MILP DEFX VOTE COMV RELV SOCV NCSV VIOL EXEC NEWS DOML FOML
-24                 -29  100  22   -22
(14)                (43) (56) (56) (56)
FS/R RADS RDCH TELE CINE LANG AREA DENS AGDS  GNP GNPC GPCH TRDE CAPF
26                            26   24
(37)                          (56) (56)
CONS GPAG LFAG AGCH NONA INDY UNWA UNWS ACHT LIFE INFD PHYS HOSP HPCH
     -24       25   27                   -29
     (56)      (50) (50)                 (31)
HIED PSED LIT LTCH MARG IMMG EMIG LNDG RENT YBFT YAFT CATH CHRS MOSL
          -25                      23   33        21
          (30)                     (38) (17)      (54)


VARIABLE 27      SOCV
VOTES FOR SOCIALIST PARTIES AS A PERCENTAGE OF TOTAL VOTE

TPOP WAPC WAGE FEMW BRTH DTHS NATR POPR PC20 20CH GGEX GGRV CGEX CGRV
     33   50        -35  -24  -22       38   -43  31   29   48   54
     (58) (53)      (50) (42) (45)      (54)      (36) (22) (23) (29) (29)
GGEM CGEM MILP DEFX VOTE COMV RELV SOCV NCSV VIOL EXEC NEWS DOML FOML
65   60             21   -50  22   100  23   -28       26        37
(12) (14)           (58) (44) (56) (58) (57) (51)      (58)      (40)
FS/R RADS RDCH TELE CINE LANG AREA DENS AGDS  GNP GNPC GPCH TRDE CAPF
               44             -30  28   37        24        39
               (45)           (58) (58) (57)      (58)      (47)
CONS GPAG LFAG AGCH NONA INDY UNWA UNWS ACHT LIFE INFD PHYS HOSP HPCH
-28  -21  -49  31   61   42        -49  -31  29   -49       -21
(46) (48) (58) (38) (51) (51)      (24) (31) (50) (37)      (58)
HIED PSED LIT LTCH MARG IMMG EMIG LNDG RENT YBFT YAFT CATH CHRS MOSL
28                  -23       25        -22       -24       -40
(58)                (31)      (30)      (40)      (18)      (56)


VARIABLE 28      NCSV
VOTES FOR NON-COMMUNIST SECULAR PARTIES AS A PERCENTAGE OF TOTAL VOTE

TPOP WAPC WAGE FEMW BRTH DTHS NATR POPR PC20 20CH GGEX GGRV CGEX CGRV
-21  -42            42        38   38                 -27  -23  -40  -39
(57) (57)           (50)      (45) (56)               (21) (22) (28) (28)
GGEM CGEM MILP DEFX VOTE COMV RELV SOCV NCSV VIOL EXEC NEWS DOML FOML
25        -35  -34  -59  -90  -22  23   100       -25
(12)      (53) (46) (57) (44) (56) (57) (57)      (54)
FS/R RADS RDCH TELE CINE LANG AREA DENS AGDS  GNP GNPC GPCH TRDE CAPF
-50                          -24                      -55       -34
(38)                         (57)                     (50)      (50)
CONS GPAG LFAG AGCH NONA INDY UNWA UNWS ACHT LIFE INFD PHYS HOSP HPCH
36                  -33   29        25   -28  -22            21   43
(45)                (51) (32)       (31) (49) (37)           (57) (48)
HIED PSED LIT LTCH MARG IMMG EMIG LNDG RENT YBFT YAFT CATH CHRS MOSL
          -21  -26  -53  41   20   34   -22  -25
          (57) (31) (38) (30) (24) (40) (39) (18)
```

TABLE B.1 (continued)

VARIABLE 29   VIOL
DEATHS FROM DOMESTIC GROUP VIOLENCE PER 1,000,000 POPULATION (L)

TPOP	WAPC	WAGE	FEMW	BRTH	DTHS	NATR	POPR	PC20	20CH	GGEX	GGRV	CGEX	CGRV
	-41	-35		55	42	39	38	-31	20	-25	-40	-32	-45
	(74)	(58)		(56)	(42)	(46)	(68)	(73)	(38)	(25)	(26)	(38)	(38)
GGEM	CGEM	MILP	DEFX	VOTE	COMV	RELV	SOCV	NCSV	VIOL	EXEC	NEWS	DOML	FOML
-63	-30	-35		-22			-28		100	-30	-35	-55	-52
(121)	(17)	(74)		(66)			(51)		(74)	(73)	(73)	(46)	(45)
FS/R	RADS	RDCH	TELE	CINE	LANG	AREA	DENS	AGDS	GNP	GNPC	GPCH	TRDE	CAPF
-40	-38	-26	-28	-25	-35				-32	-43	-43		-37
(44)	(70)	(65)	(58)	(62)	(34)				(74)	(74)	(53)		(58)
CONS	GPAG	LFAG	AGCH	NONA	INDY	UNWA	UNWS	ACHT	LIFE	INFD	PHYS	HOSP	HPCH
33	43	42	-39	-43	-44	-26	32	22	-56	47	36	36	
(52)	(55)	(69)	(42)	(58)	(59)	(34)	(25)	(39)	(55)	(36)	(71)	(74)	
HIED	PSED	LIT	LTCH	MARG	IMMG	EMIG	LNDG	RENT	YBFT	YAFT	CATH	CHRS	MOSL
-33	-39	-37		-32		-35	44	22	34	36			
(71)	(72)	(74)		(39)		(28)	(44)	(44)	(18)	(12)			

VARIABLE 30   EXEC   EXECUTIVE STABILITY—NUMBER
OF YEARS INDEPENDENT/NUMBER OF CHIEF EXECUTIVES, 1945-61 (L)

TPOP	WAPC	WAGE	FEMW	BRTH	DTHS	NATR	POPR	PC20	20CH	GGEX	GGRV	CGEX	CGRV
				-23									-31
				(64)									(38)
GGEM	CGEM	MILP	DEFX	VOTE	COMV	RELV	SOCV	NCSV	VIOL	EXEC	NEWS	DOML	FOML
-21					26			-25	-30	100		33	
(14)					(43)			(54)	(73)	(87)		(54)	
FS/R	RADS	RDCH	TELE	CINE	LANG	AREA	DENS	AGDS	GNP	GNPC	GPCH	TRDE	CAPF
21			21	23	-23						28		28
(52)			(60)	(72)	(41)						(59)		(63)
CONS	GPAG	LFAG	AGCH	NONA	INDY	UNWA	UNWS	ACHT	LIFE	INFD	PHYS	HOSP	HPCH
		-26			21								
		(78)			(63)								
HIED	PSED	LIT	LTCH	MARG	IMMG	EMIG	LNDG	RENT	YBFT	YAFT	CATH	CHRS	MOSL
							-32	27					
							(47)	(48)					

VARIABLE 31   NEWS
DAILY NEWSPAPER CIRCULATION PER 1,000 POPULATION (L)

TPOP	WAPC	WAGE	FEMW	BRTH	DTHS	NATR	POPR	PC20	20CH	GGEX	GGRV	CGEX	CGRV
	41	74	32	-73	-51	-58	-33	69		55	65	42	53
	(119)	(79)	(69)	(85)	(56)	(60)	(107)	(115)		(28)	(29)	(41)	(41)
GGEM	CGEM	MILP	DEFX	VOTE	COMV	RELV	SOCV	NCSV	VIOL	EXEC	NEWS	DOML	FOML
74	52			52			26		-35		100	85	60
(18)	(21)			(93)			(58)		(73)		(125)	(71)	(70)
FS/R	RADS	RDCH	TELE	CINE	LANG	AREA	DENS	AGDS	GNP	GNPC	GPCH	TRDE	CAPF
28	87	52	72	82	66	-25	38	27	39	80	35		49
(69)	(114)	(94)	(68)	(101)	(59)	(123)	(123)	(109)	(111)	(111)	(67)		(76)
CONS	GPAG	LFAG	AGCH	NONA	INDY	UNWA	UNWS	ACHT	LIFE	INFD	PHYS	HOSP	HPCH
-39	-75	-81		82	80	51			89	-80	-89	-74	37
(61)	(74)	(97)		(77)	(78)	(54)			(72)	(50)	(118)	(120)	(83)
HIED	PSED	LIT	LTCH	MARG	IMMG	EMIG	LNDG	RENT	YBFT	YAFT	CATH	CHRS	MOSL
74	88	88		36	34	36	-29		-32	-32	29	69	-41
(104)	(120)	(111)		(50)	(40)	(40)	(50)		(20)	(12)	(109)	(96)	(96)

TABLE B.1 (continued)

VARIABLE 32 — DOML
ITEMS OF DOMESTIC MAIL PER CAPITA (L)

TPOP	WAPC	WAGE	FEMW	BRTH	DTHS	NATR	POPR	PC20	20CH	GGEX	GGRV	CGEX	CGRV
51	75	53	-80	-30		-75	-51	65		41	52		39
(72)	(55)	(47)	(52)	(42)		(44)	(68)	(68)		(25)	(26)		(30)

GGEM	CGEM	MILP	DEFX	VOTE	COMV	RELV	SOCV	NCSV	VIOL	EXEC	NEWS	DOML	FOML
78	41			42					-55	33	85	100	67
(15)	(17)			(55)					(46)	(54)	(71)	(76)	(74)

FS/R	RADS	RDCH	TELE	CINE	LANG	AREA	DENS	AGDS	GNP	GNPC	GPCH	TRDE	CAPF
32	82	52	73	65	50		20		55	89	36		49
(72)	(72)	(66)	(43)	(69)	(35)		(73)		(75)	(75)	(47)		(53)

CONS	GPAG	LFAG	AGCH	NONA	INDY	UNWA	UNWS	ACHT	LIFE	INFD	PHYS	HOSP	HPCH
-52	-65	-80		81	78	24		-28	80	-70	-83	-72	29
(44)	(52)	(63)		(53)	(54)	(42)		(33)	(49)	(37)	(72)	(74)	(57)

HIED	PSED	LIT	LTCH	MARG	IMMG	EMIG	LNDG	RENT	YBFT	YAFT	CATH	CHRS	MOSL
62	78	82	-25	34	32	28	-25	-23			29	74	-46
(66)	(71)	(75)	(28)	(37)	(34)	(32)	(33)	(16)			(72)	(55)	(55)

VARIABLE 33 — FOML
ITEMS OF FOREIGN MAIL SENT PER CAPITA (L)

TPOP	WAPC	WAGE	FEMW	BRTH	DTHS	NATR	POPR	PC20	20CH	GGEX	GGRV	CGEX	CGRV
-39	20	73	42	-46	-49	-33	-40	54	-27	41	50	42	48
(72)	(70)	(54)	(46)	(51)	(41)	(43)	(67)	(66)	(36)	(25)	(26)	(30)	(30)

GGEM	CGEM	MILP	DEFX	VOTE	COMV	RELV	SOCV	NCSV	VIOL	EXEC	NEWS	DOML	FOML
87	64			26			37		-52		60	67	100
(15)	(17)			(53)			(40)		(45)		(70)	(74)	(74)

FS/R	RADS	RDCH	TELE	CINE	LANG	AREA	DENS	AGDS	GNP	GNPC	GPCH	TRDE	CAPF
42	59	22	50	50	37	-47	25	22		61	31	41	43
(71)	(70)	(65)	(42)	(68)	(34)	(72)	(72)	(70)		(73)	(46)	(54)	(52)

CONS	GPAG	LFAG	AGCH	NONA	INDY	UNWA	UNWS	ACHT	LIFE	INFD	PHYS	HOSP	HPCH
-41	-72	-66		78	68			-22	58	-59	-56	-62	38
(43)	(51)	(62)		(52)	(53)			(26)	(48)	(36)	(70)	(72)	(56)

HIED	PSED	LIT	LTCH	MARG	IMMG	EMIG	LNDG	RENT	YBFT	YAFT	CATH	CHRS	MOSL
30	59	48			23	48	-21					61	-22
(65)	(70)	(73)			(34)	(32)	(33)					(54)	(54)

VARIABLE 34 — FS/R
FOREIGN ITEMS SENT/FOREIGN ITEMS RECEIVED

TPOP	WAPC	WAGE	FEMW	BRTH	DTHS	NATR	POPR	PC20	20CH	GGEX	GGRV	CGEX	CGRV
		36	-23				-24	26		31	36	51	28
		(53)	(50)				(66)	(66)		(24)	(25)	(29)	(29)

GGEM	CGEM	MILP	DEFX	VOTE	COMV	RELV	SOCV	NCSV	VIOL	EXEC	NEWS	DOML	FOML
		25	21	26	39	26		-50	-40	21	28	32	42
		(51)	(52)	(52)	(30)	(37)		(38)	(44)	(52)	(69)	(72)	(71)

FS/R	RADS	RDCH	TELE	CINE	LANG	AREA	DENS	AGDS	GNP	GNPC	GPCH	TRDE	CAPF
100	28					-33	48	42		28	22	29	
(74)	(70)					(71)	(71)	(69)		(73)	(47)	(53)	

CONS	GPAG	LFAG	AGCH	NONA	INDY	UNWA	UNWS	ACHT	LIFE	INFD	PHYS	HOSP	HPCH
	-32	-41	32	34	35			-35	32		-21	-24	
	(50)	(61)	(33)	(51)	(52)			(32)	(46)		(70)	(72)	

HIED	PSED	LIT	LTCH	MARG	IMMG	EMIG	LNDG	RENT	YBFT	YAFT	CATH	CHRS	MOSL
	32	21	23	24			-40					23	
	(69)	(73)	(27)	(34)			(32)					(53)	

TABLE B.1 (continued)

VARIABLE 35   RADS
RADIOS PER 1,000 POPULATION (L)

TPOP	WAPC	WAGE	FEMW	BRTH	DTHS	NATR	POPR	PC20	20CH	GGEX	GGRV	CGEX	CGRV
	39	74	27	-69	-50	-57	-39	68		42	55	44	51
	(115)	(74)	(65)	(79)	(54)	(58)	(101)	(109)		(28)	(29)	(41)	(41)
GGEM	CGEM	MILP	DEFX	VOTE	COMV	RELV	SOCV	NCSV	VIOL	EXEC	NEWS	DOML	FOML
74	45	23		51					-38		87	82	59
(17)	(20)	(82)		(92)					(70)		(114)	(72)	(70)
FS/R	RADS	RDCH	TELE	CINE	LANG	AREA	DENS	AGDS	GNP	GNPC	GPCH	TRDE	CAPF
28	100	65	79	77	64	-25	26		32	85	31		45
(70)	(118)	(96)	(66)	(97)	(58)	(117)	(117)		(107)	(107)	(65)		(74)
CONS	GPAG	LFAG	AGCH	NONA	INDY	UNWA	UNWS	ACHT	LIFE	INFD	PHYS	HOSP	HPCH
-35	-79	-76		74	70	51		-21	86	-75	-89	-77	26
(60)	(71)	(90)		(73)	(73)	(51)		(41)	(70)	(48)	(114)	(116)	(87)
HIED	PSED	LIT	LTCH	MARG	IMMG	EMIG	LNDG	RENT	YBFT	YAFT	CATH	CHRS	MOSL
63	83	80		43	31	43					35	68	-38
(100)	(115)	(107)		(48)	(40)	(39)					(104)	(93)	(93)

VARIABLE 36   RDCH
RADIOS PER 1,000 POPULATION--AVERAGE ANNUAL INCREASE (L)

TPOP	WAPC	WAGE	FEMW	BRTH	DTHS	NATR	POPR	PC20	20CH	GGEX	GGRV	CGEX	CGRV
	40	41		-43	-21	-25	-32	37					
	(95)	(72)		(70)	(52)	(56)	(92)	(91)					
GGEM	CGEM	MILP	DEFX	VOTE	COMV	RELV	SOCV	NCSV	VIOL	EXEC	NEWS	DOML	FOML
		24		35					-26		52	52	22
		(72)		(77)					(65)		(94)	(66)	(65)
FS/R	RADS	RDCH	TELE	CINE	LANG	AREA	DENS	AGDS	GNP	GNPC	GPCH	TRDE	CAPF
	65	100	47	43	44				41	63			27
	(96)	(97)	(62)	(86)	(47)				(96)	(96)			(72)
CONS	GPAG	LFAG	AGCH	NONA	INDY	UNWA	UNWS	ACHT	LIFE	INFD	PHYS	HOSP	HPCH
-26	-54	-50		40	35	36	36		49	-22	-53	-47	
(59)	(67)	(87)		(70)	(70)	(46)	(30)		(63)	(46)	(92)	(96)	
HIED	PSED	LIT	LTCH	MARG	IMMG	EMIG	LNDG	RENT	YBFT	YAFT	CATH	CHRS	MOSL
35	52	53	-45	30			-25					35	-26
(89)	(96)	(95)	(39)	(46)			(46)					(76)	(76)

VARIABLE 37   TELE
TELEVISION SETS PER 1,000 POPULATION (L)

TPOP	WAPC	WAGE	FEMW	BRTH	DTHS	NATR	POPR	PC20	20CH	GGEX	GGRV	CGEX	CGRV
	47	74	31	-56	-41	-35	-30	54		53	54	33	30
	(68)	(57)	(52)	(56)	(42)	(45)	(66)	(67)		(21)	(22)	(30)	(30)
GGEM	CGEM	MILP	DEFX	VOTE	COMV	RELV	SOCV	NCSV	VIOL	EXEC	NEWS	DOML	FOML
70	41			40			44		-28	21	72	73	50
(12)	(15)			(61)			(45)		(58)	(60)	(68)	(43)	(42)
FS/R	RADS	RDCH	TELE	CINE	LANG	AREA	DENS	AGDS	GNP	GNPC	GPCH	TRDE	CAPF
	79	47	100	63	42				34	75	28	20	45
	(66)	(62)	(69)	(62)	(29)				(69)	(69)	(51)	(55)	(53)
CONS	GPAG	LFAG	AGCH	NONA	INDY	UNWA	UNWS	ACHT	LIFE	INFD	PHYS	HOSP	HPCH
-59	-76	-75		71	61	28		-24	78	-75	-73	-77	31
(49)	(52)	(64)		(55)	(56)	(33)		(37)	(52)	(39)	(67)	(69)	(59)
HIED	PSED	LIT	LTCH	MARG	IMMG	EMIG	LNDG	RENT	YBFT	YAFT	CATH	CHRS	MOSL
37	68	69	-31	28	39	43	-21	-22			23	60	-43
(67)	(69)	(68)	(32)	(40)	(34)	(26)	(42)	(40)			(69)	(56)	(56)

TABLE B.1 (continued)

VARIABLE 38   CINE
CINEMA ATTENDANCE PER CAPITA (L)

TPOP	WAPC	WAGE	FEMW	BRTH	DTHS	NATR	POPR	PC20	20CH	GGEX	GGRV	CGEX	CGRV
35	68	23	-52	-41	-27		62				35	28	32
(102)	(70)	(62)	(72)	(52)	(56)		(96)				(29)	(37)	(37)

GGEM	CGEM	MILP	DEFX	VOTE	COMV	RELV	SOCV	NCSV	VIOL	EXEC	NEWS	DOML	FOML
68	22		45	21					-25	23	82	65	50
(18)	(19)		(78)	(41)					(62)	(72)	(101)	(69)	(68)

FS/R	RADS	RDCH	TELE	CINE	LANG	AREA	DENS	AGDS	GNP	GNPC	GPCH	TRDE	CAPF
	77	43	63	100	59	-23	34	27	33	65	42		41
	(97)	(86)	(62)	(104)	(50)	(103)	(103)	(96)	(100)	(100)	(61)		(69)

CONS	GPAG	LFAG	AGCH	NONA	INDY	UNWA	UNWS	ACHT	LIFE	INFD	PHYS	HOSP	HPCH
-39	-59	-60		64	60	41			65	-33	-79	-59	29
(56)	(69)	(84)		(69)	(70)	(49)			(61)	(47)	(100)	(104)	(81)

HIED	PSED	LIT	LTCH	MARG	IMMG	EMIG	LNDG	RENT	YBFT	YAFT	CATH	CHRS	MOSL
66	76	71		28		37			-38	-59	22	57	-31
(90)	(102)	(99)		(47)		(39)			(20)	(12)	(96)	(80)	(80)

VARIABLE 39   LANG
SPEAKERS OF DOMINANT LANGUAGE AS A PERCENTAGE OF POPULATION

TPOP	WAPC	WAGE	FEMW	BRTH	DTHS	NATR	POPR	PC20	20CH	GGEX	GGRV	CGEX	CGRV
30	40			-32	-43			54		29	51	35	49
(65)	(36)			(37)	(20)			(61)		(12)	(13)	(21)	(21)

GGEM	CGEM	MILP	DEFX	VOTE	COMV	RELV	SOCV	NCSV	VIOL	EXEC	NEWS	DOML	FOML
		38	29						-35	-23	66	50	37
		(40)	(50)						(34)	(41)	(59)	(35)	(34)

FS/R	RADS	RDCH	TELE	CINE	LANG	AREA	DENS	AGDS	GNP	GNPC	GPCH	TRDE	CAPF
	64	44	42	59	100				27	47		-24	
	(58)	(47)	(29)	(50)	(66)				(58)	(58)		(42)	

CONS	GPAG	LFAG	AGCH	NONA	INDY	UNWA	UNWS	ACHT	LIFE	INFD	PHYS	HOSP	HPCH
	-38	-27		27	29	40			63	-41	-64	-42	38
	(37)	(43)		(34)	(34)	(29)			(33)	(18)	(61)	(65)	(43)

HIED	PSED	LIT	LTCH	MARG	IMMG	EMIG	LNDG	RENT	YBFT	YAFT	CATH	CHRS	MOSL
60	48	54	24			44	21	-59			29	46	
(51)	(62)	(57)	(22)			(20)	(22)	(22)			(58)	(51)	

VARIABLE 40   AREA
AREA (SQUARE KILOMETERS) (L)

TPOP	WAPC	WAGE	FEMW	BRTH	DTHS	NATR	POPR	PC20	20CH	GGEX	GGRV	CGEX	CGRV
59		-23		21			-22	21				-44	-38
(133)		(78)		(56)			(119)	(50)				(41)	(41)

GGEM	CGEM	MILP	DEFX	VOTE	COMV	RELV	SOCV	NCSV	VIOL	EXEC	NEWS	DOML	FOML
	-24		-22			-30				-25			-47
	(21)		(99)			(58)					(123)		(72)

FS/R	RADS	RDCH	TELE	CINE	LANG	AREA	DENS	AGDS	GNP	GNPC	GPCH	TRDE	CAPF
-33	-25			-23		100	-67	-58	45			-54	
(71)	(117)			(103)		(133)	(133)	(110)	(117)			(81)	

CONS	GPAG	LFAG	AGCH	NONA	INDY	UNWA	UNWS	ACHT	LIFE	INFD	PHYS	HOSP	HPCH
-28	25	27		-27							21		
(62)	(75)	(96)		(77)							(123)		

HIED	PSED	LIT	LTCH	MARG	IMMG	EMIG	LNDG	RENT	YBFT	YAFT	CATH	CHRS	MOSL
	-33		-35	35		-32				-55		-23	23
	(124)		(43)	(50)		(40)				(12)		(103)	(103)

TABLE B.1 (continued)

```
VARIABLE 41      DENS
POPULATION PER SQUARE KILOMETER (L)

 TPOP WAPC WAGE FEMW BRTH DTHS NATR POPR PC20 20CH GGEX GGRV CGEX CGRV
                     -31            27                          23   33
                     (83)         (119)                       (41) (41)
 GGEM CGEM MILP DEFX VOTE COMV RELV SOCV NCSV VIOL EXEC NEWS DOML FOML
 -38            29        26   28   -24                 38   20   25
 (18)          (99)      (56) (58) (57)               (123) (73) (72)
 FS/R RADS RDCH TELE CINE LANG AREA DENS AGDS  GNP GNPC GPCH TRDE CAPF
 48   26        34        -67  100  85   23   22   39
 (71)(117)     (103)      (133)(133)(110)(117)(117)(68)
 CONS GPAG LFAG AGCH NONA INDY UNWA UNWS ACHT LIFE INFD PHYS HOSP HPCH
      -29  31   27   22   30   34        28       -33
      (96) (48) (77) (78) (52) (33)     (71)      (123)
 HIED PSED  LIT LTCH MARG IMMG EMIG LNDG RENT YBFT YAFT CATH CHRS MOSL
 43   29                  25   -43       26   58        20   -30
 (124)(114)              (40) (50)      (20) (12)       (103)(103)


VARIABLE 42      AGDS
POPULATION PER 1,000 HECTARES OF AGRICULTURAL LAND (L)

 TPOP WAPC WAGE FEMW BRTH DTHS NATR POPR PC20 20CH GGEX GGRV CGEX CGRV
                              23                           27   36
                            (103)                         (40) (40)
 GGEM CGEM MILP DEFX VOTE COMV RELV SOCV NCSV VIOL EXEC NEWS DOML FOML
 -58            27        24   37                       27        22
 (17)          (83)      (56) (57)                     (109)     (70)
 FS/R RADS RDCH TELE CINE LANG AREA DENS AGDS  GNP GNPC GPCH TRDE CAPF
 42            27        -58  85   100           30
 (69)          (96)      (110)(110)(115)        (66)
 CONS GPAG LFAG AGCH NONA INDY UNWA UNWS ACHT LIFE INFD PHYS HOSP HPCH
      -25  27   21        31   33   -29
      (94) (48) (76)      (50) (32) (41)
 HIED PSED  LIT LTCH MARG IMMG EMIG LNDG RENT YBFT YAFT CATH CHRS MOSL
 32   27                       -42       28   54             -26
 (106)(110)                   (49)      (20) (12)            (82)


VARIABLE 43      GNP
GROSS NATIONAL PRODUCT, 1957, U.S. DOLLARS (L)

 TPOP WAPC WAGE FEMW BRTH DTHS NATR POPR PC20 20CH GGEX GGRV CGEX CGRV
 84   43   21        -52       -54  -28  35             34   30        27
 (117)(115)(78)      (79)      (60)(107)(110)          (28) (29)      (41)
 GGEM CGEM MILP DEFX VOTE COMV RELV SOCV NCSV VIOL EXEC NEWS DOML FOML
 27            27   28                      -32        39   55
 (18)          (81) (87)                    (74)       (111)(75)
 FS/R RADS RDCH TELE CINE LANG AREA DENS AGDS  GNP GNPC GPCH TRDE CAPF
      32   41   34   33   27   45   23        100  53   29   -59
      (107)(96)(69)(100)(58)(117)(117)       (122)(122)(68) (80)
 CONS GPAG LFAG AGCH NONA INDY UNWA UNWS ACHT LIFE INFD PHYS HOSP HPCH
 -47  -24  -37        31   35   25        39   -21  -43  -24
 (62) (75) (95)      (76) (77) (49)      (67) (50)(114)(117)
 HIED PSED  LIT LTCH MARG IMMG EMIG LNDG RENT YBFT YAFT CATH CHRS MOSL
 39   35   47   -39  55             -35       -22  -27        26   -25
 (102)(111)(117)(43)(50)           (50)      (20) (12)       (88) (88)
```

TABLE B.1 (continued)

VARIABLE 44   GNPC
GROSS NATIONAL PRODUCT PER CAPITA, 1957, U.S. DOLLARS (L)

TPOP	WAPC	WAGE	FEMW	BRTH	DTHS	NATR	POPR	PC20	20CH	GGEX	GGRV	CGEX	CGRV
	48 (115)	76 (78)	31 (69)	-76 (79)	-41 (56)	-59 (60)	71 (110)			53 (28)	58 (29)	37 (41)	47 (41)

GGEM	CGEM	MILP	DEFX	VOTE	COMV	RELV	SOCV	NCSV	VIOL	EXEC	NEWS	DOML	FOML
83 (18)	50 (20)		46 (87)			24 (58)			-43 (74)	80 (111)	89 (75)	61 (73)	

FS/R	RADS	RDCH	TELE	CINE	LANG	AREA	DENS	AGDS	GNP	GNPC	GPCH	TRDE	CAPF
28 (73)	85 (107)	63 (96)	75 (69)	65 (100)	47 (58)		22 (117)		53 (122)	100 (122)	28 (68)		45 (77)

CONS	GPAG	LFAG	AGCH	NONA	INDY	UNWA	UNWS	ACHT	LIFE	INFD	PHYS	HOSP	HPCH
-44 (62)	-81 (75)	-86 (95)		84 (76)	79 (77)	29 (49)			86 (67)	-76 (50)	-81 (114)	-77 (117)	29 (89)

HIED	PSED	LIT	LTCH	MARG	IMMG	EMIG	LNDG	RENT	YBFT	YAFT	CATH	CHRS	MOSL
58 (102)	80 (111)	80 (117)	-25 (43)	41 (50)	45 (41)	36 (40)	-26 (50)		-40 (20)	-30 (12)	31 (117)	68 (88)	-44 (88)

VARIABLE 45   GPCH
ANNUAL GROWTH OF G.N.P. PER CAPITA

TPOP	WAPC	WAGE	FEMW	BRTH	DTHS	NATR	POPR	PC20	20CH	GGEX	GGRV	CGEX	CGRV
	45 (68)	27 (60)	32 (54)	-49 (55)	-35 (43)	-27 (46)	-44 (68)	27 (66)	26 (38)		31 (25)	53 (31)	60 (31)

GGEM	CGEM	MILP	DEFX	VOTE	COMV	RELV	SOCV	NCSV	VIOL	EXEC	NEWS	DOML	FOML
25 (13)		30 (59)	55 (59)	55 (40)				-55 (50)	-43 (53)	28 (59)	35 (67)	36 (47)	31 (46)

FS/R	RADS	RDCH	TELE	CINE	LANG	AREA	DENS	AGDS	GNP	GNPC	GPCH	TRDE	CAPF
22 (47)	31 (65)		28 (51)	42 (61)			39 (68)	30 (66)	29 (68)	28 (68)	100 (68)		57 (58)

CONS	GPAG	LFAG	AGCH	NONA	INDY	UNWA	UNWS	ACHT	LIFE	INFD	PHYS	HOSP	HPCH
-36 (51)	-34 (61)	-20 (67)		32 (59)	30 (59)			-28 (34)	44 (54)		-41 (68)	-39 (68)	

HIED	PSED	LIT	LTCH	MARG	IMMG	EMIG	LNDG	RENT	YBFT	YAFT	CATH	CHRS	MOSL
42 (68)	49 (68)	26 (35)	55 (40)				-32 (38)	-21 (42)					-32 (59)

VARIABLE 46   TRDE
FOREIGN TRADE (EXPORTS + IMPORTS) AS A PERCENTAGE OF G.N.P.

TPOP	WAPC	WAGE	FEMW	BRTH	DTHS	NATR	POPR	PC20	20CH	GGEX	GGRV	CGEX	CGRV
-69 (81)	28 (61)											31 (38)	

GGEM	CGEM	MILP	DEFX	VOTE	COMV	RELV	SOCV	NCSV	VIOL	EXEC	NEWS	DOML	FOML
30 (15)	42 (19)	-22 (69)	-26 (74)		-42 (36)		39 (47)						41 (54)

FS/R	RADS	RDCH	TELE	CINE	LANG	AREA	DENS	AGDS	GNP	GNPC	GPCH	TRDE	CAPF
29 (53)		20 (55)			-24 (42)	-54 (81)			-59 (80)			100 (81)	

CONS	GPAG	LFAG	AGCH	NONA	INDY	UNWA	UNWS	ACHT	LIFE	INFD	PHYS	HOSP	HPCH
	-24 (62)						-20 (28)	-35 (35)				-28 (80)	

HIED	PSED	LIT	LTCH	MARG	IMMG	EMIG	LNDG	RENT	YBFT	YAFT	CATH	CHRS	MOSL
-24 (78)				-41 (40)	23 (36)				22 (19)	29 (12)			

TABLE B.1 (continued)

```
VARIABLE 47        CAPF
GROSS DOMESTIC CAPITAL FORMATION AS A PERCENTAGE OF G.N.P.

TPOP WAPC WAGE FEMW BRTH DTHS NATR POPR PC20 20CH GGEX GGRV CGEX CGRV
  38   41   25  -45  -49  -30  -28   42             41   48   34   35
 (77) (67) (59) (61) (47) (51) (75) (76)           (28) (29) (39) (39)
GGEM CGEM MILP DEFX VOTE COMV RELV SOCV NCSV VIOL EXEC NEWS DOML FOML
  51   29   26        38   32            -34  -37   28   49   49   43
 (18) (20) (63)      (68) (38)           (50) (58) (63) (76) (53) (52)
FS/R RADS RDCH TELE CINE LANG AREA DENS AGDS  GNP GNPC GPCH TRDE CAPF
  45   27   45   41                             45   57        100
 (74) (72) (53) (69)                           (77) (58)      (77)
CONS GPAG LFAG AGCH NONA INDY UNWA UNWS ACHT LIFE INFD PHYS HOSP HPCH
 -77  -54  -35  -20   43   48       -23         50  -40  -42  -57
 (62) (65) (72) (43) (64) (65)      (31)       (60) (41) (75) (77)
HIED PSED  LIT LTCH MARG IMMG EMIG LNDG RENT YBFT YAFT CATH CHRS MOSL
  37   46        29   32   29  -24       -29             31  -38
 (77) (77)      (43) (37) (36) (44)      (19)           (62) (62)


VARIABLE 48        CONS
PRIVATE CONSUMPTION AS A PERCENTAGE OF G.N.P.

TPOP WAPC WAGE FEMW BRTH DTHS NATR POPR PC20 20CH GGEX GGRV CGEX CGRV
 -24  -41  -53  -23   45   39   43   29  -36        -70  -67  -39  -39
 (62) (62) (55) (50) (50) (39) (43) (61) (61)      (25) (26) (34) (34)
GGEM CGEM MILP DEFX VOTE COMV RELV SOCV NCSV VIOL EXEC NEWS DOML FOML
 -53  -31  -24  -41  -41  -22       -28   36   33       -39  -52  -41
 (14) (18) (55) (55) (57) (34)      (46) (45) (52)      (61) (44) (43)
FS/R RADS RDCH TELE CINE LANG AREA DENS AGDS  GNP GNPC GPCH TRDE CAPF
      -35  -26  -59  -39       -28                -47  -44  -36       -77
     (60) (59) (49) (56)      (62)               (62) (62) (51)      (62)
CONS GPAG LFAG AGCH NONA INDY UNWA UNWS ACHT LIFE INFD PHYS HOSP HPCH
 100   47   33       -47  -52        35        -49   56   34   54
 (62) (53) (60)      (53) (54)       (27)      (50) (34) (60) (62)
HIED PSED  LIT LTCH MARG IMMG EMIG LNDG RENT YBFT YAFT CATH CHRS MOSL
      -35  -31       -43  -28  -22   32        40        28
     (62) (62)      (37) (32) (30) (41)      (17)      (61)


VARIABLE 49        GPAG
PERCENTAGE OF GROSS DOMESTIC PRODUCT ORIGINATING IN AGRICULTURE

TPOP WAPC WAGE FEMW BRTH DTHS NATR POPR PC20 20CH GGEX GGRV CGEX CGRV
  21  -36  -68  -33   59   38   42   42  -67        -61  -64  -55  -47
 (75) (75) (61) (54) (56) (44) (47) (74) (73)      (25) (25) (35) (35)
GGEM CGEM MILP DEFX VOTE COMV RELV SOCV NCSV VIOL EXEC NEWS DOML FOML
 -75  -54  -24       -50            -21        43       -75  -65  -72
 (16) (16) (61)      (63)           (48)       (55)     (74) (52) (51)
FS/R RADS RDCH TELE CINE LANG AREA DENS AGDS  GNP GNPC GPCH TRDE CAPF
 -32  -79  -54  -76  -59  -38   25                -24  -81  -34  -24  -54
 (50) (71) (67) (52) (69) (37) (75)              (75) (75) (61) (62) (65)
CONS GPAG LFAG AGCH NONA INDY UNWA UNWS ACHT LIFE INFD PHYS HOSP HPCH
  47  100   77       -80  -71  -30        32  -73   58   69   74  -21
 (53) (75) (69)      (59) (60) (40)      (32) (55) (39) (74) (75) (64)
HIED PSED  LIT LTCH MARG IMMG EMIG LNDG RENT YBFT YAFT CATH CHRS MOSL
 -34  -69  -63   35  -31  -50  -50                       -25  -52   32
 (74) (75) (75) (37) (41) (33) (33)                      (73) (61) (61)
```

TABLE B.1 (continued)

VARIABLE 50   LFAG
PERCENTAGE OF LABOR FORCE EMPLOYED IN AGRICULTURE

TPOP	WAPC	WAGE	FEMW	BRTH	DTHS	NATR	POPR	PC20	20CH	GGEX	GGRV	CGEX	CGRV
	-42	-80	-24	65	41	43	42	-72		-52	-55	-47	-43
	(95)	(77)	(68)	(74)	(54)	(58)	(92)	(92)		(28)	(29)	(37)	(37)

GGEM	CGEM	MILP	DEFX	VOTE	COMV	RELV	SOCV	NCSV	VIOL	EXEC	NEWS	DOML	FOML
-82	-51		-43	32	-24	-49			42	-26	-81	-80	-66
(16)	(19)		(76)	(44)	(56)	(58)			(69)	(78)	(97)	(63)	(62)

FS/R	RADS	RDCH	TELE	CINE	LANG	AREA	DENS	AGDS	GNP	GNPC	GPCH	TRDE	CAPF
-41	-76	-50	-75	-60	-27	27	-29	-25	-37	-86	-20		-35
(61)	(90)	(87)	(64)	(84)	(43)	(96)	(96)	(94)	(95)	(95)	(67)		(72)

CONS	GPAG	LFAG	AGCH	NONA	INDY	UNWA	UNWS	ACHT	LIFE	INFD	PHYS	HOSP	HPCH
33	77	100		-94	-81	-29			-82	69	71	71	-37
(60)	(69)	(98)		(75)	(76)	(48)			(68)	(49)	(92)	(95)	(76)

HIED	PSED	LIT	LTCH	MARG	IMMG	EMIG	LNDG	RENT	YBFT	YAFT	CATH	CHRS	MOSL
-42	-79	-76	34	-23	-58	-34	26		39	30	-23	-56	44
(92)	(94)	(96)	(43)	(48)	(40)	(37)	(48)		(20)	(12)	(93)	(75)	(75)

VARIABLE 51   AGCH
PERCENT OF LABOR FORCE EMPLOYED IN AGRICULTURE--AVERAGE ANNUAL CHANGE

TPOP	WAPC	WAGE	FEMW	BRTH	DTHS	NATR	POPR	PC20	20CH	GGEX	GGRV	CGEX	CGRV
	23			-21		-33			-33				
	(48)			(44)		(41)			(36)				

GGEM	CGEM	MILP	DEFX	VOTE	COMV	RELV	SOCV	NCSV	VIOL	EXEC	NEWS	DOML	FOML
-21							31		-39				
(12)							(38)		(42)				

FS/R	RADS	RDCH	TELE	CINE	LANG	AREA	DENS	AGDS	GNP	GNPC	GPCH	TRDE	CAPF
32							31	27					-20
(33)							(48)	(48)					(43)

CONS	GPAG	LFAG	AGCH	NONA	INDY	UNWA	UNWS	ACHT	LIFE	INFD	PHYS	HOSP	HPCH
			100				-29			33			
			(48)				(21)			(37)			

HIED	PSED	LIT	LTCH	MARG	IMMG	EMIG	LNDG	RENT	YBFT	YAFT	CATH	CHRS	MOSL
-27							-26	24	-25			-31	
(48)							(33)	(35)	(16)			(42)	

VARIABLE 52   NONA
NON-AGRICULTURAL EMPLOYMENT AS A PERCENTAGE OF WORKING AGE POPULATION

TPOP	WAPC	WAGE	FEMW	BRTH	DTHS	NATR	POPR	PC20	20CH	GGEX	GGRV	CGEX	CGRV
	48	88	41	-72	-49	-48	-35	78		57	60	52	52
	(77)	(73)	(68)	(69)	(53)	(56)	(76)	(75)		(26)	(27)	(33)	(33)

GGEM	CGEM	MILP	DEFX	VOTE	COMV	RELV	SOCV	NCSV	VIOL	EXEC	NEWS	DOML	FOML
79	59	20		47	25	61		-43			82	81	78
(14)	(18)	(62)		(62)	(50)	(51)		(58)			(77)	(53)	(52)

FS/R	RADS	RDCH	TELE	CINE	LANG	AREA	DENS	AGDS	GNP	GNPC	GPCH	TRDE	CAPF
34	74	40	71	64	27	-27	27	21	31	84	32		43
(51)	(73)	(70)	(55)	(69)	(34)	(77)	(77)	(76)	(76)	(76)	(59)		(64)

CONS	GPAG	LFAG	AGCH	NONA	INDY	UNWA	UNWS	ACHT	LIFE	INFD	PHYS	HOSP	HPCH
-47	-80	-94	100	91	22				86	-74	-72	-75	23
(53)	(59)	(75)	(77)	(76)	(42)				(60)	(49)	(77)	(77)	(62)

HIED	PSED	LIT	LTCH	MARG	IMMG	EMIG	LNDG	RENT	YBFT	YAFT	CATH	CHRS	MOSL
23	78	76		27	45		-31		-33	-26		50	-42
(75)	(76)	(76)		(47)	(35)		(43)		(20)	(12)		(60)	(60)

TABLE B.1 (continued)

VARIABLE 53   INDY
EMPLOYMENT IN INDUSTRY AS A PERCENTAGE OF WORKING AGE POPULATION

TPOP	WAPC	WAGE	FEMW	BRTH	DTHS	NATR	POPR	PC20	20CH	GGEX	GGRV	CGEX	CGRV
	63	82	43	-78	-33	-66	-45	67		66	56	40	44
	(78)	(73)	(67)	(68)	(52)	(55)	(77)	(76)		(26)	(27)	(33)	(33)
GGEM	CGEM	MILP	DEFX	VOTE	COMV	RELV	SOCV	NCSV	VIOL	EXEC	NEWS	DOML	FOML
72	59	24	21	43		27	42	-33	-44	21	80	78	68
(14)	(18)	(63)	(59)	(62)		(50)	(51)	(59)	(63)	(78)	(54)	(53)
FS/R	RADS	RDCH	TELE	CINE	LANG	AREA	DENS	AGDS	GNP	GNPC	GPCH	TRDE	CAPF
35	70	35	61	60	29		22		35	79	30		48
(52)	(73)	(70)	(56)	(70)	(34)		(78)		(77)	(77)	(59)		(65)
CONS	GPAG	LFAG	AGCH	NONA	INDY	UNWA	UNWS	ACHT	LIFE	INFD	PHYS	HOSP	HPCH
-52	-71	-81		91	100			-23	76	-66	-71	-71	
(54)	(60)	(76)		(76)	(78)			(36)	(61)	(48)	(77)	(78)	
HIED	PSED	LIT	LTCH	MARG	IMMG	EMIG	LNDG	RENT	YBFT	YAFT	CATH	CHRS	MOSL
65	75			40			-33		-31	-28		55	-40
(77)	(77)			(46)			(43)		(20)	(12)		(61)	(61)

VARIABLE 54   UNWA
UNEMPLOYED AS PERCENTAGE OF WORKING AGE POPULATION--AVG. 1958-60 (L)

TPOP	WAPC	WAGE	FEMW	BRTH	DTHS	NATR	POPR	PC20	20CH	GGEX	GGRV	CGEX	CGRV
		25		-28		30		36					
		(45)		(40)		(33)		(52)					
GGEM	CGEM	MILP	DEFX	VOTE	COMV	RELV	SOCV	NCSV	VIOL	EXEC	NEWS	DOML	FOML
21								29	-26		51	24	
(14)								(32)	(34)		(54)	(42)	
FS/R	RADS	RDCH	TELE	CINE	LANG	AREA	DENS	AGDS	GNP	GNPC	GPCH	TRDE	CAPF
	51	36	28	41	40		30	31	25	29			
	(51)	(46)	(33)	(49)	(29)		(52)	(50)	(49)	(49)			
CONS	GPAG	LFAG	AGCH	NONA	INDY	UNWA	UNWS	ACHT	LIFE	INFD	PHYS	HOSP	HPCH
	-30	-29		22	100		83		30		-58	-35	
	(40)	(48)		(42)			(55)	(34)		(38)		(51)	(52)
HIED	PSED	LIT	LTCH	MARG	IMMG	EMIG	LNDG	RENT	YBFT	YAFT	CATH	CHRS	MOSL
52	61	39				30			50		24	41	-27
(49)	(52)	(50)				(28)			(15)		(49)	(43)	(43)

VARIABLE 55   UNWS
UNEMPLOYED AS A PERCENTAGE OF WAGE AND SALARY EARNERS (L)

TPOP	WAPC	WAGE	FEMW	BRTH	DTHS	NATR	POPR	PC20	20CH	GGEX	GGRV	CGEX	CGRV
28										-26		-28	-26
(33)										(18)		(24)	(24)
GGEM	CGEM	MILP	DEFX	VOTE	COMV	RELV	SOCV	NCSV	VIOL	EXEC	NEWS	DOML	FOML
-46	-57						-49		32				-22
(13)	(12)						(24)		(25)				(26)
FS/R	RADS	RDCH	TELE	CINE	LANG	AREA	DENS	AGDS	GNP	GNPC	GPCH	TRDE	CAPF
	36						34	33				-20	-23
	(30)						(33)	(32)				(28)	(31)
CONS	GPAG	LFAG	AGCH	NONA	INDY	UNWA	UNWS	ACHT	LIFE	INFD	PHYS	HOSP	HPCH
35		-29				83	100		35	-22		-43	
(27)		(21)				(34)	(34)		(22)	(33)		(28)	
HIED	PSED	LIT	LTCH	MARG	IMMG	EMIG	LNDG	RENT	YBFT	YAFT	CATH	CHRS	MOSL
26					-26				48		42		
(32)					(18)				(14)		(31)		

TABLE B.1 (continued)

VARIABLE 56   ACHT
INDEX OF ACHIEVEMENT MOTIVATION--CHILDREN'S READERS, 1950

TPOP	WAPC	WAGE	FEMW	BRTH	DTHS	NATR	POPR	PC20	20CH	GGEX	GGRV	CGEX	CGRV
		-20								-27	-23	-25	-30
		(36)								(24)	(25)	(29)	(29)

GGEM	CGEM	MILP	DEFX	VOTE	COMV	RELV	SOCV	NCSV	VIOL	EXEC	NEWS	DOML	FOML
						-29	-31	25	22			-28	
						(31)	(31)	(31)	(39)			(33)	

FS/R	RADS	RDCH	TELE	CINE	LANG	AREA	DENS	AGDS	GNP	GNPC	GPCH	TRDE	CAPF
-35	-21		-24					-29			-28	-35	
(32)	(41)		(37)					(41)			(34)	(35)	

CONS	GPAG	LFAG	AGCH	NONA	INDY	UNWA	UNWS	ACHT	LIFE	INFD	PHYS	HOSP	HPCH
	32			-23				100	-26				
	(32)			(36)				(41)	(32)				

HIED	PSED	LIT	LTCH	MARG	IMMG	EMIG	LNDG	RENT	YBFT	YAFT	CATH	CHRS	MOSL
			23			-21	30		-42				
			(18)			(23)	(27)		(14)				

VARIABLE 57   LIFE
LIFE EXPECTANCY--FEMALES AT AGE ZERO

TPOP	WAPC	WAGE	FEMW	BRTH	DTHS	NATR	POPR	PC20	20CH	GGEX	GGRV	CGEX	CGRV
	49	76	26	-87	-77	-59	-52	71		55	67	56	61
	(71)	(63)	(55)	(65)	(47)	(51)	(67)	(69)		(25)	(26)	(32)	(32)

GGEM	CGEM	MILP	DEFX	VOTE	COMV	RELV	SOCV	NCSV	VIOL	EXEC	NEWS	DOML	FOML
56	43	43		55			29	-28	-56		89	80	58
(14)	(18)	(60)		(63)			(50)	(49)	(55)		(72)	(49)	(48)

FS/R	RADS	RDCH	TELE	CINE	LANG	AREA	DENS	AGDS	GNP	GNPC	GPCH	TRDE	CAPF
32	86	49	78	65	63		28		39	86	44		50
(46)	(70)	(63)	(52)	(61)	(33)		(71)		(67)	(67)	(54)		(60)

CONS	GPAG	LFAG	AGCH	NONA	INDY	UNWA	UNWS	ACHT	LIFE	INFD	PHYS	HOSP	HPCH
-49	-73	-82		86	76	30		-26	100	-87	-88	-79	
(50)	(55)	(68)		(60)	(61)	(38)		(32)	(72)	(43)	(69)	(71)	

HIED	PSED	LIT	LTCH	MARG	IMMG	EMIG	LNDG	RENT	YBFT	YAFT	CATH	CHRS	MOSL
43	90	88	-24	73	38	29	-42		-29	-23		50	-45
(69)	(71)	(67)	(34)	(44)	(36)	(29)	(43)		(18)	(12)		(58)	(58)

VARIABLE 58   INFD
INFANT DEATHS PER 1,000 LIVE BIRTHS (L)

TPOP	WAPC	WAGE	FEMW	BRTH	DTHS	NATR	POPR	PC20	20CH	GGEX	GGRV	CGEX	CGRV
	-30	-55		60	55	39	35	-43		-65	-65	-36	-42
	(50)	(48)		(50)	(48)	(48)	(49)	(48)		(22)	(23)	(21)	(21)

GGEM	CGEM	MILP	DEFX	VOTE	COMV	RELV	SOCV	NCSV	VIOL	EXEC	NEWS	DOML	FOML
-63	-50	-30	-30	-37	34		-49	-22	47		-80	-70	-59
(13)	(15)	(38)	(34)	(42)	(31)		(37)	(37)	(36)		(50)	(37)	(36)

FS/R	RADS	RDCH	TELE	CINE	LANG	AREA	DENS	AGDS	GNP	GNPC	GPCH	TRDE	CAPF
	-75	-22	-75	-33	-41				-21	-76			-40
	(48)	(46)	(39)	(47)	(18)				(50)	(50)			(41)

CONS	GPAG	LFAG	AGCH	NONA	INDY	UNWA	UNWS	ACHT	LIFE	INFD	PHYS	HOSP	HPCH
56	58	69	33	-74	-66		35		-87	100	62	57	
(34)	(39)	(49)	(49)	(49)	(48)		(22)		(43)	(50)	(50)	(50)	

HIED	PSED	LIT	LTCH	MARG	IMMG	EMIG	LNDG	RENT	YBFT	YAFT	CATH	CHRS	MOSL
-39	-65	-65		-28	-37		20		29		32		22
(50)	(50)	(50)		(43)	(27)		(33)		(17)		(47)		(39)

TABLE B.1 (continued)

```
VARIABLE 59        PHYS
INHABITANTS PER PHYSICIAN (L)

 TPOP WAPC WAGE FEMW BRTH DTHS NATR POPR PC20 20CH GGEX GGRV CGEX CGRV
       -37  -64  -21   73   45   70        -69        -36  -49  -39  -49
      (123) (77) (69) (83) (55) (59)      (114)       (28) (29) (41) (41)
 GGEM CGEM MILP DEFX VOTE COMV RELV SOCV NCSV VIOL EXEC NEWS DOML FOML
 -67  -34  -23        -37                           36       -89  -83  -56
 (18) (21) (84)      (93)                          (71)     (118) (72) (70)
 FS/R RADS RDCH TELE CINE LANG AREA DENS AGDS  GNP GNPC GPCH TRDE CAPF
 -21  -89  -53  -73  -79  -64   21  -33       -43  -81  -41       -42
 (70)(114) (92) (67)(100) (61)(123)(123)      (114)(114) (68)      (75)
 CONS GPAG LFAG AGCH NONA INDY UNWA UNWS ACHT LIFE INFD PHYS HOSP HPCH
  34   69   71       -72  -71  -58  -22       -88   62  100   67  -25
 (60) (74) (92)      (77) (77) (51) (33)      (69) (50)(126)(124) (87)
 HIED PSED  LIT LTCH MARG IMMG EMIG LNDG RENT YBFT YAFT CATH CHRS MOSL
 -68  -86  -83       -58  -32  -44   22        37   33  -37  -69   40
(102)(119)(111)      (49) (40) (39) (49)      (20) (12)(110) (96) (96)


VARIABLE 60        HOSP
INHABITANTS PER HOSPITAL BED (L)

 TPOP WAPC WAGE FEMW BRTH DTHS NATR POPR PC20 20CH GGEX GGRV CGEX CGRV
  21  -48  -76  -36   74   43   60   21  -62        -56  -63  -49  -58
(126)(127) (78) (69) (84) (56) (60)(108)(117)       (28) (29) (41) (41)
 GGEM CGEM MILP DEFX VOTE COMV RELV SOCV NCSV VIOL EXEC NEWS DOML FOML
 -79  -52            -48             -21   21   36       -74  -72  -62
 (18) (21)          (96)            (58) (57) (74)      (120) (74) (72)
 FS/R RADS RDCH TELE CINE LANG AREA DENS AGDS  GNP GNPC GPCH TRDE CAPF
 -24  -77  -47  -77  -59  -42                 -24  -77  -39  -28  -57
 (72)(116) (96) (69)(104) (65)                (117)(117) (68) (80) (77)
 CONS GPAG LFAG AGCH NONA INDY UNWA UNWS ACHT LIFE INFD PHYS HOSP HPCH
  54   74   71       -75  -71  -35            -79   57   67  100  -23
 (62) (75) (95)      (77) (78) (52)           (71) (50)(124)(129) (90)
 HIED PSED  LIT LTCH MARG IMMG EMIG LNDG RENT YBFT YAFT CATH CHRS MOSL
 -43  -67  -77       -24  -33  -31   24        42       -29  -62   37
(105)(122)(115)      (50) (41) (39) (50)      (20)     (113) (99) (99)


VARIABLE 61        HPCH
INHABITANTS PER HOSPITAL BED--ANNUAL PERCENTAGE RATE OF CHANGE

 TPOP WAPC WAGE FEMW BRTH DTHS NATR POPR PC20 20CH GGEX GGRV CGEX CGRV
            37                   23        24  -27
           (62)                 (51)      (81) (40)
 GGEM CGEM MILP DEFX VOTE COMV RELV SOCV NCSV VIOL EXEC NEWS DOML FOML
  40   35  -22            -45             43            37   29   38
 (15) (16) (65)          (38)            (48)          (83) (57) (56)
 FS/R RADS RDCH TELE CINE LANG AREA DENS AGDS  GNP GNPC GPCH TRDE CAPF
  26        31   29   38                           29
 (87)      (59) (81) (43)                         (89)
 CONS GPAG LFAG AGCH NONA INDY UNWA UNWS ACHT LIFE INFD PHYS HOSP HPCH
 -21  -37        23            -43                      -25  -23  100
 (64) (76)      (62)          (28)                     (87) (90) (90)
 HIED PSED  LIT LTCH MARG IMMG EMIG LNDG RENT YBFT YAFT CATH CHRS MOSL
  36   25  -41  -40                           -22        26   32
 (88) (88) (35) (43)                          (19)      (87) (71)
```

TABLE B.1 (continued)

VARIABLE 62   HIED
STUDENTS ENROLLED IN HIGHER EDUCATION PER 100,000 POPULATION (L)

TPOP	WAPC	WAGE	FEMW	BRTH	DTHS	NATR	POPR	PC20	20CH	GGEX	GGRV	CGEX	CGRV
35	39		-56		-38	-24	56			42	50	31	33
(104)	(78)		(78)		(59)	(98)	(100)			(28)	(29)	(40)	(40)

GGEM	CGEM	MILP	DEFX	VOTE	COMV	RELV	SOCV	NCSV	VIOL	EXEC	NEWS	DOML	FOML
52	21	29	37						-33		74	62	30
(18)		(83)	(79)	(84)					(71)		(104)	(66)	(65)

FS/R	RADS	RDCH	TELE	CINE	LANG	AREA	DENS	AGDS	GNP	GNPC	GPCH	TRDE	CAPF
63	35	37	66	60					39	58		-24	
(100)	(89)	(67)	(90)	(51)					(102)	(102)		(78)	

CONS	GPAG	LFAG	AGCH	NONA	INDY	UNWA	UNWS	ACHT	LIFE	INFD	PHYS	HOSP	HPCH
-34	-42	-27	23		52	26			43	-39	-68	-43	
(74)	(92)	(48)	(75)		(49)	(32)			(69)	(50)	(102)	(105)	

HIED	PSED	LIT	LTCH	MARG	IMMG	EMIG	LNDG	RENT	YBFT	YAFT	CATH	CHRS	MOSL
100	56	59	-27	37	22	35			-40	-29	33	48	-31
(105)	(103)	(103)		(42)	(48)	(40)	(38)		(20)	(12)	(100)	(84)	(84)

VARIABLE 63   PSED
PRIMARY + SECONDARY SCHOOL PUPILS AS PERCENT OF POPULATION AGED 15-64

TPOP	WAPC	WAGE	FEMW	BRTH	DTHS	NATR	POPR	PC20	20CH	GGEX	GGRV	CGEX	CGRV
31	71	40	-74	-61	-42	-20	72			45	59	46	53
(122)	(77)	(68)	(83)	(56)	(60)	(106)	(115)			(28)	(29)	(41)	(41)

GGEM	CGEM	MILP	DEFX	VOTE	COMV	RELV	SOCV	NCSV	VIOL	EXEC	NEWS	DOML	FOML
74	42	30		53			28		-39		88	78	59
(18)	(21)	(83)		(96)			(58)		(72)		(120)	(71)	(70)

FS/R	RADS	RDCH	TELE	CINE	LANG	AREA	DENS	AGDS	GNP	GNPC	GPCH	TRDE	CAPF
32	83	52	68	76	48	-33	43	32	35	80	42		37
(69)	(115)	(96)	(69)	(102)	(62)	(124)	(124)	(106)	(111)	(111)	(68)		(77)

CONS	GPAG	LFAG	AGCH	NONA	INDY	UNWA	UNWS	ACHT	LIFE	INFD	PHYS	HOSP	HPCH
-35	-69	-79		78	65	61			90	-65	-86	-67	36
(62)	(75)	(94)		(76)	(77)	(52)			(71)	(50)	(119)	(122)	(88)

HIED	PSED	LIT	LTCH	MARG	IMMG	EMIG	LNDG	RENT	YBFT	YAFT	CATH	CHRS	MOSL
56	100	90		34	35	40	-44		-35	-33	21	63	-54
(103)	(125)	(110)		(50)	(41)	(40)	(49)		(20)	(12)	(108)	(98)	(98)

VARIABLE 64   LIT
PERCENTAGE LITERATE OF POPULATION AGED 15 AND OVER

TPOP	WAPC	WAGE	FEMW	BRTH	DTHS	NATR	POPR	PC20	20CH	GGEX	GGRV	CGEX	CGRV
49	72	51	-81	-50	-67	-37	66	22		50	64	30	47
(114)	(78)	(69)	(79)	(56)	(60)	(104)	(109)	(50)		(28)	(29)	(41)	(41)

GGEM	CGEM	MILP	DEFX	VOTE	COMV	RELV	SOCV	NCSV	VIOL	EXEC	NEWS	DOML	FOML
68	35	20		63				-21	-37		88	82	48
(18)	(20)	(85)		(87)				(57)	(74)		(111)	(75)	(73)

FS/R	RADS	RDCH	TELE	CINE	LANG	AREA	DENS	AGDS	GNP	GNPC	GPCH	TRDE	CAPF
21	80	53	69	71	54		29	27	47	80	49		46
(73)	(107)	(95)	(68)	(99)	(57)		(114)	(110)	(117)	(117)	(68)		(77)

CONS	GPAG	LFAG	AGCH	NONA	INDY	UNWA	UNWS	ACHT	LIFE	INFD	PHYS	HOSP	HPCH
-31	-63	-76		76	75	39			88	-65	-83	-77	25
(62)	(75)	(96)		(76)	(77)	(50)			(67)	(50)	(111)	(115)	(88)

HIED	PSED	LIT	LTCH	MARG	IMMG	EMIG	LNDG	RENT	YBFT	YAFT	CATH	CHRS	MOSL
59	90	100		40	24	39	-37		-30	-27	34	71	-64
(103)	(110)	(118)		(49)	(41)	(40)	(50)		(20)	(12)	(114)	(87)	(87)

TABLE B.1 (continued)

VARIABLE 65   LTCH
PERCENT LITERATE OF POPULATION 15 AND OVER--AVG. ANNUAL INCREASE (L)

TPOP	WAPC	WAGE	FEMW	BRTH	DTHS	NATR	POPR	PC20	20CH	GGEX	GGRV	CGEX	CGRV
-32		24			27	21		41					
(43)		(36)			(35)	(43)		(27)					

GGEM	CGEM	MILP	DEFX	VOTE	COMV	RELV	SOCV	NCSV	VIOL	EXEC	NEWS	DOML	FOML
					50	-25	-23	-26				-25	
					(21)	(30)	(31)	(31)				(28)	

FS/R	RADS	RDCH	TELE	CINE	LANG	AREA	DENS	AGDS	GNP	GNPC	GPCH	TRDE	CAPF
23		-45	-31		24	-35			-39	-25	26		
(27)		(39)	(32)		(22)	(43)			(43)	(43)	(35)		

CONS	GPAG	LFAG	AGCH	NONA	INDY	UNWA	UNWS	ACHT	LIFE	INFD	PHYS	HOSP	HPCH
	35	34						23	-24				-41
	(37)	(43)						(18)	(34)				(35)

HIED	PSED	LIT	LTCH	MARG	IMMG	EMIG	LNDG	RENT	YBFT	YAFT	CATH	CHRS	MOSL
-27			100		-40		21						
(42)			(43)		(21)		(25)						

VARIABLE 66   MARG
MARRIAGES PER 1,000 POPULATION AGED 15-44

TPOP	WAPC	WAGE	FEMW	BRTH	DTHS	NATR	POPR	PC20	20CH	GGEX	GGRV	CGEX	CGRV
50	30			-52	-41	-36	-36	28			54	51	38
(50)	(49)			(49)	(47)	(48)	(49)	(48)			(21)	(22)	(23)

GGEM	CGEM	MILP	DEFX	VOTE	COMV	RELV	SOCV	NCSV	VIOL	EXEC	NEWS	DOML	FOML
-39	32	50	57	53				-53	-32			36	34
(14)	(40)	(36)	(43)	(33)				(38)	(39)			(50)	(37)

FS/R	RADS	RDCH	TELE	CINE	LANG	AREA	DENS	AGDS	GNP	GNPC	GPCH	TRDE	CAPF
24	43	30	28	28		35			55	41	55	-41	29
(34)	(48)	(46)	(40)	(47)		(50)			(50)	(50)	(40)	(40)	(43)

CONS	GPAG	LFAG	AGCH	NONA	INDY	UNWA	UNWS	ACHT	LIFE	INFD	PHYS	HOSP	HPCH
-43	-31	-23		27	40				73	-28	-58	-24	-40
(37)	(41)	(48)		(47)	(46)				(44)	(43)	(49)	(50)	(43)

HIED	PSED	LIT	LTCH	MARG	IMMG	EMIG	LNDG	RENT	YBFT	YAFT	CATH	CHRS	MOSL
37	34	40		100	-25	-45	-22	-27			-34	-29	22
(48)	(50)	(49)		(50)	(29)	(33)	(37)	(17)			(48)	(41)	(41)

VARIABLE 67   IMMG
IMMIGRANTS PER 1,000 POPULATION (L)

TPOP	WAPC	WAGE	FEMW	BRTH	DTHS	NATR	POPR	PC20	20CH	GGEX	GGRV	CGEX	CGRV
		33			-22	20		50					
		(37)			(29)	(32)		(39)					

GGEM	CGEM	MILP	DEFX	VOTE	COMV	RELV	SOCV	NCSV	VIOL	EXEC	NEWS	DOML	FOML
					-55		25	41			34	32	23
					(24)		(30)	(30)			(40)	(34)	(34)

FS/R	RADS	RDCH	TELE	CINE	LANG	AREA	DENS	AGDS	GNP	GNPC	GPCH	TRDE	CAPF
	31		39							45		23	32
	(40)		(34)							(41)		(36)	(37)

CONS	GPAG	LFAG	AGCH	NONA	INDY	UNWA	UNWS	ACHT	LIFE	INFD	PHYS	HOSP	HPCH
-28	-50	-58		45			-26		38	-37	-32	-33	
(32)	(33)	(40)		(35)			(18)		(36)	(27)	(40)	(41)	

HIED	PSED	LIT	LTCH	MARG	IMMG	EMIG	LNDG	RENT	YBFT	YAFT	CATH	CHRS	MOSL
22	35	24	-40		100	66		23	-68				
(40)	(41)	(41)	(21)		(41)	(28)		(26)	(12)				

TABLE B.1 (continued)

VARIABLE 68   EMIG
EMIGRANTS PER 1,000 POPULATION (L)

TPOP	WAPC	WAGE	FEMW	BRTH	DTHS	NATR	POPR	PC20	20CH	GGEX	GGRV	CGEX	CGRV
-21	21	22			-21		-21	44		-28	-23	29	31
(40)	(39)	(35)			(30)		(39)	(40)		(20)	(21)	(24)	(24)

GGEM	CGEM	MILP	DEFX	VOTE	COMV	RELV	SOCV	NCSV	VIOL	EXEC	NEWS	DOML	FOML
67		31	45	29	-29			20	-35		36	28	48
(12)		(29)	(30)	(32)	(22)			(24)	(28)		(40)	(32)	(32)

FS/R	RADS	RDCH	TELE	CINE	LANG	AREA	DENS	AGDS	GNP	GNPC	GPCH	TRDE	CAPF
	43		43	37	44	-32	25			36			29
	(39)		(26)	(39)	(20)	(40)	(40)			(40)			(36)

CONS	GPAG	LFAG	AGCH	NONA	INDY	UNWA	UNWS	ACHT	LIFE	INFD	PHYS	HOSP	HPCH
-22	-50	-34			30		-21	29		-44	-31		
(30)	(33)	(37)			(28)		(23)	(29)		(39)	(39)		

HIED	PSED	LIT	LTCH	MARG	IMMG	EMIG	LNDG	RENT	YBFT	YAFT	CATH	CHRS	MOSL
35	40	39		-25	66	100		-27			27	33	
(38)	(40)	(40)		(29)	(28)	(40)		(15)			(39)	(33)	

VARIABLE 69   LNDG
DISTRIBUTION OF AGRICULTURAL LAND--GINI INDEX OF INEQUALITY

TPOP	WAPC	WAGE	FEMW	BRTH	DTHS	NATR	POPR	PC20	20CH	GGEX	GGRV	CGEX	CGRV
-26	-38		-27	54	20	51	41			-29	-22		-22
(50)	(49)		(42)	(45)	(37)	(40)	(49)			(22)	(23)		(29)

GGEM	CGEM	MILP	DEFX	VOTE	COMV	RELV	SOCV	NCSV	VIOL	EXEC	NEWS	DOML	FOML
	-25	-24	-39	-41		-22	34	44	-32	-29	-25	-21	
	(47)	(46)	(46)	(32)		(40)	(44)	(47)	(50)	(33)	(33)		

FS/R	RADS	RDCH	TELE	CINE	LANG	AREA	DENS	AGDS	GNP	GNPC	GPCH	TRDE	CAPF
-40		-25	-21		21		-43	-42	-35	-26	-32		-24
(32)		(46)	(42)		(22)		(50)	(49)	(50)	(50)	(38)		(44)

CONS	GPAG	LFAG	AGCH	NONA	INDY	UNWA	UNWS	ACHT	LIFE	INFD	PHYS	HOSP	HPCH
32		26	-26	-31	-33			30	-42	20	22	24	
(41)		(48)	(33)	(43)	(43)			(27)	(43)	(33)	(49)	(50)	

HIED	PSED	LIT	LTCH	MARG	IMMG	EMIG	LNDG	RENT	YBFT	YAFT	CATH	CHRS	MOSL
	-44	-37	21	-45			100				40		
	(49)	(50)	(25)	(33)			(50)				(49)		

VARIABLE 70   RENT
FARMS ON RENTED LAND AS A PERCENTAGE OF TOTAL FARMS (L)

TPOP	WAPC	WAGE	FEMW	BRTH	DTHS	NATR	POPR	PC20	20CH	GGEX	GGRV	CGEX	CGRV
			-21						-35		-22	-22	
			(46)						(34)		(25)	(31)	

GGEM	CGEM	MILP	DEFX	VOTE	COMV	RELV	SOCV	NCSV	VIOL	EXEC	NEWS	DOML	FOML
20							23	-22	22	27			
(15)							(38)	(39)	(44)	(48)			

FS/R	RADS	RDCH	TELE	CINE	LANG	AREA	DENS	AGDS	GNP	GNPC	GPCH	TRDE	CAPF
			-22		-59						-21		
			(40)		(22)						(42)		

CONS	GPAG	LFAG	AGCH	NONA	INDY	UNWA	UNWS	ACHT	LIFE	INFD	PHYS	HOSP	HPCH
			24										
			(35)										

HIED	PSED	LIT	LTCH	MARG	IMMG	EMIG	LNDG	RENT	YBFT	YAFT	CATH	CHRS	MOSL
			-22	23				100	-35				
			(37)	(26)				(55)	(18)				

TABLE B.1 (continued)

VARIABLE 71   YBFT
INCOME DISTRIBUTION BEFORE TAXES--GINI INDEX OF INEQUALITY

TPOP	WAPC	WAGE	FEMW	BRTH	DTHS	NATR	POPR	PC20	20CH	GGEX	GGRV	CGEX	CGRV
-25			34	38	22	41	21	-39	50				
(20)			(17)	(20)	(19)	(20)	(19)	(20)	(13)				

GGEM	CGEM	MILP	DEFX	VOTE	COMV	RELV	SOCV	NCSV	VIOL	EXEC	NEWS	DOML	FOML
		-57	-45			33	-24	-25	34		-32	-23	
		(18)	(19)			(17)	(18)	(18)	(18)		(20)	(16)	

FS/R	RADS	RDCH	TELE	CINE	LANG	AREA	DENS	AGDS	GNP	GNPC	GPCH	TRDE	CAPF
				-38		26	28	-22	-40			22	-29
				(20)		(20)	(20)	(20)	(20)			(19)	(19)

CONS	GPAG	LFAG	AGCH	NONA	INDY	UNWA	UNWS	ACHT	LIFE	INFD	PHYS	HOSP	HPCH
40	39	-25	-33	-31	50	48	-42	-29	29	37	42	-22	
(17)	(20)	(16)	(20)	(20)	(15)	(14)	(14)	(18)	(17)	(20)	(20)	(19)	

HIED	PSED	LIT	LTCH	MARG	IMMG	EMIG	LNDG	RENT	YBFT	YAFT	CATH	CHRS	MOSL
-40	-35	-30		-27	-68	-27		-35	100	89	47	31	-23
(20)	(20)	(20)		(17)	(12)	(15)		(18)	(20)	(12)	(20)	(18)	(18)

VARIABLE 72   YAFT
INCOME DISTRIBUTION AFTER TAXES--GINI INDEX OF INEQUALITY

TPOP	WAPC	WAGE	FEMW	BRTH	DTHS	NATR	POPR	PC20	20CH	GGEX	GGRV	CGEX	CGRV
				31	27	33	22	-35					
				(12)	(12)	(12)	(12)	(12)					

GGEM	CGEM	MILP	DEFX	VOTE	COMV	RELV	SOCV	NCSV	VIOL	EXEC	NEWS	DOML	FOML
		-26	-27	-30					36		-32		
		(12)	(12)	(12)					(12)		(12)		

FS/R	RADS	RDCH	TELE	CINE	LANG	AREA	DENS	AGDS	GNP	GNPC	GPCH	TRDE	CAPF
				-59		-55	58	54	-27	-30			29
				(12)		(12)	(12)	(12)	(12)	(12)			(12)

CONS	GPAG	LFAG	AGCH	NONA	INDY	UNWA	UNWS	ACHT	LIFE	INFD	PHYS	HOSP	HPCH
	30			-26	-28				-23		33		
	(12)			(12)	(12)				(12)		(12)		

HIED	PSED	LIT	LTCH	MARG	IMMG	EMIG	LNDG	RENT	YBFT	YAFT	CATH	CHRS	MOSL
-29	-33	-27							89	100	46		
(12)	(12)	(12)							(12)	(12)	(12)		

VARIABLE 73   CATH
ROMAN CATHOLICS AS A PERCENTAGE OF POPULATION

TPOP	WAPC	WAGE	FEMW	BRTH	DTHS	NATR	POPR	PC20	20CH	GGEX	GGRV	CGEX	CGRV
					29								
					(53)								

GGEM	CGEM	MILP	DEFX	VOTE	COMV	RELV	SOCV	NCSV	VIOL	EXEC	NEWS	DOML	FOML
23		-25	-21			21	-40				29	29	
(17)		(87)	(79)			(54)	(56)				(109)	(72)	

FS/R	RADS	RDCH	TELE	CINE	LANG	AREA	DENS	AGDS	GNP	GNPC	GPCH	TRDE	CAPF
35		23	22	29							31		
(104)		(69)	(96)	(58)							(117)		

CONS	GPAG	LFAG	AGCH	NONA	INDY	UNWA	UNWS	ACHT	LIFE	INFD	PHYS	HOSP	HPCH
28	-25	-23				24	42			32	-37	-29	26
(61)	(73)	(93)				(49)	(31)			(47)	(110)	(113)	(87)

HIED	PSED	LIT	LTCH	MARG	IMMG	EMIG	LNDG	RENT	YBFT	YAFT	CATH	CHRS	MOSL
33	21	34		-34		27	40		47	46	100	70	-43
(100)	(108)	(114)		(48)		(39)	(49)		(20)	(12)	(118)	(85)	(85)

TABLE B.1 (continued)

VARIABLE 74   CHRS
ALL CHRISTIANS AS A PERCENTAGE OF POPULATION

TPOP	WAPC	WAGE	FEMW	BRTH	DTHS	NATR	POPR	PC20	20CH	GGEX	GGRV	CGEX	CGRV
	36	60	59	-53		-40	-36	50	25		31		
	(100)	(63)	(55)	(66)		(47)	(82)	(95)	(39)		(26)		
GGEM	CGEM	MILP	DEFX	VOTE	COMV	RELV	SOCV	NCSV	VIOL	EXEC	NEWS	DOML	FOML
77	63			34							69	74	61
(16)	(19)			(79)							(96)	(55)	(54)
FS/R	RADS	RDCH	TELE	CINE	LANG	AREA	DENS	AGDS	GNP	GNPC	GPCH	TRDE	CAPF
23	68	35	60	57	46	-23	20		26	68			31
(53)	(93)	(76)	(56)	(80)	(51)	(103)	(103)		(88)	(88)			(62)
CONS	GPAG	LFAG	AGCH	NONA	INDY	UNWA	UNWS	ACHT	LIFE	INFD	PHYS	HOSP	HPCH
	-52	-56	-31	50	55	41			50		-69	-62	32
	(61)	(75)	(42)	(60)	(61)	(43)			(58)		(96)	(99)	(71)
HIED	PSED	LIT	LTCH	MARG	IMMG	EMIG	LNDG	RENT	YBFT	YAFT	CATH	CHRS	MOSL
48	63	71		-29		33			31		70	100	-64
(84)	(98)	(87)		(41)		(33)			(18)		(85)	(103)	(103)

VARIABLE 75   MOSL
MOSLEMS AS A PERCENTAGE OF POPULATION

TPOP	WAPC	WAGE	FEMW	BRTH	DTHS	NATR	POPR	PC20	20CH	GGEX	GGRV	CGEX	CGRV
	-27	-38	-73	46		41	22	-30	-42	-34	-42		
	(100)	(63)	(55)	(66)		(47)	(82)	(95)	(39)	(25)	(26)		
GGEM	CGEM	MILP	DEFX	VOTE	COMV	RELV	SOCV	NCSV	VIOL	EXEC	NEWS	DOML	FOML
-48	-23		21	-43							-41	-46	-22
(16)	(19)		(68)	(79)							(96)	(55)	(54)
FS/R	RADS	RDCH	TELE	CINE	LANG	AREA	DENS	AGDS	GNP	GNPC	GPCH	TRDE	CAPF
	-38	-26	-43	-31		23	-30	-26	-25	-44	-32		-38
	(93)	(76)	(56)	(80)		(103)	(103)	(82)	(88)	(88)	(59)		(62)
CONS	GPAG	LFAG	AGCH	NONA	INDY	UNWA	UNWS	ACHT	LIFE	INFD	PHYS	HOSP	HPCH
	32	44		-42	-40	-27			-45	22	40	37	
	(61)	(75)		(60)	(61)	(43)			(58)	(39)	(96)	(99)	
HIED	PSED	LIT	LTCH	MARG	IMMG	EMIG	LNDG	RENT	YBFT	YAFT	CATH	CHRS	MOSL
-31	-54	-64		22					-23		-43	-64	100
(84)	(98)	(87)		(41)					(18)		(85)	(103)	(103)

A brief commentary may identify some of the more important points that emerge from this table, including some relationships that might have been expected but do not appear.

Human Resources. The primary relationship here is the high correlation between two of these indices—wage and salary earners and population in cities—both with each other and with a broad range of variables indicating several aspects of economic development. These latter include most of the communications indices, G. N. P. per capita, labor force in industry and nonagricultural labor force, the health and well-being indicators, and most of the education indices. (Some of these correlations are negative, since a high degree of development implies low inhabitant–hospital bed and inhabitant–physician ratios, and low infant mortality rates.) Unlike primary and secondary education or literacy, the correlation with higher education enrollment is quite low. Similarly the vital statistics indices—birth, death, and to a lesser degree natural increase rates—show a negative correlation with development. These variables together, then, form a quite consistent cluster indicating the state of a nation's economic growth. To a substantial extent these indices are interchangeable, and missing data for a particular country can be estimated by knowing the country's standing in other series. In any attempt to use indices interchangeably, of course, one does lose some information about the particular qualities of a given case, the amount of information lost being roughly proportional to 1 minus r^2. Since r^2 is often only about .50, we know that there are nevertheless important differences even among the correlated series, and interesting deviant cases.

The remaining population series do not fit in the economic development cluster. For instance, female wage and salary earners shows a moderate, but only moderate, correlation with most of the economic development variables. Percentage of population of working age shows a fair correlation with the vital rates, as one might expect, but otherwise is not closely related to development. Total population is correlated with area and G. N. P., indicating that big countries are usually big in several ways. The average annual increase rate for cities shows no correlation with economic development, though one might reasonably have expected it to do so, at least in the developing countries. It does, however, show a rather moderate correlation with most of the other change rates—for G. N. P., labor force in agriculture, inhabitants per hospital bed (negative correlation of course), and literacy. But there is no relationship between increase in cities and increase in radios, which suggests that they often reflect different stages of development.

Government and politics. Perhaps the most striking relationship is that between all of the various indices of government size—expenditure, revenue, and employment, for both general and central governments—and most of the economic development indicators. The government employment percentages, it should be noted, tend to correlate more highly with development than do the financial ones, though one cannot be sure how much of the difference is due to the fairly different composition of the samples. Government employment and finance, especially those of the central government, tend rather strikingly to be correlated with socialist vote, though not with communist vote. Communist vote is highly correlated with total voting percentage, and negatively correlates with votes for other parties. The extent to which these relationships are attributable to the presence of the communist one-party states could not be known without first eliminating the communist-governed countries from the sample. (This kind of analysis, studying a relationship in two different groups of countries, will be illustrated in a later section.)

Total vote as a percentage of voting-age population is found to be correlated, fairly weakly, with most of the economic development variables. The correlation is stronger with literacy and with primary and secondary enrollment. There is also a rather high correlation between total vote and government size, suggesting a (causal?) connection between wide popular political participation and wide government involvement in the economy. (Recall that the government size figures are for noncommunist states only.) We also note a clear correlation between vote and G. N. P. change, though the strength of that relationship must remain unknown until communist countries, which have high voting percentages and high growth rates, are analyzed separately.

Our measures of military effort—defense expenditure and military personnel—are notable for the absence of any strong and theoretically interesting correlations. Military effort seems not to be related, at least in any simple way, with size or economic development, with political orientation (party votes), or with political stability or violence. Any attempt to account for military effort must allow for the effect of two or more independent variables, and perhaps must include some variables—military alliance, external assistance, geographical region—which are not included in Part A. Some further analysis of these questions will be carried on in the sections below.

The relationships between both executive stability and domestic violence and other variables are almost equally complex. Absolutely no important simple correlations appear for executive stability. Violence seems fairly mildly related (negatively) to government size and to economic development, but the correlations are so low as to emphasize the need for further exploration. Probably the most striking is the negative one between life expectancy and deaths from domestic group violence (which are too few by themselves to affect life expectancy). Expectation of life is of course itself highly correlated with G. N. P. per capita, but to some very moderate degree also reflects the equality with which the health and welfare benefits of a society are distributed. This suggestion—and without more rigorous analysis it still is not more than that—that violence is related to equality as well as to the level of development is supported by the modest correlations between it and the four measures of inequality: land distribution, rented land, and income before and after taxes. Violence is also negatively correlated with the foreign mail ratio, suggesting that relatively isolated countries are more susceptible to unrest.[2] Perhaps one of the most important things to note about violence and executive instability is their low linear correlation with each other—only 30 (in Table B.1 the correlation

---

2. Cf. Seymour Martin Lipset's indication (*Political Man*, Garden City, N. Y., 1960, pp. 233–52) that this relationship holds within countries.

between violence and *stability* is −30), supporting our original contention that these two indices are measuring quite different aspects of political stability and are complementary to each other.

Communications. Most notable here is the inclusion of most of these variables, including newspapers, domestic and foreign mail per capita, radios, television sets, and cinema attendance, in our larger economic development cluster. The correlations between development and cinema attendance and foreign mail sent are a little lower than the others. The first supports our original hypothesis, in Part A, that cinema attendance is not highest in countries with very high incomes, but rather is partially supplanted by other modes of communication and recreation. For foreign mail we can be sure that, in addition to development, political and economic aspects of a nation's foreign relations play a role. Foreign mail sent is related moderately (but *only* moderately, 41) to the foreign trade ratio, despite the fact, as we shall see below, that the foreign trade ratio bears no linear relation whatever to G. N. P. per capita. The other mail series—foreign items sent−foreign items received—shows virtually no important correlations. It is *not*, for instance, related to development, even though one might have suspected that rich countries would "export" more mail, especially in the form of commercial mailings, than they would "import." The only rate of change given in this series, for radios, shows a much closer relationship with the absolute level of G. N. P. per capita than do any of our other change rates, indicating that the richest countries add radios the fastest. One more variable that turns out to be moderately related to G. N. P. per capita—and this relationship was not so obvious—is speakers of the dominant language as a percentage of total population. This is so even though a number of Western European countries which are both rich and of quite uniform language composition (and so would raise the correlation) were omitted from the series because precise data on their language characteristics were unavailable. Very possibly this is in part a causal relationship—countries of diverse linguistic composition face a special hurdle in development—but the relationship between linguistic diversity and development is so complex, including the power of economic development to force assimilation to the dominant (or even sometimes a minority) language, that the question demands further inquiry.

Wealth. In addition to the now-familiar development cluster, the following correlations and absent correlations may be identified: Area is positively correlated with total population, but very negatively with density—physically big countries do have larger populations than smaller ones, but their man−land ratio is still much lower. Population per square kilometer is not notably related to G. N. P. either negatively (high density as pressing on a small resource base and thus producing relative poverty) or positively (density, by lowering transportation and communication costs, as an aid to development). The G. N. P. growth rates show a substantial correlation with government size, especially with government revenue (do high taxes *increase* the push behind economic development?). Growth rate is also, predictably, correlated with gross capital formation, and both are negatively correlated with private consumption. Capital formation is also correlated positively with government size, again suggesting that there is nothing incompatible—perhaps quite the contrary—between big government and rapid development in noncommunist states. Note, however, that the correlation between growth and capital formation is not as high as one might have expected, only 59. Perhaps this is due to essentially random errors in the underlying data; perhaps too it indicates the varying importance of social, noneconomic factors in promoting development whatever the investment rate.

The foreign trade ratio seems quite unrelated, at least in a simple linear fashion, to development, even though we suggested in Part A some reasons why the relationship might be negative. We did hypothesize, however, that the relationship might be neither simple nor linear. Nevertheless we do find clear negative relationships between foreign trade and size—population, total G. N. P., and area. The unemployment indices show some relation to economic development, but the correlations are generally low and may well be only a result of incomplete reporting in poorer states. In any case they do not reflect underemployment, which is greatest in less-developed countries. We do find a relationship between unemployment and income inequality before taxes, suggesting an even wider set of social problems. For the other two variables, annual average change in agricultural labor force and index of achievement motivation, there are no high correlations. Agricultural labor force change seems not to be associated with any of the other change rates, and, even more surprisingly in terms of what it is trying to measure, the achievement motive is not correlated with economic development or with rates of development. Perhaps the index is inadequate, or perhaps the relationships are more complicated than simple linear ones.[3] The strongest relationship that appears here is the *negative* one between the achievement motive and income inequality. Where income is distributed very unequally the desire to achieve may be dulled, not stimulated.

Health. All four of these indices fit well into the economic development cluster. The correlations between infant deaths and the development indices tend to be somewhat weaker than those for the other health indices, probably because of the sensitivity of the infant mortality rate to the equality of distribution of medical services within a country, as well as to a nation's wealth.

Education. Literacy and primary education also belong at the heart of the development cluster, but the fit for higher education is not quite as good. Some of the reasons for this are noted in Section 2; in addition to problems of definition they undoubtedly include cultural differences and the rapidity with which some underdeveloped states build up their higher education facilities. Higher education, it will be noted, is not correlated too highly with either primary and secondary education (56) or with literacy (59). Average annual increase in literacy shows a fairly consistent, though not high, set of correlations with the other change rates, but it seems somewhat negatively correlated with development. This is after all reasonable—countries showing the greatest improvement in literacy are those

3. David C. McClelland (*The Achieving Society.* Princeton, 1961, p. 98) reports a moderate correlation between the achievement motive and growth in electrical output 1952–58. We should not, after all, demand a high correlation between the achievement motive and *past* growth—it may be much more useful as a predictor of *future* development.

already developing a little but still far from developed (and, presumably, far from total literacy).

Family and social relations. One of the most striking correlations here is the *negative* one between births and marriages. The sample is not too large (49) and is composed primarily of European and Latin American states, but it points out the relation between casual unions and high birth rates in some areas. For migration patterns, we see a high correlation between emigration and immigration, and of both with economic development. Substantial international migration, probably like internal migration, requires a fairly high level of development. One interesting difference between the two sets of correlations is that the negative one between income inequality and immigration is much higher than that between inequality and emigration. This correlation, in fact, is much higher than that between immigration and G. N. P. per capita. Not only wealth, but an *opportunity* to achieve wealth, seems necessary to attract immigrants.

Distribution of wealth and income. The clearest relationship in this set is the negative relationship between unequal distributions of land, and especially of income, and economic development. Poorer states tend to be those in which the relative gaps are widest. Certainly there is no positive relation between inequality and either development or rates of development or capital formation. If surplus capital for productive investment is available in poorer countries (as the high inequality would lead one to suspect) it tends not to be used for that purpose. Note also that there is some correlation between inequality and domestic violence, and a negative one between inequality and executive instability. The correlation coefficients are not high, however, and both in Part A and in sections below we discuss some of the complexities.

Religion. Most of the relationships here are more or less what one would expect; for example, very high correlations between percentage Christian and most development indices, and moderate negative correlations between percentage Moslem and development. The negative correlation between Moslems and female wage and salary earners, however, is much greater (-73) than the positive relationship between Christians and female workers (59), indicating the strength of Islamic culture, as well as of underdevelopment, in reducing the female labor force. Possibly the most interesting relationships are those that do *not* appear. For instance, percentage Roman Catholic seems not to be highly correlated at the worldwide level with anything (except percentage Christian), not even with birth rates, or negatively with economic development or development rates or achievement motivation as the famous Weberian "Protestant ethic" theory would indicate.

2. "Stages" of Economic and Political Development

Several economists have hypothesized that there are rather clearly discernible stages in the economic development of nations. The idea is by no means universally accepted; serious difficulties arise, for example, when one suggests that there may be "thresholds" separating quite different kinds of economic activity. Nevertheless, if one thinks of stages theory not in any rigid sense, but in terms of seeking consistent patterns and relationships at various levels among variables, it would be rash to dismiss it before a careful examination of relevant data. We have found, for example, a high correlation among such indicators of economic and social development as the percentage of the population in cities of over 20,000, the percentage literate, the proportion of the population enrolled in higher education, the inhabitant–physician ratio, the number of radios per 1,000 population, and G. N. P. per capita. The relationship between per capita G. N. P. and more explicitly political variables, however, is not so close. There is a moderate correlation between per capita G. N. P. and the percentage of the population voting, but only very slight ones between per capita G. N. P. and such variables as the relative size of the armed forces or the expenditure of the central government (including social security and public enterprises).

Table B.2 shows some of the details of these relationships. All the political units (107) for which we have data on most of these variables are divided into five groups or "stages" as identified by levels of per capita G. N. P., with the cutting points chosen so as to maximize the internal consistency of the groups. If labels are desired, they might be identified as "traditional primitive" societies, "traditional civilizations," "transitional societies," "industrial revolution societies," and "high mass-consumption" societies. These labels of course are very imperfect and in particular cases, especially for the first two stages, are sometimes quite inaccurate; nevertheless they may be helpful as a general guide. At the far left of the table is given the number of states (N) in each stage, though data are not available for each variable for every country; data for the three political variables particularly are often missing. It will be noted that for the first five variables the means for each stage advance substantially with each higher G. N. P. level. (The mean for inhabitants per physician declines, but because of the way the ratio is constructed a lower figure indicates greater welfare.)

For the last three political variables, however, the relationship is much less clear. The mean for stage V is appreciably higher than that for stage I, but the intermediate steps are fairly indistinct, marked in each case by at least one reversal. The reversals, or declines at a higher stage, are not substantial, and given the small size of the sample for these last three variables are never statistically significant. Still, simply the absence of a clear increase is itself a notable contrast with the economic development variables.

Note the rather sharp discontinuities in the pattern of these political variables. For both military personnel and central government expenditure

TABLE B.2

"Stages" of Economic and Political Development

Summary Table

Stage	N =		G.N.P. per Capita	% Urban (20,000)	% Adult Literacy	Higher Ed. per 100,000	Inhabitants per Physician	Radios per 1,000	% Voting	% Mil. (15–64)	% Exp. of Central Govt. +
I	11	Range:	45–64	0–18	3–48	5–63	5,800–117,000	1–63	0–55	.20–2.52	8–29
		Mean:	56	5.8	12.9	27.3	46,073	11.7	29.9	.84	18.9
II	15	Range:	70–105	0–19	1–68	4–251	5,200–95,000	3–78	0–83	.15–2.00	12–27
		Mean:	87	9.6	23.9	86.3	22,160	20.2	49.4	.79	16.9
III	31	Range:	108–239	6–72	3–91	3–976	1,394–48,000	7–161	0–95	.05–11.11	9–48
		Mean:	173	20.6	41.6	165.3	5,362	56.5	41.1	1.68	26.2
IV	36	Range:	262–794	7–82	38–99	42–1,192	400–6,400	37–348	0–100	0–4.84	14–38
		Mean:	445	34.3	76.8	385.8	1,630	157.5	69.4	1.40	27.8
V	14	Range:	836–2577	30–70	96–99	36–1,983	765–1,089	215–948	28–92	.15–3.62	15–40
		Mean:	1,330	45.3	98.0	650.0	875	351.9	77.8	1.52	29.6

I "Traditional Primitive" Societies

Country	G.N.P. per Capita	% Urban (20,000)	% Adult Literacy	Higher Ed. per 100,000	Inhabitants per Physician	Radios per 1,000	% Voting	% Mil. (15–64)	% Exp. of Central Govt. +
Nepal	45	4.4	5.0	56	72,000	1.7		0.86	
Afghanistan	50	7.5	2.5	12	41,000	8.0		0.81	8.0
Laos	50	4.0	17.5	4	100,000	4.3		2.52	
Togo	50	4.5	7.5		58,000	4.5			
Ethiopia	55	1.7	2.5	5	117,000	5.6		0.28	
Burma	57	10.0	47.5	63	15,000	11.4	54.5	0.49	
Angola	60	4.7	2.5		14,000	11.4		0.49	29.1

Libya	60	18.4	13.0	49	5,800	63.1		0.69	17.6
Sudan	60	5.0	9.0	34	40,000	.9	0.0	0.20	20.9
Tanganyika	61	3.3	7.5	9	18,000	3.6	33.8		
Uganda	64	.1	27.5	14	15,000	13.8	31.0		
II "Traditional Civilizations"									
Mozambique	70	13.9	1.0	165	20,000	5.7	0.0	0.37	12.3
Pakistan	70	11.8	13.0	69	8,670	3.0		0.57	
China (Mainland)	73	10.0	47.5	220	8,700		52.6	0.15	13.9
India	73	12.0	19.3	83	5,200	5.0		2.00	
South Vietnam	76		17.5		29,000	8.9	40.4		
Nigeria	78	10.5	10.0	4	32,000	4.0	28.9		26.9
Kenya	87	3.8	22.5	5	10,000	8.0	64.8		
Madagascar	88	7.6	33.5	21	8,427	22.4			
Congo (Leopoldville)	92	9.1	37.5	4	63,000	2.5			
Thailand	96	7.7	68.0	251	7,500	6.2	51.4	0.90	15.2
Bolivia	99	19.4	32.1	166	3,900	72.7		0.47	16.1
Cambodia	99	16.0	17.5	18	95,000	6.5	82.9	1.49	
Liberia	100	0.0	7.5		16,000	77.5		0.88	
Sarawak	100	7.0	21.0		15,000	55.3			
Haiti	105	5.1	10.5	29	10,000	4.9	74.2	0.29	
III "Transitional" Societies									
Iran	108	21.0	15.0	90	3,800	65.3	29.1	1.94	
Paraguay	114	15.2	65.8	188	1,800	60.8	58.8	0.96	
Ceylon	129	11.4	63.0	56	4,500	38.4		0.05	
Jordan	129	25.5	17.5		5,800	37.7		4.34	47.5
Indonesia	131	9.1	17.5	62	48,000	7.4	92.0	0.24	
Rhodesia & Nyasaland	135	9.2	16.1	3	7,400	17.6	1.9		
Egypt	142	29.1	19.9	399	2,600	65.8	0.0	0.67	36.1
Morocco	142	24.2	12.5	40	9,400	45.5		0.48	
Surinam	142	72.4	72.5	109	2,000				
South Korea	144	18.5	77.0	397	3,700	129.9	31.3	4.58	

TABLE B.2 (continued)

III "Transitional" Societies (continued)

Country	G.N.P. per Capita	% Urban (20,000)	% Adult Literacy	Higher Ed. per 100,000	Inhabitants per Physician	Radios per 1,000	% Voting	% Mil. (15–64)	% Exp. of Central Govt. +
Iraq	156	23.6	10.0	173	5,600	21.2	0.0	2.02	32.5
Nicaragua	160	20.1	38.4	110	2,800	65.5	92.7	0.43	
Taiwan	161	24.0	54.0	329	1,500	69.5	0.0	11.11	
Saudi Arabia	170	9.5	2.5	6	13,000	12.1	0.0	0.81	
Ghana	172	6.4	22.5	29	21,000	22.2	43.9	0.20	
Syria	173	38.8	27.5	223	4,600	57.3	27.6	1.71	
Tunisia	173	19.9	17.5	64	8,200	63.5	49.9	0.54	
Albania	175		60.0	145	3,500	33.6	94.6	4.12	
Algeria	178	14.1	19.0	70	6,096	54.1			
Peru	179	13.9	47.5	253	2,100	77.9	39.2	0.24	13.1
Ecuador	189	17.8	55.7	193	2,600	40.6	28.4	0.69	
Guatemala	189	11.2	29.4	135	6,400	54.3	27.5	0.37	
Honduras	194	11.5	44.0	78	4,800	66.1	36.5	0.27	
Barbados	200	54.7	91.1	24	3,000	161.0			
El Salvador	219	12.9	39.4	89	5,400	92.0	29.3	0.21	
Philippines	220	12.7	75.0	976	5,555	22.3	55.1	0.28	9.2
Turkey	220	18.2	39.0	255	2,800	52.5	72.5	3.06	23.8
Portugal	224	16.5	55.9	272	1,394	98.1	18.5	1.35	21.2
Mauritius	225	27.4	51.8	14	4,500				
British Guiana	235	17.9	74.0	27		72.2	52.1		
Dominican Republic	239	12.2	59.9	149	3,900	33.8	63.6	1.12	

IV "Industrial Revolution" Societies

Country	G.N.P. per Capita	% Urban (20,000)	% Adult Literacy	Higher Ed. per 100,000	Inhabitants per Physician	Radios per 1,000	% Voting	% Mil. (15–64)	% Exp. of Central Govt. +
Mexico	262	24.0	50.0	258	1,700	96.9	34.6	1.92	
Colombia	263	22.4	62.0	296	2,400	139.5	40.2	0.27	
Yugoslavia	265	18.6	77.0	524	1,637	98.6	91.4	3.48	

Hong Kong	272	81.9	57.5	176	3,300	55.3	34.4	0.71	13.7
Brazil	293	28.1	49.4	132	2,100	64.3	0.0	2.39	16.5
Spain	293	39.8	87.0	258	1,000	90.0	71.2	0.39	34.5
Japan	306	43.1	98.0	750	930	106.7	70.6		
Jamaica	316		77.0	42	4,300	87.9	56.2	0.00	
Panama	329	33.1	65.7	371	3,200	159.0	73.3	2.52	23.6
Greece	340	38.4	80.0	320	800	89.9	54.8	1.37	
Malaya	356	22.7	38.4	475	6,400	36.5	57.6	0.00	
Costa Rica	357	15.4	79.4	326	2,600	66.1	97.9	1.79	
Romania	360	18.0	89.0	226	788	117.0	48.0	0.15	
Lebanon	362	23.0	47.5	345	1,100	60.8	99.2	3.07	
Bulgaria	365	15.3	85.0	456	740	202.0			
Malta	377	7.3	57.6	142	980	222.0			
Chile	379	46.3	80.1	257	1,700	130.2	37.4	1.06	
South Africa	395	32.9	42.5	189	2,000	66.2	10.4	0.11	31.1
Singapore	400		50.0	437	2,400	88.3	82.3		
Trinidad & Tobago	423	75.1	73.8	61	2,300	84.1			
Cyprus	467	13.6	60.5	78	1,400	178.0	92.8	1.67	
Poland	475	31.9	95.0	351	1,100	183.0	58.3	0.45	
Uruguay	478		80.9	541	870	286.0	61.8	0.81	
Argentina	490	48.3	86.4	827	660	175.0	93.5	1.14	17.0
Hungary	490	37.0	97.0	258	650	231.0	92.9	1.42	
Italy	516	30.3	87.5	362	746	170.0	71.6	0.77	34.2
Ireland	550	35.6	98.5	362	1,000	176.0	73.3		31.1
Puerto Rico	563	32.0	81.0	1,192	2,200				
Iceland	572	40.5	98.5	445	840	279.0	86.6	0.95	
East Germany	600	36.2	98.5	395		348.0	97.3	3.02	
U.S.S.R.	600	35.5	95.0	539	578	205.0	99.6	0.49	
Venezuela	648	47.2	52.2	355	1,300	186.0	83.8	0.32	27.2
Austria	670	39.8	98.5	546	695	288.0	90.4	2.54	36.4
Czechoslovakia	680	25.3	97.5	398	620	263.0	98.1	4.84	
Israel	726	60.9	93.7	668	400	194.0	88.0	1.51	38.2
Finland	794	31.2	98.5	529	1,600	289.0	72.8		30.1

TABLE B.2 (continued)

V "High Mass-Consumption" Societies

Country	G.N.P. per Capita	% Urban (20,000)	% Adult Literacy	Higher Ed. per 100,000	Inhabitants per Physician	Radios per 1,000	% Voting	% Mil. (15–64)	% Exp. of Central Govt. +
Netherlands	836	49.8	98.5	923	900	263.0	92.1	2.00	37.0
West Germany	927	55.1	98.5	528	798	319.0	86.9	0.90	30.6
France	943	29.8	96.4	667	1,014	282.0	89.4	3.62	40.0
Denmark	1,057	48.5	98.5	570	830	365.0	84.0	1.46	21.4
Norway	1,130	32.8	98.5	258	946	286.0	,78.8	1.62	28.6
United Kingdom	1,189	66.9	98.5	460	935	289.0	78.0	1.86	38.8
Belgium	1,196	32.0	96.7	536	819	298.0	87.6	1.46	34.6
New Zealand	1,310	69.7	98.5	839	700	242.0	86.4	1.05	39.8
Australia	1,316	57.3	98.5	856	860	215.0	85.3	0.79	18.0
Sweden	1,380	40.8	98.5	401	1,089	378.0	83.1	1.52	39.1
Luxembourg	1,388	30.6	96.5	36	910	319.0	71.1	1.32	
Switzerland	1,428	29.9	98.5	398	765	272.0	28.0	0.15	15.2
Canada	1,947	39.4	97.5	645	900	451.0	74.2	1.16	21.3
United States	2,577	52.0	98.0	1,983	780	948.0	64.4	2.36	21.0

the differences between stages I and II, and among III, IV, and V, are slight and can be ignored. But the difference between stage II and stage III is very striking. The role of the central government, both in overall spending and in military mobilization, seems to increase sharply at this level. This suggests that an expanded role of government is "normal" in a developed economy, and must more or less be expected. On consideration this seems fairly plausible, especially by comparison with the predominant role played by subsistence agriculture in the typical underdeveloped economy. It is not easy to bring the agricultural sector very heavily under government ownership or control, and this is especially true of subsistence farming. Industry or commerce, on the other hand, are much more typical objects of government ownership, and in countries where industry is greater the role of government tends to be larger.

The finding about the size of the military establishment is significant in other ways. A fairly commonly held image is that of the underdeveloped country which tries to make up in quantity what it lacks in military quality, the image of the poor state which fields hordes of badly equipped soldiers in an effort to overwhelm its enemy by sheer numbers. Our data provide no support for this image; (proportionately) very large armies are to be found only in economically advanced states. Of the really underdeveloped "traditional" societies represented in this table (stages I and II), none have military participation ratios as high as those for 11 more advanced nations in the higher stages. A certain level of economic development (perhaps on the order of $125 per capita G. N. P.) is required to support a large military establishment, and even at this level the only countries with large armies are those, such as South Korea, Jordan, and Taiwan, which receive very great external military assistance.

The model implicit in this presentation is in some degree a longitudinal one, for we at least partially assume that as a country develops, as its G. N. P. rises, the values of the other indices also rise. Stage III, for instance, in some way shows what a country now in stage II may look like some years hence. Clearly there are important difficulties inherent in these assumptions. We cannot be sure of uniformities in the developmental process, and conditions and technology change. Even a highly developed country would not, thirty years ago, have had a radios per 1,000 population ratio as high as that now typical for stage IV states. A more direct and dependable method for examining stages would be to look at developmental data for many countries over long periods of time, to substitute longitudinal for cross-sectional data. We have computed rates of change for some variables, and these rates were given in Part A and will be referred to again in some tentative projections in Section 6. Yet data for changes over time are still hard to obtain in any reliable form; the rates given in this book are for fairly short periods and in no case apply to more than a one-stage transition. Even outside this book there are virtually no data for the transition of countries over the entire span. It may be useful therefore, in the absence of better longitudinal data, to use the cross-sectional data we have as if they in some way applied to development over time.

In doing so, and aware of the implications and limitations, we may compute income elasticities to estimate the amount of change in any variable that can be expected with a given increase in per capita G. N. P. Such a computation forms the basis for Figure B.1. Along the horizontal axis are measured the percentage increases in per capita G. N. P. associated with each of the stages. Thus stage II represents a 55% increase over stage I, stage III a 99% increase over stage II, etc. To express it differently, the lines perpendicular to the horizontal axis at various points along it mark the percentage increase in G. N. P. for each stage *over that for the previous stage.* Points on the vertical axis are placed in the same manner on the same scale. Thus if some other variable increased by the same percentage as per capita G. N. P. between stage I and stage II (55%), the slope of

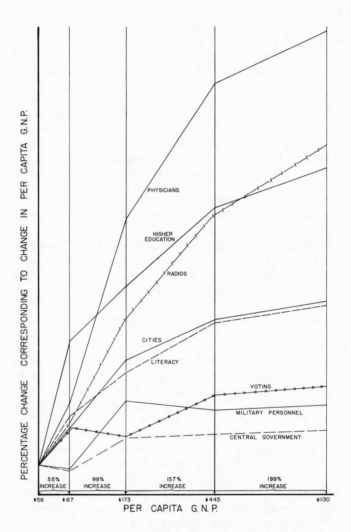

Figure B.1 Income "Elasticities" for Aspects of
Economic and Political Development

the line would be exactly 45°.[1] From the slopes we therefore can derive elasticities; a slope of more than 45° would indicate that the percentage increase in the variable was, at that range, greater than the equivalent increase in G. N. P.

This procedure brings out the *amount of change* characteristic of any particular range, and the amount of change to be found at *particular levels.* It is not a surprise, for example, to be told that urbanization and G. N. P. are highly correlated; it may be more interesting to know *how much* urbanization is associated with *how much* G. N. P. Overall, the number of physicians is most sensitive to G. N. P. per capita, and literacy is the least sensitive of the economic variables. Breaking the elasticities down into elasticities for different subranges is useful in other ways. Examination of Figure B.1 shows, for instance, that between the first two stages the percentage increase in students in higher education is by far greater than that for any other variable. Development implies the existence of an educated elite. Between stage IV and stage V, however, the slope for radios per 1,000 (a key component of high mass consumption) is steeper than that of any other variable. At this level literacy and urbanization are no longer sensitive to greater wealth. It is clear also that for all the economic variables the elasticity is greatest at the lower levels and declines as higher income levels are reached. To the extent that the assumptions in our longitudinal use of this cross-sectional data are appropriate, we may predict the amount of increase in any variable to be expected from any given change in per capita G. N. P., and make that prediction appropriate to the present position of the country in question.

We may also use the graph to gain some appreciation of the magnitude of social change that is associated even with the beginnings of economic development. Up through stage III, for instance, each doubling of the G. N. P. per capita implies a doubling of the proportion of the population living in cities (and, incidentally, a doubling of the proportion engaged in non-agricultural occupations). The new city dwellers are often completely uneducated, or sometimes barely literate. They are usually leaving their families for the first time; men often come into the cities alone in search of work, leaving their wives behind for months or even years. Employment may be hard to find. Living conditions may be squalid, perhaps substantially worse than on the farms, and at best they will be strange. The new urban citizen must adjust to a very different way of life, to regular hours under someone else's direction. He may for the first time use money for exchange instead of bartering goods; he will be exposed, at least from a distance, to newspapers, motion pictures, and radios to a degree far greater than before. And he will be exposed to new people, new ways of life, and, in the hands of others, a kind of wealth he has never imagined. The consequences may be enormously unsettling for the social and political life of the country.

Our analysis of stages and of the relationship among variables at different points in their ranges can be useful in at least one further way, the identification of "deviant" cases. If a particular level of urbanization is usually associated with a given income, what are the exceptions or devi-

---

1. Inhabitants per physician is inverted to physicians per inhabitant to make a higher ratio indicate an advanced economy.

ants? An apparently deviant case may arise for either of two reasons—some item or items of data are in error, or the country departs for particular reasons from the general pattern established elsewhere and is therefore a true deviant. In these cases we must look to a revision or expansion of our theory. A brief examination of a few of the more striking deviants in Table B.2 will illustrate these points.

Some of the clearest departures from the expected pattern arise with respect to enrollments in higher education. In each of the three higher stages the mean of the higher education enrollment ratio is much nearer the lower end of the range than the upper end, and in fact the country at the upper end in each case stands out as at least 45% above the next highest at its stage. The countries in question are the United States, Puerto Rico, and the Philippines. Puerto Rico is followed at some distance by Argentina and then by Japan; after the Philippines, Egypt is second and South Korea is third. It is obvious here that American influence makes a very great difference. Countries long under American tutelage (Philippines and Puerto Rico) seem to have quite thoroughly adopted the American system of mass higher education, rather than the system typical of Britain and much of the European continent where higher education is considered to be basically for the future elites. Countries which have not had long experience of American control but which nevertheless underwent major revisions in their social and educational systems as a result of post-World War II occupation (Japan and South Korea) show a lesser but still very distinct American influence.

A different kind of deviation arises for Burma. By virtue of its low G. N. P. per capita Burma was placed in stage I, but the fit is not a particularly good one. For inhabitants in cities of over 20,000 and inhabitants per physician Burma ranks somewhat better than the stage I mean; for literacy and pupils in higher education the Burmese data form the top of the range. Possible explanations include error in the G. N. P. estimate, or explanation in terms of reasonably accurate data but peculiar circumstances. Burma has throughout the postwar period experienced substantial civil unrest and strife; it is generally agreed that the Burmese economy has remained relatively stagnant. Perhaps some of Burma's achievements, especially the educational ones, have their origins in an earlier period of a growing and more prosperous economy.

Yet these explanations are not entirely satisfactory, especially when one notes that the situation of Burma's neighbor, Thailand, is much the same in stage II. Thailand's urbanization rate is low, but its inhabitants per physician ratio is good and the Thai figures for the two educational rates form the top of their ranges. Possibly both economies have stagnated; possibly the G. N. P. of both is underestimated; possibly too the cultural peculiarities of this part of Southeast Asia are manifested in high literacy and educational attainments. Yet another interesting deviant case of this sort is Israel which, though at a higher level, in some respects resembles Burma. Except for G. N. P. and radios per 1,000 Israel's pattern is that of a high mass-consumption society, not of an industrial revolution society. Possibly here too the explanation lies in a mistaken estimate of G. N. P. More likely, however, the difference is a reflection of the high educational achievements (including many physicians) of Israel's postwar immigrants.

If so, and if many economists are correct in emphasizing the great importance of human resources in economic development, Israel's potential for
future growth would seem extraordinarily high.

An imbalance in development can have important political consequences
too. Venezuela's huge resources of oil and, to some degree, iron ore,
have given it the highest per capita G. N. P. in Latin America, but its politics have been neither stable nor, except for the past seven years, democratic. A look at the Venezuelan pattern offers insight if not a full
explanation. Venezuela's per capita G. N. P. is near the top of the stage IV
range. One prime indicator of social mobilization, urbanization, is also
relatively high, and the ratios for radios and physicians are slightly better
than the stage IV mean. For higher education, however, Venezuela is below
the mean, and for literacy well below it.

A rather different pattern emerges for Malaya, a country that has been
fairly stable recently but previously was racked by major guerrilla warfare. Malaya's per capita G. N. P. is high enough to place it in stage IV,
and its higher education enrollment ratio is above the stage IV mean. But
for literacy, physicians, radios, and urbanization Malaya ranks low, and
except for urbanization is even below the mean for stage III. The rise in
income, it would seem, has not been matched by an equivalent increase in
many of the amenities of life found in other industrial revolution societies.

These deviations are of course not conclusive, but they can point out
cases of considerable practical and theoretical significance. Close examination of Table B.2 will identify other such cases, as will the addition of
more variables to this or similar models of stages. Any set of variables
evidencing fairly high intercorrelations is subject to this kind of analysis.[2]

---

2. We are grateful to Alexander Eckstein for suggestions regarding this section.

3. Changing Relationships Between Variables

In Section 1 we presented the *linear* correlations between all pairs of variables. In a linear correlation it is assumed that the relation between one variable and another remains essentially the same throughout the ranges of both variables. It means, for instance, that a regression line for radios per 1,000 population and G. N. P. per capita will retain the same slope at all points; if an increase in per capita G. N. P. from $100 to $200 is associated with an increase of approximately 50 radios per 1,000 inhabitants, then an increase of from $500 to $600 will also be associated with a 50-radio change. For some relationships this assumption does not do serious violence to the facts; for radios and G. N. P. it does not in fact depart too seriously from the truth. But always to use a linear model is frequently to distort or obscure the true relationships.

An excellent example is the correlation between annual rate of increase in population and literacy, which is shown in Table B.1 as only −.37. Considering the conventional wisdom about vital rates and social and economic development, this correlation is slighter than one might expect. Close examination of the data, as plotted in the scattergram for Figure B.2, shows why. The rate of population increase is relatively low at low levels of literacy, but in countries where literacy is somewaht higher, so is population growth. Clearly widespread illiteracy is associated with high birth rates and high death rates; as literacy rises death rates fall much faster than birth rates. This is shown by the higher linear correlations between literacy and the *components* of population growth—births per 1,000 (−.81) and deaths per 1,000 (.56). Still, that is hardly the end. Above literacy rates of approximately 40%, one finds a sharp negative correlation between population increase and literacy, with a decline from a growth rate of over 3% to below 1.5%. In other words, population growth and literacy are positively correlated below 30% literacy, negatively correlated above 40% literacy, and remain unchanged at a high level between those two percentages.

Use of a linear regression model totally obscures this relationship but a curvilinear regression, with the curve plotted on Figure B.2, brings it out very plainly.[1] The linear regression line is also given so that the two methods can be compared. Use of the curvilinear regression raises the correlation coefficient fairly substantially, from −.37 to −.49.[2] The curvilinear relation between these variables may be known to demographers,

---

1. All the regressions in this section are computed from either second- or third-order polynomials; i.e., from the original data either squared or cubed. In some cases an even better fit could have been obtained with fourth-order polynomials, or even higher, which would have produced curves with additional "kinks" to account better for points far from the curves given by lower-order computations. But given the relatively small "sample" of countries such attempted precision would be misleading.

2. The correlation would undoubtedly be even higher except for our need to use the annual rate of population increase from all causes. Migration tends in some instances to blur the relationship between literacy and birth and death rates; reliable *natural* increase rates for countries below 35% literacy exist in only four cases. Most of the countries with population growth rates well above the "expected" level are states that have experienced substantial net immigration in recent years, as the three low states clustered together (Portugal, Cyprus, and Malta) have experienced high net emigration.

but to other social scientists it should serve as a warning about uncritical use of linear correlation coefficients, and especially against the too hasty *rejection* of the hypothesis that two variables *are* related.

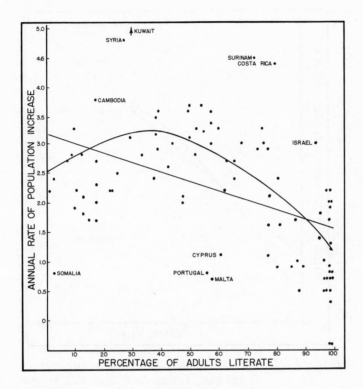

Figure B.2 Population Increase Is Fastest at
              Middle Levels of Literacy

It is quite impossible to exhaust here all the possibilities for improving explanation by employing curvilinear models, but their utility may be further illustrated with several politically relevant variables. First, note Figure B.3, with votes as a percentage of voting-age population plotted against logarithms of G. N. P. per capita. Here we find a rather high linear relationship (r = .46), but a curve improves the fit somewhat to .51. Though there is much variation, it is clear that at low G. N. P. levels voting and G. N. P. per capita are positively related. Low voting rates tend to be found with low income, and the two rise together until a per capita G. N. P. of roughly $700 is reached. After that voting levels off and then turns down again with income levels of over $900. From this cross-sectional view, at least, it would appear that very high voting rates are to be expected at middle levels of development, but are unusual when economic growth is in either its early or late stages.[3]

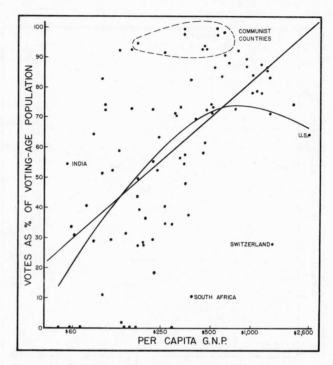

Figure B.3   Voting Turnout Tends to Be Highest in
Developed Countries, but Not in the
Richest Ones

Another interesting relationship appears when logarithmic transformations for violent deaths per 1,000,000 population are plotted against logarithms of G. N. P. per capita. The linear correlation coefficient was –.43 and a glance at Figure B.4 will show why even a curvilinear fit only raises the correlation slightly (to –.47)—the variation around any possible regression line is great, as most sophisticated political scientists would expect. Even so a general pattern does emerge, the most striking feature of which is the low level of violence associated with high economic development (G. N. P. equal to more than $800 per capita). Furthermore, violent deaths seem to be less frequent at extremely low G. N. P. levels than at

3. Though this relation is strengthened by the communist countries, with their middle G. N. P. per capitas and high voting rates, it would still hold in a scattergram which excluded them. The peak of the curve would still come between $500 and $900, although it would be around 5% lower. Note too that though Switzerland helps pull the curve down in the later stages because its low rate stems in part from the disenfranchisement of women, even if doubled to 56% the Swiss figure would still be very low.

somewhat higher stages. All of the nine states with G. N. P. per capita under $100 rank below eight middle-income nations in violent deaths. There
are a number of moderate-income countries with very high violence rates,
but on the average after about $200 per capita the incidence of violence
declines sharply, rarely going over one death per 1,000,000 population for
a G. N. P. above $800 per capita. This would suggest—to the extent that
our cross-sectional model provides useful insights for change over time—
that underdeveloped nations must expect a fairly high level of civil unrest
for some time, and that very poor states should probably expect an increase, not a decrease, in domestic violence over the next few decades.
The reasons, of course, are not hard to suggest. In a traditional society
knowledge is limited, aspirations are limited, and expectations as to the
proper activities of government are limited. All this changes with development.

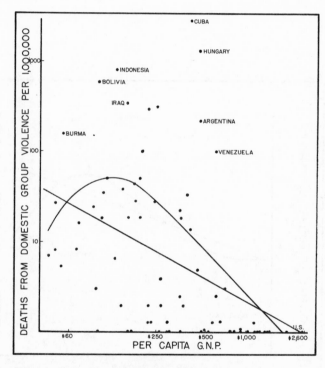

Figure B.4 Economic Development Is Associated with Political Violence, at
Least in the Early Stages

In a related vein, notice how in Figure B.5 the role of government in the
national economy tends to increase up to a per capita G. N. P. of approximately $600, then levels off and declines somewhat for the United States
and Canada at the far right-hand of the scattergram. Such a curve raises
the correlation coefficient to .56 from the original .47 for a linear correla-

tion. Our use of *revenue* in this graph given a better fit than government *expenditure* because the data for revenue exclude foreign aid which, in one or two cases (e.g. Jordan) produces extraordinary spending. Had we used *general* instead of *central* government the relative decline of public activity in advanced countries would be less (because of the importance of state or provincial governments in Australia, Canada, Switzerland, and the United States), but the curvilinear relationship would still be present.

Our graph shows that central government revenues (including those of social security and public enterprises) tend to be low in poor countries where so much of the economy is subsistence agriculture. But in more fully developed states, with industry, modern communications, utilities, and a labor force that expects welfare benefits, the role of the government expands very substantially.[4] Within limits this pattern is without exception; no developed state, for example, shows a government revenue percentage of less than 15%, although such a figure is fairly

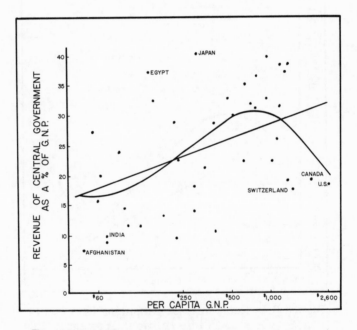

Figure B.5 The Central Government's Role in
the Economy Increases with Development, but May Diminish at Very
High Levels

4. Note W. W. Rostow's description of the vital role of government in creating the preconditions for take-off (*The Stages of Economic Growth*, Cambridge, England, 1960, p. 25).

common in countries with less than \$300 per capita G. N. P. It would seem that a modern economy cannot operate without substantial government economic activity. Still, the relative role of the public sector may well decline in high mass-consumption societies, especially in very rich states. A very prosperous economy can perhaps provide the necessary resources to government while keeping a growing proportion in the private sector.

One final example of the kind of relationship often brought out by curvilinear regressions is Figure B.6 for G. N. P. per capita and annual growth in G. N. P. At very low G. N. P. per capita levels the rate of growth tends to be slow. But the curve rises quickly to a peak at about \$300 per capita and continues high until about \$1,000 per capita G. N. P., after which it begins to fall. At the top of the income scale, for the United States and Canada, the rate drops to well under 3%. The curvilinear regression raises the correlation coefficient from .28 to .39.

Without a careful check of intervening variables an explanation of this pattern can only be tentative, yet certain obvious points must be made. One is about the countries with per capita G. N. P.'s of less than \$250. No country in this group shows an increase rate of as high as 6%, even though such a rate is not uncommon for somewhat richer nations. In fact, in all but two cases the growth rate is no higher than 4% and the mean is only 1.8%. These are traditional societies, or at best states which have only very recently entered into what W. W. Rostow has termed the take-off phase of economic development.[5] In this phase capital investment tends to take but a small percentage of national product. (Rostow suggests that, at take-off, productive investment as a proportion of Domestic Product rises from on the order of 5% to over 10%; according to our data the mean gross capital formation percentage of G. D. P. is 14.5%, but most of the countries for which we have data already seem to have begun "take-off.") Once an industrial base has been established, habits of investment are formed, and the per capita product level has reached a point sufficiently above subsistence to make a substantial surplus available for investment, the pace may quicken and a country may have the capacity for self-sustained growth. This is indicated by the uniformly positive and fairly high growth rates for countries of over \$500 per capita G. N. P.[6] Once they accumulate sufficient technically competent manpower, present-day economies sharply increase their rate of growth by permitting adaptation of the scientific advances which have been or are currently being employed in the developed states.[7] But finally, it would seem, there comes a point (currently to be found perhaps at about \$900 per capita G. N. P.) when previous fast rates of development no longer can be matched. The ability to adopt or adapt the technology of more developed countries diminishes as the gap lessens; more scientific advance must be self-generated. At this point too, according to Rostow, comes the stage of high mass consumption, when the demands for leisure

---

5. Ibid.
6. One could say above \$250 except for Argentina, whose recent economic development has been damaged by particularly serious political disruption.
7. Certain states currently noted for their scientific and military achievements in some fields are still heavily dependent upon—or have not yet even adopted—other states' technological developments in different fields.

and the diversion of resources away from investment to consumption slow down the rate of growth.   In part this can be attributed to greater equality of income distribution in these states, as those who would save more income earn proportionately less than in the past.   It may be attributable also to the expansion of the welfare state as benefits come to be expected and demanded.   The United States and Canada, the world's richest economies, do indeed show a relatively low growth rate.

At least one third variable may be noted—many of the states with the highest growth rates have Soviet-type economies.   Five of the nine countries whose growth rates have been 6% or higher are communist.   To some degree the communist countries' success is surely attributable to their organization and their ability to maintain high investment percentages. Certainly their average is above the mean growth rate for their income group.   Still, five of the top nine—Japan, Austria, Jamaica, West Germany, and Trinidad—are noncommunist nations, and all of the communist countries with very high growth rates are in the middle-income range which characterizes those economies that are in "take-off" or "the drive to maturity."   Very likely their efforts are assisted by the fact that for a variety of social and economic reasons this income level is one at which capital accumulation is relatively easy.   How much their rate of growth may be expected to diminish as they reach higher income levels cannot be known; recent reports of a moderate slowing in the Soviet Union's growth rate may possibly be indicative of things to come.

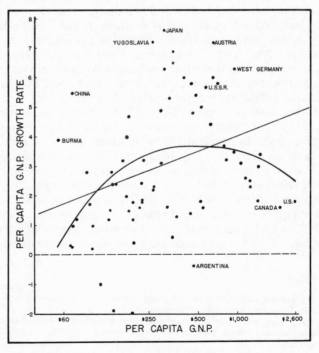

Figure B.6 G. N. P. Tends to Grow Fastest at
Middle Levels of Development

4. Multifactor Explanations of Social Change

A number of the correlations in Section 1 were lower than we might have expected. Sometimes the correlation could be raised by allowing for a curvilinear relationship, but this was by no means always the case. Often it is impossible adequately to explain one variable in terms of only one other, and it is necessary to use some method that shows the effect of several variables, or factors, operating independently upon a single "dependent" variable. One such method is multiple regression. It allows one to identify the amount of variance in a variable "explained" by two or more other variables. Thus squaring the multiple correlation coefficient (r^2) tells us the explanatory strength of a linear *combination* of the independent variables. This technique also produces values, to be discussed below, by which one can identify the distinctive explanatory power of each independent variable, controlling for the others. One can tell which of the several independent variables in a regression equation produces the most change, whether we are talking about equally sized or equally probable changes in the independent variables.

We will illustrate this method with several equations, expressed in two forms. The first type "explains" deviations in y in terms of deviations in each of the independent variables about their means:

$$\hat{y} - \bar{y} = b_1(x_1 - \bar{x}_1) + b_2(x_2 - \bar{x}_2) \ldots + b_n(x_n - \bar{x}_n) \tag{1}$$

In this equation $\hat{y}$ indicates the value of the dependent variable predicted by the regression equation. The mean values of y and of each of the n independent variables are denoted by barlike superscripts. For each of the independent variables there is a coefficient (b_i, called a "b-weight") which indicates the predicted change in y due to a unit change in the independent variable, controlling for all the other independent variables. The b-weights are of course the same whether we describe departures of the independent variables from zero or (sometimes more conveniently) from their individual means. It is clear that equation (1) represents a linear model for explaining y additively in terms of several independent variables. If one assumes each explanatory variable is an independent *cause* of the dependent variable, equations in this form also suggest how much and in which direction each might be manipulated to produce a particular desirable or undesirable outcome.[1]

As in our original presentation of the simple correlations, we have found it desirable in many instances to transform the original raw data into logarithms. Not only does this procedure produce a more statistically normal

---

1. From a policymaker's point of view, the cost and desirability of such manipulations would vary greatly. Political sophistication might also help one decide which of the "causal" variables were truly independent of each other (our model is really quite simplified) and what time lag, if any, is best for producing the intended result. An advantage of multifactor explanations (if they are appropriate) is that the decision-maker has several possible influence paths from which he can choose the ones most socially acceptable in his particular context. "Predicting" results from such policies also depends on the assumption that the b-weights will remain constant over time.

This section has been written by Hayward R. Alker, Jr., and Bruce M. Russett.

distribution in the case of highly skewed variables, it affects the nature of our explanatory model. In deciding to log a particular variable we felt that a *proportionate* change in the variable would explain more than an *absolute* change. Thus for some variables we believed that a doubling from 10% to 20% in a value (like the percentage of a country's population in cities) was more important in a political and social sense than a change of equal absolute magnitude from 50% to 60%. G. N. P. per capita provides another good example of a variable which is highly skewed and which, in addition, shows a range that is artificially wide in terms of what one is usually trying to measure. Thus we discussed, in Part A, the reasons why the difference between the living standards of very rich and very poor countries is exaggerated (perhaps by a factor of four) by the usual figures for G. N. P. per capita, especially when standardized with foreign exchange rates. At the same time, one intuitively feels that a country's increase from $50 per capita to $100 is likely to have more profound effects than the increase from $2,000 to $2,050. Using the logarithms of G. N. P. per capita we assume greater explanatory power—and better "predictions"—will result from proportionate rather than from absolute changes.

The equations below combine both logged and unlogged variables. A method for interpreting the general formula above therefore must be provided for four different cases.

A. *If the dependent variable is a logarithm:*

1. *If the independent variable is also logged.* In this case we are predicting a proportionate change in y from a proportionate change in x. The b_i tells us the change in the *log* of y resulting from a unit change in the *log* of x_i. *Adding* b_i to the logarithm of y is the same thing as *multiplying* y itself by the *antilog* of b_i (i.e. the number of which b_i is the log). In this case b_i may also be interpreted as an elasticity, the ratio of the proportionate change in $\hat{y}$ resulting from a proportionate change in x_i.[2]

2. *If the independent variable is not logged.* In this case b_i is the increment to log y resulting from a one *unit addition* to x_i. The *antilog* of b_i is the *multiplication* factor deviating y from an average value when x_i is one unit higher than its mean in absolute value.

B. *If the dependent variable is not a logarithm:*

1. *If the independent variable is a logarithm.* In this case a *doubling* of x_i results in an *addition* of b_i units to the value of y.

2. *If the independent variable is also not logged.* Under these circumstances a unit *increment* in x_i results in an *increment* of b_i units in y.

Thus we are assuming an additive or multiplicative model in the original unlogged data depending upon which is more appropriate to the variables in question. To repeat, this model in a form facilitating dynamic or manipulative interpretations "explains" or "predicts" changes in the dependent variable from its mean produced by given changes (unitary increase or doubling, as the case may be) above or below the means of each independent variable.

Still, there are differences in scale involved. Even when taken about

---

2. The general formula for an elasticity (E) is $E = \Delta y/y / \Delta x/x$. It will be convenient below to report b_i's for logged terms corresponding to a doubling of their x_i's. This is equivalent to using logarithms to the base 2 rather than (as we otherwise have done) to the base 10.

their means, some variables are measured in dollars, others in units such as number of people. The range of variation differs greatly, as between votes as a percentage of voting-age population and defense expenditure as a percentage of G. N. P. If one wants, then, to measure the relative *weights* of each variable in the regression equation, in terms of the relative contribution it makes to explaining the dependent variable, one must have a standardized unit and talk about equally probable changes in the x_i. If each variable (about its mean) is divided by its standard deviation we obtain adjusted values which are then comparable. These standardized values are often called "standard scores" or "z-scores." Equation (2) presents the relation among these transformed variables that corresponds to the earlier form of equation (1).

$$Zy = \beta_1 Z_1 + \beta_2 Z_2 + \ldots + \beta_n Z_n \tag{2}$$

The new coefficients (β_i), called "beta-weights" are equal to the old b_i's times the ratio of the standard deviation of the appropriate x_i divided by the standard deviation of y.

Rather than the concrete and policy-oriented interpretations suggested for equation (1), this new form lends itself to theoretical discussions of the relative importance of each of the independent variables. Each β_i indicates the amount of change in Z_y produced by a change of one standard deviation in Z_i. The standardized form of equation (2) allows us to measure the theoretical relative importance of statistically equally probable changes in each of the independent variables; it also facilitates comparing different variables in different equations derived from different sets of data. This usage will perhaps be clearer in the discussion of some actual cases.[3]

1. *Explaining crude birth rates.* There is substantial evidence that fertility varies inversely with economic development through most of the range from developed to underdeveloped countries, but that with highly developed countries, such as those in North America and Oceania, the relationship becomes positive again, as families in some sense choose more children in preference to greater acquisition of such goods as consumer durables (e.g., home appliances, furnishings). Thus it is reasonable to include G. N. P. per capita in our regression equation. Another major influence on childbearing is education, which is also generally inversely related to birth rates (again with a reversal for well-to-do individuals in some of the highly developed states). Because we wanted to see whether it might exert an effect independently of income levels, we included the level of adult literacy in our prediction equation.[4] There is also a significant amount of theoretical literature on the interrelation between income growth rates and fertility. It is commonly argued that an above-average rate of population growth hinders development by diverting funds from investment to consumption; on the other hand it is sometimes maintained that high

---

3. For a helpful introduction to regression equations, cf. Hubert Blalock, *Social Statistics* (New York, 1961), pp. 326–46.

4. For a discussion of some of these theoretical considerations, as well as a highly skillful use of regression analysis, cf. Irma Adelman, "An Econometric Analysis of Population Growth," *American Economic Review*, 53 (June 1963), 314–39.

fertility may spur development either by increasing the potential market or, on the individual level, by increasing responsibilities and so providing a greater impetus to economic activity and achievement.[5] In this instance the causal argument is *from* fertility *to* economic growth, so we cannot properly discuss manipulating what for the regression equation is labeled the "independent" variable (economic growth) to affect the "dependent" one (fertility). But if we are interested in knowing what factors are *associated* with high fertility, and to what extent, we may still put annual rate of change in G. N. P. per capita in our regression equation. We were also intrigued by the negative correlation between birth rates and marriages per 1,000 population aged 15–44, and so included it in the analysis. Finally, we wanted to investigate the effect, if any, of Roman Catholic religion on fertility. Catholic doctrine is opposed to certain methods of family restriction, but in at least some Catholic countries (e.g., Ireland and Austria) the birth rate is very low. We therefore also used Roman Catholics as a percentage of total population in our attempt to measure the separate effects of these five independent variables. For an equation of form (1) the coefficients for the amount of deviation from the mean of the dependent variable produced by a change (unitary or doubling, depending on whether the variable is logged) in the independent variables are as follows. We use the same four-letter abbreviations to identify the variables as were employed in Section 1.

b-Coefficients of for BRTH:	$\log_2$GNPC	LIT	GPCH	MARG	CATH
	−3.61	−.29	−2.12	.62	.01

The number of countries for which we had data on all variables (N) was 38 (most of the underdeveloped were from Latin America); the r^2 of .81 indicates that we have explained over four-fifths of the variance in BRTH. The individual effects of the variables may be described according to the method discussed above. When G. N. P. per capita is doubled the birth rate falls by only 3.61 births per 1,000. For example, if a country with a per capita G. N. P. of $200 and a birth rate of about 46 per 1,000 were to double its income, the birth rate would probably decrease only about one-sixth of the way toward the moderate fertility rate of the United States (25 births per 1,000). For countries enjoying the Age of High Mass Consumption, Rostow has argued that higher incomes bring more babies, suggesting that this b-weight might eventually reverse its sign.[6]

Much larger changes in birth rates are likely to result from increases in national literacy rates (a 1% increase in literacy on the average seems to be associated with a decline of .29 units in the birth rate. This finding is of considerably greater significance if, for instance, population planners feel making an additional 50% of the population literate is more feasible than doubling or tripling the G. N. P. Our equation suggests that 50×.29 or about 15 fewer births per 1,000 would result. Such an educational effort over time might be sufficient (if the model continued to be accurate) to

---

5. Cf. Albert O. Hirschman, *The Strategy of Economic Development* (New Haven, 1958), pp. 176–82.
6. Adelman found that logged per capita G. N. P. has a small *positive* coefficient for birth rates. Like our results, however, she found literacy to have a much higher depressant effect.

change the birth rate from that typical of most high birth rate societies to that of the United States. It should be noted, however, that in all countries of over \$650 per capita G. N. P. literacy is virtually complete, and beyond this point one must depend on other influences, such as delayed marriages, to reduce fertility. One must be careful to check that the linear additivity assumption is appropriate to the variable ranges being discussed.

Also in this equation we see a negative relationship between the rate of economic growth and the crude birth rate. While there are few theoretical grounds for thinking that rapid growth *causes* a decline in births, the association between the two is apparent, with an increase of 1% in the growth rate being associated with 2.12 fewer births per 1,000. Possibly the causal relationship works the other way, or at least a decline in the birth rate makes rapid economic growth feasible. In any case we find no support for the idea that high birth rates are often likely to spur growth.

As for marriage rates, when other variables are controlled we find a positive though not substantial relationship with fertility. (One more marriage per eligible 1,000 leads us to expect .62 more births per 1,000.) This rather more plausible result modifies the impression given by the negative *simple* ecological correlation for births and marriages. And we find also a small positive relationship between percentage Catholic and fertility, with other variables controlled. A 1% increase in the Catholic population seems to cause a .01 unit addition to the birth rate. These coefficients must now be revised to β-weights, to allow for the great variation in the ranges and standard deviations of the variables.

β-Coefficients of	$\log_2$GNPC	LIT	GPCH	MARG	CATH
for BRTH	−.34	−.54	−.43	.19	.05

We now see that the major effect (always with the other variables controlled) is produced by variations in literacy, but that each of the other variables except percentage Catholic bears an important relation to birth rates. But rather surprisingly, with this group of countries Catholicism makes very little difference to the birth rate.

2. *Explaining items of foreign mail per capita.* In Part A we presented some arguments for the relevance of foreign mail rates to international politics. The consequences of a high rate of intercountry transactions, as measured by foreign mail ratios, may vary with the circumstances, but there is good reason to believe that a high ratio indicates a high *sensitivity* (whether favorable or antagonistic one cannot tell) to external events, that a high rate of transactions would at least produce a high potential for international cooperation.[7] Thus we should like to have some knowledge of what factors are associated with a high rate of transactions.

We began with the knowledge that the foreign mail ratio was correlated (.61) with G. N. P. per capita, and assumed that any explanation of this variable would have to include such a measure of development. It also

---

7. Cf. Karl W. Deutsch, "Shifts in the Balance of Communication Flows: A Problem of Measurement in International Relations," *Public Opinion Quarterly, 20* (Spring 1956), 143–60; and Bruce M. Russett, *Community and Contention: Britain and America in the Twentieth Century* (Cambridge, Mass., 1963), chs. 2, 7.

seemed reasonable that foreign mail would be related to the ratio of foreign trade to G. N. P.—the maintenance of a high level of foreign commerce
would require and stimulate a high level of postal exchange (and perhaps
vice versa). Finally, we noted the negative correlation between total population and the foreign trade ratio—large countries tend to engage less in
external transactions. We wished to measure the relative effects of these
three independent variables. The coefficients for this equation (form (1))
are:

b-Coefficients of	$\log_2$GNPC	TRDE	$\log_2$TPOP
for log FOML	.32	.11	−.04

The number of countries for which we had data on all variables was 54, and
the fit of the regression model is reasonably good (r^2 = .55). That the
resulting r^2 is above the simple r^2's for each of the independent variables
acting alone is fair evidence for a linear additive explanatory model.[8]
When G. N. P. per capita is doubled and the other variables are held constant, it produces a .32 increase in the foreign mail ratio. The elasticity
of the relationship (for logs to the same base) is .32 $\times \log_2$10 or 1.07; that
is, in the appropriate ranges, our model suggests that a doubling of per
capita G. N. P. will of itself produce slightly more than a doubling of the
foreign mail items per capita.

A 1% change in the foreign trade ratio, again with the other variables
controlled, gives a full .11 increment in the logarithm of the foreign mail
ratio (actually a multiplicative 18% increase). And a doubling of the population produces a .04 *decrease* in the logged foreign mail ratio (which
means, roughly, that the mail ratio will be about 90% of what it was before).
When revised to β-weights, the coefficients become:

β-Coefficients of	$\log_2$GNPC	TRDE	$\log_2$TPOP
for log FOML	.37	.33	−.13

Thus the major effects are produced by income levels and by foreign
trade, or at least by some variable like past or current colonial status
which is associated with trade. Insofar as we can generalize from this
cross-sectional model to a longitudinal one, we may say that as economic
development progresses in the world the level of international transactions
will increase substantially, and that contacts through foreign mail will also
be increased by greater foreign trade. But these trends will be countered
to some extent by the expectable growth in world population, and furthermore would be countered by any tendency toward the agglomeration of
small political units into fewer large units—European or Latin American
integration, for example.

3. *Explaining items of domestic mail per capita.* The preceding example becomes more instructive if we compare it with a similar model for
domestic mail. As in the first instance, we noted a high correlation between domestic mail and G. N. P. per capita. And, conversely to the first

---

8. That a quadratic term in log GNPC might still improve this model, however, is suggested by
the curvilinear relationship found between log GNPC and a logged foreign trade ratio in K. W.
Deutsch, A. Eckstein, and C. I. Bliss, "Population, Sovereignty and the Share of Foreign Trade,"
Economic Development and Cultural Change, 10 (July 1962), 353–66.

situation, we hypothesized that, other things being equal, a larger than average population would result in a higher than average domestic mail ratio—in effect, that in large countries some attention would be shifted from foreign to domestic contacts. We also hypothesized that there would be a relationship, over and above that found from G. N. P. per capita, between the percentage of literate adults and domestic mail. Finally we hypothesized that the domestic mail ratio might be related to population density, as suggested by a low positive (.20) correlation between density and domestic mail in Section 1. Perhaps relatively short physical distances between people might occasion greater contacts through the mails. The values for the equation this time are:

b-Coefficients of	$\log_2$GNPC	LIT	$\log_2$TPOP	$\log_2$DENS
for log DOML	.41	.002	.04	−.003

We had data for 71 countries. The r^2 is an extremely high .82 indicating that these four variables (three actually, for as will be apparent below density makes virtually no independent contribution) predict most of the variance in domestic mail. In the unstandardized coefficients the major effect is again produced by G. N. P. per capita, with a doubling in that value producing a 41% increase in the dependent logarithm (actually over a 150% increase in the domestic mail rate).

The β-weights appropriate to this equation are:

β-Coefficients of	$\log_2$GNPC	LIT	$\log_2$TPOP	$\log_2$DENS
for log DOML	.79	.08	.12	−.01

Again the most important contribution to predicting proportionate changes in the dependent variable is made by G. N. P. per capita, though literacy and total population also have effects. Although highly correlated with per capita G. N. P., literacy makes a notable improvement in explaining domestic mail. Population density may safely be disregarded, leaving a model with three independent variables. This equation is perhaps most interesting when viewed in the context of the preceding one, for foreign mail. We indicated that increases in G. N. P. would, if we may properly extrapolate from our cross-sectional model, produce a rise in the number of items of foreign mail, and so a rise in this form of transaction across national boundaries. But they will also produce a rise in domestic mail, in intranational contacts. And although our sample in one case is larger than in the other, and thus not strictly comparable, it would appear that G. N. P. increases will produce a greater effect on the latter variable than on the former. Further economic development would, therefore, while bringing increases in both, mean a shift in the balance from foreign to domestic communications. It would be a factor hindering, not promoting, one important kind of internationalist influence.[9]

4. *Explaining total vote.* In Part A we suggested that within countries there were powerful reasons for associating, at the individual level, high

9. A similar argument regarding the causes of foreign trade decline using *longitudinal* (time-series) data may be found in K. W. Deutsch and A. Eckstein, "National Industrialization and the Declining Share of the International Economic Sector, 1890–1959," *World Politics*, 13 (January 1961), 267–99.

rates of political participation with high socioeconomic status, that voting turnout was strongly correlated with income. We further indicated, and referred to some available evidence, that this same relationship held, but not so strongly, when comparing nations. In general, rich nations have higher voting turnouts than poor ones, but there are many important exceptions. An essential variable for our prediction attempt is thus G. N. P. per capita, but we cannot stop there. Another useful variable in this instance might be vote for the communist party as a percentage of total vote, primarily because of the virtually complete turnout observable in all communist nations. Communist vote also seemed an important variable for another reason, however. In Western democracies a vote for the communist party is a protest vote, an action directed against perceived severe injustice and deprivation. In Part A we also referred to some evidence that political participation tended to be higher (and occasionally, sometimes much lower too) in situations of social and political tension, that within countries voting turnout rose in times of crisis. Communist vote in part tapped this dimension also, but more direct measures were offered by our two measures of different aspects of political stability—deaths from domestic group violence and executive stability (the latter indicating positive stability of sorts, the former instability). The b-weights in a regression model of this interpretation are as follows:

b-Coefficients of	$\log_2$GNPC	COMV	$\log_2$VIOL	$\log_2$EXEC
for VOTE	8.46	.34	.35	−1.74

The number of countries in this instance is 40, and r^2 is a creditable .66, which is far higher than that achieved by any of the independent variables alone. The β-weights are:

β-Coefficients of	$\log_2$GNPC	COMV	$\log_2$VIOL	$\log_2$EXEC
for VOTE	.46	.58	.05	−.08

G. N. P. per capita is, as usual, a major element in the predictive equation, as is the percentage of the vote accruing to communists. The b-weights suggest, however, that a doubled per capita G. N. P. will be twice as effective in producing turnout as an increase of communist voting from 10% to 20%. Such a likelihood is of course improbable because of the negative relationship at the individual level between income and communist vote in most areas. Executive stability is negatively related to voting turnout and violence is positively associated with voting. Though the coefficients are small, "peaceful" polities *tend* not to have high levels of political involvement. The result with the others, however, is to support the hypotheses derived from intracountry comparisons. Voting turnout is positively related both to socioeconomic status and to tension levels.

5. *Explaining military personnel as a percentage of working-age population.* In asking what kinds of countries put more of their manpower resources into military service, we again hypothesized that the dependent variable, military participation, would be positively related to G. N. P. per capita even with other variables controlled. The simple correlation in Section 1 was not high enough even to be included in Table B.1, but nevertheless it seemed that richer states might be more able to shift resources into what is usually (though not always) in most economic senses a nonpro-

ductive channel. We further hypothesized that there would be some relation between army size and political instability, though the direction of the
possible relationship to the indicators was not clear. One might expect
large armies to be organized to suppress domestic unrest, but their success would be reflected in an inverse relation between army size and *in*-
stability, whereas their failure might be shown by a positive relation. To
explore the question we included the same two indices used in the preceding
equation, deaths from domestic group violence and executive stability. We
also added votes for communist party (partly in knowledge of the fact that
communist countries have large armies, and partly again in the belief that
in noncommunist states a high communist vote indicates unrest) and private consumption as a percentage of G. N. P. The latter variable obviously
was included to discover how incompatible are guns and butter. The b-
weights for the equation are:

b-Coefficients of	$\log_2$GNPC	$\log_2$VIOL	$\log_2$EXEC	COMV	CONS
for log MILP:	.14	−.08	−.11	.01	.01

N is 33 in this instance, and r^2 is .48. We thus can, with these variables,
go almost half way toward predicting military participation, at least in the
more-developed countries from which data are primarily drawn. Of the
five, four (including consumption) deal with *internal* politics. Thus a fairly
high level of prediction can be achieved without explicit reference to relations *between* nations, including influences like foreign aid, alliance, or
geographical region. More striking in this equation is the lack of a negative correlation between consumption and military participation. The
policy-relevant conclusion is that in general guns and butter are not competitive, at least in peacetime, and that if there is any competition for
scarce resources it may be between guns and factories—capital formation.
The relative importance of different influences will be clearer when we
examine the β-weights.

β-Coefficients of	$\log_2$GNPC	$\log_2$VIOL	$\log_2$EXEC	COMV	CONS
for log MILP:	.37	−.46	−.25	.60	.17

Each of the first four independent variables plays an important role in explaining military participation, though the most powerful variables are
political violence and communist vote. Thus we do find, when other influ-
are held constant, that military participation does increase with income.
We also find that military participation is inversely related to deaths from
domestic group violence, suggesting that the motive behind the creation of
many large military establishments may well be the suppression of domestic dissent, and that dissent is not so likely to be manifested in violence
when this is done. On the other hand, executive stability is also negatively
related to military participation; i.e., large armies and rapid executive
turnover go together. Possibly this reflects the role of the army in some
Latin American and Middle Eastern states.

6. *Explaining deaths from domestic group violence.* The final regression to be presented shows our attempted explanation of domestic violence,
with which there were relatively few high simple correlations in Table B.1.
We shall here see whether a multivariate model will be more successful in
interpreting it. In this equation we used G. N. P. per capita, to correspond

with the common hypothesis that, all other things being equal, economic development promotes political stability. We also included the annual rate of change in G. N. P. per capita to see which, if either, of two contradictory causal hypotheses might be correct. One is that a rapid rate of growth may serve to channel energies, relieve dissatisfactions, and promote stability. The opposite idea is that a rapid growth rate implies a rapid rate of social change, dislocation, and potential instability. Another variable included was votes as a percentage of voting-age population, again in line with the hypothesis that a higher than average voting turnout indicates dissatisfaction (and perhaps potential violence). We added life expectancy on the theory that it would prove a useful supplement to G. N. P. per capita as a measure not only of the wealth of a nation but of the distribution of welfare within a society.

In addition we included the Gini index of inequality for agricultural land to test the hypothesis that above-average inequality promotes above-average social and political discord or, conversely, that substantial equality means the existence of a large and relatively prosperous middle class which will support the existing political system. Data on income inequality were available for too few countries to include them in a regression analysis, but we do have fairly extensive data on the distribution of what is in most countries a prime source of wealth and income—agricultural land. This enabled us in turn to specify the hypothesis as one generally considered plausible but seldom tested with care—that a prosperous peasantry, a sturdy yeomanry, is especially likely to support the existing regime, but that a deprived peasantry, such as that of nineteenth-century Russia, is a particular source of political discontent. To make this hypothesis applicable to a broad range of countries, however, it was necessary to add to the equation the percentage of the labor force employed in agriculture. It seemed reasonable that the political effects of inequality in land distribution would be much more important in a predominantly agricultural country than in a chiefly industrial one.[10] The coefficients for the regression model follow:

b-Coefficients of	$\log_2$GNPC	GPCH	VOTE	LIFE	LFAG	LNDG
for log VIOL:	−.10	−.16	.01	−.03	.01	1.34

For this equation N is 33 and r^2 is .60. The b-weight equation is quite rich in its policy insights regarding the path of peaceful development. We find that both an increase in the *level* of G. N. P. per capita and a rise in its growth *rate* are associated with domestic tranquility; i.e., they are negatively associated with violence. This negative relation between wealth and violence may not, however, hold at the lowest levels of development. Furthermore, a useful *political* benefit of early emphasis on relatively noncontroversial and widespread social welfare policies improving individual health and life expectancy is its depressant effect on domestic violence. The remaining b-weights suggest the need to lag urbanization and mass political participation behind positive contributors to political sta-

---

10. For a discussion of some of the relevant theory cf. Bruce M. Russett, "Inequality and Instability: The Relation of Land Tenure to Politics," *World Politics*, *16* (April 1964).

bility. An increase in the inequality of land distributions (land reform) appears also to be a potent pacifier. By taking the antilog of .0134, we find that within certain ranges, a one-point (out of 100) decrement in the land Gini index has the effect of decreasing domestic violence by 3%.

Turning to the β-weights we can make the following theoretically significant comparisons:

β-Coefficients of for log VIOL:	$\log_2$GNPC	GPCH	VOTE	LIFE	LFAG	LNDG
	$-.13$	$-.34$	$.27$	$-.32$	$.20$	$.22$

It appears that the "causes" of political violence are numerous and that the relationship is complex. G. N. P. per capita, though it has an effect, is the least important of the independent variables used. The rate of change in G. N. P., however, is a powerful factor. Since both G. N. P. per capita and its change rate show a negative relationship with violence, it is clear that the optimists carry the day: economic development will, *ceteris paribus* as usual, tend to reduce the amount of political violence as that term is used here. As we would by now expect, voting turnout is rather strongly associated with violence (probably the high voting rate, like violence, is an expression of discontent). A major surprise comes from the size if not the direction of the coefficient for life expectancy, in its role as a composite index of welfare. And the two agricultural variables turn out to have important explanatory power. There would appear to be much truth in the common beliefs about land inequality and democratic instability. The *distribution* of wealth may be more relevant politically and theoretically than its *level*.

One general substantive point should perhaps be made about all these regression equations. In all our examples economic development, as measured by G. N. P. per capita, bore a major explanatory role. But it was in every case only a partial explanation, which, to produce satisfactory predictions had to be supplemented by other variables. In only two instances was it the variable with the greatest theoretical explanatory power. Economic analysis cannot adequately explain many of the situations that interest social scientists most, and economic factors must be used in conjunction with other factors such as those measured by the social and political indices in this *Handbook*.

5. Regionalism Versus Universalism in Comparing Nations

When we *describe* Peru as a Latin American country, we are simply locating it in a particular geographic region. If, however, we attempt to *explain* certain things about Peru, such as its *personalismo* in politics or its low per capita income, by saying that it is a Latin American country, several interpretations of this remark are possible. The simplest, which we shall call the geographic interpretation of regionalism, is that being a Latin American nation means having a lower per capita income than, say, North American countries, or means having considerable *personalismo* in its politics.[1] If the tables in Part A had been presented separately for each of the world's major regions this kind of geographic analysis of the broadest ecological sort, comparing different regions with respect to their typically different social and political characteristics, would have been facilitated.

Another way of interpreting the regional clustering of national data for cross-national comparisons would be to make explanations in terms of generalized cultural, political, or social variables which correlate with regional groupings. Thus, instead of talking about East European states, one can refer to communist countries and mean nearly the same thing. At some stage Mainland China and Castro's Cuba would also merit such a label. Even more generally, as this *Handbook* has done, one might describe such states in terms of a very high percentage of the electorate voting for communist political parties. Again it is clear that European nations (and a smaller number of Asian states, some of which do not have elections) are the ones particularly involved. Although highly concentrated in Europe and North America, economic development is another important generalizable regional phenomenon.

Describing nations in terms of such universalistic variables might be called "sociological regionalism." This conceptualization of regional phenomena implies important substantive and methodological assumptions. As done in this *Handbook*, applying such additive techniques as simple, curvilinear, or multiple correlation and regression or factor analysis to the world's entire population of nations is considered appropriate and desirable. This universalistic focus on national behavior in general terms leads to the view that regional clusterings of data familiar from the geo-

---

1. Drawing on theoretical formulations by Juan Linz, Robert Alford conceives "political regionalism" within a nation to occur when "political parties exist which are peculiar to a given region" or "when a national party consistently draws a disproportionate support from a given region" or "when regions shift from election to election in opposing directions, thus indicating that the impact of national political currents affects regions in contradictory ways." (*Party and Society*, Chicago, 1963, pp. 42–43.) The present cross-national interpretation of "geographic regionalism" corresponds quite closely to Alford's first and second concepts; the concepts of "sociological regionalism" and "configurative regionalism" as social facts and explanatory methods defined below may be considered generalizations of the second and third aspects of Alford's "political regionalism."

This section was written by Hayward R. Alker, Jr., in response to several methodological questions raised by Paul Lazarsfeld, Mattei Dogan, René Bassoul, and Juan Linz. See Stein Rokkan, et al., "Summary Report of the International Conference on the Use of Quantitative Political, Social and Cultural Data in Cross-National Comparisons," *Social Science Information, 2* (January 1964).

graphic approach can best be explained by other equally general variables. Domestic unrest in a particular country in Latin America would be explained not by anything peculiar to Latin America but rather by such conditions as the degree of concentration of land and the country's level of development. (See Section 4 above.) In this view region is a *composite index* of variables of a nonregional sort. Sometimes regions additively summarize other variables; sometimes they additively explain them.[2]

As a research focus and a political fact regionalism may mean more than a clustering of geographically proximate states on *Handbook* profiles, and more than the description or explanation of regional political and social phenomena in terms of sociological variables. A good deal of the literature of social science suggests that *relationships between variables will be different for data from different geographic or cultural contexts.*[3]

The best approach to these possibilities of "configurative regionalism" is a heightened sensitivity on the part of those who do universalistic analyses to possible regional or cultural differences. Regional specialists, on the other hand, should make continual distinctions between local events and worldwide patterns, they should state their findings in the most universal terms possible. There is a need to use and develop more adequate formal models of the various ways in which particular regional contexts influence configurations.

These basic distinctions in regional analysis pose the same questions as the study of ecological correlation, Lazarsfeld's well-known technique of elaborating a relationship, and the multivariate statistical technique

---

2. The *Encyclopedia of the Social Sciences* suggests that "regionalist problems arise only where there is a combination of two or more such factors as geographic isolation, independent historical traditions, racial, ethnic or religious peculiarities and local economic or class interests." Structurally, however, it also describes regionalism as "a counter-movement to any exaggerated or oppressive form of centralization." See Hedwig Hintze's article on "Regionalism," *ESS* (New York, 1948), 3, 208–18.

Brian J. L. Berry, a geographer, used additive techniques (regression, factor and discriminant analysis) in "regionalizing" economic development. After reducing 43 technological and demographic indices to four distinct factors explaining over 90% of the original variance, he found that most of the world's regions can be distinguished from each other on the basis of their scores on two of these factors. See his "An Inductive Approach to the Regionalization of Economic Development," in N. Ginsburg, ed., *Essays on Geography and Economic Development* (Chicago, 1960), pp. 78–107. A shortened and more widely distributed form of this article may be found in N. Ginsburg, ed., *Atlas of Economic Development* (Chicago, 1961).

3. From a developmental perspective, an early example of this viewpoint is Harold Lasswell's remark that "Each specific interpretation is subject to redefinition as the structural potentialities of the future become actualized in the past and present of participant observers." See his "The Configurative Analysis of the World Value Pyramids," ch. 1 of *World Politics and Personal Insecurity* (1934) reprinted in Lasswell, Merriam, and Smith, *A Study of Power* (Glencoe, Ill., 1950). Lipset repeatedly distinguished between European or English-speaking countries and Latin America in discussing the relationship between economic development and democracy in Chapter II of *Political Man* (Garden City, N.Y., 1960). Paul Lazarsfeld and Wagner Thielens in *The Academic Mind: Social Scientists in a Time of Crises* (Glencoe, Ill., 1958), found that faculty expectations of university support in times of crisis increased with the quality of secular schools but decreased with the increasing quality of traditional schools.

known as the analysis of covariance.[4] Simply put, each of these analytical techniques takes a hard look at a particular simple relation between two variables, breaking it down into relations within and between different sub-groupings such as geographic regions or stages of economic development. The measure of association between the independent variable x and the dependent variable y may be a correlation coefficient as presented in Section 1, a coefficient of covariation or, as Lazarsfeld has suggested, a term involving cross-products in a 2×2 table. We shall now show how each of these mathematical techniques distinguishes between our three kinds of regional analysis.

For expositional purposes it will be convenient to talk about cross-products between x, y, and a dichotomous control variable c. Let us consider a relationship between land inequality (x) and domestic violence (y) in a hypothetical universe of 100 developed and 100 underdeveloped nations. We shall denote the *absence* of violence, inequality, and development by a barlike superscript in the following arrays and formulas:

Developed countries				Underdeveloped countries				All countries		
	x	$\bar{x}$			x	$\bar{x}$			x	$\bar{x}$
y	40	20	60	y	50	20	70	y	90	40	130
$\bar{y}$	10	30	40	$\bar{y}$	10	20	30	$\bar{y}$	20	50	70
	50	50	100		60	40	100		110	90	200

Identifying each cell with up to three subscripts referring first to its x class, then to its y class and finally to its state of development (c or $\bar{c}$), and omitting subscripts when a certain distinction is being ignored we define the cross-product of x and y (xy) as follows:

$$(xy) = \frac{N_{xy} N_{\bar{x}\bar{y}} - N_{\bar{x}y} N_{x\bar{y}}}{N^2} \tag{1}$$

As might be expected we find positive associations between inequality and domestic violence in both developed and underdeveloped countries. $(xy)_c =$ .100, $(xy)_{\bar{c}} = .080$, $(xy) = .093$. Comparing the "regional" relationships with the universal one, however, we find that the relationship between inequality and violence is *stronger* for developed countries and *weaker* for under-developed countries than the universal relationship would suggest.

A simple formula relates these different cross-products:

$$(xy) = \frac{N_c}{N} \cdot (xy)_c + \frac{N_{\bar{c}}}{N} \cdot (xy)_{\bar{c}} + \frac{N^2 (xc) \cdot (cy)}{N_c \cdot N_{\bar{c}}} \tag{2}$$

---

4. The discussion that follows is based on W. S. Robinson, "Ecological Correlations and the Behavior of Individuals," *American Sociological Review, 15* (1950), 351–57; Paul Lazarsfeld, "Evidence and Inference in Social Research," in Daniel Lerner, ed., *On Evidence and Inference* (*Daedalus, 87,* Fall 1958), 99–130; H. Walker and J. Lev, "Analysis of Covariance," ch. 15 of their *Statistical Inference* (New York, 1953); H. M. Blalock, *Social Statistics* (New York, 1960), Part III; and G. Yule and M. Kendall, *An Introduction to the Theory of Statistics* (14th ed. London, 1958), chs. 1–3 and 9–14.

In words, we find that the relationship between x and y can be broken down into proportionately weighted relations between x and y in either developed or underdeveloped countries and a term involving the relations of both x and y to the level of development. On the right side of the equation the terms associating x with y in each region are called the "partials" and the final term a "marginal" or "ecological" relationship between groups.[5]

In the light of our previous discussion of geographic, sociological, and configurative analysis, we can make the following comparisons. Geographic interpretations, like ecological correlations, focus on differences in regional marginals and averages. Sociological analyses emphasize relations between individual nations for an entire universe. Configurative analyses pay greater attention to the structure of partial, within-region relationships. Sociological analyses are often necessary to correct the "ecological fallacy" of generalizing to individual behavior from aggregate data; configurative analyses are often necessary to correct the "*universal fallacy*" of inferring anything about particular regions or stages of development from universalistic relationships.[6] Some examples of configurative analysis are given below.

Achievement motivation and per capita gross national product.   It has already been suggested in Section 1 that McClelland's achievement motivation index derived from children's readers shows no relation to per capita G. N. P. and that it correlates only slightly, but negatively, with contemporaneous national growth rates. A configurative analysis, however, suggests that educationally induced motivations may be of unequal relevance to growth rates in different regions. If we accept McClelland's evidence regarding the reliability of his need for achievement data, it still

---

5. Let C denote a covariation, E a correlation ratio, the subscripts b and w refer to between and within group relations, and r_{ec} be an ecological correlation. Then the corresponding equations of ecological and covariance analysis are

$$r_{xy} = \sqrt{1 - E_{xc}^2} \cdot \sqrt{1 - E_{yc}^2} \cdot r_w + E_{xc}E_{yc}r_{ec} \tag{3}$$

$$C_{xy} = C_{xyw} + C_{xyb} \tag{4}$$

The first term of equation (4) sums products of deviations in x and y from their universal means; the second does the same with respect to subgroup means; and the third does this for group means compared to overall means in very much the same manner as an ecological correlation. That equation (2) is analogous to equation (3) is clear when we realize first that the two partials are really just a weighted average of a within-group relationship and secondly that the marginal term is equivalent to a weighted cross-product for two estimates of x and y derived from the marginals of the within-region arrays given above.

Covariations, covariances, correlations and cross-products are also closely related. Covariances are average covariations; product-moment correlations (r's) are covariances divided by the standard deviations of x and y. If for a 2 × 2 table we assign a numerical value of 1 to x and y and 0 to $\bar{x}$ and $\bar{y}$, and take deviations about the "middle" of the table, $r_{xy} = 4 \cdot$ (xy) whenever the marginals are all equal.

6. Erwin Scheuch has referred to an "individualistic fallacy" in his contribution to Richard Merritt and Stein Rokkan, ed., *Comparing Nations* (New Haven, Conn., forthcoming). He makes the same point, that contextual variables may change individual relationships. It should be added, however, that except in the case of nonadditive contributions by a control variable, *regression* analyses such as those in Section 4 need not suffer too severely from either the ecological or the universal fallacy. Nor should it be implied that sociologists, with their special interest in mechanisms for maintaining sub-system boundaries, are especially likely to "sociologize" regional variables. See Leo A. Goodman, "Some Alternatives to Ecological Correlation," *The American Journal of Sociology, 64* (1959), 610-25, and the discussion below. In a recent excellent paper, Raymond Boudon, "Propriétés individuelles et propriétés collectives: un problème d'analyse écologique," *Revue Française de Sociologie, 4* (1963), 275-99, has suggested several other ways of approximating individual relations from ecological correlations.

may be true that higher average achievement scores within the developed regions, and sociological analysis, are concealing interesting *within-group* relationships. Another possibility suggested by McClelland is that achievement scores, which do not correlate with current income levels or growth rates, will correlate with future ones.

Separate correlations and regressions between achievement motivation and per capita G. N. P. are summarized in Figure B.7 for (1) Western European states, the United States, Canada, Australia, and New Zealand ("Europeans"); (2) Eastern European countries (excluding Finland, Greece, and Turkey, but including Yugoslavia); (3) Latin American states; and (4) African and Asian nations. We see that the overall correlation between per capita G. N. P. and the achievement motivation index (too small to appear in Section 1) is meager and negative: $r = -.13$. Within each of our four rather crude regional groupings, however, there are considerably different intercepts, slopes, and correlations.

Assuming the predictive validity of achievement scores, these different relationships between achievement motivation (in 1950) and per capita income (in 1957) are quite suggestive. Higher achievement motivation may be taken to indicate a higher than average future growth rate. Within those areas with a high *positive* correlation between current achievement motivation and current income, the rich nations will get richer and greater inequality of income levels should develop; in those areas with a *negative* relationship the "laggards" should tend to catch up in the future. Figure B.7 suggests, for instance, that on a worldwide scale between-nation income difference may diminish in the long run (a conclusion supported by better evidence in Section 6 below). And among wealthier "European" states, as the economic growth rates also suggest, income levels appear likely to grow more slowly. But *within* Eastern Europe, Africa, and Asia no such conclusions are warranted. For the small sample of Latin American states we find a rather strong *positive* relationship between ACHV and GNPC, suggesting that inequality will increase. In a culture area where McClelland's index might be especially appropriate, only a few states have established the psychological preconditions of economic take-off.[7]

Regional varieties of Catholic ruralism. Section 1 also suggested that, if anything, Catholic countries are *less* agricultural than non-Catholic ones, thus casting doubt on the Weberian notions of Protestant influences on industrial development. An immediate retort would be that the relationship is spurious, that it results simply from the *ecological* fact that Catholics and other Christians are found more often in the more developed countries, where, of course, there are fewer agricultural workers. It is true, for instance, that the product corresponding to (xc) · (cy) in equation (2), using the somewhat incomparable correlations in Section 1, is +.27. Assuming a similar lower level of agricultural labor force for all developed countries, the partial correlation $r_{xy\cdot c}$ between Catholicism and ruralism (under these assumptions analogous to the sum of the partial relationships

---

7. Had we excluded America and Canada from our "European" grouping, the within-Europe relationship would have been stronger. The Latin American results (N = 5) are of course extremely dependent on Argentina's higher income and better current methods of inculcating achievement motivation. See the comments on validity, population size, and statistical significance below.

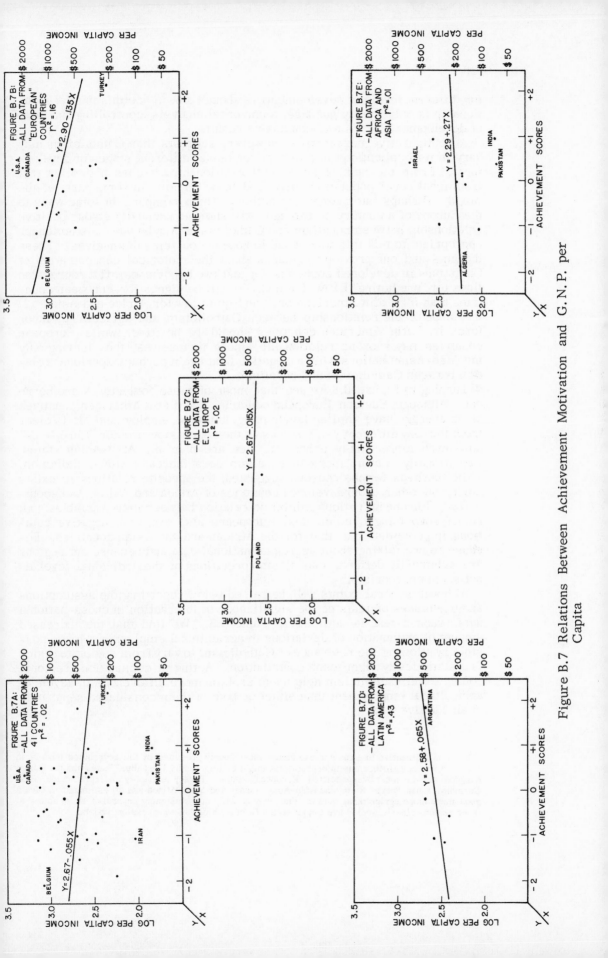

Figure B.7 Relations Between Achievement Motivation and G.N.P. per Capita

for different levels of development) is about +.08. Since this partial relationship is only weakly *positive*, a universal analysis, controlling for level
of development, leads to inconclusive results.

A configurative perspective, however, suggests that Catholicism may
vary in its implications in different regions at different stages of development. From the lack of an overall relationship, it does not follow that
traditional rural populations may tend to be Catholic in some parts of the
world. Perhaps Latin American nations, which compare in some ways to
the Europe of a century or two ago, will show an unusually strong positive
relationship between ruralism and Catholicism. Maybe *now* it is no longer
appropriate to talk this way about European countries themselves. These
thoughts and our previous remarks about the ecological concentration of
Christians in developed countries suggest two hypotheses: (1) regression
lines for "predicting" LFAG from CATH will be higher for European countries than for Latin American ones and quite low for Africa and Asia; (2)
the slope of the relationship between Catholicism and agricultural labor
force in Latin American countries should be positive, while European
countries may show no relationship among themselves, thus leaving only
the Afro-Asian nations with a negative (and again perhaps spurious) relation between Catholicism and ruralism.

Turning to Figure B.8 we see that most of these conjectures are borne
out. Although Eastern European countries and Latin American countries
on an average have similar levels of agricultural employment, it is clear
from the very different y-intercepts of the regression line for "Europeans"
how much more highly urbanized they are than the Afro-Asian states.
Directionally, Latin American ruralism does increase with Catholicism,
while (perhaps for the reasons suggested) the opposite relationship exists
among the other underdeveloped countries of Africa and Asia. As hypothesized, "European" nations exhibit no relation between these variables and,
rather surprisingly, communist Europeans also exhibit a negative relationship somewhat like that for the African and the Asian countries. Because we are talking about aggregate national data and because our regions
are arbitrarily defined, causal interpretations at the individual level do
not seem appropriate.[8]

Although several points will be raised below regarding the assumptions
and usefulness of tests of the significance of interaction in cross-national
data, such a test is outlined in Table B.3. We find that the increased
amount of explanation of deviations in agricultural employment made possible by allowing the relevance of Catholicism to vary from region to region
is a statistically significant contribution. Acting in conjunction, regional
contexts and Catholicism help us to explain more differences in levels of
agricultural employment than either or both of them considered separately
in an additive way.

---

8. It is instructive to look at those states most poorly predicted by the regression models in
Figure B.8 to see whether our interpretations might be improved. The United States and the United
Kingdom are the most overpredicted "European" states; Turkey is greatly underpredicted. East
Germany, Latin Puerto Rico, and Afro-Asian Israel and South Africa are all estimated to have a
good many more agricultural workers than they actually do. Assigning several of these states to
other regions clearly would have improved the fit of each of these regression models.

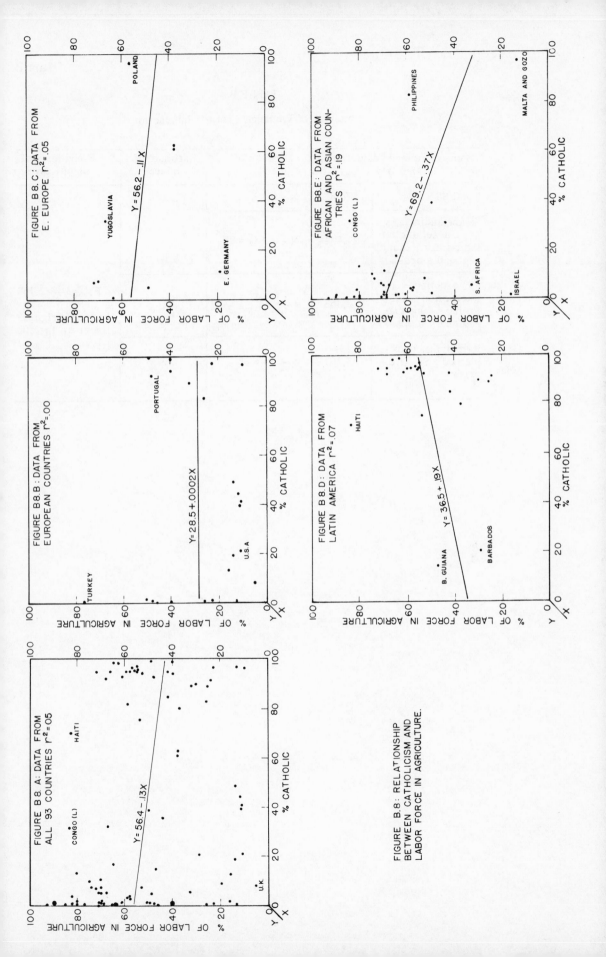

FIGURE B.8.A: DATA FROM ALL 93 COUNTRIES $r^2 = .05$

$Y = 56.4 - .13X$

FIGURE B.8.B: DATA FROM EUROPEAN COUNTRIES $r^2 = .00$

$Y = 28.5 + .0002X$

FIGURE B.8.C: DATA FROM E. EUROPE $r^2 = .05$

$Y = 56.2 - .11X$

FIGURE B.8.D: DATA FROM LATIN AMERICA $r^2 = .07$

$Y = 36.5 + .19X$

FIGURE B.8.E: DATA FROM AFRICAN AND ASIAN COUNTRIES $r^2 = .19$

$Y = 69.2 - .37X$

FIGURE B.8: RELATIONSHIP BETWEEN CATHOLICISM AND LABOR FORCE IN AGRICULTURE.

TABLE B.3

Analysis of Variance Test for Interaction

Sums of squared deviations (SS) in y		Degrees of freedom	Estimate of variance	F and level of significance
Total SS	47,681	$N - 1 = 92$		
SS unexplained by x or c assuming no interaction (equal regional slopes)	27,734	$N - (4+1) = 88$		
SS explained by interaction (allowing unequal regional slopes)	2,465	$4 - 1 = 3$	821.5	$F = \dfrac{821.5}{297.3} = 2.763$ which is significant at the .05 level
Remaining unexplained SS (i.e. error)	25,269	$N - 2 \cdot 4 = 85$	297.3	

Popular longevity and executive stability. In Section 4 we found that life
expectancy, more than per capita income, contributed importantly and
additively to reducing the frequency of domestic violence. It also turned
out that high levels of voting are associated with violence. Here we can
look at the relationship between these variables and our alternative index
of political instability—executive turnover. If we interpret longevity
to be an indicator of a society's healthiness, the question arises whether
or not the positive association between well-being and stability is characteristic of all kinds of political systems. Health-oriented political systems
might be defined as those showing such a positive relationship (other variables being controlled); no relationship between executive tenure and popular longevity would define a class of political systems within which popular
well-being is not related to executive stability. We might hypothesize that
in the more participant societies the possibility of medical care (unlike its
cost) is no longer a political issue.

Separate regression analyses were performed for the subgroup of nations
with more than 80% voting, for societies with voting levels between 50% and
80%, and for a third group with popular political participation below 50%.

Turning to Figure B.9 we find that a strong health orientation is largely
confined to the class of political systems (most of them underdeveloped)
with low levels of political participation. This relationship seems especially true of Latin America and Western European states like Spain, Portugal, and Switzerland. The effect of increasing political participation is

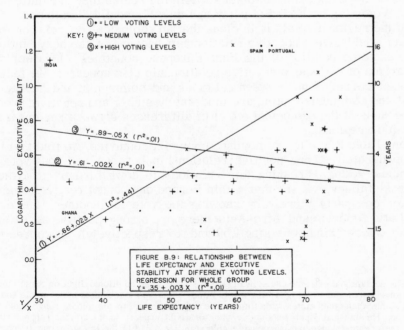

Figure B.9 Relationship Between Life Expectancy and
Executive Stability at Different Voting Levels

to reverse or nullify this relationship. In systems not encouraging popular participation, welfare policies appear politically expedient as a means of promoting executive stability; otherwise there is no compensatory payoff, presumably because it is not a determinative issue. In fact, there is even a slightly negative relationship among highly participant systems, which is probably due to democratically induced executive turnover in the most developed of these societies.[9]

The structure of national political choice. A full-scale configurative analysis of voting alternatives within different regional and developmental contexts might well involve curvilinear and multivariate analyses within the appropriate groupings to detect different structural relationships. Because such analyses would go beyond the illustrative intent of this section, we shall confine ourselves to a discussion of the marginal, partial, and universal relationships between two pairs of voting alternatives: communism versus socialism and communism versus religious party support. These relationships provide a good example of data where both the ecological and the universal fallacy may occur.

The average levels of support for each of these three kinds of parties within four regional contexts are given, with their standard deviations, in Table B.4. The averages are only for those countries with data available on each of these series. The first striking result is the size of all the standard deviations except that for Eastern Europe. Within every other region these deviations appear to indicate that voting levels go below zero. The reason for this strange result is readily explainable by looking at the original data within each of the regions; in some countries these kinds of parties do not even exist; in others within the region they are quite prominent. Votes for each kind of party are thus bimodally distributed. Comparing the regional totals it is clear that an ecological correlation for all the data would give a negative relationship because of the heavy influence of the extreme position of the East European countries. In a worldwide comparison of nations, a negative relationship also appears. In fact, the universal correlations between religious and communist and between socialist and communist voting are moderately strong and negative, probably just because of the ecological effect of differences between regions (rather than within regions).

From Table B.5, after removing communist countries, we find that there is a moderately strong positive relationship between religious votes and communist voting. Breaking this relationship down further, to avoid the universal fallacy, we see that within Europe one cannot really predict the vote for one party merely by knowing the vote for another, but that in both Latin America and Afro-Asia there are strong positive associations between the two kinds of voting (.69 and .87 respectively). Of course these

---

9. The deviant and extreme cases in Figure B.9 shed some additional light on these interpretations. Among societies with high voting levels West Germany is a good deal more stable and France is less stable than other states with similar life expectancies; in the middle range India is more stable and Panama and Japan less stable than we would expect; in the lowest range Switzerland enjoys the greatest longevity and considerable stability. Within the lowest group it appears that among medically advanced societies Portugal and Spain enjoy more stability than one would expect, while underdeveloped Ghana has also been remarkably stable.

TABLE B.4

Average Regional Votes $\pm$ Their Standard Deviations for Religious,
Communist, and Socialist Parties

	RELV	COMV	SOCV
"Europe" (N = 20)	16.2 ± 20.1	5.7 ± 7.9	29.4 ± 16.0
East. Europe (N = 9)	0.0 ± 0.0	99.2 ± 1.0	0.0 ± 0.0
Latin America (N = 9)	8.8 ± 10.7	3.1 ± 3.6	8.5 ± 15.3
Africa & Asia (N = 5)	14.6 ± 18.5	7.4 ± 5.5	25.6 ± 12.6

TABLE B.5

The Regional Structure of National Political Choice

(Correlation coefficients within boxes are for regional data only)

A. Relations Between Votes for Communist Parties and
for Religious Parties

COMV

	Communist countries	Others
RELV	− 1.00* (N = 9)	+.24 (N = 34)

r = − .29 (N = 43)

COMV

	"Europe"	E. Europe	L. America	Afro-Asia
RELV	.07 (N = 20)	− 1.00* (N = 9)	+.69 (N = 9)	+.87 (N = 5)

r = − .29 (N = 43)

B. Relations Between Votes for Communist Parties and
for Socialist Parties

COMV

	Communist countries	Others
SOCV	− 1.00* (N = 9)	− .05 (N = 35)

r = − .50 (N = 44)

COMV

	"Europe"	E. Europe	L. America	Afro-Asia
SOCV	− .23 (N = 20)	− 1.00* (N = 9)	.02 (N = 10)	− .29 (N = 5)

r = − .50 (N = 44)

* Strictly speaking these correlations are indeterminate unless those who did not vote "yes" are assumed to have voted for another party. r = − 1.00 corresponds to the case where all other votes went to the opposing party.

underdeveloped countries provide only a small part of the data available for this analysis, but at least we can conclude that inferring a negative universal relationship would be highly misleading. In some cases both kinds of votes may represent the growing pains of modernization.

Regarding socialism or communism, we again find that outside the communist world the overall negative correlation of – .50 in voting patterns is meaningless. Within Europe and Afro-Asia, but not Latin America, there is some indication that these two choices tend to coincide. In the already developed European area, socialism and communism appear as national alternatives.[10]

Configurative analysis is based on the assumption that events or social processes may vary in their meaning from context to context. If structural differences in relationships are found, regional interpretations must be considered; if not, universal comparisons have been justified. For instance the presence of a strong Catholic Church may or may not be associated with rural populations. Similarly different levels of popular participation in politics shape the issues that determine executive stability. Developed countries are more often forced to make a choice between religious, socialist, and communist parties than underdeveloped ones. On the other hand, several important universalistic relationships, ones in which additive models appear appropriate, were also mentioned. Political regionalism affected only the level and not the form of relationships between per capita income and urbanization and between military participation ratios and domestic group violence.

Causal variables explain substantial variation in a dependent variable even after the effects of other independent variables have been controlled (see Section 4).[11] In cross-national comparisons, the assumption of con-

---

10. Although the details will not be presented here, a few words on the other analyses of covariance and nonadditive interaction in *Handbook* data completed to date may be appropriate. The relationship between violence and military participation ratios previously discussed was found to be very similar in *form* at all levels of communist voting, but at a higher *level* in communist societies. Such an effect could be discovered by additive partialing procedures like regression analysis. K. Deutsch, C. Bliss, and A. Eckstein, "Population, Sovereignty, and the Share of Foreign Trade," *Economic Development and Cultural Change*, 10 (July 1962), 353–66, found foreign trade ratios to decrease in a curvilinear way with increasing national population size. A repeated test of this hypothesis (not assuming curvilinearity) found this decrease to be true for older and newly sovereign states. Ex-colonies were also more likely to trade, as found before. A more subtle impact of the colonial experience, however, was suggested by the *less rapid decrease* in outside contacts for the larger-sized ex-colonies.

Labor force in agriculture turned out to be a crucial condition reversing the overall positive relationship (r = .44) between land inequality and domestic violence (the subject of our hypothetical example above). The relationship between land inequality and violence is steepest and strongest for moderately rural nations, somewhat less so among urbanized states and slightly negative (r = –.18, N = 10) for very rural societies. In sum, a little urbanization is a dangerous thing.

Finally, per capita income and urbanization (measured by PC20) show a similar form of positive relationship of identical strength (the within-group and universal slopes are all about .70) for each of the four regions used above. Regional differences only account additively for different intercepts (levels) for these relationships.

11. In a similar way, Lazarsfeld, "Evidence and Inference in Social Research," pp. 120ff. describes x as causally related to y "if we have a relationship between x and y, and if for any *antecedent* test factor the partial relationships between x and y do not disappear." Even more generally (p. 124) he says that "explanation consists of the formal aspect of elaboration and some substantive ordering of variables." This substantive ordering could be a temporal one, theoretical plausibility, our related notion of "independence" and "dependence," or a hierarchy of levels of analysis.

textual variability suggests the importance of exploring conditional relationships that may or may not independently be of causal importance.

Different kinds of conditional relationships. A number of important distinctions concern the different kinds of conditional relationships.[12]   When we noted that two different kinds of political systems differed from each other in the level of violence associated with a particular size of military establishment, we meant that the political system was a *discriminating condition* affecting this relationship.   Similarly, when we found that the level of political participation within a society changes or reverses the sign or slope of a relationship, we called this variable a *directional condition*.   *Associational conditions* are those which change degrees of association between variables.   *Threshold conditions* are a special mixture of directional and discriminating conditions.   They serve to change slopes and levels, but only once, and that from a position of no relationship. Thus, for example, we seemed to pass a threshold of national health's relevance to political stability as we decreased the level of popular political participation.   Unlike independent causes, or discriminating variables, *"causal" conditions* are variables making irreducible directional changes in a relationship.

The earlier discussion about region as a sociological or a configurative variable may be reinterpreted to ask whether it is a discriminating or a directional conditioner.   Even when measured on a nominal scale, discriminating variables could be broken down into a number of separate categories, scored as zero or one and used in a multiple regression analysis in addition to the other possibly causal independent variables.   Directional conditioners on the other hand specifically violate the assumption of additivity in regression analysis, requiring analysis of variance and covariance techniques and suggesting, as we shall see below, multiplicative formalizations.[13]   To repeat, interaction between two variables (such as region and religion) occurs whenever they explain more when considered jointly than as the sum of their independent effects.

---

12.   Lazarsfeld distinguishes various types of conditional relationships on the basis of an equation like (2) above.   These are based on the relative time of occurrence of the condition variable and whether or not it makes the marginals or the partials disappear.   The case of vanishing partials corresponds to the situation where the control variables wash out spurious relations between x and y.   When the marginals disappear we know there is no ecological correlation resulting from unequal distributions of the variables.

If we define a "slope" (b_{yx}) for covariances using marginal products

$$b_{yx} = \frac{(N_{xy} + N_{\bar{x}y})\ (N_{x\bar{y}} + N_{\bar{x}\bar{y}})}{(N_{\bar{x}y} + N_{\bar{x}\bar{y}})\ (N_{xy} + N_{x\bar{y}})}(xy)$$

we see that the slopes of both partials and the universal relationship in the hypothetical example above are different: $b_c = .096$, $b_{\bar{c}} = .070$, $b = .084$.   Using the correlation coefficient ϕ as a measure of association in a 2×2 table, Hubert Blalock has suggested using differences between proportions to measure slopes.   In his example and in ours, the analogy of the equation $r^2 = b_{xy}b_{xy}$ in regression analysis holds.   See his letter to the Editor, *American Sociological Review*, 28 (December 1963), 988–89.

The most important distinction we are suggesting is whether or not the partials' slopes are equal. If they are, partialing corresponds to additive multiple regression; if they are not, nonadditivity occurs and the "elaboration" of a relationship means the analysis of its covariance and interaction. Lazarsfeld offers the same interpretation in his more recent "The Algebra of Dichotomous Systems," in H. Solomon, ed., *Studies in Item Analysis and Prediction* (Stanford, 1961).

13.   See Daniel Suits, "The Use of Dummy Variables in Regression Equations," *Journal of the American Statistical Association*, 52 (December 1957), 548–51.

The relative importance of different kinds of explanations. The analysis of variance test for interaction given above suggests more than a way to compute the statistical significance of the interaction sum of squares. By breaking up the variation in y as is done there, one can state precisely what part of this variation is explained by a universal regression line, what additional part is explained by using several parallel regional regression lines, and finally, the additional sum of squares (SS) attributable to the independent and the control variable acting jointly.[14]   Several examples of this kind of analysis are given in Table B.6.

Among the breakdowns of sums of squared deviations in the table only land inequality as an independent variable contributes sizably toward explaining its dependent variable, domestic group violence. Except in the case of executive stability, within region or subgroup variation contributes most substantially to the interpretations. Predicting executive stability from life expectancy appears to be the least successful overall explanation (which suggests caution in the formalization of the related model below), but the interaction term as discussed above contributes most of what explanation there is. In general these two-variable models are fairly successful and explain approximately half of the variation involved. As evidence for the usefulness of regionalism as a sociological composite index, which of course needs further exploration, we cite the dominant role it plays in explaining the agricultural employment and per capita income figures. In both cases a regional variable explains around 50% of the variation in the data.

Formalizing conditional relationships.   For theoretical purposes the relationship between agricultural employment and Catholicism, including both the discriminatory and the directional contributions of regional variables, may be formalized as follows: Let x stand for percentage Catholic, y for the percentage of the labor force employed in agriculture and r be a variable equal to 1, 2, 3, or 4 representing the region we are discussing. Furthermore, let a and b be the y-intercept and the slope of the overall relationship given in Figure B.8. $L(r)$ and $d(r)$ indicate deviations in these numbers for each region r. If we set $K_1 = a + l(r)$ and $K_2 = b + d(r)$, then we may summarize all four equations in Figure B.8 using a *single* equation:

$$\hat{y}(x,r) = K_1(r) + K_2(r) \cdot x \tag{5}$$

The predicted value of y, $\hat{y}(x,r)$, is immediately seen to depend *additively* on the various levels of ruralism induced by each regional context as well as *multiplicatively* on any directional implications implied by a structural concept of regionalism. Depending on the relationships between a and $l(r)$ and b and $d(r)$, one can infer from this formalization each of the special kinds of conditioning relationships discussed above. In other words for

---

14. In their "Problems in the Analysis of Survey Data, and a Proposal," *Journal of the American Statistical Association, 58* (June 1963), 415–34, James N. Morgan and John A. Sonquist develop some of the distinctions made here and present a method for uncovering interaction in survey data; the method helps them explain two-thirds of the variance in individual income, using groupings which as additive variables in regression analysis explain only 36% of the variance. The similarity of their analysis to the "pattern analysis" technique suggested by Sewall Wright and the recent development by Hubert Blalock of Simon's method for making causal inferences from spurious correlations represent a converging research focus in the multivariate analysis of social data.

TABLE B.6

Universal, Regional, and Interaction Explanations of per Capita
Income, Executive Stability, Labor Force in Agriculture,
and Domestic Group Violence

Dependent variable	GNPC (L)	EXEC (L)	LFAG	VIOL (L)
Independent variable	ACHV	LIFE	CATH	LNDG
Conditioning variable	Region	VOTE	Region	LFAG
SS explained by one regression	1.7%	1.3%	5.4%	19.7%
Additional SS explained by parallel regressions	50.2	1.2	36.4	18.4
Additional SS explained by nonparallel regressions (Interaction SS)	4.2	13.0	5.2	2.9
Unexplained SS (Error)	43.9	84.5	53.0	59.0
Total SS	100.0%	100.0%	100.0%	100.0%

any given r, the equation is identical with its counterpart in Figure B.8. A by no means obvious theoretical use of this kind of equation concerns temporal relations among the variables. Consider the case of stable coefficients and assume that the model in equation (5) remains valid over time. The projection of a decrease in traditional religion (say, according to an equation of the form $x = 100 \cdot e^{-.01t}$ which decreases a population by about two-thirds every hundred years) would allow us to make configurative predictions of the resulting effect on ruralism in each regional area.

As a slightly more complicated formalization let us consider the previously discussed ralationship between logged executive stability (log y), life expectancy (x), and voting level (v). Again the relationship involves directional and discriminatory conditional effects of public political participation and coefficients like K_1 and K_2 above.

Formally we may summarize *all three* of the subgroup equations in Figure B.9 as follows:

$$\widehat{\log y}(x,v) = K_1(v) + K_2(v) \cdot x \qquad (6)$$

From our previous data plots, we can say how accurately this summary equation fits the data as a function of x and v.

Logarithms were used with the stability data because closer fitting relations resulted. Taking logarithms of equation (6) in the case of a continuous function $K_2(v)$ would also eliminate the product term that causes non-additive interactions between x and v to occur. Such transformations are frequently used by statisticians to approximate the additivity assumptions of many statistical techniques. Taking the opposite route, however, from statistically convenient terms to those we actually measure, leads to interesting results once the researcher is reasonably satisfied with his transformation. Equation (7) is a solution to Equation (6) in terms of x and y and v.

$$\hat{y}(x,v) = 10^{K_1(v) \cdot x + K_2(v)} \qquad (7)$$

With this equation it is possible to see a good many more ways in which voting levels and welfare levels interact to influence executive stability than was possible with the original equation. For example, we can see how x and v exponentially influence the growth of y. As yet not tested or interpreted in more detailed structural terms, this model relating welfare policies and political participation is, of course, rather speculative. Nonetheless, it provides a simple and plausible example of mathematical formalizations possible from empirically derived statistical descriptions. One could argue, for instance, that the logarithmic transformation was inappropriate; certainly other transformations of the data should be explored as to the statistical helpfulness and their assumptions. Sampling problems and levels of significance for testing the model would be difficult, but not impossible, to deal with.

The meaning of statistical significance. These remarks return us to a consideration of the meaning and relevance of statistical significance in cross-national comparisons. It is important to use statistical tests based on the proper levels of measurement and appropriate assumptions about the universe from which a sample is drawn and the way the sample was selected. For bivariate comparisons, a possible approach is to use nonparametric statistics. These measures do not depend on any assumptions about the nature of the universe from which the data are drawn, and therefore are of special usefulness for samples of political data. But unfortunately, significance levels for multivariate comparisons are either hard to calculate or nonexistent, and even then our data have not been selected by random procedures. Usually the results are descriptive summaries about that half of the entire world for which the data are available. Furthermore, in the real political world the usual assumption of an underlying bivariate normal distribution is clearly artificial—note in particular the bimodal distributions of Catholics and political parties in the previous analysis. Norms and ideal types are essential in comparative analysis. But talking *as if* data were drawn from a bivariate normal universe loses much of its value when we realize that in the *statistician's* "best of all possible worlds" communists and Catholics are normally distributed!

What appear to be the more important contributions of statistical analyses in comparing nations? They include (1) clear and precise descriptions; (2) means of controlling for the effects of other variables, including random error; (3) concepts or theoretical formalizations; (4) the possibility of choosing from among several plausible explanations the one that best fits a greater variety of data; and (5) some notion about the reliability or validity of the research findings. The validity of certain indices can be established by comparisons with those indices or observations that are already established. The reliability of a research finding is the extent to which it is found again by repeating the research operation. When we want to describe the world we actually live in, questions about reliability translate themselves into legitimate questions about the nature of the missing data, the validity of our methods and indices, their operational meaning, and the likelihood that similar results would be obtained from random subsamples of nation-states in various historical periods and different contexts. For these reasons we have taken care to mention the sizes of the populations being studied, the possibilities of configurative analysis, and the comparability of our results with other research findings using various indices and different methods of analysis. Further studies including the missing data, new variables, and differently conceptualized indices would certainly be appropriate.

6. Projections to 1975

In Section 2 we discussed stages of economic and political development, and displayed the data for elasticities of change in such variables as urbanization and physicians per inhabitant. This is one way of making projections about future conditions, but it is a method based on the use of cross-sectional data to make statements about changes over time. One is in some sense saying that country X, with a higher per capita G. N. P. than country Y, really represents country Y after N years have elapsed. This can be an extremely useful procedure, but the hazards involved in the assumption are obvious.

Another procedure available for use with a mass of aggregate data is to compute the rates of change in a variable over some past time and project those rates into the future. Assume, in other words, that the situation in the future will change at the same rate as in the past. Such a procedure is naturally one of *projection,* not of *prediction.* It says what would happen *if* the rates remained unchanged, but does not predict that they *will* be unchanged. It is therefore essentially a *null* approach to estimating future conditions, a method of "persistence forecasting." By its very nature this method of course cannot identify any change in trends, and is therefore less useful the longer the projection one attempts.

In this section we have attempted projections for a moderate time span, to 1975, using the rates given in Part A for changes during the recent past. In doing so we see what the world distributions of a number of values would look like in 1975 *if* past trends continued. Because some past trends cannot or will not continue, this procedure will produce some anomolies, but it can nevertheless assist us in identifying problem areas and particular trends of consequence. First we present Figures B.10 and B.11, showing the Lorenz curves for the world distributions of six variables: urbanization (population in cities over 20,000), radios, labor force employed in agriculture, literacy, hospital beds, and G. N. P. The first four are meant as indices of social mobilization, of access to modern communications; the fifth is one measure of health; the sixth is in some sense an overall measure of welfare and wealth.[1] The first set of curves is for the late 1950s (cf. the exact dates in the appropriate tables) and the second set is for 1975. At the bottom of each graph are the Gini indices for the cumulative distributions. The sample of countries is the same in both graphs for each variable, though the sample for any one variable does not correspond exactly to that for another. In every case, however, it includes over half the world's population, and the differences are not so great as seriously to affect the comparability of the Gini calculations or the Lorenz curves.

Following the Lorenz curves are tables for the rankings of the countries in 1975. Two variables for which Lorenz curves could not be drawn—population and G. N. P. per capita—are included in the set of tables. A discussion follows.

---

1. Obviously a *low* percentage of population employed in agriculture would, *ceteris paribus,* indicate *high* social mobilization.

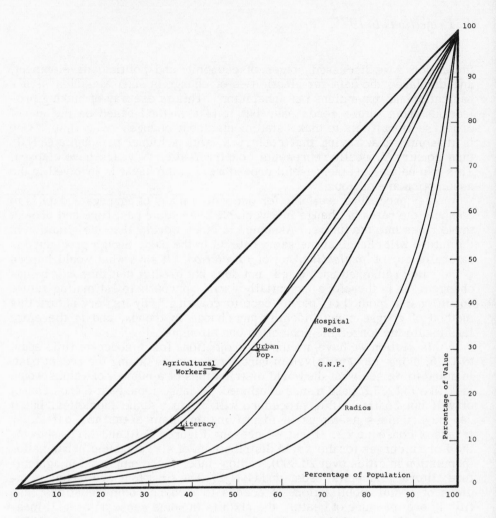

Figure B.10 Distribution c. 1959

Gini Indices:

Literacy	27.0
Agricultural workers	27.3
Urban population	30.2
Hospital beds	46.0
G. N. P.	63.6
Radios	70.4

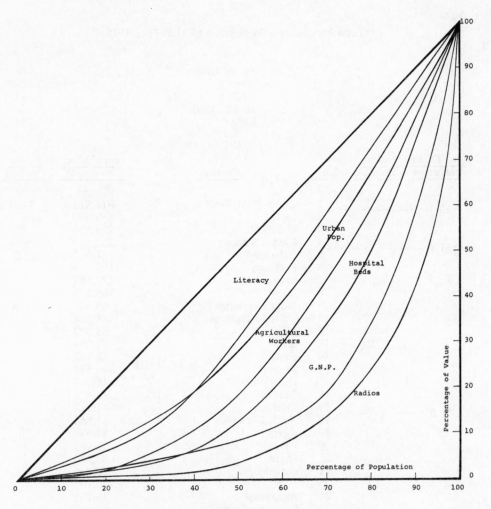

Figure B.11   Projected Distributions in 1975

Gini Indices:

Literacy	23.3
Urban population	27.4
Agricultural workers	38.5
Hospital beds	49.0
G. N. P.	61.3
Radios	65.0

TABLE B.7

Total Population, Projections to Mid-Year 1975

No. of Cases	110
Mean	35,578.0
Median	9,597.5
Modal Decile	X
Range	915,750

% of Table Population	Case Deciles	Rank	Country	Population (thousands)	Range Deciles
23.4 - - - - - - - - - - -	I	1	China (Mainland)	915,982	I–III
		2	India	599,689	IV–VI
		3	U.S.S.R.	279,850	VII
51.8 - - - - - - - - - - -		4	United States	232,649	VIII
		5	Indonesia	131,512	IX
		6	Pakistan	126,475	
		7	Brazil	120,163	
		8	Japan	106,619	
		9	West Germany	63,846	X
		10	United Kingdom	58,354	
		11	Mexico	55,337	
	II	12	Italy	53,031	
		13	France	52,829	
		14	Nigeria	46,530	
		15	Philippines	45,257	
		16	Turkey	42,678	
74.5 - - - - - - - - - - -		17	Thailand	41,113	
		18	South Korea	37,863	
		19	Egypt	37,575	
		20	Poland	36,403	
		21	Spain	35,126	
		22	Burma	28,796	
	III	23	Iran	26,181	
		24	Argentina	25,761	
		25	South Vietnam	24,807	
		26	Canada	24,775	
		27	South Africa	23,274	
		28	North Vietnam	22,326	
		29	Yugoslavia	21,686	
		30	Afghanistan	21,484	
		31	Romania	21,048	
		32	Congo (Leopoldville)	20,159	
		33	Colombia	19,587	
	IV	34	Taiwan	18,245	
		35	Sudan	17,824	
		36	Morocco	17,553	
		37	Czechoslovakia	15,189	
		38	East Germany	15,184	
		39	Ceylon	14,763	
		40	Australia	14,303	

TABLE B.7 (continued)

% of Table Population	Case Deciles	Rank	Country	Population (thousands)	Range Deciles
		41	Algeria	14,301	
		42	Peru	14,276	
		43	Netherlands	13,943	
		44	North Korea	12,388	
	V	45	Tanganyika	12,065	
		46	Nepal	12,051	
		47	Venezuela	12,008	
		48	Rhodesia & Nyasaland	11,875	
		49	Kenya	11,507	
		50	Iraq	11,442	
		51	Malaya	11,092	
		52	Chile	10,909	
		53	Hungary	10,753	
		54	Portugal	10,053	
		55	Belgium	9,848	
	VI	56	Uganda	9,671	
		57	Greece	9,524	
		58	Syria	9,451	
		59	Cuba	9,274	
		60	Mozambique	9,018	
		61	Bulgaria	9,004	
		62	Cambodia	8,992	
		63	Madagascar	8,209	
		64	Sweden	8,063	
		65	Austria	7,384	
		66	Switzerland	7,152	
	VII	67	Ecuador	6,924	
		68	Angola	6,787	
		69	Guatemala	5,958	
		70	Haiti	5,762	
		71	Tunisia	5,386	
		72	Hong Kong	5,214	
		73	Denmark	5,090	
		74	Finland	4,994	
		75	Dominican Republic	4,976	
		76	Ivory Coast	4,475	
		77	Bolivia	4,252	
	VIII	78	El Salvador	4,103	
		79	Norway	4,037	
		80	Sierra Leone	3,557	
		81	Israel	3,305	
		82	New Zealand	3,193	
		83	Chad	3,080	
		84	Puerto Rico	3,008	
		85	Honduras	2,863	
		86	Singapore	2,805	
		87	Laos	2,686	
		88	Ireland	2,661	
	IX	89	Albania	2,615	

TABLE B.7 (continued)

% of Table Population	Case Deciles	Rank	Country	Population (thousands)	Range Deciles
		90	Paraguay	2,525	
		91	Nicaragua	2,470	
		92	Kuwait	2,306	
		93	Somalia	2,269	
		94	Costa Rica	2,238	
		95	Jordan	2,229	
		96	Jamaica	2,036	
		97	Panama	1,610	
		98	Central African Republic	1,596	
		99	Libya	1,560	
	X	100	Sarawak	1,524	
		101	Mongolian People's Republic	1,464	
		102	Trinidad & Tobago	1,281	
		103	Mauritius	965	
		104	British Guiana	880	
		105	South West Africa	724	
		106	Cyprus	672	
		107	Surinam	594	
		108	Malta & Gozo	362	
		109	Luxembourg	236	
		110	Netherlands Antilles	232	

TABLE B.8

Percentage of Population in Cities Over 20,000, Projections to 1975

No. of Cases		50
Mean		38.3
Median		39.0
Modal Decile		VI
Range		71.8

% of Table Population	Case Deciles	Rank	Country	% Pop. in Cities over 20,000	Range Deciles
	I	1	New Zealand	78.8	I
		2	United Kingdom	68.3	
		3	Israel	66.4	
		4	Venezuela	65.3	
		5	West Germany	64.5	II
	II	6	Barbados	63.0	
		7	Japan	55.9	III
		8	United States	55.6	
		9	Chile	53.8	
		10	Denmark	53.3	
	III	11	Spain	50.8	
		12	Iceland	50.2	IV
24.6		13	Panama	49.2	
		14	Cuba	48.1	
		15.5	Greece	46.9	
	IV	15.5	U.S.S.R.	46.9	
		17	Sweden	46.4	
		18	Ireland	46.1	
		19	Poland	45.4	
		20	Canada	42.5	V
	V	21	East Germany	42.3	
		22	Finland	40.9	
		23	Puerto Rico	39.8	
		24	Hungary	39.3	
		25	Mexico	39.1	
	VI	26	South Africa	38.8	
		27	Austria	38.7	
52.8		28	Brazil	35.2	VI
		29	Italy	34.9	
		30	France	34.8	
	VII	31	Mauritius	33.9	
		32	Nicaragua	32.7	
		33	Luxembourg	31.8	
		34	Switzerland	31.6	
		35	Belgium	31.2	
	VIII	36	Czechoslovakia	29.6	
		37	Malaya	28.8	
		38	Yugoslavia	25.5	VII
		39	Turkey	23.4	

TABLE B.8 (continued)

% of Table Population	Case Deciles	Rank	Country	% Pop. in Cities over 20,000	Range Deciles
		40	Morocco	21.4	VIII
	IX	41	Dominican Republic	19.0	
		42	British Guiana	17.9	
		43	Portugal	17.8	
		44	Congo (Leopoldville)	17.6	
65.5		45	Honduras	17.0	
	X	46	India	16.3	
		47	Mozambique	14.3	IX
		48	Pakistan	13.6	
		49	South West Africa	7.1	X
		50	Malta & Gozo	7.0	

TABLE B.9

Radios per 1,000 Population, Projections to 1975

	No. of Cases	96
	Mean	208.2
	Median	131.8
	Modal Decile	X
	Range	1,592.8

% of Table Population	Case Deciles	Rank	Country	Radios per 1,000 Population	Range Deciles
	I	1	United States	1,596.0	I–IV
		2	Canada	830.0	V,VI
		3	East Germany	552.4	VII
		4	Uruguay	514.8	
		5	West Germany	492.6	
		6	Denmark	486.8	
		7	Belgium	485.6	
		8	Luxembourg	481.4	
		9	Sweden	469.0	VIII
	II	10	Finland	427.6	
		11	Austria	426.6	
		12	France	424.8	
		13	Hungary	424.2	
		14	Bulgaria	388.2	
		15	Cyprus	379.0	
		16	Venezuela	378.0	
		17	Norway	374.2	
		18	Netherlands	368.0	
		19	Switzerland	363.0	
	III	20	Czechoslovakia	362.4	
		21	United Kingdom	353.4	
		22	Malta & Gozo	352.2	
		23	Poland	339.8	
		24	Israel	333.2	
		25	Iceland	312.6	IX
		26	Barbados	312.2	
25.2		27	Italy	301.6	
		28	Cuba	292.0	
	IV	29	Colombia	282.0	
		30	Ireland	279.6	
		31	Surinam	273.9	
		32	New Zealand	253.2	
		33	Panama	247.0	
		34	Argentina	245.5	
		35	Romania	226.2	
		36	Greece	206.7	
		37	Netherlands Antilles	202.7	
		38	Jamaica	190.3	
	V	39	Yugoslavia	188.2	
		40	Spain	187.7	

TABLE B.9 (continued)

% of Table Population	Case Deciles	Rank	Country	Radios per 1,000 Population	Range Deciles
		41	Portugal	180.7	
		42	Chile	175.0	
		43	Australia	173.0	
		44	Mexico	171.1	
		45	Taiwan	156.3	X
		46	Singapore	149.9	
		47	Trinidad & Tobago	147.1	
	VI	48	British Guiana	133.8	
		49	Iran	129.7	
		50	Syria	129.3	
		51	Egypt	128.8	
		52	Nicaragua	124.3	
		53	Honduras	120.7	
		54	Japan	119.3	
		55	Sarawak	118.3	
		56	Tunisia	118.1	
		57	Costa Rica	113.7	
	VII	58	Peru	111.5	
		59	Guatemala	106.1	
		60	Aden	105.6	
		61	Lebanon	104.3	
		62	Bolivia	102.1	
		63	Algeria	100.6	
		64	Hong Kong	97.3	
		65	Turkey	95.9	
		66	South Africa	92.8	
	VIII	67	Jordan	88.7	
		68	Morocco	86.1	
48.5 ----------------		69	Ecuador	85.4	
		70	Brazil	83.9	
		71	Malaya	77.0	
		72	Paraguay	76.8	
		73	Ceylon	76.2	
		74	Albania	72.6	
		75	South West Africa	69.2	
		76	Dominican Republic	57.8	
	IX	77	Philippines	51.1	
		78	Ghana	51.0	
		79	Iraq	45.2	
		80	Uganda	37.8	
		81	Rhodesia & Nyasaland	34.4	
		82	Angola	24.9	
		83	Indonesia	17.0	
		84	Kenya	15.5	
		85	Mozambique	11.7	
65.5 -----------------		86	Burma	11.6	
	X	87	India	11.0	
		88	Haiti	9.1	
		89	Nigeria	8.5	

TABLE B.9 (continued)

% of Table Population	Case Deciles	Rank	Country	Radios per 1,000 Population	Range Deciles
		90	Sierra Leone	8.1	
		91	Tanganyika	7.8	
		92	Thailand	7.7	
		93	Pakistan	6.0	
		94	Congo (Leopoldville)	5.7	
		95	Laos	3.8	
		96	Afghanistan	3.2	

TABLE B.10

Gross National Product, $U.S., Projections to 1975

No. of Cases	68
Mean	39,730
Median	7,620
Modal Decile	X
Range	826,189

% of Table Population	Case Deciles	Rank	Country	G. N. P. (million $)	Range Deciles
	I	1	United States	826,369	I–IV
		2	U. S. S. R.	455,316	V–VII
16.2		3	West Germany	177,747	VIII
		4	China (Mainland)	174,953	
		5	Japan	121,866	IX
		6	United Kingdom	104,454	
	II	7	France	92,504	
49.5		8	Italy	70,478	X
		9	Canada	64,167	
		10	Brazil	60,922	
		11	India	52,173	
		12	Poland	47,688	
		13	Czechoslovakia	29,467	
	III	14	Romania	25,173	
		15	Spain	24,342	
77.3		16	Indonesia	22,489	
		17	Mexico	21,803	
		18	Netherlands	20,538	
		19	Yugoslavia	20,081	
		20	Sweden	18,940	
	IV	21	Switzerland	18,638	
		22	Belgium	18,367	
		23	Austria	17,286	
		24	Venezuela	16,883	
		25	Philippines	15,251	
		26	Turkey	12,931	
		27	Hungary	12,248	
	V	28	Argentina	11,721	
		29	Bulgaria	10,202	
		30	Pakistan	9,359	
		31	Denmark	9,320	
		32	South Korea	8,330	
		33	Greece	8,200	
	VI	34	Finland	7,621	
		35	Colombia	7,619	
		36	Norway	7,238	
		37	Israel	6,617	
		38	Algeria	5,806	
		39	Thailand	5,345	
		40	Chile	5,215	

TABLE B.10 (continued)

% of Table Population	Case Deciles	Rank	Country	G. N. P. (million $)	Range Deciles
	VII	41	Taiwan	5,163	
		42	Nigeria	4,467	
		43	Malaya	4,392	
		44	Puerto Rico	4,073	
		45	Portugal	3,961	
		46	Peru	3,341	
		47	Burma	3,254	
	VIII	48	Congo (Leopoldville)	3,044	
		49	Rhodesia & Nyasaland	2,624	
		50	Ceylon	2,347	
		51	Ireland	2,017	
		52	Jamaica	1,932	
		53	Ecuador	1,800	
		54	Morocco	1,755	
	IX	55	Trinidad & Tobago	1,546	
		56	Guatemala	1,394	
		57	Tunisia	1,330	
		58	El Salvador	1,235	
		59	Syria	1,087	
		60	Cambodia	1,061	
		61	Albania	926	
	X	62	Panama	704	
		63	Luxembourg	668	
		64	Honduras	596	
		65	Bolivia	434	
		66	Cyprus	403	
		67	Paraguay	240	
		68	Iceland	180	

TABLE B.11

Gross National Product per Capita, $U. S., Projections to 1975

No. of Cases	68
Mean	901.4
Median	492.9
Modal Decile	X
Range	3,478.8

% of Table Population	Case Deciles	Rank	Country	G. N. P./Capita	Range Deciles
	I	1	United States	3,553	I,II
		2	West Germany	2,784	III
		3	Switzerland	2,607	
		4	Canada	2,591	
		5	Sweden	2,349	IV
		6	Austria	2,342	
	II	7	Israel	2,003	V
		8	Czechoslovakia	1,941	
		9	Luxembourg	1,914	
		10	Belgium	1,865	
		11	Denmark	1,831	
		12	Norway	1,794	
		13	United Kingdom	1,790	
	III	14	France	1,752	VI
		15	U. S. S. R.	1,627	
		16	Finland	1,527	
		17	Netherlands	1,474	
		18	Venezuela	1,407	VII
		19	Puerto Rico	1,355	
		20	Italy	1,330	
	IV	21	Poland	1,311	
25.2 ---------------		22	Trinidad & Tobago	1,207	
		23	Romania	1,197	
		24	Japan	1,144	
		25	Hungary	1,140	
		26	Bulgaria	1,134	
		27	Jamaica	949	VIII
	V	28	Yugoslavia	926	
		29	Greece	861	
		30	Iceland	761	
		31	Ireland	758	
		32	Spain	693	IX
		33	Cyprus	600	
	VI	34	Brazil	508	
		35	Chile	478	
		36	Argentina	456	
		37	Panama	438	
		38	Algeria	407	
		39	Malaya	397	
		40.5	Portugal	395	

TABLE B.11 (continued)

% of Table Population	Case Deciles	Rank	Country	G. N. P. /Capita	Range Deciles
	VII	40.5	Mexico	395	
		42	Colombia	389	
		43	Albania	355	
		44	Philippines	337	X
		45	Turkey	303	
		46	El Salvador	302	
		47	Taiwan	284	
	VIII	48	Ecuador	261	
		49	Tunisia	247	
		50.5	Guatemala	234	
		50.5	Peru	234	
		52	Rhodesia & Nyasaland	222	
		53	South Korea	221	
		54	Honduras	209	
44.6	IX	55	China (Mainland)	191	
		56	Indonesia	171	
		57	Ceylon	160	
74.5		58	Congo (Leopoldville)	151	
		59	Thailand	130	
		60	Cambodia	118	
		61	Syria	116	
	X	62	Burma	114	
		63	Bolivia	103	
		64	Morocco	101	
		65	Nigeria	97	
		66	Paraguay	95	
		67	India	87	
		68	Pakistan	74	

TABLE B.12

Percentage of Labor Force Employed in Agriculture, Projections to 1975

	No. of Cases	49
	Mean	30.4
	Median	25.9
	Modal Decile	X
	Range	74.6

% of Table Population	Case Deciles	Rank	Country	% Labor Force Emp. in Agric.[1]	Range Deciles
	I	1	Thailand	77.6	I
30.4		2	India	73.6	
		3	Turkey	72.0	
		4	Morocco	66.6	
	II	5	Guatemala	62.3	II, III
		6	Yugoslavia	56.0	
		7	Malaya	55.8	
		8	Nicaragua	55.5	
		9	Mexico	51.4	IV
	III	10	Bulgaria	49.9	
		11	Panama	49.0	
		12	El Salvador	48.0	
		13	Poland	47.8	
		14	Brazil	46.0	
	IV	15	Portugal	45.5	
		16	Egypt	44.4	V
50.3		17	Honduras	44.2	
		18	Philippines	40.1	
		19	Czechoslovakia	39.3	
	V	20	British Guiana	37.4	
		21	Cyprus	34.7	VI
		22	Japan	31.6	
		23	Hungary	30.5	
		24	Austria	26.2	VII
	VI	25	Ireland	25.6	
		26	Colombia	23.6	
		27	U. S. S. R.	21.4	VIII
		28	Dominican Republic	21.0	
	VII	29	Chile	20.3	
		30	Trinidad & Tobago	19.2	
		31	Iceland	18.8	
		32	Finland	18.5	
75.0		33	Venezuela	17.0	
	VIII	34	France	15.9	
		35	Denmark	15.0	
		36	Norway	14.8	IX
		37	Italy	10.0	
		38	New Zealand	9.4	
	IX	39	Australia	7.9	
		40	West Germany	7.8	X

TABLE B.12 (continued)

% of Table Population	Case Deciles	Rank	Country	% Labor Force Emp. in Agric.[1]	Range Deciles
		41	Switzerland	7.1	
		42	Belgium	5.8	
		43	Netherlands	5.6	
	X	44	United Kingdom	3.6	
		45	Sweden	3.3	
		47.5	Canada	3.0	
		47.5	Puerto Rico	3.0	
		47.5	South Africa	3.0	
		47.5	United States	3.0	

[1] It was assumed that no state would have less than 3% of its labor force in agriculture, and no projections were carried below that point.

TABLE B.13

Inhabitants per Hospital Bed, Projections to 1975

	No. of Cases	90
	Mean	488.0
	Median	221.5
	Modal Decile	X
	Range	6,277

% of Table Population	Case Deciles	Rank	Country	Inhabitants per Hospital Bed[1]	Range Deciles
	I	1	Taiwan	6,347	I
		2	Afghanistan	5,713	
		3	Aden	2,281	II–VI
		4	Haiti	1,863	VII
25.0		5	India	1,615	VIII
		6	Laos	1,390	
		7	Nigeria	1,371	
		8	British Guiana	1,075	IX
		9	Indonesia	916	
	II	10	Cambodia	782	
		11	Burma	770	
		12	Ecuador	758	
		13	Kenya	715	
		14	Honduras	709	
		15	El Salvador	696	
		16	Sierra Leone	672	
		17	Nicaragua	661	
		18	Madagascar	588	X
	III	19	Lebanon	580	
		20	Ruanda-Urundi	468	
		21	Uganda	443	
		22	Malaya	426	
		23	South Vietnam	417	
		24	Peru	410	
		25	Singapore	403	
		26.5	Dominican Republic	400	
		26.5	Egypt	400	
	IV	28	Thailand	378	
		29	Iran	376	
		30	Chile	371	
		31	Somalia	369	
		32	Jordan	366	
		33	Surinam	357	
		34	Paraguay	353	
		35	Tanganyika	339	
		36	Syria	333	
	V	37	Algeria	315	
		38	Costa Rica	284	
		39	Iraq	269	
		40	Colombia	259	

TABLE B.13 (continued)

% of Table Population	Case Deciles	Rank	Country	Inhabitants per Hospital Bed[1]	Range Deciles
		41	Uruguay	257	
		42	Panama	250	
		43	Ceylon	247	
		44	France	241	
		45	Guatemala	222	
48.7	VI	46	Hong Kong	221	
		47	Brazil	220	
		48.5	Turkey	217	
		48.5	Togo	217	
		50.5	Tunisia	214	
		50.5	Philippines	214	
		52	Venezuela	199	
		53	Denmark	185	
		54	Barbados	164	
	VII	55	Argentina	160	
		56.5	Hungary	150	
		56.5	Israel	150	
		58.5	United Kingdom	143	
		58.5	Rhodesia & Nyasaland	143	
		60.5	United States	139	
		60.5	South Africa	139	
		62	Switzerland	132	
		63.5	West Germany	128	
75.0	VIII	63.5	Congo (Leopoldville)	128	
		65.5	Portugal	123	
		65.5	Poland	123	
		67	Yugoslavia	110	
		68	Belgium	107	
		69	Iceland	100	
		70	Finland	94	
		71.5	Australia	90	
		71.5	New Zealand	90	
	IX	73	Norway	89	
		74	Puerto Rico	88	
		75	Cyprus	87	
		76	Austria	84	
		77	Canada	82	
		78	Sweden	80	
		79	Netherlands Antilles	76	
		80	Czechoslovakia	74	
		81	Greece	73	
	X	86	Albania	70	
		86	Ireland	70	
		86	Italy	70	
		86	Japan	70	
		86	Liberia	70	
		86	Luxembourg	70	
		86	Netherlands	70	
		86	Romania	70	
		86	U.S.S.R.	70	

[1] It was assumed that no state would achieve an inhabitant–hospital bed ratio better than 70, the lowest ratio for any state c. 1959, so no projections were carried below 70.

TABLE B.14

Percentage Literate of Population Aged 15 and Over, Projections to 1975

No. of Cases	59
Mean	84.4
Median	98.5
Modal Decile	I
Range	95.0

% of Table Population	Case Deciles	Rank	Country	% of Pop. Literate[1]	Range Deciles
	I	16	Albania	98.5	I
		16	Australia	98.5	
		16	Austria	98.5	
		16	Belgium	98.5	
		16	British Guiana	98.5	
		16	Bulgaria	98.5	
	II	16	Canada	98.5	
		16	Czechoslovakia	98.5	
		16	Denmark	98.5	
		16	East Germany	98.5	
		16	France	98.5	
		16	Finland	98.5	
	III	16	Hungary	98.5	
		16	Iceland	98.5	
		16	Ireland	98.5	
		16	Italy	98.5	
		16	Japan	98.5	
		16	Mauritius	98.5	
	IV	16	Netherlands	98.5	
		16	New Zealand	98.5	
		16	Norway	98.5	
		16	Philippines	98.5	
		16	Poland	98.5	
		16	Romania	98.5	
	V	16	Sweden	98.5	
		16	Switzerland	98.5	
		16	Trinidad & Tobago	98.5	
		16	United Kingdom	98.5	
		16	United States	98.5	
		16	U.S.S.R.	98.5	
	VI	16	West Germany	98.5	
49.9		32	Spain	98.0	
		33	Panama	96.5	
		34	Costa Rica	93.7	
		35	Puerto Rico	92.7	
		36	Chile	92.3	
	VII	37	Dominican Republic	91.6	
		38	Greece	90.8	
		39	Jamaica	90.0	
		40	Cyprus	89.5	

TABLE B.14 (continued)

% of Table Population	Case Deciles	Rank	Country	% of Pop. Literate[1]	Range Deciles
		41	Yugoslavia	87.5	
	VIII	42	Thailand	86.5	
		43	Cuba	83.4	II
		44	Ceylon	77.7	
		45	Venezuela	77.2	
		46	Portugal	73.7	III
		47	Colombia	73.3	
	IX	48	Mexico	66.3	IV
		49	Brazil	61.4	
		50	Turkey	58.6	
		51	Singapore	57.4	
		52	El Salvador	56.2	V
		53	Malaya	54.1	
	X	54	Honduras	49.2	
		55	Guatemala	44.2	VI
71.8 ------------------		56	Egypt	32.8	VII
		57	India	25.8	VIII
		58	Algeria	23.2	
		59	Mozambique	3.5	IX,X

[1] It was assumed that no more than 98.5% of any state's population would be literate, and no projections were carried above that point. A few countries which had 98.5% literate in the 1950s, but for which we had no rate of change, were assumed to remain at 98.5% for the purpose of the projection.

The curves for different values vary greatly. We find the flattest curves—and thus the greatest equality—for literacy, followed fairly closely by urban population and agricultural (and therefore nonagricultural) workers. In other words, three basic elements in social mobilization are now fairly widespread, and will be so in 1975. These measures are of course indicators of a fairly rudimentary level of accomplishment—literacy does not mean technical skill, nor does living in a city of over 20,000 or holding a nonfarm job necessarily mean close involvement in modern life. But each of these usually does carry with it substantial exposure to modern life, involvement in a money economy, potential participation in politics, and frequent interaction with others; in short, most of the phenomena which contribute to the "revolution of rising expectations."

If these projections are even approximately accurate, furthermore, literacy and urbanization will be even more equally distributed in 1975 than they have been in the recent past. The developed countries' populations are already almost 100% literate and they can do little more in promoting this basic skill, but many of the poorer countries will also attain fairly high literacy levels by 1975, closing the present gap somewhat. Half the total population of Table B.14 will live in countries with almost complete literacy.[2] Much the same applies to the percentage of the population in cities, where there is a tendency for urbanization to increase more rapidly in the underdeveloped areas than in the richer states. Employment in agriculture, however, is declining faster in the developed than in the underdeveloped countries, a reflection of the increased mechanization and capital-intensiveness of modern agriculture. For this variable the present worldwide gap will widen, not diminish.

The other three values for which we have Lorenz curves are much more unequally distributed in both the time periods under consideration—of the three, the hospital beds curve is the flattest and that for radios the most concave.[3] Our table of projections for hospital beds in one important respect looks odd—several of the countries with very low (i.e., favorable) inhabitants–hospital bed ratios are underdeveloped states, and their ratios would have been even lower were it not for our use of 70 as the cutoff point for a level not likely to be bettered. With a few exceptions for individual countries, most of the projections in the tables previously discussed looked plausible; some do not and this is almost surely our most unreliable set of projections. The reason lies in the extraordinary efforts which some underdeveloped countries have recently made to improve their health levels. These efforts were reflected in very high rates of change over the past decade but, once a fairly high absolute level is reached, they are unlikely to continue. If we are to have an approximate picture of the real world of 1975, then, these projections ought to be modified. Note, never-

---

2. It is of course true that many important underdeveloped countries are unrepresented in the table because rates of change are unavailable. They include China, Indonesia, Pakistan, and virtually all of Africa. The Gini indices are nevertheless calculated for the same "sample" of countries in both years, and the Gini for 1975 is notably lower (i.e. the distribution is more equal) than in the 1950s.

3. In the table note the ratio of one and one-half radios to each member of the population of the United States. This may seem peculiar, but given the booming popularity of transistor radios and the wide use of automobile radios it would appear within the realm of possibility.

theless, that even given the implausibly favorable levels for some under-developed countries, the overall degree of worldwide inequality, as measured by the Gini index, grows greater.

We find G. N. P. distributed somewhat more equally in 1975 than in 1957, with some quite surprising changes in the tables. In the projections for total G. N. P. (which despite its faults is perhaps the best available overall measure of power) China very clearly rises into fourth place behind only the U. S., the U. S. S. R., and West Germany. Japan and Italy also rise substantially; the United Kingdom drops from third to a poor sixth, and India falls from eighth to eleventh place. And while the United States remains first, the gap between it and the U. S. S. R. changes from a factor of almost four to a factor of less than two. As a group, the countries of the European Common Market fall not far short of the Soviet Union.

We· repeat the caution expressed in Part A about G. N. P. figures: the rankings are more reliable than the totals, which almost certainly exaggerate the difference between developed and underdeveloped countries. Also, there is no reason to believe that these projections will actually be borne out just as they appear here. It would seem reasonable, for example, to expect the growth rate for several Western European countries to decline somewhat as postwar recovery is completed and the early stimulation of the Common Market wears off. Perhaps the rate of growth for the communist countries of Eastern Europe will also decline as they approach the production levels of contemporary Western Europe.[4] Yet these projections are probably more nearly right than wrong; the situation in 1975 will almost certainly be more like that of the projections than that of the base year from which the projections are made. If so, important changes in the world distribution of welfare, and of power, will occur.

Note also the changes implied in the other two tables, for G. N. P. per capita and for total population. If the projections are at least approximately accurate, by 1975 the Soviet Union and Eastern Europe will have a per capita product (though not necessarily a standard of living) not far short of the projected average for Western Europe, and well above the current Western European average. Communist China will have made very significant gains, but India and Pakistan will lag far behind. Israel also would appear on the verge of a very high per capita product level. Some of the projections appear odd and probably will not occur—Canada's drop to fourth, for instance, behind West Germany and Switzerland, and the very high level projected for Austria—but in general they are not implausible and imply some major changes. In the table of projected populations we note relatively few major changes in the rankings, except for the very clear exchange between the relatively stable population of Japan and the rapidly growing one of Brazil. Mainland China, however, shows a population of just a little under a billion, and it is generally believed that the rate of increase upon which our projection is based (2% per annum) is a rather conservative one.

---

4. The U. N. Economic Commission for Europe (*Economic Survey of Europe in 1962,* Part I, New York, 1963, ch. 1, p. 1) reports a much slower growth in Eastern Europe in 1962 than in previous years. The 1962 rates given for increase in national (material) product averages, when adjusted to a per capita basis, to only about one-half the rates given in Part A of this book for earlier years.

To recapitulate: our projections indicate appreciably more equal world-wide distributions of most basic aspects of social mobilization (literacy, urbanization, and radios, though not nonagricultural labor force). Furthermore, we find a modest but clear decline in inequality of G. N. P.—the income gap between the advanced countries and most underdeveloped nations will diminish, not grow. And since these are *projections* of rates from the recent past we see that at least since the early 1950s the gap *has been* decreasing, despite a widespread impression to the contrary.[5] It has not, however, been narrowing rapidly. For our basic and imperfect indicator of health, inhabitants per hospital bed, we find an increase in world inequality. It is difficult to know just what the relation between changes in the worldwide distribution of income and changes in social mobilization must be to maintain a reasonably stable international society, but one can reasonably believe that income must not lag.

------

5. Simon Kuznets has nevertheless convincingly demonstrated that the gap grew between the 1900s and mid-century. Cf. his "Regional Trends and Levels of Living," in Philip M. Hauser, ed., *Population and World Politics* (Glencoe, Ill., 1958), pp. 79–117.

Index

Page numbers underlined refer to pages of tables in Part A.

365

DATE DUE

JUL 26 70		
APR 5 1981		
GAYLORD		PRINTED IN U.S.A.

of traditional detective work in clearing crimes.[13] On the basis of these pioneering experiments, David Farmer concluded that "police agencies are at the beginning of a revolution in operating practices."

4 *Police discretion.* The exercise of discretion is now recognized to be both a fundamental aspect of routine policing and the source of many police problems. The factors governing the exercise of discretion—in the case of arrests, for example— have been examined in detail. Fyfe's study of the use of deadly force provides systematic data on the circumstances under which police officers make this fateful decision. Perhaps even more important, Fyfe's study suggests the manner in which discretion can be effectively controlled through administrative policy.[14]

Impact These are only the highlights of the information explosion. An abundant and steadily growing body of literature exists on other aspects of policing. The information explosion has altered the way we think about the police. Discussions of police operations and problems now take place on a more informed level than they did fifteen years ago. Many old stereotypes (the cop as crime fighter) have been laid to rest. The knowledgeable student of the American police has no excuse for indulging in old myths and clichés.[15]

The new knowledge base also provides a starting point for innovation and reform. Experiments with the use of police officers' time, for example, rely upon the existing body of knowledge about what officers do on the job. To give two specific examples, the Worcester, Massachusetts, experiment with police service aides (PSA's) and priorities for patrol car dispatches are based on the finding of several researchers that the police handle a large number of routine, nonemergency service calls.[16]

Police Unions Police unions were not mentioned in the commission report. At the time, relatively few police departments had collective-bargaining agreements with employee organizations. Today, however, as many as 75 percent and virtually all the officers in large police departments are members of unions.

Police unions have brought about a hidden revolution in police management. Prior to the advent of unions, police administrators had virtually a free hand (subject only to existing civil service departments) in managing their departments. Today, however, many important issues of management are governed by legally binding collective-bargaining agreements. Collective bargaining is a process of shared management, in which rank-and-file police officers, through their union, share in the decision-making process.[17]

Unions have had an impact in many areas of policing. They have contributed to a substantial improvement in police salaries and benefits. Even more important, the unions have altered the process and the prospects for planned change. Traditionally, police departments were professionalized through the efforts of a strong-willed chief executive. Parker in Los Angeles, Vernon in Oakland, Kelley in Kansas City, and Wilson in Chicago effected change almost single-handedly. But these reforms occurred in the preunion era. Future reforms along the same lines must take into account the role of the police unions.[18]

Areas of Moderate Change

In a number of other areas there has been an important, although not major degree of change since the mid-1960s. These include the following:

Expenditure and Employment   Expenditure and employment for all law enforcement activities increased significantly from the mid-1960s through the end of the 1970s. Between 1971 and 1977 alone total expenditures on police protection by all levels of government increased by 92.5 percent, from $6,164,918 to $11,864,875. The total number of employees increased by 20 percent in the same period.

In particular cities, the increase was even more dramatic. The number of police officers in Washington, D.C., for example, increased from 2347 in 1956 to 4695 in 1975.[19]

Impact   The impact of increased expenditure and employment has been complex. There is no reliable evidence that increased number of sworn officers enhances the ability of the police to deter crime. As the data indicate, expenditures rose faster than the number of persons employed. This was due in part to substantial increases in police salaries. On the one hand, higher salaries and improved fringe benefits made law enforcement a more attractive career. The President's Commission noted in 1967 that salaries were lagging behind occupations in the private sector, and that many departments were unable to attract qualified applicants.[20] By the late 1970s salaries were very competitive, and departments were able to raise their recruitment standards.

On the other hand, increased expenditures on law enforcement (and for all other public services) contributed to a severe fiscal crisis for local governments. The result has been a boomerang effect in employment. Many police departments have been forced to reduce the number of sworn officers in order to hold down expenses. The New York City Police Department shrank by almost one-third, from nearly 30,000 sworn officers in the early 1970s to about 22,000 by the end of the decade. The Cleveland Police Department was operating at about one-third its authorized strength in 1980: Detroit, Philadelphia and other cities also laid off many officers.

In short, the long-term trend in expenditure and employment since the mid-1960s represents a radical shift from rapid expansion to stagnation and, in some cases, contraction.

Personnel Standards   Related to increases in expenditure and employment are significant improvements in personnel standards. The President's Commission called for increased emphasis on education and training. While the commission's goal of having all officers hold B.A.s has not been attained (and does not appear likely in the near future), the number of police officers with some college experience did increase. The National Manpower Survey found a generation gap between the educational levels of officers hired before and after 1970.[21]

Additional improvements have been made in the area of training. Particularly important is the movement toward state-mandated training for all officers, which was pioneered by New York and California in 1959. By 1976, thirty-nine states required training of all law enforcement officers, either by statute or by state law. The number of hours of formal training ranged from a low of 150 to a high of 560.[22]

The Control of Discretion   As late as the mid-1960s many police departments put their officers on the street with no guidelines for the exercise of discretion in such important decisions as arrest and the use of deadly force. The President's Commission recommended that "Police departments should develop and enunciate policies that give police personnel specific guidance for the common situations requiring exercise of police discretion."[23]

Police departments have made slow but steady progress in correcting this problem. Many professionalized departments have elaborate procedure manuals, detailing the proper action to take in specific situations. Some departments have improved on existing procedures, making the guidelines clearer and more specific. (See for example, the New York City Police Department's guidelines on the use of deadly force).[24]

In general, the issue of discretion has been recognized as a major problem in policing, and there is a general recognition of the need to provide officers with guidance. Important is the development of model rules for the exercise of discretion. The Texas Law Enforcement Commission developed such rules, the function of which is to facilitate the development of operational rules by law enforcement agencies.[25]

Experiments in Organization and Management   Contrary to popular myths, the American police have not been resistant to experiment and innovation. James Q. Wilson argues that "A few police departments in this country have shown themselves to be remarkably innovative, experimental, and open to evaluative research. There are not as yet many prosecutors or courts about which one can say the same thing."[26]

The important point is not that significant innovations have been found and implemented, but that the search for innovation has been conducted. The most notable innovation in the 1970s was team policing. The President's Commission gave the concept a strong endorsement. As a result, many police departments attempted team-policing experiments. The results, however, have been mixed. Researchers have been unwilling to conclude that team policing makes a substantial difference in the overall effectiveness of a police department's operations, although there appear to be some positive contributions.[27]

Despite these mixed results, the quest for innovation has continued. Gerald Caiden reviewed the most notable efforts in his study of *Police Revitalization.* He cites the Kansas City Police Department as an agency with a strong commitment to innovation. Kansas City produced the important preventive-patrol experiment and the response-time study. The use of task forces to generate new ideas is also significant. Caiden cites the reorganization and decentralization of the Los Angeles Police Department in the 1970s under Chief Ed Davis.[28]

Areas of Little or No Change

In certain areas there has been little or no change. Problems persist either because they are beyond the control of the police or because efforts to make improvements have been inadequate. The principal areas of little or no change include:

The Police Role The role of the municipal police is complex and ambiguous. The police are responsible for a multitude of tasks, many of which are vague and some of which conflict with other tasks. The complexity and ambiguity surrounding the police role is the source of many police problems. It is difficult to specify performance objectives for law enforcement agencies when it is not clear what they are supposed to be doing in the first place. Relations with the public are complicated by the fact that citizens have confused, unrealistic, and often conflicting expectations about the police. Finally, it is difficult to recruit, train, and supervise police personnel when the nature of the job itself is not clear.

To a certain extent, the complexity and ambiguity of the police role is inescapable. There will always be crime and disorder, and it is reasonable to assume that society will always have some agency to respond to these problems.[29]

Even if the order-maintenance function were transferred to another agency, that new agency would face the same problems the police now face: public agents, vested with a certain amount of coercive power, would enter ambiguous situations and be expected to make critical decisions about law, order, and justice in the face of confused and conflicting public expectations.

A realistic understanding of the possibilities for police reform, then, begins with a somewhat fatalistic recognition that certain police problems will remain.

While the nature of the police role is likely to remain complex and ambiguous, progress could be made in enhancing public awareness of this fact. Many experts, from the National Advisory Commission on Criminal Justice Standards and Goals to Herman Goldstein, recommend that police agencies develop formal statements regarding the police role. Goldstein argues that improvements in policing must begin with a more realistic understanding—by the public and by the police themselves—of the police role.[30]

Police-Community Relations The President's Commission began and completed its work in the midst of one of the worst periods of domestic violence in American history. Between the summer of 1964 and the spring of 1968 riots erupted in the black urban ghettos in every part of the country. The police-community relations crisis, which the riots represented, were only one part of a larger problem of racism in American society.

Little progress appears to have been made in either improving police-community relations or in eradicating American racism. Superficial evidence of progress does exist. Most police departments established and continue to maintain police-community relations units. Rioting did end in 1968 and disappeared for twelve years. This evidence of progress, however, is outweighed by evidence to the contrary. Relations between the police and minorities remain tense in most cities. Complaints about unwarranted use of physical and deadly force continue. Rioting returned in 1980 in Miami, Florida. Other evidence suggests that white Americans are reducing their support for civil rights (in the areas of education, affirmative-action employment, etc.) in the 1980s.

THE FUTURE

Using the events of the recent past as a baseline, we can begin to make educated guesses about the future of the police. Predicting the future, of course, is a hazardous enterprise. Guesses, however educated, are still only guesses. Experience seems to teach us that we are often overtaken by unexpected events. With respect to the police, for example, few people foresaw the riots of the mid-1960s, the sudden rise of police unions in the late 1960s, or the impact of chronic inflation in the late 1970s. The past, then, provides only a limited guide to the future.

Areas of Continuity

In certain respects, basic elements of American policing are likely to remain unchanged for the foreseeable future. The major areas of continuity involve the *social and political structure* of American society and its impact on the *police role*.[31]

Barring some unforeseen upheaval, the dominant features of the American social structure will remain unchanged. In addition to great extremes of wealth and poverty, including chronic poverty among part of the population, there will continue to be cultural diversity, conflict over moral standards, ethnic prejudice, racism, and sexism.

As a consequence, the police role will continue to be complex and ambiguous. The municipal police function as a twenty-four-hour, catchall social-service agency. They are called upon to respond to the many social problems associated with chronic poverty. Thus, the police will continue to play a major peacekeeping and social-service role in addition to the more clearly defined law enforcement role.

The cultural diversity of American society will continue to impose difficulties concerning proper police actions. The meaning of disorder has always been a matter of dispute, with the officer on the street faced with the task of mediating between conflicting public expectations. At same time, different individuals and groups will disagree over law enforcement priorities. As they have in the past, the police will be faced with conflicting public attitudes about the seriousness of various kinds of criminal activity.

The American political structure will also affect the police in the way it has in the past. First, the American political system is relatively open in the sense that many different groups are able to exercise political influence with varying degrees of effectiveness. The result is that the police will continue to be subject to the winds of political pressure. As has been true in the past, political pressures will have an important effect on the management of law enforcement agencies.

Second, the American political structure is highly decentralized. Responsibility for law enforcement and order maintenance is distributed among 20,000 separate agencies. Many experts believe that the fragmentation of police services, and the consequent lack of coordination, is a major problem. Although the consolidation of police agencies has been recommended for more than fifty years, little progress in this direction has been made. It is likely that little additional progress will be made in the foreseeable future. Substantial political obstacles stand in the way. Moreover, other experts now question whether consolidation would in fact result in greater efficiency.

The persistence of racism and racial discrimination, a major feature of the American social structure, will also result in the persistence of major political controversy over the police. The police play a symbolic role as the guardians of the status quo. As a result, they will be regarded by minorities as the enforcers of a discriminatory system. In the past few decades questions of police activities (arrest patterns, the use of deadly force), and recruitment practices have been primarily racial controversies. Given the symbolic role of the police and the apparent persistence of racism, these controversies are likely to continue in the foreseeable future.

The Enduring Features of Police Work   The continuities in the American social structure and in the police role mean that routine police work will also remain essentially unchanged. In his essay on "The Future Policeman," James Q. Wilson observes that

> Men and women will continue to value their property and their privacy, to have differing standards of public and private virtue, and to disagree with many government decisions. Whoever responds to the distress or manages the disputes of these people will of necessity have to take many, if not most of his cues as to proper action from the immediate circumstances of excited demands of individuals and primary groups.[32]

In short, the police role will continue to be complex and ambiguous and individual officers will continue to exercise enormous discretion in dealing with an infinite range of human situations.

An awareness of these continuities in policing provides perspective for a consideration of changes that might occur in the future. It is important to recognize the extent to which policing will *not* change.

Areas of Change

The Economy   The state of the American economy may be the most important force for change in the immediate future. In the late 1970s chronic inflation began to have a major impact on the police in many cities. Inflation imposes a double bind on the police. On the one hand it generates demands for higher police salaries, as officers seek to keep pace with the rising cost of living. On the other hand it generates political pressure for limitations on government spending.[33]

Several cities responded to the economic crisis by reducing the size of their police departments. The magnitude of the problem is illustrated by comparing the current situation with the 1960s: in 1967 the President's Commission declared a crisis because police departments were generally 5 percent below authorized strength.

The economic crisis has a number of potential effects. Reductions in personnel generate pressure for improved efficiency in the use of existing personnel. Productivity gains might be achieved through innovations in patrol: stacking calls for service, directed patrol, use of cadets or police service aides. Improved productivity could be an unanticipated benefit of the economic crisis. At the same time, however, the economic crisis could provoke union-management conflicts and result in more police strikes. Or the reduction in personnel and the simultaneous reduction in the number of promotional opportunities could seriously damage police officer morale.

Criminal Activity   The police are affected not only by the total amount of crime, but by the relative amounts of different types of criminal activity and by public attitudes toward various kinds of crime.

The upsurge in serious crime beginning in the early 1960s profoundly affected the police. Not only did it increase their workload, but it increased public pressure on the police to "do something" about crime. Also, the general increase in violent crime manifested itself in terms of more assaults on police officers and more officers killed on duty.

After the great increase from the early 1960s to the mid-1970s, the crime rate appeared to stabilize. Two schools of thought exist concerning the direction of crime rates in the 1980s. Some criminologists anticipate a reduction in crime as a result of demographic changes. Part of the increase in crime during the 1960s was due to the baby boom. The number of persons in the crime-prone age group of 14–24 years old was disproportionately high. Now that the baby boom has matured, the number of persons in that age group will be disproportionately low in the 1980s. The result could be a reduction in crime and delinquency.[34]

Others argue that crime is likely to continue at high rates, and possibly even increase in the 1980s. According to this school of thought, street crimes (particularly robbery and burglary) are strongly correlated with unemployment. If the economy worsens in the 1980s, with higher levels of unemployment, we can anticipate higher levels of crime.

Shifts in the relative frequency of different types of crime or changes in public attitudes toward certain crimes may also affect law enforcement priorities. Between 1969 and 1978, for example, arrests for Part I offenses rose by 42 percent while arrests for drunkenness declined by 46.5 percent.[35] In part this can be explained in terms of a logical shift in priorities by police: to put less emphasis on minor offenses in order to concentrate on the more serious felonies. It can also be explained in part by changing public attitudes and a changing legal environment. The laws governing many victimless crimes (vagrancy, public drunkenness, etc.) were in many instances ruled unconstitutionally vague or simply repealed.

Changes in public attitudes about various crimes could have a major impact on the police. The decriminalization of possession of small amounts of marijuana or continued deemphasis on public-order offenses such as vagrancy and public drunkenness could substantially reduce the workload of the police and, at the same time, eliminate sources of tension with certain elements of the community.

Police Organization and Management   One of the lessons of the past decade is that police organizations are not easily changed. Ten years ago team policing appeared to be a promising alternative to traditional organizational practices. Yet today, it is clear that *implementing* the team-policing concept, translating it into an operational reality, is an extremely difficult task. The Police Foundation, which set out ten years ago to bring about significant change in American policing, concluded its efforts in Dallas with an essay on "The Limits of Organizational Reform."[36]

A police department in a medium-sized city is a large bureaucracy, and bureaucracies are not easily changed. Moreover, as *public* bureaucracies, police departments are limited by civil service laws. Nonetheless, even with these limits in mind, possibilities for significant changes in police organization and management do exist. The past few years indicate not only the limits but also the possibilities of change.

Changes in police organization and management fall into two broad categories. The first involves change along *traditional* lines. The quality of police management still falls far short of the ideal. Since police chiefs are primarily promoted from within, many chiefs assume their jobs without any previous management training or experience. As a result, many departments have failed to implement modern concepts of management. Pressure for improvement in management technique and in police chief selection is likely to have an important impact on many departments.

One of the main features of American police administration is the fact of *uneven development*. Because policing is administratively fragmented, with no central coordination or control, individual departments progress (or fail to progress) at very different rates. In 1973, Lawrence Sherman pointed out that in the 1960s many police departments were just discovering the principles of management set forth in O. W. Wilson's *Police Administration.* At the same time, however, some departments which had adopted Wilson's principles long before were beginning to look for alternatives.

The second broad category of change in police organization and management, then, can be called *nontraditional*. The most promising innovations involve some form of decentralized authority within the traditional structure. Caiden cites the decentralization of the Los Angeles Police Department in the 1970s as a significant development.[37] Task forces involving officers from all ranks is another promising way of tapping unutilized talent and energy within police departments.[38]

The role of the police unions in police organization and management is one of the most important questions for the 1980s. Since collective bargaining is a process of shared management, the unions already have a substantial voice in police administration. For the most part, however, this continues to involve an adversary relationship between union and management. The National Symposium on Police Labor Relations recommended that union and management jointly seek improvements in policing. The Symposium proposed that joint committees on police be established. Such a development would bring the rank and file more directly into a management role and offer a significant change in traditional managemnet practice.[39]

Police Operations As we have already suggested, basic police operations will not undergo any fundamental change. The police will still have the responsibility for dealing with crime, maintaining order, and providing miscellaneous services to the public. In all probability, patrol will remain the basic manner in which police services are delivered to the public, and police officers—working alone or in pairs—will continue to exercise enormous discretion.

Nonetheless, the past few years indicate that significant improvements in some police operations are possible. The major force for change will probably be the demand for greater productivity, itself a product of the economic crisis.

New approaches to police patrol have been proposed and, in some cases, tested. Research has clearly indicated that a large proportion of police contacts with the public are of a nonemergency nature. It has been suggested that the police workload could be substantially reduced through one of three methods, or by a combination of the three: (1) stacking calls and responding to nonemergency calls on a delayed basis, when time and resources permit; (2) taking reports over the phone or requiring citizens to make the complaints in person at the police station; or (3) assigning nonemergency duties to paraprofessionals or cadets.[40]

Reducing the burden of nonemergency calls creates the possibility of improved productivity through more effective use of police officers' time. One new technique that needs thorough evaluation is directed patrol, in which officers are freed from the responsibility of responding to calls and use their time carrying our preplanned activities (such as intensive surveillance of high-crime areas, etc.).[41]

Recent research has also indicated that most criminal investigatory work is routine and relatively unproductive. More effective use of detectives' time, or even deemphasis of the detective altogether, are among the changes indicated by this research.[42]

Improvements in police operations are likely to be small, however. The primary objectives of policing are beyond the direct control of the police. Research indicates that patrol has, at best, a marginal effect on criminal activity.[43] Improvements in patrol are not likely to increase the deterrent effect substantially. Criminal activity remains a social phenomenon largely beyond the control of the police. At the same time, improvements in the detective function are not likely to increase the clearance rate substantially. The very nature of many crimes (especially crimes where the offender is not known to the victim) puts limits on the ability of the police to solve them.

Accountability The demand for greater accountability of the police is also likely to continue in the near future. Rising public expectations about police performance is only one part of a more general "consumer revolution" affecting all aspects of society.

How will the demand for greater accountability be met? Internal mechanisms of accountability have shown substantial improvement in recent years. Studies indicate that police discretion can be effectively controlled through the development of written policy guidelines and the enforcement of these policies. Documentation of the impact of written guidelines—as in the case of the New York City policy on firearms discharges—will probably lend added support to demands that departments develop similar guidelines.[44]

External means of accountability have a problematic future. Civilian-review boards have not been widely adopted, and the political opposition to this concept (largely through police unions) appears to be stronger than the political support (mainly minority communities and their white allies).

The future role of the courts in reviewing police conduct is also a matter of some uncertainty. The U.S. Supreme Court emerged as one of the principal external mechanisms of accountability. The Warren court looked at many previously unexamined police practices and defined new standards of due process. In the 1970s, the Burger court did not develop a clear or consistent policy. In some respects it modified the standards set by the Warren court—defining a series of exceptions to the exclusionary rule, for example. But in other respects it continued in the same direction as the Warren court, establishing some new limits on police powers and ruling in favor of the rights of individual citizens.

Whether the Supreme Court will continue to play a prominent role in police accountability depends, to a great extent, on the changing composition of the Court itself. Much depends on the appointments that President Reagan will make in the 1980s.

Police Personnel   The recent past suggests that police personnel standards will continue to change but only rather slowly. Minimum standards for recruitment rose during the 1960s and 1970s, resulting in police officers with generally higher levels of educational achievement than in the past.[45] This trend is likely to continue, although it is doubtful that sufficient political pressure exists to implement the commission's recommendation that a college degree be required of all recruits.

The most important issue in the area of recruitment involves equal employment opportunity. Minorities and women are underrepresented in the ranks of American law enforcement agencies. Failure to make substantial progress in the immediate future will undoubtedly lead to continued litigation, as women and minorities file discrimination suits. For many agencies, recruitment standards and practices will be dictated by the courts.

Implementation of equal employment opportunity has been sought through the concept of affirmative action—the idea that the agency itself has responsibility for correcting past discrimination. Preference for particular categories of applicants— minorities and women—raises the thorny question of reverse discrimination. Affirmative-action programs have been challenged in the courts by white males alleging discrimination against them. At this point, the questions surrounding affirmative-action programs remain unsettled. The Supreme Court, in the *Bakke* and *Webber* decisions, did not clearly resolve the question of reverse discrimination.[46]

To a great extent, the future of equal employment opportunity, of affirmative-action programs, and of recruitment standards in general, are in the hands of the courts. The uncertainty is compounded by the prospect of a changing composition of the Supreme Court in the 1980s.

The personnel issue that began to receive increased attention in the 1970s was the question of career development. Existing police personnel systems are extremely rigid. Promotional opportunities are circumscribed by civil service regulations. Generally an officer must spend a number of years in rank before becoming eligible to even take a promotional examination. At the same time, the economic crisis which limits police recruitment has the parallel effect of limiting promotional opportunities (departments that are expanding need to add supervisory personnel; and many departments reduce costs by not replacing supervisory personnel who retire).

Compunding these problems is the fact that police departments have not developed methods for meaningful performance evaluation. The traditional objective measures of arrests bear little relationship to the bulk of police work. Officers who do a competent job, day in and day out, frequently do not receive adequate recognition.[47]

The result of these various problems is a serious morale problem among the police. Too many officers receive little recognition for good work and are trapped in routine jobs with little chance for either promotion or more creative use of their talents.

Experts generally recognize the need for greater flexibility in police personnel systems. The term *career development* is used to describe alternate systems for recognizing and rewarding good performance. One proposal calls for allowing police officers to specialize in a particular area of expertise and to remain in that area throughout his ot her career (much as lawyers specialize in particular kinds of legal work.

Related to the idea of career specialization is the proposal for a broader, merit-based salary schedule within particular ranks. An officer might remain at the rank of police officer but earn salary increments based on meritorious performance. Thus, there would be incentives for good performance unrelated to the question of promotion.

A final personnel issue involves police pension systems. A major crisis looms because of the shaky financial condition of many pension plans. The problem is not unique to the police. The social security system faces a similar crisis: future obligations for pensions may bankrupt the system under current financing arrangements. There is some evidence that local government pension systems are in even worse shape. Local officials have found it expedient to grant generous pension benefits without facing the issue of providing sufficient revenue to pay for them. The pension system crisis could become one of the major police problems of the 1980s.

Accreditation In the near future, these and other issues may be dealt with through accreditation.

The concept of accreditation is new to criminal justice, but it has a long history in other fields. Minimum standards are defined and then used to evaluate the quality of individual agencies. Those that meet the standards are accredited. Accreditation is a peer-review process, since the development and enforcement of standards is done by professionals working in that field. Colleges, for example, are accredited by groups of professionals from the field of higher education. Particular disciplines, such as social work or clinical psychology, are accredited by professionals from those fields.

Accreditation is a voluntary process, thus the denial of accreditation carries only indirect sanction. A college that is not accredited can continue to operate, but the value of the degrees it grants are greatly weakened. Federal funding indirectly supports accreditation. Veterans' benefits and other forms of federal support are often not available to nonaccredited institutions.

The accreditation of law enforcement agencies would involve the development of minimum standards in such areas as personnel recruitment, utilization of community resources, support services, internal discipline, and so on. In 1979, LEAA awarded $1.5 million to four professional organizations to develop accreditation standards: the International Association of Chiefs of Police (IACP), the National Organization of Black Law Enforcement Executives (NOBLE), the National Sheriffs' Association, and the Police Executives' Research Forum (PERF). The project is being coordinated by the Commission on Accreditation for Law Enforcement Agencies (CALAE), and is to be completed in five years.[48]

Accreditation is further along in the area of corrections. Primarily through the efforts of the American Correctional Association, minimum standards for adult and juvenile institutions have been developed and published.

The impact of accreditation is uncertain. Since accreditation is a voluntary system, there would not necessarily be any sanctions for agencies that failed to meet the standards. A police department that failed to develop adequate recruitment standards, for example, would suffer no penalty. Accreditation would become more meaningful if it were related to federal funding. The Justice Department, for example, could adopt accreditation standards as prerequisites for federal funding.

With the elimination of LEAA in 1982 and the reduction of federal financial assistance to the criminal justice system, however, the future of the accreditation movement is in doubt.

A Final Note: Police Revitalization

In the end, the future of the police depends upon initiatives taken by the police themselves. The critical issue is leadership. In *Police Revitalization,* Caiden cites the example of departments which have taken the lead in initiating change, notably Los Angeles and Kansas City. James Q. Wilson also offers a cautiously optimistic observation: "The long and growing list of . . . major police innovations demonstrates the impressive willingness of many police administrators to take risks, incur costs, and devote energy to the difficult process of inducing their organizations' members to accept new ways of doing things."

The financial problems being experienced by all government agencies will be an important factor. On the one hand, budget reductions restrict the ability of the police to innovate. Existing personnel cannot be diverted from basic tasks for new projects. With the elimination of LEAA, external sources of funding have been ended. On the other hand, a budget crisis can be an opportunity for innovation. It can force agencies to seek new and more efficient ways of operating, in the process challenging traditional assumptions.

Finally, police revitalization depends on leadership. Improvements in policing will result only when key actors take the lead. One hopeful sign is the leadership taken by the Police Executive Research Forum in developing new guidelines for police accountability. The research forum consists largely of police executives dissatisfied with the failure of the IACP to provide adequate leadership. The role of rank-and-file police officers is also critical. Hans Toch argues in favor of "Mobilizing Police Expertise." Based on his own experiments in Oakland, Toch believes that rank-and-file police officers' "experiences and personal impressions are immensely relevant" to innovative projects. Involving the rank and file enhances the commitment of the entire organization to the project and increases the possibility of success.[49]

REVIEW

1 Explain the different types of change and how they relate to the police.
2 Evaluate progress in policing since the Wickersham Commission report in 1931.
3 Describe the most significant changes in policing since the 1967 report of the President's Crime Commission.
4 What are the major contributions of the police research revolution?
5 Evaluate the impact of police unions on the future of the police.
6 Explain why the police role is unlikely to change in the near future.
7 What impact will the state of the economy have on the future of the police?
8 Describe three new ways of handling the police service-call workload.
9 What is meant by career development for police officers?
10 What is the role of national professional associations in promoting change and innovation in policing?

REFERENCES

1 Project STAR, *The Impact of Social Trends on Crime and Criminal Justice* (Cincinnati: Anderson Publishing, 1976).
2 James Q. Wilson, "The Future Policeman," in *Issues in Police Patrol,* eds. Thomas J. Sweeney and William Ellingsworth (Kansas City: Kansas City Police Department, 1973), pp. 207–221.
3 Herbert Packer, *The Limits of the Criminal Sanction,* (Stanford: Stanford University Press, 1968), chap. 8.
4 Samuel Walker, *Popular Justice* (New York: Oxford University Press, 1980), pp. 173–178, 232–236.
5 National Commission on Law Observance and Enforcement, *Police* (Washington, D.C.: U.S. Government Printing Office, 1931); National Commission on Law Observance and Enforcement, *Lawlessness in Law Enforcement* (Washington, D.C.: U.S. Government Printing Office, 1931).
6 President's Commission on Law Enforcement and Administration of Justice, *The Challenge of Crime in a Free Society,* (New York: Avon Books, 1968).
7 David J. Farmer, "The Research Revolution," *Police Magazine* (November 1978): 64–65.
8 President's Commission on Law Enforcement, *The Challenge of Crime in a Free Society,* p. 249.
9 James Q. Wilson, "Police Research and Experimentation," in *Progress in Policing: Essays on Change,* ed. Richard A. Staufenberger (Cambridge: Ballinger Publishing, 1980), p. 146.

10 U.S., Department of Justice, *Expenditure and Employment Data for the Criminal Justice System, 1977* (Washington, D.C.: U.S. Government Printing Office, 1979); U.S., Department of Justice, *Trends in Expenditure and Employment Data for the Criminal Justice System 1971-1975* (Washington, D.C.: U.S. Government Printing Office, 1977).

11 Albert Reiss, *The Police and the Public* (New Haven: Yale University Press, 1971); Donald J. Black, *The Manners and Customs of the Police* (New York: Academic Press, 1980).

12 George L. Kelling, et al., *The Kansas City Preventive Patrol Experiment: A Summary Report* (Washington, D.C.: Police Foundation, 1974).

13 Peter W. Greenwood, et al., *The Criminal Investigation Process,* vol. 1, *Summary and Policy Implications* (Santa Monica: Rand Corporation, 1975).

14 David J. Farmer, "The Future of Local Law Enforcement: The Federal Role," in *Crime and Justice in America: Critical Issues for the Future,* eds. John T. Obrien and Marvin Marcus (New York: Pergamon Press, 1979), p. 94.

15 Herman Goldstein, *Policing a Free Society* (Cambridge: Ballinger Publishing, 1977), chap. 2.

16 James M. Tien and Richard C. Larson, "Police Service Adies: Paraprofessionals for Police," *Journal of Criminal Justice* 6 (Summer 1978): 117–131; U.S., Department of Justice, *Improving Patrol Productivity,* 2 vols. (Washington, D.C.: U.S. Government Printing Office, 1977).

17 International Association of Chiefs of Police, *Guidelines and Papers from the National Symposium on Police Labor Relations* (Gaithersburg, Md.: IACP, 1974).

18 Robert Fogelson, *Big City Police* (Cambridge: Harvard University Press, 1977), pp. 241–268.

19 Jerry V. Wilson, *The War on Crime in the District of Columbia, 1955–1975* (Washington, D.C.: Department of Justice, 1978).

20 President's Commission on Law Enforcement, *Task Force Report: The Police* (Washington, D.C.: U.S. Government Printing Office, 1967), pp. 133–134.

21 U.S., Department of Justice, *The National Manpower Survey of the Criminal Justice System,* vol. 2, *Law Enforcement* (Washington, D.C.: U.S. Government Printing Office, 1978), p. 3.

22 U.S., Department of Justice, *Sourcebook of Criminal Justice Statistics 1979,* (Washington, D.C.: U.S. Government Printing Office, 1980), p. 210.

23 President's Commission on Law Enforcement, *The Challenge of Crime in a Free Society,* p. 267.

24 Lawrence W. Sherman, "Restricting the License to Kill—Recent Developments in Police Use of Deadly Force," *Criminal Law Bulletin* 12 (1978): 577.

25 Texas, Criminal Justice Council, *Model Rules for Law Enforcement Officers: A Manual on Police Discretion* (Gaithersburg, Md., IACP, 1974).

26 James Q. Wilson, *Thinking about Crime* (New York: Basic Books, 1975), p. 97

27 Lawrence W. Sherman, *Team Policing: Seven Case Studies* (Washingtion, D.C.: Police Foundation, 1973).

28 Gerald E. Caiden, *Police Revitalization* (Lexington: Lexington Books, 1977).

29 Wilson, "The Future Policeman."

30 Herman Goldstein, *Policing a Free Society* (Cambridge: Ballinger Publishing, 1977). chap. 2.

31 Wilson, "The Future Policeman."

32 Ibid., p. 209.

33 International City Management Association, Urban Data Service, "The Era of Fiscal Restraint" (Washington, D.C.: Author, 1979).

34 Wilson, *Thinking About Crime*. chap. 1.

35 U.S., Federal Bureau of Investigation, *Crime in the United States 1978* (Washington, D.C.: U.S. Government Printing Office, 1979), p. 188.

36 Mary Ann Wycoff and George L. Kelling, *The Dallas Experience: Organizational Reform* (Washington, D.C.: U.S. Government Printing Office, 1978).

37 Caiden, *Police Revitalization,* p. 111.

38 Thomas C. Sweeney, "A Report on the Use of Task Forces for Change in the Kansas City Police Department," in Chauncey Bell, ed., *Changing Police Organizations: Four Readings* (Washington, D.C.: National League of Cities, 1973), pp. 13–29.

39 IACP, *Guidelines and Papers from the National Symposium on Police Labor Relations.*

40 U.S., Department of Justice, *Improving Patrol Productivity,* chaps. 2 and 3.

41 Ibid., chap. 4.

42 Greenwood et al., *The Criminal Investigation Process.*

43 Kelling et al., *The Kansas City Preventive Patrol Experiment.*

44 James J. Fyfe, "Administrative Interventions on Police Shooting Discretion: An Empirical Examination," *Journal of Criminal Justice* 7 (Winter 1979): 309–323.

45 U.S., Department of Justice, *National Manpower Survey of the Criminal Justice System,* vol. 2, p. 3.

46 *Regents of University of California v. Bakke,* 438 U.S. 265 (1978); *U.S. Steelworkers v. Neber,* 443 U.S. 193 (1979).

47 Frank J. Landy, *Performance Appraisal in Police Departments* (Washington, D.C.: Police Foundation, 1977).

48 Caiden, *Police Revitalization;* Wilson, "Police Research and Experimentation," p. 131.

49 Hans Toch, "Mobilizing Police Expertise," in *The Police and Violence,* ed. Lawrence W. Sherman, *Annals* 451 (November 1980): 53–62.

INDEX